W9-BVL-972

Bargaining Across Borders

How to Negotiate Business Successfully Anywhere in the World

Dean Allen Foster

Boston, Massachusetts   Burr Ridge, Illinois
Dubuque, Iowa   Madison, Wisconsin   New York, New York
San Francisco, California   St. Louis, Missouri

Dedicated to
Sheryl, Wendy, and Sylvia

McGraw-Hill

A Division of The McGraw·Hill Companies

Library of Congress Cataloging-in-Publication Data

Foster, Dean Allen.
    Bargaining across borders : How to negotiate business successfully anywhere
in the world / Dean Allen Foster.
        p.   cm.   .
    Includes index.
    ISBN 0-07-021647-9(hc)   ISBN 0-07-021656-8(pbk)
    1. Negotiate in business.   2. International trade.   I. Title.
HD58.6.F67   1992
658.4–dc20   91-45342
                                                                         CIP

Copyright © 1992 by McGraw-Hill, Inc. All rights reserved. Printed in the
United States of America. Except as permitted under the United States
Copyright Act of 1976, no part of this publication may be reproduced or
distributed in any form or by any means, or stored in a data base or retrieval
system, without the prior written permission of the publisher.

First McGraw-Hill paperback edition, 1995

6 7 8 9 0   DSH/DSH   0 1 0 9 8 7 6 5 4

ISBN 0-07-021647-9 (HC)
ISBN 0-07-021656-8 (PBK)

*The sponsoring editor for this book was David Conti, the editing supervisor was
Kimberly A. Goff, and the production supervisor was Donald F. Schmidt. This
book was set in Baskerville. It was composed by McGraw-Hill's Professional
Book Group composition unit.*

Contents

Part 2. Americans at the International Negotiating Table

Part 3. Successful International Communication

Preface

This book is meant to serve as a guide on your journeys. Inevitably, the most beneficial journeys are the ones that occur within yourself. This book practically insists that to reach out we must first reach within. Therefore, this book is meant to help you to begin looking inward. The first step to looking outward when negotiating with those across the table is understanding oneself.

In this sense, the book has a behavioral bias. Throughout the book, wherever possible, we have tried to present academic or theoretical information in a manner that relates to practical business issues. The purpose of making the information as practical as possible is to enable you to *behave* more effectively. Therefore, you will have ample opportunity to analyze, compare, and generally test yourself, your own tendencies, and your own ways of negotiating and doing business against other ways of Americans and non-Americans alike. This will help you to identify your own style and your options and to make intelligent and effective choices. We hope that by the end of the book you will have increased your behavioral options, thus enabling you to be well-armed when walking into a negotiation with people who do business differently.

While the word *bargaining* appears in the title, we want to quickly state that bargaining is not being used as a substitute for *negotiating*. In fact, bargaining is just one aspect of the larger process of negotiating. However, for many Americans negotiation and bargaining are the same. Hopefully, by highlighting this conflation right up front we are already beginning an intelligent discussion of just one of the many formidable differences of perception that can arise between cultures when they sit down to negotiate – or bargain – with each other. This book is not meant to be just one more guidebook to bargaining, to negotiation, or to international business. Rather we would hope that many of the topics discussed in this book could be used as guides to better *communication* cross-culturally, between yourself and your "foreign" associates. In this sense, as negotiation is but one aspect of the larger issue of international business communication, we could have just as easily called the book *Business Across Borders*.

In trying to make the book practical, we have used as many "critical incidents" or "snapshots" of business and social scenarios as possible to highlight cross-cultural communication and negotiation problems. In turn, our hope is to allow you the opportunity to analyze and to develop the necessary perceptual skills to "read" international business situations. In light of this goal, many of the international snapshots we have used have, by necessity, been altered, simplified, or modified in some way to draw attention to (or in some cases, to mask) the specific issues being discussed. For this reason, these scenarios may appear skewed or may carry an air of simplified unreality. Certainly, no retelling of these kinds of events can carry with it all the complexities of human interaction and communication and, fortunately, our goal here is to eliminate much of these elements that are external to the issues being examined. We hope you will grant us the license to make these modifications. They exist solely to assist you in your goals of achieving better communication and negotiating skills.

We have put much effort into limiting the prescriptive nature of the book since one of its premises is that prescribing appropriate and effective behavior regarding international business communications is not the preferred method for developing success. We would rather that this book helps you to build on the methods, styles, and successes you already have. Most of us have had a good deal of experience negotiating in life with our work associates, spouses, friends, family, children, and so forth. We have, no doubt, already developed particular styles of our own, certain notions of proceding, and ways in which we are more comfortable in handling these situations. The purpose of the book is not to invalidate these conclusions, built up so carefully through the rough and tumble of real-life trial and error. We hope instead that you can build on what you already bring to the table, recognize some things about what you already do, and make some reasonably intelligent decisions about it. In addition, we hope to help you discover possible options that you may not have realized you had or employ options in ways that you had not previously recognized. In short, we hope this book puts more on your quite possibly already large plate.

The book is divided into three parts, paralleling, we hope, the journey that we need to make when attempting to do business with people from other cultures. First, we need to be aware that differences, primarily cultural, affect our ability to do business with each other, and in Part 1, we discuss this issue of business and culture. Then, to understand "them," we need to first understand ourselves. Part 2 is devoted to looking at some very key "American" behavioral traits and comparing their effects in business with the behavior, attitudes, and underlying values of other important cultures. Part 3 takes a much closer look at negotiation per se and attempts to apply the information from the previous chapters specifically to the processes of international negotiation.

By the end of the book, you will have increased your cross-cultural business and negotiation options. We hope you will also have increased your appreciation for the diversity of possibilities of human behavior that exist when we venture forth out into new cultures—and the expanded difficulties, yes—but also the expanded opportunities that such diversity provides when we begin to do business with each other.

Dean Allen Foster

Acknowledgments

First, to our grandparents, their grandparents, and their grandparents' grandparents. They not only have provided each of us with our own individual rich cultural heritage, but in so doing, also have provided me with the premise for this book. While today I cannot thank them, I acknowledge their immense contribution.

I have had the privilege in my field to work with the best, and for this I am profoundly grateful. It is rare for one to be continuously guided, taught, and acknowledged by those whom others have acknowledged to be leaders in their field. I trust this was a karmic accident which shall never be repeated again in my life, and therefore, I have unashamedly seized the opportunity to make a career and to write this book. To all of those who have put their faith in me, helped me, and lent their support (the great number of people this represents is merely an indication of the amount of faith, help, and support I have needed), I am truly thankful.

Within the ranks of those whom I am privileged to count as my colleagues, I would be remiss not to acknowledge certain individuals (and organizations) who truly have been, and in many cases literally, at my side during the inspiration for and the writing of this book. These individuals no doubt deserve my apologies as well as my thanks. They have provided me with the highest calibre grist for whatever creative mill I have chosen to put their thoughts through, and I am eternally thankful for their contributions. I also apologize for any mangling of their contributions in the process. No doubt I have mangled more than a few. It is not intentional. My failures are my own; any success is theirs.

Ellen Raider, of Ellen Raider International, one of the wisest risk-takers I know, took a risk one day when she agreed to accept my assistance in her already successful and important work on international negotiation. I hope someday that she will have the pleasure to know that such a risk proved to have been a wise one. I have already had the great professional pleasure to have worked with her, to have sought her counsel, to have rejoiced and grieved with her over the highs and lows of life, and to have had, in the process, most wonderfully built and sustained a friendship that I count as very, very dear.

The fact that I probably cite John Bing, President of ITAP, International, Princeton, New Jersey, more often throughout this book than any one else, is because he perhaps is simply more citable than anyone else I know. His lifetime experience in international management and training and his willingness to share his wisdom, knowledge, and friendship have been an enduring source of support for me; and I am indebted.

I have had the pleasure to work with many people in the field of international business—in the corporate trenches, in their homes with their children and spouses, in warm far-away places, in cold and rarified academe, around late-night hotel coffee tables—planning, discussing, reworking, sometimes only to start over again. Their insistence on maintaining the highest professional levels, of stretching me to my limits, and of forcing me to look within to better deal with what is without, needs to be acknowledged. If international negotiating and mediating were only an art, Susan Coleman, my co-trainer on so many programs would be Mary Cassatt. Thank you for your insights, your patience, and your insistence on excellence. Yves Speeckaert helped me understand the American inside me by showing me the European inside him. *Merci, mon ami.* Cynthia Milani of Milani Associates reminds me always, even in my darkest moments, through her life and good humor that real cross-cultural understanding *is*, despite appearances, still possible. All of these people, and so many others, have contributed in word and spirit to this book. I only hope I have taken what they have so freely offered and done justice to it.

In the course of this kind of career, there are clients and there are clients. They all present a challenge, and I thank them for that. Some insist on challenging me to ensure that there will always be a relationship, for that I thank them very much. It is from challenging relationships that I have gleaned much of the material for this book. Many thanks, therefore, go to the international training and education departments at AT&T, Johnson & Johnson, American Cyanamid, General Electric, the Square D Corporation, the World Trade Institute of the Port Authority of New York and New Jersey, and many others, who have provided me with the rich and varied experiences that are the heart and soul of this book.

Beyond the material and experiences reflected within the book, however, lies the making of the book itself, and for this I have many to thank. Thanks go to my editor, David Conti, for his belief in the viability of the book, and his gentle, but firm handling of the problems my schedule and shortcomings constantly caused. I am sorry; never was there a more wise and patient man. Thanks as well to his assistant, Alison Collier, for being there whenever I called and to the excellent editing staff headed by the very able Kim Goff. Only after reading the edited versions of my work did I begin to truly develop an appreciation for the talent and effort required to make the unintelligible clear. Hats off to all.

To Bob Stein, my dear friend and perceptive attorney, I send my qualified thanks. I am still not certain that his suggestion to wrestle with the tortures of writing a book was based on the kind of personal concern for me one expects from a friend. On second thought, a true friend knows what's best for you. Therefore, thanks, Bob...unqualified.

To my agent, Jane Dystel of Acton and Dystel, thanks is given for her guidance and support throughout every stage of this work. Her suggestions, prodding, and sincere concern for this, my maiden literary voyage, are very much appreciated.

To my father, whose confidence in my achievements was matched only by his patience with my failures, I send my enduring love and appreication. He was always there for me. No one could ask for more.

To my daughter, Leah, who at fourteen, had the kindness to reassure me that my absences from family life were worth it and the fortitude to plough through math and French alone, my devotion and thanks. Leah, there were far too many sunny August days that I missed with you while writing this book and I only hope that the result of such sacrifice may someday be worth it.

Finally, to my wife, my greatest supporter, who has seen me at my worst and yet always manages to remember me at my best, my deepest respect, love, and appreciation. She was always willing to share in any agony, always provided perspective, and always cared enough to help me find a way out. This book would not have been written without her.

I hope that anyone I have omitted understands that such omission is one of mercy; it should not be construed as intentional.

Dean Allen Foster

Bargaining
Across Borders

PART 1

On Doing Business Internationally

1
Introduction

A Global Homecoming for Americans

Recently, I have come to recognize a vague discomfort whenever I consult with a group of American businesspeople on the ins and outs of doing business with other countries. There I am, sitting with a group of people wearing name tags that read "Ramirez," "Schwartz," "Guttbaum," "Wang," "Johnson," "Wiczsniczski," "O'Donnell," and "DiAngelo," yet I am being asked questions about what's it like for Americans to do business with people from other cultures. "Who am I?" I ask myself, "to offer information about other countries to *them*? Why do they think they need *me*? Americans usually come to such programs seeking a laundry list of do's and don'ts regarding business customs, manners, and procedures in other countries. But more often than not, such programs become an exploration of what it means to be an American. And significantly, the best answers usually come, not from me, a book, or someone else's anecdotes about life abroad, but from the participants themselves.

It is an irony that the United States, perhaps the most multicultural society in the world (along with—another irony—the former Soviet Union), has long had an inferiority complex when it comes to doing business internationally. This has been the case for many reasons, not the least of which has been the need, during the first two-thirds of our history, to focus most of our energies on the new society growing within our borders. Our focus on developing this country has gone hand in hand with the process of becoming American that millions of Americans-to-be (former "thems," if you will), immigrants and slaves alike, have experienced. Whatever the reasons (and we will explore many of them in the following chapters), many Americans feel insecure and ill-equipped to face the challenges of business with "foreigners." This book will make many suggestions for overcoming this insecurity, while also providing much information about other cultures. But its most important recommendation will be that Americans begin by looking within themselves.

"Know Thyself"

Socrates said it. It's in the Bible and the Koran. It's central to Confucianism and a driving force in Buddhism. According to Freud, its absence is at the heart of many modern men and women's problems. Why, then, should it not also be a central concern for international business? For our purposes, "know thyself" also means "know your own culture." And there are several reasons why knowing your own culture is the primary condition for learning how to do business in someone else's.

To begin with, we cannot understand another culture without also understanding our own. We must start by recognizing our own points of reference—the values and assumptions we ourselves operate within. Creating a list of the cultural expectations that affect business in other lands is meaningless until we recognize the cultural expectations that affect business right here. Generalizations about business practices in Japan, for example, mean nothing unless we can compare them with generalizations about business practices in the United States. Without understanding the *ways* in which business can be different, we cannot understand the *hows*. We need overarching, defining structures by which differences can be compared, by which the distance between our ways and those of other countries can be specifically identified and measured.

Understanding why we do something can also provide us with an insight into why "they" do something. When we understand our own history, when we discover the reasons why we do what we do, we can look at the history of another country and find the reasons why its citizens act as they do. Suddenly, within the larger context of history, behavior that at first seemed irrational begins to make sense. We think and act as we do because of our cultural past—because of who we are and what has happened to us as a people. The same is true for the citizens of other countries. Our histories are different, so of course we act differently. But when I understand my history, I begin to understand myself; and when I understand your history, I begin to understand you.

Knowing ourselves better has a special meaning for Americans because we can often find the reasons for "foreign" behavior in our own cultural background. Most of us are just one or two generations away from being foreign ourselves. Indeed, many of us have become Americans within our own lifetimes. (One of the chief characteristics of American culture is its dynamism, the fact that we are, as a society, still in the process, at a fairly high social level, of defining what it means to be "American.") As Americans, we have a unique and often overlooked advantage when it comes to doing business with people from other cultures because not too far back in our family histories, most of "us" came from somewhere out "there" too.

While we will provide key facts about various cultures, their business styles, and their negotiating preferences, tactics, and strategies, it would be futile to try to discuss all aspects, even the important ones, of every culture in this book. That is a task for an encyclopedia, and a shallow one at that. Creating a laundry list of meaningful cultural distinctions is probably impossible. It is certainly of questionable value, because such lists often only reinforce stereotypes. The individual you negotiate with may be very different from the "average person" profiled on the list.

The better negotiators, the more successful global businesspeople, are not those who have memorized hundreds or thousands of do's and don'ts. Rather, they are those who have developed an international feel, a global mind-set, an empathic approach toward doing business with people from other cultures. Certainly, the better international negotiators do try to learn about the people of the country they are negotiating with. And, certainly, those more experienced with one particular country will have an advantage over those less experienced in that country. But, first and foremost, the better negotiators understand the larger process of achieving effective communication with business associates whose cultural baggage is different from their own. And they know the importance of understanding cultural differences in order to prevent such differences from undermining their negotiations.

The Value of a Global Mind-Set over a Global Miscellany

Developing a good working knowledge of the culture you'll be negotiating in before you hop off the plane to begin doing business there is always a good idea. We're certainly not going to downplay the importance of knowing as much as you can about the culture of the people you'll be working with. How much do you need to know about it? The answer, of course, is "as much as possible." The more you understand about the history, art, music, literature, politics, economics, religion, psychology, sociology, anthropology, and mythology of a people, the more likely you will be to succeed in communicating with them. But while it is difficult to know enough details about one culture, it is next to impossible to know more than a smattering about several cultures. Yet, inevitably, the American venturing forth into the new global marketplace is probably not going to be limited to one particular culture, or even to one or two countries. The nature of the new global order is that we are doing business with the world, with scores of different cultures and countries, so that the task of learning enough about all the cultures one will be doing business with becomes a challenge of impossible proportions. It is crucially important to learn all one can about other cultures, of course, but given the enormity of the challenge, it is best to begin by understanding the one culture we can truly master, our own, and becoming aware of the ways it affects the process of working with others at the negotiating table. We need to recognize that most Americans have a lot of catch-up work to do when it comes to detailed, current information about other countries, but we can only take one step at a time, and this book suggests another way around. First, Americans need to develop an international *cultural perspective*, an appreciation of the ways things may be different abroad in relation to our own culture. Second, we need to develop an understanding of the contents of our own cultural baggage. Third, and finally, Americans need to fill in the gaps with as much information as we can get about the cultures with which we are working. But our first priority should not be the gathering of a miscellany; our first priority needs to be the development of a larger, deeper, and more empathic approach to doing business with other cultures.

A point here about the third step, gathering culture-specific information about the countries you'll be doing business with: No one can know everything about someone else's culture, just as you cannot gather every fish in the sea. The third step is more like a journey. It is possible, for example, after much time—after living in someone else's culture perhaps—to learn a great deal, to become an "expert," from an outsider's point of view. But you will never know it like an insider, like the person sitting across the table from you. And while you may never need to know (and certainly never *will* know) as much as your foreign associates know about their country, you *do* need to know a great deal about how *your* culture affects what happens at the table. Your foreign associates' strength lies in their knowledge about themselves, which you cannot match. However, your strength lies in your knowledge of yourself, which *they* cannot match. At the negotiating table, you want to maximize your strengths and minimize your weaknesses. So it seems to make sense to start first with the steps that *can* be mastered, those stages of learning that we can truly become expert at which and that will have a real effect at the negotiating table abroad. Unfortunately, when they realize their need for information about business life abroad, many Americans try to master the last step overnight, an impossibility, while ignoring the more important, and more attainable, first two steps. This book is about reordering these priorities.

Mastering the details about a culture merely allows you to predict a possibility; the information can only serve to point out tendencies. Individuals can be very different from the way they are supposed to be. No one is a typical, perfect representation of his or her country. Cultures and individuals are enormously complex, and while I may very much be the model American in some ways, in other ways I am sure I am not. It is the same abroad. Since there are so many cultures we need to learn about, the nature and size of the task limits the amount of information we can learn to simple generalizations or to pat lists of facts. And along the way what we learn is reduced in meaning and applicability.

We rarely meet, in real life, an individual from any culture who looks or acts anything like the pithy little summary of the "average" person. In fact, we are often confronted abroad with individuals who aren't behaving according to the norm we have been told to expect, creating confusion where there perhaps needn't have been any. Worse still, we tend to look for the behavior we were told to expect, so we seek out only those individuals or aspects of individuals that match the stereotypes we have in mind. In fact, such short summaries of the way people are supposed to be serve only to puzzle us when we meet real flesh-and-blood people who are human enough to confound our neatly packaged expectations.

In addition, specific cultural facts are always shifting. Globalization means there is a lot of change going on, both within and among cultures. As soon as we make a statement about a cultural norm being this way or that, there is evidence to prove that the opposite is true. Much of what has been said about Japan, for example, is really a generalization about an "over-forties Japan"; the "under-forties Japan" is considerably different. Much of what we say about Americans is true more perhaps for certain groups of Americans than for others and even their beliefs and habits are undergoing considerable change. These change despite the fact that research seems to indicate that traditional values have a much more powerful hold over us than we might think.

As we watch whole societies going through what appears to be revolutionary change today, we see that cultures can be quite dynamic, some more dynamic than others. And, of course, there is concern for the pos-sible homogenization and watering-down of cultures as the world grows smaller through technology and globalization. (The French, as well as many other Europeans, have given this a lot of thought.) I suspect that we will see the development of some particular supranational cultural identities and ways of doing business and a simultaneous digging in of certain other traditional national values. The point is that cultures do change, and in today's world, apects of them can change very fast.

Relying on a laundry list of do's and don'ts about a particular culture more often than not reveals nothing more than the well-intentioned goal of not wanting to offend, but being nice isn't what negotiations are all about, and being nice isn't the only appropriate behavioral response. It takes more than not offending the other side to succeed at the nego-tiating table. It takes knowing how to be proactive in a productive sense.

Do's and don'ts too often seem to be about how Americans can avoid being American. This is nonsense. You cannot be who you are not, and the worst thing you can do is try to be less who you are and more like others. It's demeaning to you and insulting to them. Besides, as a for-eigner in someone else's country, you are very often forgiven a multi-tude of sins, just as we forgive non-Americans when they make mistakes here. Most breaches of do's and don'ts are fairly innocuous. They don't make or break negotiations. What will, however, determine your success at the table with your associates abroad is your ability to identify and respond flexibly to deep differences in world views, perhaps culturally determined, so that these differences do not undermine or get in the way of accomplishing the business at hand. The global mind-set is a be-havioral skill for effective, productive handling of cross-cultural situa-tions. It needs to be a gut-level response to a gut-level understanding.

Developing a Global Mind-Set

The question is, how can Americans develop a global mind-set? Also, why is it that Americans have tended to miss seeing what I believe to be out natural advantage in dealing effectively in the global arena? Rather than looking for answers in neat, sterilized summaries of customs in this country or that, Americans should be looking at customs in our own country, for once upon a time, almost everyone "here" came from somewhere out "there." Besides, despite what we may feel in the midst of our own internal national debates, we already know ourselves infi-nitely better than we are likely to know other nationalities.

There is something telling about Americans' preference for quick and easy answers, and it is important in our work with associates abroad to understand this. Rather than look inward for the answers, we often seek the authority of others to provide us with solutions. Knowing that a negotiation involves us and other people, we want first to understand "them," completely ignoring the requirement of understanding how "we" affect "them" in the process. If we do acknowledge our own involvement at all, we do so only grudgingly and secondarily. Moreover, we don't seem to have time to comprehend what we learn about "them" fully enough to give the information real applicability. Rather, we are satisfied with the most superficial tips, which we just hope will shed a little light on the actual person sitting opposite us. (The word *tip* itself is telling, for it calls to mind the image of an iceberg and the dangers of believing that the only reality is the little we can actually see.)

We come from a country more culturally diverse than almost any other on earth, yet profess an ignorance of other cultures abroad when the information we need is all around us at home. It strikes me that we Americans have unnecessarily chosen, for a variety of reasons, to keep our blinders on, to maintain the darkness, when this simply does not have to be. Many of the same traditions and values (the content of our cultural baggage) that determine our behavior at the negotiating table abroad also drive us to opt for the quick and dirty solution, the packaged answer, the external, generalized "truth" that has long lost any down-to-earth meaning.

Americans have tended to overlook those aspects of our own culture that can help us as individuals to develop a global mind-set, in an effort to quantify, categorize, and rationalize the rest of the world, to get a fix on things. Perhaps it is an American tendency to understand things in such fashion (not uniquely American, by the way), but there are many paths to understanding, and, as a first lesson in dealing internationally, it's important to recognize that there will be people at the negotiating table who do not understand things this way. Perhaps it is the cult of the expert, the myth of the professional, and the specialist in America that drive us to accumulate detail, to see the trees but not the forest, to rely on the technician but not the teacher. But people from other cultures see things differently, and the better international negotiators recognize that our American way of knowing is only one way of knowing. They acknowledge the futility of trying to be expert at every culture. They are *generalists,* who, in place of a database of cultural prescriptives, have worked at developing behavioral skills that acknowledge and then transcend cultural variances. This is what we mean by a global mind-set.

Our Secret Weapon: Our Multicultural Heritage

Americans have a good shot at understanding what drives the rest of the world at the negotiating table by simply looking at what drives the many peoples of America. Because of our own particular immigrant and multicultural history, we have a unique, built-in advantage when it comes to doing this. The question is, why don't we?

Part of becoming an American in the past has included a denial of our multiculturalism, and, among the many problems this denial has caused, it has prevented us from seeing the hidden advantage that we, as Americans, have in working with people abroad. Too often, to become an American has meant ignoring one's cultural past, putting aside differences, deemphasizing roots. Only within the last decade or so have the emphasizing of cultural differences, the celebration of diversity, and the rediscovery of heritage become important (and the reasons for these trends, curiously, parallel the requirement for Americans to develop an international outlook in business and elsewhere). How many of us lost the opportunity to speak a second or third language (something so valuable when doing business internationally, despite the institutionalization of English as the language of business) because of the stigma attached to speaking the language of our parents' or our grandparents' country? Often, in the process of becoming American, we have been required to adopt values, attitudes, and ways of being that may be very different from those of our root country. Through a complex process of adaptation, assimilation, and adjustment, many of our culturally original ways of being have been masked, repressed, hidden, or reshaped to fit the larger set of definitions that, for the moment at least, described "being American."

In the past, this process helped us to do business with each other by forging a unified domestic business environment. If we all, as Americans, could expect each other to act in predictable, mutually accepted ways, we could do business together. In an effort to create an American business culture that all Americans could understand in a new and growing country, we subsumed our differences under what we believed was the greater American way.

In today's global world, however, it is exactly this past part of ourselves, our unique differences, our pre-Americanized selves, that we need to rediscover, to strengthen and renew, in order to succeed with people in other cultures. We need to dig deep and find the "foreigner" within, to become reacquainted with our grandfathers and grandmothers and their ways. This is the special edge that Americans can have in international business: not in looking outside for the answers, but in looking within. If people in much of the rest of the world have centuries of experience to guide them in doing business with each other, it is precisely America's lack of history that is our advantage. We are still so close to where we came from, we have *the advantage of remembering*. Too often we have focused on where we were going, ignoring where we came from. In order to build a new America, our grandparents were eager to forget the old country, the old language, the old ways. Today, in order to succeed in where we are going, we need to shine a light on where we came from. That outside world, which we now warily approach as alien and unknown, was our first home. If we are to do well in the new global future, we first must reclaim our multinational pasts.

The Importance of Behavioral Skills

As we've been saying, purely intellectual, factual knowledge is of limited use, chiefly because it tends to stay right there, in the intellect. But taking facts and translating them into useful, productive behavior at the international negotiating table is another matter. A major goal of this book, therefore, is to show you how to apply information productively, in ways appropriate to your work. Knowing, for example, that the French tend to think deductively and that Americans tend to think inductively is a statement of cultural fact. But how does that affect *your* negotiation with the French? And how does that affect what *you* will do at the table with them? How will knowing that the Japanese place great emphasis on protocol and seniority affect your behavior with them next time *you* are in Tokyo? Our primary concern is to help you to assess your responses, and how to go about changing them, if you decide it is important to do so. In this sense, we are concerned with helping you to build international negotiating skills, not just a bank of international negotiating facts.

This emphasis on skill-building comes from our experience in the training room. It is very difficult to build behavioral skills, for behavior can be rooted in lifelong patterns and based on deeply held cultural values. Skills development takes time and practice, and certainly won't result from simply studying facts. There needs to be a way to practice change, to connect the mind with the heart, for such learning to be effective. Developing international business skills is not something that occurs overnight. It is an ongoing process of self-assessment and experimentation that can be taken along on one's journeys. Like learning any skill, its mastery takes time, but improves with each successive opportunity to practice it.

It is the purpose of this book, therefore, first and foremost, to help Americans to develop an understanding of our associates abroad at a level deep enough to effect appropriate, constructive behavior in response to the business at hand. Our concern is to help Americans develop an empathic understanding of our opposite numbers' behavior in cross-cultural business circumstances. It allows for appropriate, constructive behavioral responses that advance the negotiation, that emerge naturally from within the individual. It is nonprescriptive, because behavior cannot be prescribed. A global mind-set transcends the details of culture-specific differences by recognizing up front the areas in which differences between cultures might exist, and then helps individuals respond appropriately and constructively to the behavior of their opposite numbers by first identifying that behavior in themselves.

Effective International Behavior

We've been using terms like *empathic, appropriate, constructive,* and *authentic.* Let's take a closer look at what empathy actually means and how the other terms relate. Webster's defines *empathy* as "the action of understanding, being aware of, being sensitive to, and vicariously experiencing the feelings, thoughts, and experience of another." To understand other people empathetically is to be in sympathy with them, to comprehend their needs and motives almost as well as if they were your own.

Empathic understanding, of course, is enhanced by accurate, culture-specific information, but it is not handicapped without it. Understanding empathically enables you to use the information, power, and abilities already within to solve the cross-cultural problems without. It helps you to understand deeply, because you are putting yourself in the other person's place, so that your responses are more naturally appropriate. But more importantly, your responses are also more authentic, that is, they reflect your way of responding, given who you are as a person, and, hence, will probably be much more effective, and more constructive. These three aspects of the global mind-set—reacting appropriately, authentically, and constructively—are critical skills at the international negotiating table and can be developed and learned. Intellectual understanding, on the other hand, while providing some awareness of appropriate and constructive behavior, offers no method for translating this limited information into effective, authentic behavior. Often, the negotiator without a global mind-set is left stranded at the table with a head full of cultural information bytes and no plan for acting on them.

Empathic Versus Intellectual Understanding

As an American, I like to come straight to the point. I like to zoom in to the bottom line and I have little patience for long-winded explanations unrelated to the issue at hand. I especially disdain pomp, protocol, and people who expect me to fall all over them just because they're older or hold a higher position than I. Now let's say I find myself at the negotiating table with someone whose behavior tells me that he expects to take all the time he wants giving me endless background notes, that he is completely uninterested in talking about terms and price at this stage of the negotiation, and that it is very important to him that I demonstrate lots of deference to his higher title and greater age.

In a worst-case scenario, I would have arrived without any cross-cultural information. I would soon become angry, frustrated, and mystified, and there's a very good chance the negotiation would fail at its outset. In a better situation, I would have arrived with some facts about his culture under my belt. But even if I had armed myself with this information ahead of time and knew that people in his country tend to value detail, formality, and seniority, the best I might be able to do with this *intellectual* understanding would be to come prepared with more notes, find someone who could spend an hour or so coaching me on etiquette and protocol in that country, and exercise a lot of patience. Not a bad start, but all of these responses are limited in their appropriateness, constructiveness, and certainly in their authenticity.

It would simply be very difficult for me to exercise the patience required and just as hard for me to remember all the protocols called for under various circumstances in dealing with this person. All these actions would require that *I act according to that person's values*. Worse, this behavior would go *against* my own values. The problem with merely understanding intellectually is that it leaves us stranded without a way to respond behaviorally that's constructive, appropriate, and authentic. All too often the choice before us becomes one of tolerating behavior that we don't understand and may not appreciate, or of accommodating such behavior, but at the risk of losing ourselves in the process. In both cases, there is no constructive, positive movement forward. At best, intellectual understanding points out some of the dangers facing us without providing any information about how to maneuver through them effectively.

Empathic understanding, on the other hand (or, for our purposes, responding to the international business situation with a global mind-set), focuses on my behavioral response to the situation as the important consideration. I consider this the best way. In the above example, I use my global mind-set to understand that there are several business areas in which my foreign associate and I might have different expectations of each other. I know I cannot change his values or his behavior; I have control only over mine.

Here's where a global mind-set—acknowledging another's values and finding them within yourself—comes in. I don't necessarily want to be

like him, and I certainly can't make him like me. I simply want to operate effectively with the "givens" of who we both are, in order to prevent our differences from getting in the way of our business goals.
Where are my values in conflict with his? Aren't there aspects of me that
value detail (I like precision, and disdain sloppy work), formality (a
good hierarchy lets everybody know what to expect), and seniority (I
don't mind when my subordinates give me the respect I deserve)? Now
I can understand where this man across the table is coming from, and
can *authentically* respond to his expectations, for I know how to act according to these values, too. More importantly, I can move comfortably
toward my own goals for this negotiation, knowing now that cultural
differences are not going to undermine the communication or the process of finding a way to make a deal.

Taking Control over the One Thing You Can Control

What, after all, are the goals of cross-cultural understanding in relation
to negotiating business internationally? Why is it important enough for
whole shelves of books to be written about it? This book's point of view
is that we need to understand culture's impact on business in order to
prevent cultural differences from getting in the way of good negotiation. Our goal at the negotiating table is not to give up our values in the
face of our international associates' values, nor to make "them" negotiate "our" way, or to avoid or discount the impact of differences. Our
reason for seeking cross-cultural information is not to learn how to be
more like them or force them to be more like us. Nor is it to accommodate ourselves to their ways, or to make life any more or less pleasant
for them, just because they are negotiating with us.

We should not seek cultural facts about them in order to feel more
secure about ourselves when we're with them. While feeling more secure is important at the negotiating table, cross-cultural information of
the intellectual kind offers a false security. Knowing the etiquette,
avoiding a social *faux pas*, imitating their behavior, might be reassuring
to you for the moment, but it does not address the deeper areas where
cross-cultural misunderstandings make or break good negotiations. Inadvertently crossing your legs or shaking hands incorrectly, or not being able to use chopsticks in China will, more than likely, be shrugged
off, or laughed at, at least, the first time you do it. It will not, I suspect,
seriously affect your business negotiation. (Should you build a real relationship with these individuals, however, and have reason to meet often, it *is* important to learn these things eventually. After all, how many

times can people forgive you for not picking up their customs? After a while, it will grate on your associates, just as non-American behavior by non-Americans in the United States will, after a while, engender negative reactions. At the very least, they may come to question your sensitivity to their country and its ways, and resent your unwillingness to learn.) Real security comes, not in behaving as they would expect you to behave if you were one of them, but rather in being yourself, in being true to your own values, in trusting to your own behavior—and always with a sensitivity to the ways in which they might be very different from you.

The goal of understanding cultural differences, therefore, in the context of international business negotiations, is, quite simply to enable us to get on with the show, to carry out the business at hand that has brought the two parties together. The surest way to accomplish that is to recognize and acknowledge the differences that are at the table and to work with them. And the best way to do *that* is to find the place within where the differences begin to make some sense, where we can relate to them, where they do not seem so "foreign."

When we find that place in ourselves where we can connect in some meaningful way with what at first seemed odd and foreign about our associates, not only do the differences cease to be a threat to the negotiation, but at that point they may actually become a factor contributing to its success. When differences are understood deeply (when I can identify them in myself and can know why you act as you do), it is also possible to acknowledge their possible value. When I see your side, your way, your point of view, I have increased the options available to me (and vice versa). I have grown; I have learned something I did not know before. There may, after all, be another way to look at the problem, another way to slice the pie, another way to skin the cat. Your way might be valuable to me. Understanding where the other person is coming from has never weakened anyone's position at the negotiating table. It does not mean that you give up your own. It simply means you've got more options to consider. It might enrich your possibilities for the immediate negotiation, and it certainly adds to your global mind-set for the future. You might not win every international negotiation you participate in, but you can certainly learn from them.

Preempting and Preventing
Versus Prescribing

Cross-cultural understanding in negotiations is very much about preemptive action. Many of the horror stories of cultural misunderstandings one hears in business describe situations already past the point of no return. The errors have been made; the wrong actions have already been taken. In these cases, the best one can hope to do is exercise damage control, redeem what is left, pick up the pieces, learn from the mistakes, and try again later. But cross-cultural understanding should not have to be used for damage control. It should be used instead to guide preemptive action—to make it possible to plan, anticipate, get a sense of what might be in store, *in order to do something about potential problems before they develop*. I emphasize this final point because this is where empathic understanding comes in and intellectual understanding leaves off. Intellectual understanding provides precious little in the way of helping us decide in advance what to *do* about the circumstances we are about to face. A global mind-set, on the other hand, allows us to focus on this aspect first and permits us to exercise the only real control we have in the situation—over ourselves. By better understanding our own cultural habits and expectations, we can more deeply understand those of our negotiating partners and respond more constructively and authentically in order to avoid, prevent, preempt, and in a sense *transcend* the cultural differences.

All good international negotiators recognize their opposite numbers in themselves. But Americans have the unique advantage of having an intimate connection with most of the people they will be negotiating with abroad, because Americans came from "there" not too long ago. Deep inside us is a place where we can remember what it is like to walk in their shoes. Therefore, this book hopes to help Americans develop this understanding of our "foreign" associates by helping us recognize the foreigner in ourselves. It is the best way to truly understand your foreign associates, and it is available to every American automatically.

Negotiation as Communication

Throughout this book, we will alternately refer to *communicating* with our foreign associates, *bargaining* with our associates abroad, *doing business with*, or *managing*, local country nationals, and, of course, *negotiating* with them. Bargaining is just one possible component of negotiating, and, like doing business, managing, and communicating just naturally intertwine with negotiation. Negotiation is essentially about communication, and nowhere is that more clear than in business dealings across cultures in an international setting. All business between individuals is a negotiation in one form or another. And ideally, all negotiation involves clear communication.

When we speak of *negotiating* in this book, we will be using the term in its broadest possible application.

One can have a preference for negotiating a particular way, but that way is just *one* way to negotiate. It does not define *negotiation*. One might see the negotiation process merely as an opportunity to bargain, but that, too, is but one definition. One might view a negotiation as the meeting itself, but that is limiting, too. In fact, how one defines the process of negotiating is culturally determined. Some cultures see it only as an opportunity to bargain, others as the establishment of a lifetime relationship that goes beyond the occasional meetings, still others as an opportunity to demonstrate their capacity for eloquence and debate. Some do not see negotiation as a process at all. We will look, in fact, at how different cultures view the idea of negotiation later in the book, in order to see how it fits with our own American notions. Differences in the fundamental definition of the act itself can be so basic that they often, if unrecognized, remain the source of the most profound problems in business. It is doubly important, therefore, when discussing negotiation in the multicultural global context, to keep the meaning of the word as flexible as possible.

Because all business is ultimately a negotiation, the examples you'll find throughout this book will all be representations of negotiating, even if they may not look that way at first. They may not fit your initial expectations of what negotiation should look like precisely because they involve non-Americans. Should a negotiation be a formal meeting, or can it be a casual conversation at a café? Does it include outsiders or only privileged power holders? Is it an occasion for running off with the goodies before the people on the other side knows what hit them, or is it an opportunity to establish collaborative, long-lasting personal and business relationships? Do we exchange information or keep it close to the vest? Is it one on one or group to group? Can an informal argument in the back room, an office Christmas party, a late night out at the bars after work, or a welcoming reception be a negotiation, too? In the international arena, all of these must be open for consideration until we are quite clear about how each particular culture perceives the negotiation. For now, all business is negotiating, and all negotiating is communicating. Remember, this book is about how to do business across borders.

Culture Is Nonnegotiable

One final word about negotiating and values: you can negotiate business, but you cannot negotiate values. Values, like the different cultures they're a part of, are nonnegotiable. You don't have to like them, you don't have to make them your own, but you will not be able to change them—at least not at your negotiation. Changing another's values should not be the goal of a business negotiation anyway, unless your business is that of changing hearts and minds (and that's another book). If you make the decision to sit down at the table with people from another culture, you're implicitly acknowledging their values. You don't have to agree with them, but in order for you to be successful in your negotiation, you do need to respect them, and you have the right to expect that your foreign associates will respect your values as well. (This may sound easier than it is.)

In fact, you may not know what the values of your associates are until they begin to reveal themselves through the course of negotiation. That, after all, is one of the reasons why we need cross-cultural information ahead of time. We may not be able to anticipate how we will feel in response to certain behavior and values, and we may find ourselves in uncomfortable situations dealing with individuals whom we come to discover we do not like. Based on values alone, we might find these people very disagreeable if we met them at a party, for example. The point, though, is that a business negotiation requires a professional relationship. You don't have to like each other to be able to do business together, and that's true even in those cultures where personal relationships are important to the business deal. If the values of the people on the other side strike you as so reprehensible that you cannot sit down at the table with them, because doing business with them would mean seriously compromising your own values, ethics, or beliefs, you must face the fact that negotiation—and the business that depends on it—may be out of the question. Fine. Just do not expect to do business *and* change those values. There may be situations where you have to make this kind of choice; it is probably better to make the decision to walk away than try to change the other person's values at the table. As we will see later, making the values of the person on the other side of the table part of what you are negotiating will probably derail the entire negotiation.

In the midseventies, the United States and the former Soviet Union had several negotiations over the sale of wheat. Some of the original negotiations failed because both the Soviets and the Americans made cultural values part of what was being negotiated. During high-level initial negotiations, both parties focused on positions and postures, rather than on the issues at hand. In effect, the Americans were saying that they could not negotiate with the Soviets because the Soviets were communists, and the Soviets were saying that they could not negotiate with the Americans because the Americans were capitalists. Both sides allowed their different beliefs to enter into and become part of the negotiation. This is an all-too-frequent occurrence at international governmental negotiations and an all-too-frequent pretext for ending negotiations that were perhaps not entered into in good faith in the first place. Unfortunately, the real issues get put aside in favor of less central, and ultimately irreconcilable cultural differences. In the case of the Soviets and the Americans, the negotiation did not really begin until both sides refocused their concerns away from each other's economic and social value systems and onto the issue of the wheat being offered for sale. Once the purchase of wheat became the central concern, the negotiations proceeded—and relatively smoothly, at that.[1]

The moral of the story is that it is very difficult to change the values of the other side, and it is best, at the negotiating table anyway, not to try. If the other side's values are so intolerable to you that you cannot ignore them, you may want to decide that you cannot negotiate with them. Perhaps we are making more of an issue over this point than we need to, but businesses in the global arena now face, and will increasingly face, similar issues all the time. It may not be that far removed from you and your business. How, for example, would you feel being asked to pay what you consider a bribe in order to get a contract approved? How would you react to a business opportunity with a government known for its human rights or environmental abuses? What if you are a woman, or an African-American, or a Jew, and need to do business with a culture in which women do not do business with men, in which African-Americans are not taken seriously, or in which Jews are hated? These are not farfetched possibilities in a world where all sorts of businesses are meeting all sorts of cultures. You need, ahead of time, to know how you will respond under these, and other, ethically challenging circumstances, for yourself, your associates, and your company. We will discuss ethical problems throughout the book. For now, suffice it to say that values are nonnegotiable and must be acknowledged as legitimate at the negotiating table, in order for both parties to be able to proceed with the business at hand.

How the Global Homecoming Exercises© Work

Since we have been emphasizing the "doing" part of understanding as opposed to the "knowing" part, it's only right that this book challenge you to "do" as well as "know." Therefore, keeping these experiential learning goals in mind, you will find a special section called a Global

---

[1]This example was developed and analyzed by Ellen Raider of International, Inc.

Homecoming Exercise° at the end of many chapters. Each exercise begins with a scenario involving an American businessperson and his or her non-American associates. In each case, the American is having a problem, but it's your job to figure out what he or she is doing wrong, what cultural factors are in conflict, and what might be the best way to solve the problem. Some of the scenarios might be familiar to you if you've been doing business abroad. Some might be new to you. Certainly, if you are already familiar with business in the cultures represented in these scenarios, you will probably have an easier time identifying what's going on and what to do about it.

The primary benefit of each exercise is the opportunity offered to you to work on developing a global mind-set—to identify with the non-Americans in the situation by relating aspects of your own experience to their behavior and putting yourself in their place in order to understand why they are doing what they do. In fact, the Global Homecoming Exercises° that might be of most value to you could be those involving cultures about which you have no information and with which you have had no experience. The purpose of these exercises, after all, is to help you develop the skills necessary to deal with any cross-cultural business situation in a safe way—with or without previous knowledge of the culture *before* you go out and endure the bumps and bruises of the cold, hard world. Whether or not you are already knowledgeable about the particular countries represented in the Global Homecoming Exercises°, we believe they can help you determine a culturally appropriate and positive solution, because the exercises are designed to help you develop a global mind-set.

Each Global Homecoming Exercise follows a five-step process of recognizing, retracing, reclaiming, reframing, and resurfacing°. The goal of Step 1, recognizing, is to sharpen your ability to identify conflicting cultural values. Since each exercise is designed to reflect the cultural issues discussed in the chapter preceding it, you'll have a chance to take the information you have just read and apply it to a real-life business scenario. Step 2, retracing, asks you to identify individuals in your own past with values similar to those of the foreign characters in the business case. Step 3, reclaiming, asks you to recall the response you had to these people in your past, your feelings about them, and interactions with them. Step 4, reframing, asks you to reevaluate that past situation—including the people involved and your reactions to them—in the light of who you are now and what you now know. If you were back there today, what would you do? Would you act differently? How? Finally, Step 5, resurfacing, asks you to apply this information to the business case at hand. How can you best use your past experiences to guide you through current situations and help you resolve cultural conflicts more appropriately, authentically, and constructively?

There is no time limit for the Global Homecoming Exercises°, although you should be able to go through all five steps of each exercise in less than an hour. The exercises are a personal journey. They are meant to help you discover and develop the tools you need for a genuine understanding of your foreign associates, whether or not you are familiar with their cultures, by finding similarities between them and yourself. In the appendix at the end of the book, you will find detailed analyses of each Global Homecoming° scenario, providing culture-specific information, as well as a chance for you to see how your empathic solution stacks up against the analysis.

The Global Homecoming Exercises° are not the only experiential practice in the book. In keeping with our belief that real understanding of cultural differences at the negotiating table needs to be more than intellectual, you will find many examples of Americans attempting to do business abroad. Most of these examples are based on my own experiences or on the experiences of associates and friends. Each example highlights an important point being made in the chapter, and each is analyzed in detail. However, most will be presented in a way that will enable you to test your own analytical skills first. That is, the analysis will come after the example, so that you will always have the chance to interpret on your own before the book does it for you. As you develop your global mind-set, your own analyses will get swifter and sharper.

Most chapters will also contain cultural measurement scales, helping you to get a fix on your own cultural baggage and on your perceptions of other cultures as they relate to key areas of business. As various issues are discussed, you will also have the opportunity to judge how near or how far, how different or similar, your beliefs and attitudes are to those of businesspeople from different cultures.

We will try throughout the book to look at as many different key cultures as possible. In this sense, we will be taking a world tour of important countries in order to explore how their cultures have affected the ways they do business and in what ways American approaches tend to differ. Since Americans do more business in some areas of the world than in others, we will try to focus the majority of our remarks on the following key regions: Japan and the Pacific Rim; Western, Southern, and Central Europe; Latin America and the Caribbean; the Arab world and South/Southwest Asia; Australia; and developing Africa. Our apologies go out to readers looking for information about countries and cultures we have omitted. Would that there were time, space, and knowledge enough to cover them all!

A word of caution: The many cultures we will be looking at will be covered in no particular order. You will not be able to find, for example, a chapter on Japan or one on sub-Saharan Africa. In keeping with the central philosophy of the book, we are not setting out to provide a culture-by-culture list of prescriptives and generalizations. Rather, we will be highlighting important country-specific information as illustrations of the topics discussed. You will find that the cultural examples throughout the book provide a significant amount of information about many parts of the world. It is important to know as much as possible about the countries you do business with, and we'll be making many observations about the business behavior of other cultures. At all times we will try to ensure that the generalizations we make about a country's business behavior are as valuable as the historical factors driving that behavior.

Let's Agree on Some Terms

A brief note about terminology. First we will try, whenever possible, to be consistent in using the most appropriate and current terms. By the time you read this, however, no doubt some of the terms will already be out of date; such is our modern, changing world. Nevertheless, some important points need to be made about the terms we've used and why. First, to all my Canadian, Mexican, Guatemalan, Cuban, Puerto Rican, Brazilian, Argentinian, and Ecuadorian readers—in fact, to all readers anywhere in the Western Hemisphere—I extend my apologies for the use, throughout the book, of *American* to mean *U.S.-national.* As a U.S.-national, myself, I am as guilty as most of my fellow citizens in casually coopting the term *American.* However, since the word *American* is used almost as often by citizens of other nations in the Western Hemisphere when referring to U.S. nationals, and since there isn't an alternative term, I shall use the term *American* to mean "U.S. national." I welcome any and all suggestions for alternative phraseology. In addition, my British friends have assured me that referring to "the Brits" is just fine, although "Scotch" is only a noun when it refers to a whiskey. When referring to the people of Scotland, therefore, I shall use the word *Scots.*

For our purposes, *North America* will be used to mean Canada and the United States taken together, exclusive of Mexico and the Caribbean. *Latin America* will be used to mean all the countries from Mexico to Argentina and Chile, again exclusive of the Caribbean (Hispanic cultures in the Caribbean being noticeably different, in terms of business customs and expectations, from those in South and Central America).

Western Europe will mean the United Kingdom, Scotland, Ireland, France, Germany, the Benelux countries, Switzerland, and Austria. We will use the term *Nordic countries* when referring to the countries of Scandinavia as well as to Iceland and Finland. *Mediterranean or Southern Europe* will refer to Portugal, Spain, Italy, and Greece. (Yugoslavia is a non-Mediterranean, Slavic culture and will be considered part of Central Europe.) Since Eastern Europe is no longer within the former Soviet sphere, the area will be referred to as *Central Europe* (its pre–Cold War description), while the term *Eastern Europe* will be reserved for those republics of the former Soviet Union east of Central Europe and west of the Urals. This includes Russia. The *Baltics* remains the reference for the countries of Lithuania, Estonia, and Latvia.

Since *the Middle East* is in no way an accurate cultural reference, that area of the world will be referred to as *Southwest Asia,* encompassing Turkey, the Arab and Gulf states, Israel, and Iran. *South Asia* will refer to India, Pakistan, Afghanistan, Bangladesh, Nepal, Bhutan and Sri Lanka. *China* will be used to mean the People's Republic of China (as distinct from Taiwan). The *Pacific Rim* will mean those countries in the region now experiencing or likely soon to experience the economic boom of that region. This includes Japan and "the four dragons" of Korea, Singapore, Hong Kong, and Taiwan, as well as the Philippines, Brunei, Thailand, and Malaysia. *Southeast Asia* will mean those countries in the region that have not yet experienced an economic boom, such as Indonesia, Papua New Guinea, Vietnam, Kampuchea, Laos, and Myanmar (Burma). Sometimes Australia and New Zealand are included in the term *Pacific Rim,* but I prefer to refer to them as *Austral regions,* since their cultures are significantly unrelated to both their Pacific Rim and Southeast Asian neighbors.

For our purposes, *North Africa* refers to all Saharan countries, as well as to Egypt and the Sudan. *West Africa* refers to African nations of the sahel, such as French-speaking non-Saharan Africa and Nigeria, Ghana, Liberia, Sierre Leone, Togo, Benin, Guinea, etc. *Sub-Saharan Africa* refers to the central tropical African countries. *East Africa* covers Ethiopia, Somalia, Tanzania, Malawi, Uganda, the Malagasy Republic, Kenya, and Rwanda-Burundi. *South Africa* means South Africa, Angola, Lesotho, Swaziland, Zambia, Zimbabwe, Botswana, Namibia, and Mozambique. I am sure I have offended someone, either by inclusion or omission. Believe me, no offense was intended.

One final remark about terminology. Throughout the book, we will be using several different terms to refer to non-Americans (i.e., non-U.S. nationals). Among these terms are *foreigners, foreign associates, associates abroad,* and simply "non-Americans" or "non–U.S. nationals." Each of these terms has its drawbacks, but since no better terms have come to mind, I shall quite arbitrarily use them all, thereby spreading the damage equally. *Foreigners,* of course, are only foreign to their own country when they are not *in* their own country; in fact, the Americans doing business abroad are the foreigners, not the people they are negotiating with. Nevertheless, we will be referring to the non-Americans in these situations as the foreigners, since the book has the American's point of view. *Foreign associate* is a bit softer, I suppose, but still doesn't really solve the problem. *Associate abroad* is better, but a bit weak (notice we will also avoid the word *overseas,* since you can go to another country without having to cross an ocean, as when U.S. nationals visit their Canadian, Mexican, or Peruvian friends). *Non-Americans* requires the caveat that we are excluding all non-U.S. American nationals, and *non-U.S. nationals* is abominably awkward. There you have it. If anyone has any suggestions to clear this up, I welcome all ideas!

The Plan of the Book

Part 1 will begin by taking a close look at what it means for Americans to be working in the rest of the world and what our American cultural baggage looks like from out there. We'll discuss important concepts in cross-cultural understanding in order to better understand the problems that arise when two different sets of baggage conflict at the negotiating table. Part 2 will give you the chance to identify your American values, behavior, attitudes, and traditions as they affect important areas of business in various cultures around the world. In Part 3 we'll look first at the global mind-set of the ideal international negotiator, discussing the behavior used in successful international negotiations. Then we'll explore the impact of culture on those areas of business especially critical to the negotiation process. Part 3 will also help you to identify those aspects of the global mind-set that are already part of our experience as Americans. Additionally, Part 3 will discuss various theoretical models of effective negotiation and integrate the various cultural components into those models.

Throughout the book, we will be working from these premises:

- That developing the capacity for appropriate, authentic, and constructive responses to cross-cultural differences is the most important task facing the international negotiator

- That culture-specific intellectual information is most useful when it enhances a preexisting global mind-set

- That the unique multicultural American heritage provides a special

advantage when it comes to developing an empathic approach because Americans abroad are not explorers of alien lands; instead, they
are returning home

In summary, then, this book is meant as a kind of training guide and
roadmap. Tuck it into your "baggage," along with your values and traditions, and it will provide meaningful clues for understanding the non-
Americans you are doing business with. As we've discovered through
our training sessions and consultations, the best answers are often contained within ourselves. We simply need a way of letting them out, of
discovering and applying them. Hopefully, this book will help you do
just that. Let's begin our journey.

2
Some Basic Cross-Cultural Ground Rules

That Sinking Feeling

"Something wasn't going quite right." "I had a sinking feeling that what I said and what they heard were two different things." "I didn't feel as if I was really connecting with them." "They were nice enough, but it was as if we were talking beyond each other." "It seemed to me that we should have been a lot further along than we were." "Despite my best intentions, I felt as if nothing I did was right."

A fish out of water. A bull in a china shop. A stranger in a strange land. These are just some of the phrases used by Americans to sum up their experience of doing business in foreign countries. The obvious differences (a five-hour time-zone difference, for example) are distressing enough. But even more troubling are the subtle, unexpected differences that creep up on us unaware when we're abroad, keeping us constantly off balance and unsure of how to react. It's often our inability to locate a cause, to nail down a reason, for the gnawing discomfort we feel that's most disturbing of all. At the negotiating table, things might seem to be going well. To all appearances, there is nothing wrong, nothing that can be identified as the source, or reason, for the fact that, despite the smiles and good intentions, the negotiations are falling apart. And that's when things are going well! Equally common is the situation in which, despite your own best intentions, clarity of thought, positive expectations, and best efforts, the other side seems determined to be belligerent, obstinate, suspicious, stubborn, and uncooperative. As with much of human reality, ways of understanding, ways of negotiating, and ways of communicating are culturally determined. How we think, how we view ourselves in relation to others, and how we view success are all conditioned, to greater and lesser degrees, by the world around us. That world — our culture, our society — is the environment in which we were raised and currently live. It flows through the patterned interaction of virtually all the stimuli we receive. It speaks through the values, beliefs, and attitudes of everyone we know, from the members of our family to the newsmakers we read about and see on TV. If society has a profound effect on so many aspects of our lives, it's logical to assume that it also has a profound effect on how we behave in business.

Our goal is to isolate this area and identify how our own culture, our American society, has determined our attitudes, values, perceptions, and behavior when it comes to work, business, and negotiations. The tricky part is that the same kind of cultural programming we've undergone in the States has also been at work on our associates abroad. They, too, have a particular perception of reality, formed significantly by the patterned interaction of combined social forces in their own countries. When life in the United States and our associates' countries is basically similar, our beliefs, attitudes, outlooks, and expectations tend to mesh easily. Opposite each other at the negotiating table, our styles of communication and negotiation will have much in common. We'll each know what to expect, play by more or less the same implicit rules, have similar priorities, and find it easy to understand their actions — perhaps even their motives, needs, and objectives.

But often the circumstances of life in our own and our associates' countries are very different. In these cases, the outlooks, expectations, and behaviors of the two parties will be just as dissimilar, and we'll probably have trouble interpreting each other's behavior at the negotiating table. Not knowing the ground rules by which the other operates, we'll have a hard time making accurate assumptions about their motives, needs, expectations, or objectives. And to complicate things further, since we each know only our own way, we'll each tend to interpret the other's behavior through our own cultural perspectives, quite likely piling misunderstanding on misunderstanding.

Our culture gives us our world view, and this includes not only the specifics of how we operate, but even the fundamental categories into which these specifics fall. It would be difficult, for example, to understand a particular *way* of doing something if we didn't first have a basic category in which those ways could vary. It's like trying to know the difference between the colors blue and red, without first establishing the

category of "color". It's the same with cross-cultural differences. Sometimes the cultural differences, the backgrounds of the people, and the
lives they live in their respective countries are so dissimilar that there
are not even comparable larger categories under which to define the
specific differences between us.

At the negotiating table, for example, Americans might expect a
meeting to begin and end at a certain time, with a series of important
points discussed in between. Our Latin counterparts, however, while
agreeing to this format, might arrive much later than the time stated
and expect to discuss a great many things in addition to or perhaps instead of what was on the agenda, even if it means keeping the Americans and the meeting going long beyond its stated end-time. There are
clearly immediate differences over scheduling practices. But on a
deeper level, there are also basic category differences: the Latins have
certain ideas about business relationships that Americans simply do not
have, which in turn, affect the way they handle their schedules. And it's
most often conflicts over these deeper cultural differences that create
"that sinking feeling."

How do you know you've got a cross-cultural problem? Well, if you're
lucky, it might be obvious: neither of you speaks the other's language;
you eat lunch at noon, and they eat lunch at 2 p.m.; you want to get
straight down to business, and they want to take you to their local
shrine. The solutions to these kinds of differences are easy to prescribe,
precisely because the problems are immediately identifiable. The differences are specific within mutually shared categories: in this case, you
both have a language, only yours is different; you both eat lunch, only
at different times; and you both recognize the importance of religion,
only he or she, more so. Instead of a sinking feeling in the pit of the
stomach, one's reaction to these kinds of differences is more like a brisk
nod of the head.

But, how do you come up with a prescription for some of the more
subtle problems highlighted above—where things aren't going well
and you simply don't know why? This time, the reasons are not specifically identifiable, because there are categorical differences between yourself and your opposite number. This is where that sinking
feeling comes in. Check it out. It is a sign that deep differences exist
between you and your opposite numbers. You may not know what
the differences are, but identifying the problem is the beginning of
the solution. How to sort out those specific and categorical differences between the way you're thinking and the way the person opposite you is thinking is what this book, and this chapter in particular, is
all about.

The Purpose of Cross-Cultural Information

"I don't want to do anything stupid." "I don't want to offend them." "I don't know anything about how they behave." "I'd like to be able to do things the way they do things, so we'll all feel comfortable with one another."

These are some of the more common goals people give when stating why they attend training and consulting workshops on cross-cultural orientation and international negotiation. Sometimes people are more candid and say things like, "If I know how they're thinking, I'll know what to do." I'm never quite sure if the speaker here should be praised for his or her desire for in-depth understanding or considered suspect for his or her manipulativeness. In any event, some of the motives for cross-cultural understanding in business need to be examined closely.

Cross-cultural information is not about turning you into them, turning them into you, or making you more like one another. It's not about "my way" versus "your way," or "good" versus "bad." It is about the adjustment of expectations, about preventive versus curative action, and, ultimately, about increasing your own options.

The most disruptive cross-cultural problems tend to emerge over deep cultural misunderstandings rather than over specific behavioral differences. (A particular behavior might spark a breakdown in communication or understanding, but it is more often based on deeper misunderstandings that have been at work previously.) There is a significant distinction to be made between "deep culture" and customs. Not knowing that it is impolite to do this or that will generally not make or break a negotiation, but deeply misunderstanding the other side's intent by not understanding the thought processes could have serious repercussions for the negotiation.

A passing note here: Certainly, it is appreciated when one demonstrates an awareness of and a sensitivity to the customs of another country. It can go far in helping to develop an ongoing business relationship, so I am not discounting its value. I am, however, trying to minimize the possibility of serious damage when such sensitivity is not demonstrated. It is simply more important to focus on the deep cultural differences. If I accidentally forget my manners and tap a Malay's head, show the sole of my shoe to my Arab associate, or give the OK sign to my Brazilian business partner, it may not be appreciated. But all other things being equal, it won't seriously affect our ongoing business relationship. If I were to remain ignorant of important customs over a period of time in which I could reasonably be expected to become familiar with them, my associates *would* probably become annoyed. It is for this reason that information regarding etiquette, customs, etc. can be very useful. Sometimes, after all, things are not always equal, and a small breach of etiquette in a tenuous set of circumstances can be the straw that breaks the camel's back. But this is the exception rather than the rule.

Curiously, though, it is just such do's and don't's, or concerns for surface issues such as etiquette and customs, that many negotiators-to-be see as primary information to be digested before going off to their foreign associates. There are probably many reasons for this basically misguided effort, not the least of which is that it's simply easier and more efficient to believe that all one needs to do is get a few interesting pointers under one's belt to be off and running. It's also unsettling to focus on deep-culture issues because it involves an exploration of the unknown. We are, after all, talking about fundamental categorical differences between the way you and someone else might be viewing essential facts of life. Behavioral responses to such basic differences in this case ask us to enter the unknown, and this is not as easy as learning which fork to pick up or whether to bow or shake hands. I suspect that the issue is one of personal security, and the way Americans often seem to resolve this issue when with non-Americans is to try donning new customs like a new suit of clothes.

While we've stated this before, it bears repeating here: People cannot be who they are not. And nothing is more damaging to a blossoming relationship than inauthenticity. Real security abroad comes not in mimicking customs in order to avoid offense, but rather in more deeply understanding the other side while remaining true to oneself. The task of understanding the other side, of recognizing the differences and plumbing the depths of one's own behavior to find responses that are authentic, is admittedly a daunting activity. It's certainly not as simple as picking up a few quaint and curious facts about the other side's culture. It takes commitment, self-assurance, time, and energy.

The gut reaction to this challenge is often: "Why do we have to learn so much about them?" "Are they learning as much about us?" "Shouldn't they have to accommodate to us a little, too?" What's the purpose of going over all this anyway? The world is getting so small, we're all going to be the same anyway."

Well, the answer, like most things in a complicated world, is "yes" and "no." First of all, cross-cultural awareness is not about changing anybody. Just as you shouldn't have to become like your international associates, you cannot expect them to become like you. Therefore, any cross-cultural training they might be receiving, any preparation they might be getting for negotiating with Americans, if meaningful, will not make them more like you in any deep important way. If it is good training, it will help them understand why you do what you do and help them adjust their own expectations in response to who you are, in order to move the negotiation forward and avoid shoals of misunderstandings along the way.

The fact is that they probably already know a lot more about you than you know about them. It is simply in our best interests to put the time, energy, and money into learning about them, if only to balance the scales and give ourselves a fighting chance. American popular culture is one of our greatest exports. Most of the rest of the world has received a great deal of information about us as a society through Hollywood, our music, TV, etc. Although much of it is stereotypical and misinformational, its sheer volume has been so great that a lot of valuable information about Americans has gotten out there. Americans are also very mobile, not only within our own borders, but throughout the world. We have, for better or for worse, also personally carried American culture with us in our travels to other countries. Many nations have also experienced American culture through our military involvements in their countries, beginning with World War I. And there is no denying that English has become a significant second language throughout the world, taught in schools and used (at least in snatches) in everyday life.

English has also become, to all intents and purposes, the first language of business. And since language is such a significant cultural difference (certainly the most obvious), many Americans tend to feel that there is no need to learn more about "them," since we're already speaking English together. But that's just the point. "They" have already gone more than halfway toward meeting us: they've learned our language, while we rarely bother to learn theirs. They've learned about our culture (often unintentionally) while we have received little information about theirs. If it were merely for the sake of being courteous, it would be important for us to learn more about our foreign associates before sitting down to do business with them.

Many of the cultures we are doing business with in the rest of the world are significantly more conservative, more cautious, in their business attitudes than we, as a culture, generally are. This means, among other things, that their need for information, their need to be certain before making decisions, before taking action, can be greater than similar needs in ourselves. This fact has important repercussions for our discussion. Having a greater need to be sure, being less able to feel comfortable with risk, means that the people of many of these cultures devote considerably more time and energy to finding out about us than we, being less conservative, more daring, if you will (along with, perhaps, more time-conscious), will want to devote to finding out about them. This means that, when dealing with people from many of these cultures, you might be sitting opposite someone who has amassed a considerable amount of information about you and your company, who knows a great deal about who you are and what you've been up to. Americans have a tendency to "wing it," to "shoot from the hip," to "run it up the flagpole just to see if anyone salutes." We're comfortable taking a certain amount of risk, and this means that, under certain conditions, of course, we don't need as much information in order to make a decision or take action. This is often not true of the people you are negotiating with. It is usually a safe bet that your opposite numbers have devoted considerable resources to investigating you and your company before you first get together.

All this adds up to a lot of information on their side about who we are, what we want, and how we might behave and not too much similar information about them on our side. In preparing people for assignments to represent their firms in the United States, the Japanese might typically provide cross-cultural training and then send them to live in the United States without expecting any measurable results for a full year. Instead, these individuals (and sometimes their families, too) are expected to learn about America and Americans, to settle in, to develop ties, networks, and a working knowledge of how business in their field is done here. The Japanese, having a much longer-term view than is typically American, do not expect real results during this learning and adjustment period; rather it is viewed as a training period, during which information is gathered and evaluated.

Americans, on the other hand, can be sent off on foreign assignments with a minimum of notice, advance planning, or preparation and with the expectation that real and measurable business results will commence within the first three months of their arrival. The idea of providing orientation training for themselves and their families, of helping them to better do their job, and adjust to possibly very different ways of life is a relatively new one. Traditionally, adjustment was seen as a "soft" requirement, not to be taken quite so seriously. It is something that could just as easily be handled by connecting the expatriates and their families to someone already settled in "over there" to hold their hands and "mentor" them along. As American business has gotten more involved in the global arena, however, the need for a more formal and systematic approach to providing cross-cultural information, not only for American expatriates, but for the families whose happiness is critical to the expats' peace of mind and effectiveness, is more often being given serious consideration. Nevertheless, our overall attitude toward learning about "them," whether in preparation for living abroad or merely to become a more effective negotiator (here *or* there), is significantly less pressing than in many of the cultures American businesspeople do business with. For a variety of reasons, Americans are, comparatively speaking, still much less prepared about international associates than they are about us.

As for the argument that we don't have to learn about how different we are now because the world is getting smaller so rapidly that we are really all going to be the same soon anyway, I suppose the best response is, "Well, it hasn't happened yet!" Whether we should be preparing for this coming utopia with joy or despair is open to speculation. Whether it is even going to happen is the stuff of debate. As stated previously, I personally suspect that we will see the development of certain pan-regional (perhaps even panglobal) business behavior, but that the traditional national values of individual businesspeople will be very much with them, and consequently, with us, for some time to come. In fact, faced with economic homogenization, cultural distinctions are often highlighted as important guideposts to identity. We see this happening in Europe today, where, despite the economic unity of 1992, there is the simultaneous development of pan-European values and business behaviors and the digging-in of individual national identities. Studies have shown traditional values to be deeply rooted and difficult to change, whatever current events may suggest. In any case, we have to do our business in the world of the here and now, and none of this is in the imminent future. Right now we are dealing with people who do business differently from the way we do. So how are we going to handle it? Ultimately, presenting an argument for not learning about differences because of our growing similarities is an excuse for denial. And that gets us nowhere.

On a deeper level, I also suspect that those who say we are all becoming the same really mean that we are all becoming American, which is merely the latest version of the old chestnut repeated by inexperienced Americans abroad that "if you scratch a foreigner, you'll find that he or she is really American deepdown." This is ignorant chauvinism. Scratch a non-American and you'll more likely get scratched back by a non-American.

"When in Rome..."

One question I often get asked is, "What can we expect of our foreign associates when they come to the States to negotiate with us? After all, if they become our guests—if the shoe is on the other foot, so to speak— shouldn't we be able to expect them to conform to our ways, much as we are trying to conform to theirs when we are in their countries?" Again, the question is really one of to what degree either side should expect the other to change in cross-cultural business situations, and the answer, again, is that neither side should expect the other to change in any really important ways. It's not possible, and it's also not desirable. We might reasonably expect our foreign associates to be aware, when they visit us here, of certain basic customs. (They're probably already familiar with them anyway, given the ubiquity of American popular culture abroad.) Beyond that, we'll probably be forgiving of any breaches and appreciative of all efforts. And this is what we can realistically expect of them in return, when we are doing business in their country.

We need not attempt to mirror or replay any of their preferences or customs while they are in the United States unless we consciously choose to do so, and I would suggest *not* doing so unless you decide there is a tangible and real benefit in doing so. Most of the time, such paralleling of others' ways in our country comes off as just plain "odd." Unless such activity will really go a long way toward solving some problem or easing an uncomfortable situation for your guest, I suggest not bothering. Usually, when we try to "be more like them," we wind up making fools of ourselves. It's like the Japanese who reach out to shake hands with the Americans visiting Tokyo as the Americans simultaneously attempt to bow. The gesture is appreciated, but it can cause confusion. I am reminded of the story of the Englishman who comes to America. He is told ahead of time, of course, that Americans are very informal so he arrives at his first business meeting in New York casually dressed — no tie, a sport coat, etc. Of course, all in attendance are wearing dark, conservative business suits. Thinking to himself that his information about Americans was perhaps wrong, he is careful to wear his perfectly English dark suit to his next meeting in Texas, where, of course, everyone shows up in cowboy boots, hats, and string ties. I really cannot imagine any Englishman messing up in quite this way, so maybe it is an old and exaggerated story. But the point is well worth noting. The most useful application of cross-cultural information is not to enable you to be like your international associates, but to know how they behave in order to more comfortably be yourself. It is a matter of adjusting expectations, not behavior. In fact, for many of the reasons we have highlighted above, most foreign associates do a better job of adjusting their expectations when they come to the United States than we do of adjusting our expectations when we go to their countries.

Much of the time, foreign associates relish the opportunity to experience real American life when they come to our shores. Of course your French associates eat French food in France. But when they come to the United States, they don't expect to be taken to the finest French restaurants every night; what they might really appreciate, however, is a down-home American barbecue, something they can't get so easily in France. Of course your Japanese associates will exchange expensive gifts with you when you visit them in Tokyo. But when they come here, what they might actually appreciate receiving is something truly representative of the United States, something that might be difficult, expensive, or unattainable in Japan, even though it might be inexpensive and attainable here. In fact, one of the best gifts I've ever heard of Americans giving to their Japanese associates — although it was sent over to Tokyo after the visit — was a box of grapefruit (several dozen of the excellent kind that are shipped by speciality fruiterers). Apparently, grapefruit is very expensive and not easy to come by in Japan. Sending a quantity as a gift to one individual allowed that person to pass the rest among his associates there, a fact that meshed well with the Japanese value of group orientation. When in America, your guests generally will appreciate learning from you about American ways; you should try to maintain those ways, with a respect for the fact that the ways and needs of your guests might be different. (Your Chinese guests, for example, despite their possible curiosity about American food, will probably appreciate dining on good Chinese food simply because American food is so different from what they are used to.)

Some final thoughts on the purposes of cross-cultural information in negotiations. As we've stated earlier, information about how foreign associates negotiate differently is most useful in a preemptive, or preventive, way. Information allows you to control your own behavior, reactions, etc. so that problems can be avoided. Once they've occurred, it can often be difficult to roll back the consequences. At that point, sometimes the most one can expect is "damage control." Hindsight and "should have done" are hard lessons in real life. It we can learn about differences and their consequences and experiment with reacting appropriately, constructively, and authentically to them in a safe, controlled learning environment *prior* to experiencing them in real life, we might be able to avoid them. All international negotiators have horror stories, and no doubt you will have a few of your own. It is a difficult skill, this informed mastering of one's own reactions to unfamiliar behavior, but the better negotiators take their experiences and learn from them. We will discuss in depth some of the more effective international negotiator qualities in Part 3. Here, suffice it to say that it is perhaps more of a process than a final accomplishment, and the more you can become tuned into the process, the more you will learn, and the more effective you will become. Inevitably, effectiveness is equated not with how well you maneuver through an already bad situation but with how well you can prevent a bad situation from developing, while creating a positive one in which to negotiate.

Increasing Your Options

There can be a series of stages that people go through as they become familiar with doing business (and really conducting life in general) with people from other cultures.

The Denial of Differences

When people are in this mode, one hears things like "common sense," "common decency," "common courtesy," "people are basically the same everywhere," etc. Let's take a closer look at these statements. First of all, what is "common," whether it is sense, courtesy, or decency, is common only within the culture of the people being observed. While one can find many cultures subscribing to what appear to be similar values and behavior, these values and behavior may be caused by very different conditions, which can make the people who adhere to them very different from you. Additionally, there are many beliefs, values, and behaviors that are acceptable in one culture, that add up to "common sense" or "decency" there, but that would never be considered so in other cultures. The marriage of first cousins is common decency in some places, not so in others; directing all remarks to the oldest man in the room is common courtesy in some places, not so in others; spending most of the time during a negotiation visiting famous historical sites is common sense in some places, not so in others. It's a different world out there. And while people do share basic common needs, how they achieve the satisfaction of those needs can be very different. In fact, it is the way that people go about ordering their lives and viewing their world, in an effort to take care of their needs, that distinguishes one culture from another. While our needs might be the same, we are not.

The Acceptance of Differences

In this stage, a general attempt is made to develop a workable strategy, in life and in business, for the successful accommodation of differences. In business, this means learning about the business styles (including negotiation patterns) of the other side, developing models of domestic, regional, and global corporate responsibilities, building supranational structures that help integrate regionally accepted differences into the larger corporate entity. At this stage, there is often much concern for domestic, regional, and global authority, autonomy, responsibility, etc. Also at this stage, differences are acknowledged (sometimes grudgingly, and only as a problem), but they are regarded as requiring management in order to keep them from mucking up the works. Moving on to the third stage usually resolves these issues.

The Valuing of Differences

Here, there is a general attempt to develop a workable strategy, in life and in business, for successful growth, because of—not in spite of—the existence of differences. In business, this means valuing other business styles (including other negotiating patterns) for their possible selective application to your own business issues. Supranational corporate structures support the dialectical development of a larger global entity using input from the autonomous regions that make up the global corporation. At this stage, differences are valued and perceived not as problems, but as alternate solutions to problems and additional opportunities for growth.

The point here is that becoming familiar with the methods and practices of people who do business differently from the way we do ultimately presents us with opportunities to improve the way we do what we do, even back home. If we deny differences, we learn nothing. If we accept them, but only as problems to be managed, we learn little. But if we can see and value the way someone else approaches a problem, seizes an opportunity, and deals with a situation, we can learn from it and perhaps put it to use ourselves to resolve our own work issues. We simply increase our options. Ultimately, learning how someone else does business gives us additional tools for doing our own business. Admittedly, there are many ways others conduct their business and view their business world that would be inappropriate and unconstructive if we were to transfer them directly to our domestic business issues. Similarly, when we require others to adopt our ways, we are often asking them to go through the same impossible and unproductive process. Of course, what works for someone else might not work for you, and what works over there might not work over here, but then again…it just might. And at the very least, if we recognize, understand, and value how things are done somewhere else, it may point the way to solutions to problems we'll face tomorrow, even if it has limited applicability to the issues we face today. Learning is not about setting limits. It's about expanding possibilities. That's the reason we learn how others do business, and it should ultimately be the reason why we try to understand how others negotiate.

Values, Attitudes, and Behavior

In many of our training programs, we talk about culture as if it were an iceberg, with the behavior of individuals represented only by that part of the iceberg above the water line—the tip, as in "just the tip of the iceberg." Individual behavior is the perceivable manifestation of culture's effects. However, the major weight and substance of culture is hidden below what is perceptible to us through our senses. That is, the determinants of the behavior we see—the more fundamental attitudes, beliefs, and world views—are below the "waterline." Attitudes, beliefs, and world views don't announce themselves; they need to be deduced from the individual behavior exhibited. Still further below the surface, and occupying the greatest volume of this cultural iceberg, are the basic values that determine the attitudes, beliefs, and world views. Values lie very deep, and they are the least easy to recognize immediately. The moral of the iceberg analogy, admittedly simplistic, is that what we see on the surface as behaviors often is determined by what we can't readily see. Values are not necessarily explicit, and we can run into unseen value conflicts without knowing it. This analogy supports the point that concern for visible behavior—the customs, if you will—should not be our primary emphasis. The possibility of value conflicts at deeper, unknown levels is where we should be focusing our attention when we want to improve our communication, negotiation, and all-round work relations with people from other cultures.

All forms of input from all aspects of our environment contain messages that transmit information about the values of the society we grow up in. This information becomes such a central part of our core being while we are still young. As adults, we are often unaware of how much it is part of how we define ourselves. It is for this reason that culture's effect on us, as well as on our foreign associates, remains invisible. Since culture and its attendant values are so central to our own definitions of ourselves, it is difficult for us tease out those aspects that were once external, that are not "natural" to us, but rather were given to us by society as we developed. We are indeed our society's children. In this sense, our own culture can be relatively invisible to us. However, if the values of others are significantly different from our own, the two respective cultures can suddenly become very visible, outlined in bold relief by the differences between them. It is when this occurs that we can see how unalike cultures truly can be, how different from one another individual societies can make us.

It is usually only at such moments of comparison that we realize culture's effects on us. Whether we go to other cultures, or people from other cultures come to ours, we see that what we grew up thinking of as "natural" and perhaps the "only way" is really just one way among many, and natural only to us and others of our culture. It's like being a fish: when in the water, the fish is unaware of any possible alternate environments. The water surrounding the fish is all it knows of the universe: hence, the whole universe must be made of water. Only when the fish is removed from the water does it perceive a different environment, and then, should it be an extremely smart fish, it might even conclude that it had been wrong to assume that its previous existence in water was the only possible way to be.

When we travel from one culture to another, we often feel like a fish out of water. And while we may not know exactly what the differences are between our former environment and this new one we find ourselves in, we perceive that things are different—perhaps better, perhaps worse, but certainly different. Sometimes this perception can be so strong that it debilitates us. We feel disoriented. We don't know our way around. Suddenly, all the subtle, almost unconscious cues we get from the environment we trust and feel so comfortable in are gone. It feels as though the supports that get us through the day have been knocked out from under us—and indeed, our cultural underpinnings are often so unconscious that we don't realize they're there until we leave them behind when we go somewhere else. Whole sets of rules, attitudes, values, world views are different, and since they form so central a core of our being, their sudden absence feels as if some major geological shift has occurred directly under our feet. We don't quite know where we are or what to hold onto. If seriously disoriented, we can actually fall physically ill. Most of the time, though, we are simply put out of sorts, depressed. This is known as culture shock. It is the result of serious conflicts of values at deep unseen categorical levels in the iceberg.

Most people get over culture shock (some need to return home for a while) given enough time and the right kind of support. No matter how many times you've been to another culture, you may still be susceptible to the shock of difference. And it can occur as soon as you step off the plane or may never occur at all, no matter how long you stay away. It is important, therefore, for anyone traveling to another culture to be able to recognize the signs of culture shock, even if one is just traveling for a three-day negotiation. And while we are not concerned in this book with issues of expatriate adjustment to overseas life, we are very much concerned with the impact of cultural differences on our ability to do business with each other. And at the table, the differences at these very deep levels can be startling.

At the negotiating table, deep value differences can determine behavior that is immediately and integrally part of the negotiation process. And since values in a particular culture do not operate independently of each other, they combine in ways unique to the culture to produce behavior and sets of behavior that play themselves out right at the table.

Differing concepts of time, for example, will affect how quickly the negotiation moves along, how much time is devoted to various stages of the negotiation, how much emphasis is given to certain activities. Notions of socializing in business will determine the emphasis placed on developing relationships. Beliefs regarding hierarchy, status, age, and position will determine both the style and content of protocol at the table, affecting everything from the use of business cards, to gift giving, table manners, greetings, dress, etc. Beliefs regarding sex roles will affect the power and presence of both women and men at the table. Differing beliefs regarding relationships with authority will affect who can speak with whom and when. Language differences and external cultural differences (such as legal holidays and political conditions) will automatically set parameters of action at the table, as will attitudes and values regarding the taking of risk and the need for information. Concepts of decision making and the role of the individuals versus the group will affect how and what is decided and communicated at the table. There are values that have an impact on the consensus-building process as well as on the concession-making process: Different cultures respond to different motivations, and people judge things according to different criteria provided by their respective societies. Finally, the way all of the above is communicated will also be affected by culture, most overtly in the participants' different languages and the means they use to pass along information verbally (face to face, over the phone, by fax, by letter, or by memo) and also in their nonverbal communication styles (their use of gestures, body language, and personal space; their manipulation of silence; their degree of physicality; etc.). Clearly, the differences, as they show up at the negotiation table, can be many and mind-boggling.

Fact Versus Fancy

If we are to explore this murky realm of values and fundamental categorical differences that lies below the surface, we want to be able to do so with as much security, safety, and information as possible, and we need as much light on the subject as we can get. Unfortunately, in the world of international business, most of the information about negotiating and doing business across cultures has thus far been anecdotal, often in the form of very funny personal incidents told by the guy down the hall who just got back from who-knows-where and is relaxing over drinks at the end of the day. Similarly, these incidents often take the form of horror stories from returning (or recalled) expats or individuals who come back covered with scrapes and bruises from the international negotiation arena. Most of the time, the anecdotes have some kernel of truth in them, and at best, they're entertaining. At worst, however, they tend to support stereotypes. It's difficult not to conclude that because XYZ happened to Smith in Sri Lanka last September, the same will happen to us when we go over there in May.

Fortunately, there has been some recent, scientific research in the field that can shed some real, objective light on our investigations. While anecdotal information is limited in its usefulness because it is so specific, hard data can provide a good guide to what we may expect. It is important to remember, however, that even the best social scientific research also has its limitations. For one thing, most of the best information available can only point out patterns, trends, norms, and tendencies. We don't want to say, and are pleased that the best information does not attempt to say, that all individuals of a particular culture act a certain way. But objectively studying tendencies, norms, and patterns *can* provide us with a possible explanation for why something is turning out the way it is, or why someone is behaving in a certain way.

As a way of clarifying the future references to this research in this book, I'd like to introduce some of the leaders in the field, whose work is reflected throughout the book.

The distinguished anthropologist, Edward T. Hall, has devoted much of his research to the effects of culture and people's behavior in the world of business, mainly for our purposes through his concept of "cultural context." We'll discuss context and its meaning for negotiation in Part 3. Suffice it to say here that the concept of cultural context allows us to organize cultures (and consequently anticipate behavior) according to the ways in which the cultures communicate information; this has a striking importance at the negotiating table. We'll also be referring to the work of Geert Hofstede, who conducted one of the first surveys of work preferences around the world. Using his research we can anticipate possible behavioral tendencies in our foreign business associates that can immediately affect the negotiation process. In Part 3 we will also be looking at the work of Stephen Weiss and some of his associates, who have identified certain basic aspects of the negotiation process and how they differ among key countries around the world. We're thankful for the important work that these people have done in the field, and we will be bringing their research forward throughout the book wherever appropriate.

Separating fact from fancy is important if we are first to make accurate and reliable generalizations and then make decisions about our behaviors. By balancing personal experience with the best and most current data available, we can arrive at a rounded and valuable picture of the challenges and options facing us when we negotiate around the world.

Cross-Cultural Crisscrossings

Let's look at how some fundamental value differences can create problems at the international negotiating table. Each of the following situations reflects a particular type of cross-cultural business problem. Identifying some of the pitfalls frequently encountered at the international negotiating table will help you prepare for the real-life situations you may find yourself facing when you do business across borders.

Attribution

Charlie Hampton, a Texas oil broker, was astonished when Sven Stephenson, the buyer for a large Scandinavian oil refinery, would not even attempt to meet his price. Charlie stated what he hoped to sell his oil for. Sven was at first silent, and then added slowly that he was not authorized to agree to anything outside of the world market price as published daily. Hampton knew, of course, that the price he was quoting was much higher than market, but it was, after all, just his first opening price. This was the first time Charlie had ever dealt with Sven, and he did not expect this kind of cold indifference to his opening offer. "What kind of man is this Swede anyway?" he thought to himself. "If he won't bargain with me, I'll never be able to justify the price I'm eventually willing to settle for." In fact, Charlie was willing to settle for a figure much nearer the world market rate, if it came to that. "He's giving me no room to maneuver; he's not serious about negotiating anything," Charlie thought.

Sven was very wary of dealing with this American. He had been told that Americans had a way of first asking one price and then putting forward another. Sven felt that Charlie was not to be trusted and frankly was very uncomfortable doing business with him. "How can I do business with such a man?" he thought to himself. After much fruitless prodding on Charlie's part and much adamant resistance on Sven's, the two men agreed to part company; perhaps they could strike a deal next time.

The Attribution Process

This is an example of how two people can misinterpret the meaning of each other's actions by using criteria that are inapplicable within each other's cultural context. It is the result of the misguided process we refer to as *attribution*. Attribution is a common cross-cultural phenomenon, and we need to become aware of its occurrence in common intercultural business situations.

Here's how attribution works. As a basic cross-cultural dynamic, both sides interpret the other's behavior from their own cultural perspectives, or through their own "cultural filters." That is, Charlie perceives Sven's behavior through his American culture filter and makes some decisions about Sven based on this perception. In turn, Sven perceives Charlie's behavior through his Swedish cultural filter, and makes some decisions about Charlie. If culture determines to a great degree how we view reality, seeing things through our own culture is like looking at the world through a pair of tinted glasses—in our own case, "American-tinted" glasses. Others, wearing *their* culturally tinted glasses, would see the same world, and view the same reality, but they would see things differently. The attribution problem develops because both sides view the same reality but make different decisions about what they see and what it means based on the particular tint of their cultural outlook.

In the example above, Sven perceives and assesses Charlie's behavior through the filter or tinted glasses of his Swedish background and values. The same is true of Charlie, who, in the absence of other cultural information, can only assess Sven's behavior according to his own American background and values. The result, of course, is that the behavior of people in one culture is judged in terms of the standards of another. It's a mixing of apples and oranges, or at least, the assumption that an orange is an apple just because it's also round. Bargaining is not highly valued in Swedish culture; those who bargain, who attempt to negotiate by offering a higher price in order to concede to a lower price, can be viewed as untrustworthy, inefficient, or perhaps out for personal gain at the expense of others. In the end, they are suspect. In American culture, bargaining is generally valued more favorably. It can range from out and out horse trading to the give and take of finding an appropriate middle ground. But those who refuse to bargain are viewed as cold, as having alternative secret agendas, and of not really being serious about business. In the end, they are suspect. After attributing, or applying, Swedish values (or standards) to American bargaining behavior, Sven decides that the American is not to be trusted. Similarly, after attributing American values to Swedish nonbargaining negotiating behavior, Charlie concludes that the Swede is not to be trusted.

Attribution is the projection of our own values onto the behavior we perceive in individuals of other cultures. We attribute meaning to their behavior that may not exist. We account for what they do according to our own standards, instead of matching their behavior against the standards of their own culture, the environment in which their behavior developed.

Attribution is not uncommon. In fact, along with many of the other cross-cultural processes we discuss in this section, it can be a virtually automatic and fairly unconscious process that we revert to in the absence of additional information. When we perceive behavior that is uncommon, disagreeable, or mystifying to us, we try to find a reason or explanation for it based on the only available information we have. This, in most cases, is nothing more than the information already in our heads about our own culture, and as you can see in the case of Sven and Charlie, it can lead to mistaken conclusions.

How do you avoid attributing the wrong meaning to the (culturally) right behavior? Don't assume that the behavior of individuals and groups from other cultures means the same thing as similar behavior does in the United States. Rather, start from the position that the behavior of people and groups from other cultures might have very different meanings from similar behavior in the United States. Then go about finding out what such behavior, within that culture, really does mean.

The misinterpretations of attribution are often highly noticeable in connection with nonverbal behaviors. We will discuss nonverbal behaviors in more depth when we discuss cultural context. For now, let's look at some examples that illustrate the way misunderstandings can arise as . a result of the attribution process.

An Arab who stands "too close" is a good example. Personal space, or the acceptable distance that individuals place between themselves and other individuals, can vary from culture to culture. Let's say that during a break in a meeting, an Arab and an American are standing too close for comfort for the American, who unconsciously backs away. In response, the Arab moves closer again, for now the American is too far away for the Arab's personal comfort. The American backs away again, this time less unconsciously, aware of an uncomfortable feeling of being "pushed" across the floor. The American attributes hostility and combativeness to the Arab, for in American culture, someone moving that close that fast may be considered dangerously aggressive. The Arab, on the other hand, attributes an unwillingness to engage on the part of the American, a hesitancy to develop a relationship, a resistance to doing business, perhaps. All other things being equal, the American has no such motives: the American is merely trying to reestablish his personal-space comfort zone.

Similar personal-space preferences are also noticeable between Latins and *Norte Americanos*. An Argentine friend of mine told me of a party he attended recently where a low-railed balcony had been roped off-limits specifically because, in the past, several Americans had inadvertently fallen off as they had backed onto the balcony in conversations with their Argentine associates! Fortunately, in this case, the Argentine management did not attribute *Norte Americano* behavior as a predilection for falling off of balconies, but rather, supplied with accurate cross-cultural information about personal-space differences between Argentines and *Norte Americanos*, understood correctly what the problem was and took appropriate measures to overcome it.

Here's another example of faulty nonverbal behavior attribution. An American businesswoman attributes an unwillingness to engage in frank conversation on the part of her Indian associate because each time the American confronts her, the Indian looks away. The Indian, on the other hand, attributes to the American an attempt to control and dictate by means of direct physical confrontation. In fact, the Indian is looking away because to do so is a sign of showing respect in her culture. In America, one shows respect by forthrightly confronting the speaker, and this often takes the nonverbal form of providing full attention and direct eye contact. Therefore, instead of interpreting the Indian behavior as a sign of respect, the American attributes it as an intent to avoid.

Eye contact between Americans and the French is very different, however. In the same kind of conversation, the eye contact of the French person could be much more intense than that of the American. In fact, the French often outdo Americans when it comes to the "look-me-in-the-eye" approach. American businesspeople, made uncomfortable by the direct and intense French gaze, might attribute aggressiveness, stubbornness, and perhaps even a conscious attempt to make them uncomfortable to their French associate. The French person, meanwhile is likely to attribute weakness, casualness, and perhaps insincerity to the American when the intense gaze is either not returned or avoided.

The American who gives the index finger-to-thumb hand gesture sign for OK to a group of Brazilian associates may be astonished to find the Brazilians offended. The American attributes to the Brazilians a supersensitivity that he or she finds annoying. For their part, the Brazilians attribute to the American an aggressiveness and insensitivity to their ways that was never intended.

An American businessperson whose hand is suddenly taken by a Thai associate, or who is embraced by a Latin business partner, might attribute a sexual meaning where there is none. In turn, the Thai or Latin associate, meeting American resistance to these nonverbal gestures, might attribute a coldness and indifference to the American where such is not the case.

For the reasons given above, nonverbal behavior is constantly being misjudged in the cross-cultural business arena. But verbal behavior, too, is subject to misinterpretations. There are two kinds of attribution: The kind that occurs when we misinterpret a particular behavior because that behavior also occurs in our culture but has another meaning; and the kind that occurs when we perceive behavior that is not common in our culture, but, in an attempt to understand it, attribute a wrong meaning to it that we assemble from available information in our own culture. It is, of course, much easier to explain the behavior we recognize; it is more difficult to surmise the meaning of behavior we do not recognize. The result, when we try to interpret it, is the same in both cases: We attribute a false meaning to what we see.

We must be especially vigilant to guard against this process by admitting the possibility that certain behavior, whether recognizable or not, may have different meanings from those we at first attribute to it. It is simply safer to assume that there may be differences, rather than similarities. While this might feel uncomfortable, because it raises more questions than it provides quick and easy answers, it is, nevertheless, a more accurate way of understanding what might really be going on.

Selecting Out

Thomas felt as if he were getting mixed signals. Whenever he asked a question or inquired about the status of things, the Singaporeans would assure him that everything was going well, as planned, even better than anticipated. For months, in several face-to-face meetings, and in communications by phone and fax, Thomas was always reassured that things were fine. "Be comfortable. We want you to be comfortable," was what his Singaporean associates often said.

In fact, Thomas started out quite comfortable, but, in the absence of the kind of information he was waiting for, was slowly becoming less so. In the past, he had never had any problems with the Singaporeans. He could feel confident that things would turn out as he had been told they would, there were hardly any delays, things moved along quickly and smoothly. But now Thomas did have some concern regarding various knotty problems with the project. Specifically, Thomas had some questions about one of the new Singaporean chiefs, Yeo, whom the Singaporeans had assigned to a recent phase of the project. Thomas had never met the man and didn't know anything about him, really. Thomas's relationships with the Singaporeans in the past had been so good, in fact, that he hadn't at first felt it imperative to get to know Yeo himself.

However, now that these sticky problems were coming up, Thomas felt he needed to know more about Yeo and how he and the Singaporeans in general were moving along. Each time he inquired, however, he was told to relax, that things were under control. He appreciated the reassurance and waited for more information, which sometimes arrived and sometimes didn't arrive. When it didn't, Thomas would call again, and get the same kind of reassurances. Once he asked about Yeo directly, wanted to try to schedule a meeting with him on his next trip over, and his Singaporean associate made a point of telling Thomas that he shouldn't be so worried about not knowing Yeo; that Singaporeans in general and Yeo in particular (having been educated at a U.S. university), were really just like Americans. Thomas began to notice a pattern developing here. Whenever he questioned his Singaporean associate's abilities or competence, whether directly, or even indirectly, by merely implying some concern, he was immediately met with forceful reassurance that things were under control. However, he was increasingly unable to get real evidence of this.

The Selecting-Out Process

This is an example of another cross-cultural business dynamic that can be referred to as *selecting out.* This is the process by which we recognize familiar behavior but fail to recognize or correctly interpret unfamiliar behavior. Obviously, selecting out is a relative process. The more unfamiliar a behavior is and the further it is from our cultural reference, the less likely it is that we will recognize it. In reverse, the more familiar a behavior is and the closer to our own cultural reference it is, the more likely it is that we will recognize it. In both cases, however, our selecting out a particular behavior for recognition does not necessarily mean that we recognize it correctly. Our correctly understanding it is still dependent on whether or not we attribute our own meaning to it. In this sense, selecting out can often be a process that occurs even before attribution.

Selecting out is based on natural psychosociological reflexes. It's difficult to see accurately beyond our own cultural filters. In the case of selecting out, it is especially difficult to see—let alone correctly interpret—a foreign cultural behavior if it simply doesn't exist in our own. Our cultural filter provides us with our frame of reference; it is difficult, perhaps nearly impossible, to see things that our cultural frame of reference does not predispose us to see. And like attribution, selecting out goes on at a fairly automatic and unconscious level.

For example, there may be forty different words for snow in a particular Eskimo culture, each word describing snow of a different texture and condition. It would be difficult for most New Yorkers, and more difficult still for people completely unfamiliar with snow, to perceive these forty varieties of snow when looking at them, simply because non-Eskimos do not have the cultural filters that enable them to make these distinctions. As you can see, what determines our cultural filters is often what is of most importance to our survival, given our culture's unique environmental requirements. The non-Eskimo, while looking at a Nordic landscape, might only be able to perceive snow, ice, rain, and slush. The Eskimo, looking at the same landscape, might perceive the presence of 36 additional types of snow because it is particularly important to their long-term survival to know these distinctions. The non-Eskimo, in perceiving the landscape, selects out only those features their cultural filter allows them to understand, to the exclusion of other possibilities.

In fact, in any culture, it is the people who can see things others cannot—the people who frame their perception of reality differently and who, for a variety of reasons, can reassemble the facts of their world to make something new that no one else has seen before—who are either written off as crazy or revered as geniuses. In both cases, there is a perception of reality that is new and different from the one defined by their society. The fact that we regard geniuses as so rare, or that when we mere mortals experience moments of "higher consciousness," or momentary revelation, we consider them so precious, is an indication of the power that our culture has over our ability to see reality in all of its potential. The genius breaks out of these bounds, and, in so doing, achieves immortality. Our humanness is created by our culture, but our culture usually limits what we can see.

In international business, we tend to select out that behavior for perception in our foreign associates that most closely match what our cultural filters have already predisposed us to see. We are less likely even to notice that behavior in our foreign associates that is outside our cultural experience, let alone to understand it accurately if we do notice it. In this sense, selecting out prevents us from seeing the full spectrum of what our counterparts are really all about, simply because we do not have the same lens for viewing reality as they do.

This has significant ramifications in business negotiations. For one thing, it means we might always be missing part of what really is going on; there may be invisible aspects of our foreign associates' behavior that we are simply not tuned into. It's like having a TV that can only pick up certain channels; the frequencies we can get limit the information we can receive, and, because we don't get the other channels, we are unaware of the possibilities of what appears on them. Our foreign associates miss a great deal of what is going on with us, again because of the selecting out process. This is another reason why we must always be sure to confirm mutual understanding at the negotiating table (see Chapter 7).

Our foreign associates, because they are outside the limits of our cultural parameters, are seeing things differently, and, while sometimes problematic, this can also be profitable. Their view, being different, may provide new insights, new ways of looking at things, new ways of solving old problems, a new and different perspective. We should anticipate the process of selecting out that occurs on both sides, try to compensate for it with confirmations of clear understanding, and accept and celebrate the real possibility that the other side may see problems-solving opportunities in the situation that we do not.

In the above example, Thomas, the American, was selecting out the behavior exhibited by his Singaporean associates that he most easily identified: the direct, positive reassurance that things were OK. Once he had selected out this behavior, he relied on his culturally influenced interpretation to provide him with an understanding of the situation. However, since he selected out this behavior precisely because of its similarity to American values and behavior, it did not provide him with any additional understanding of his Singaporean associate. In fact, it blinded him to other behavior his Singaporean associates were also exhibiting that, if interpreted correctly, would have given him more information as to what was really going on. Instead, the more familiar behavior was selected out, while other, more important, behavior remained unseen.

Singaporeans place a high value on being able to maintain control and harmony in all situations. In this case, the constant reassurances that things were OK and that there was nothing for Thomas to worry about should have been interpreted as a red flag. Singaporeans, like most Asians, place a great value on saving face; therefore, despite their apparent directness, forthrightness, and speed of response, real and meaningful communication may take time simply because it may be more indirectly delivered if it is not the positive, good news they hope always to be able to deliver. Anything that might indicate a lack of competence, a problem on their part, or a difficulty they may have might not be communicated or might be communicated indirectly, surreptitiously, in a form not easily read. Good news moves very quickly in Singapore. For Thomas' Singaporean associates to put such energy into reassuring him, while often being unable to provide any real information was their way of indirectly communicating bad news. But, because of selecting out, Thomas saw only the direct communication. And, because of attribution, he could not accurately read the bad news in the selected out behavior.

Selecting out also can be a process of reinforcing stereotypes. If we see only that behavior we are culturally predisposed to see, then we see only that behavior in our foreign associates that support our preconceived expectations of who they are and how they will behave. The American's expectation that all Parisians are gruff, cold, insolent, arrogant, and indifferent is supported primarily because, when Americans go to Paris, they select out that behavior exhibited by busy, rushed, stressed-out Parisians that tends to support this expectation. In turn, Parisians select out only that behavior in the Americans they interact with that supports what they already are predisposed to believe of Americans: that they are boorish, uncultured, tasteless, and loud. I suppose one could summarize and say that you get what you expect in this world. But you pay the price of never getting any more than what you are already primed to expect. The challenge of international negotiation is to be able to get more — more out of the situation and more out of your counterpart — for international negotiation presents a unique opportunity to deal in a much larger world, a world of increased problems, to be sure, but also a world of increased possibilities. The skill to be learned is that of helping your international associate help you get what you want by maximizing their strengths and minimizing their weaknesses. And maximizing their strengths often means making their world view, together with their particular culture filter, work for you.

Ethnocentrism

Paul Sanders, the American vice president of advertising, was attempting to convince his British associates in the London office of the importance of the direct mail and telephone advertising campaign he had come over to promote. His presentation at this meeting included significant data that demonstrated how direct marketing via telephone and through the mails had dramatically increased retail sales for the company in the United States.

His British associates sitting around the table were, as a group, unimpressed. Nigel Simpson, whose approval was critical, was against any of Sanders' suggestions because last year's advertising in the United Kingdom, based primarily on print ads, had produced disappointing results. For Nigel, the print ads were much too direct, too hard-sell, and that, for Nigel and his committee, was the reason the ads had not produced the projected target sales in the United Kingdom.

Paul did not agree. He felt that if the ads had not produced, it was because they were not hard-hitting *enough*; certainly they had been nowhere near as hard-hitting as the American counterparts.

Nigel definitely did not want to move forward with a telemarketing and direct mail campaign based on the American model. He warned Paul that the British public would never react favorably to such an "intrusive" advertising scheme. Paul was extremely frustrated, feeling that he was having to work with one hand tied behind his back. He said angrily that it was no wonder Britain's economy was in such bad shape, since the British obviously never wanted to try anything new, especially if it had been proven to work in the States.

The Pitfalls of Ethnocentrism

Those cultural glasses we wear provide us not only with our perspective on the rest of the world, but also with perspective on ourselves. Culture not only prescribes parameters by which we view the rest of the world, but also prescribes how we see and define ourselves. Culture provides us with a major source of our own identity. We are proud of our heritage, proud of who we are, of our country, our ethnicity, and our backgrounds. We, as Americans, might be merely "American" to our overseas associates. But more often than not, we are "African-American," or "Italian-American," or "Hispanic-American," or "Asian-American" to ourselves and each other. We see ourselves and the world according to these identities, according to these labels that we willingly wear. We must be careful, however, not to allow our pride in our identity to blind us to the cultural filters of our international associates or to the requirement that we respect their cultural perspective.

Ethnocentrism is pride in one's culture at the expense of others. It is the belief, as the word indicates, that one's own culture is central, and that all others are more or less peripheral. Ethnocentrism can be overt or very subtle. The French vintner who insists to his Italian or Californian associates that his wine is the best simply because France makes the best wine in the world is clearly and overtly ethnocentric. The world map that used to hang on the schoolroom wall in U.S. high schools was more subtly, and therefore perhaps more effectively, ethnocentric, too; it often placed the Western Hemisphere directly in the middle of the flat world, with the rest of the world on either side of the United States. (More precisely, it placed Chicago right in the middle of the world.) On these maps, China and India were sometimes cut in half; Asia was given less importance than certain Polynesian islands; the distances between North America and Europe were often reduced (suggesting, I suppose, the connection between Mother Europe and colonial America); and Canada and the United States were disproportionately extended — all in order to place the States at the center of the world. To be fair, I have also seen world maps made in Australia, in which Australia is placed at the center of the world, with the major hemispheres laid out on either side of the continent. No one culture is immune to or has an exclusive lock on ethnocentrism, and all cultures are ethnocentric in some fashion and to some degree. The point here is that, despite its degree, shape, or form, ethnocentrism is dangerous: it denies the respect the other side is due; it breaks down communication by generating anger and resentment (and defensive ethnocentrism, in kind, from the other side), and it keeps people from the truth about one another. Perhaps it is the biggest danger in business.

In the example above, Paul Sanders, knowing that telemarketing and direct mail had worked well in the United States, simply assumed that it would also work well in the United Kingdom. Because of his own ethnocentrism, he reasoned that, "If it works here, it's got to work there." Ethnocentrism implies a basic disregard for the fact that other cultures are different. It also implies that "different" is "less than," that it is not as good. All too often it takes the form of self-righteous superiority: Since our way is better, you'd better listen to us. In the years following World War II, Americans often displayed this kind of ethnocentrism toward Europeans and the Japanese. When the people of other countries refused our good advice, we would get angry and view them as ungrateful and arrogant. It was an ignorant approach then and a ridiculous approach now.

In fact, telemarketing and direct mail, as Nigel Simpson knew, can be ineffective advertising schemes in the United Kingdom because of cultural attitudes regarding selling, advertising, and marketing, and the impact of these activities on privacy and the individual. Most of the time, the U.S. style of advertising and marketing is too direct, obvious, and intrusive. British people tend to recoil from this approach; they are often offended by it. Calling their attention to a product in this manner might actually ensure that they will *not* buy it. Americans, on the other hand, while sometimes getting annoyed with the direct, intrusive, fact-filled hard-sell, accept it most of the time and sometimes actually welcome the information. By not being aware of his own ethnocentrism, Sanders was prevented from understanding the problem the British were having with his proposal. Instead of receiving the information about cultural requirements for advertising in Britain that might have enabled him to proceed with an effective campaign, he was left with bitter and reinforced stereotypes about the Brits and the way they do business. More important, he was left with no campaign.

It is in the realm of advertising, marketing, and sales that we often see wonderful and unfortunate examples of ethnocentrism at work in business. The stories are legion. For example, a U.S. auto manufacturer learned too late while trying to market its car in Spain and Latin America that the name of the car when translated from English into Spanish meant "no go" — not quite the name you want to use to sell a car. More recently, an airline with routes to Japan had to remove its very expensive TV advertisement because it pictured a woman in a kimono. There was nothing inherently wrong in this, particularly for an ad referring to Japan. However, the kimono was tied with the sash going in the wrong direction, tied in the direction one ties a kimono when attending a funeral. Ethnocentric assumptions about the ad's content and the amount of background research it needed, prevented the producers of the TV spot from fully understanding the requirements of their work. A soft-drink manufacturer, in an effort to advertise its drink in China, had its current domestic English advertising slogan translated into Mandarin, which came out, roughly translated, as something like "drink our soda and may your ancestors come out of their graves." It was ethnocentric on the part of the advertiser to assume that English would translate acceptably into Chinese, and that, since the slogan worked in the United States, it would just as easily work in China.

Perhaps the most overt form of ethnocentrism, however, is the display of disinterest often exhibited by individuals from different cultures when they come together. Foreign visitors often show disinterest, intentionally or not, simply because they feel lost, out of touch, perhaps a little frightened, without adequate handles for understanding the language, life, and people of the country they find themselves in. Sometimes these feelings provoke defensive behavior. People who feel all at sea in another country defend themselves by downplaying the values, behavior, and lifestyles of the other culture in order to minimize the impact on their own already wounded system. It's a kind of "belittling of the other" in order to stay above the fray.

The host national, also intentionally or not, may display disinterest, too, only reinforcing the sense of alienation the foreigner is already experiencing. Host nationals, being members of the in-group the foreign visitor wants to penetrate, will often, in order to preserve the unity, power, sanctity, etc., of their group, treat the visitor as a foreigner, as a real outsider. It's not that visitors are unwelcome, but that, being from somewhere else, they are members of an "out-group" and can never know us as we know each other. These two reactions combine to create a vicious circle, each reinforcing the other, so that both sides are actually cooperating in pushing each other away.

It is important to recognize the fact that the visitor, whether it is you going abroad to negotiate, or a foreign national coming to the United States to negotiate, is automatically at the disadvantage of being an outsider. It is the outsider who is at a loss about how things are done in the country where he or she is trying to do business. As a member of an out-group, one must expect a sense of alienation, of being cut off. It is access to cross-cultural information, a recognition of the foreigner within, and the building of relationships with individuals on the other side who can mentor and guide you that will help alleviate the feelings that accompany out-group status. But the first step is to acknowledge and accept this status when it occurs.

Ethnocentrism in this case takes the form of in-group/out-group identification and labeling. "I'm not one of them, so I am alone," or "They're not one of us, so we cannot let them in." The identification and labeling most often starts with the mutually acknowledged perception that "I don't speak your language," or that "they don't speak our language." And it is perhaps language differences that are the first obvious, and most critical, cross-cultural crisscrossings we need to consider.

Some Words on Language

Many people who do business internationally start out thinking that all they need to do is to learn the language of their international associates. Of course, they haven't really got the time to accomplish this, and, even if they do master enough of the language to negotiate in it, they usually do it badly, and then only too late to learn that the real issues, the real problems at the table, had very little to do with differences in language and everything to do with differences in culture beyond language. Remember, this is not a book on language differences. While language differences can be the first, most obvious, and most critical factor separating people when they come together to do business, we want to keep our focus on the larger culture. The reason is simple: While there are some things we can do about language differences (and we will discuss them), they are basically few. However, there are many things we can know and do about larger cultural differences. And, after we deal with language differences in whatever form we choose to handle them, we are still left with the profound effect of the larger culture on business negotiations.

That said, let's look at several considerations regarding language in international negotiations.

English as the Language of Business

Yes, English is becoming the international language of business, but that doesn't mean everyone speaks it. And even when people speak it, we English-speakers must remember that it is still their second language. The point is that it is important not to assume that everyone out there speaks English. Most of the people in countries where English is not the primary language do not speak English. It's that simple. If your associates do, that's your good luck. But you should not expect it. It is important to confirm this before the meeting, so that you know what you are walking into and can make arrangements for interpreters, etc. if you choose to. The Japanese, for example, may find English as difficult to speak as we find Japanese. Nevertheless, because English is so important in world business and affairs, English is a major language in Japanese education. Despite this emphasis, the Japanese often feel inadequate when using their English and have an inferiority complex about speaking the language. This can make them appear reticent and hesitant to us, when we negotiate with them in English — we who are already making judgments about how closed and distant the Japanese appear to be. Their language difficulties only enhance our stereotyped ideas of them. However, we are not offering Japanese in our schools, and the only explanation I can think of is that we are trying to justify the abysmally low academic expectations we have of our students by applying an ethnocentric view of language in business. That is, since everyone is having to learn English anyway, why should our kids have to learn Japanese? Well, the answer is that the Japanese are only speaking to us in English because in the past they have had to. (But they may not have to for long!)

Learning a second language as an adult can be a very difficult thing; learning it well enough to conduct business in it is even more difficult. Think of your high school French or Spanish. Most likely, unless you have had additional opportunities to apply it continuously, it is difficult for you to speak it and more difficult to follow someone speaking it fluently. Trying to speak your high school language can give you some idea of what it might feel like when your foreign associates attempt to speak English with you. And yet they have had to learn. They have already met us halfway. Americans, for a variety of reasons including our geography and immigrant experience, are notoriously language-ignorant. (The joke in Europe has long been: "What do you call someone who speaks three languages? Trilingual. What do you call someone who speaks two languages? Bilingual. What do you call someone who speaks one language? An American.") However conscious we may now be of the need to improve our foreign language skills, we remain the ones who do not speak our international associates' language, while they do speak ours. It is only appropriate that we respect this effort of theirs through our own attempt to speak their language where and when we can, and through making a genuine effort to understand their ways. This is most true when we go to *their* country to negotiate.

A final note about English. Just because you might be negotiating with individuals from countries where English is spoken as a first language, it is important not to assume that cultural differences *don't* exist. In fact, negotiating with individuals from countries like the United Kingdom, Australia, New Zealand, and even Canada can be a doubly frustrating experience for Americans precisely because we are not expecting differences to surface at the table. And they do surface. Speaking the same language does not ensure similarities in culture. When we attempt to negotiate with someone from Japan, for example, and we do not speak Japanese, we are already sensitized to the fact that there are many differences between the two of us, language being only one of them. And the significant differences in language serve to remind us throughout our communication of the degree of difference that separates us. However, when we negotiate with people from English-speaking countries, the same process works to our disadvantage. That is, we hear English and are lulled into a false belief that since there is no language difference, we can expect no cultural differences. This can be a great mistake.

There are significant differences between the United Kingdom, for example, and the United States, which have a profound effect on our ability to negotiate and understand each other, despite the fact that, to all intents and purposes, we speak the same language. The United Kingdom is a profoundly class-conscious society, based on a history of aristocracy and royalty. The United States is inherently egalitarian, with a history shaped and formed in rebellion against class and royalty. The British tend to be formal in their personal presentation, while the Yanks are notoriously informal. Americans have an inherent belief in the future and in "doing"; the British are not so sure tomorrow is going to be any better than today, and are suspicious that anything of real substance can be obtained merely through hard work. The list goes on and on; in fact, in comparison, despite the fact that we speak the same language, Americans are as different from the British as we are from the French. Oscar Wilde once said that Americans and the British are cousins separated by a common language. This is never more true than at the negotiating table.

A Little of Their Language Goes a Long Way

Just a small amount of knowledge of another's language goes a long, long way. Think of how thrilled you are when someone who clearly speaks very little English uses a few words to introduce themselves to you. It leaves you feeling as if he or she really cared about making contact with you. It's the same in reverse. Learning even just a few common expressions of the other side's language goes a long, long way in establishing the all-important relationship between you. You may never use the words again, or you may use only these few words over and over again, but the effect can be profound. Perhaps nothing so small has so much power. It is absolutely essential to learn a few basic phrases, such as hello, goodbye, good morning, good evening, I'm happy to meet you, please and thank you, I would like, and so forth.

Even if it appears that your efforts are not appreciated, you should continue to make the effort. In such cases, you might merely be misreading the verbal and nonverbal cues of the others, not knowing their culture. Many Americans, for example, complain that the French do not respond positively to their attempts to use French in France. The French, it must be acknowledged, have a particular love affair with their own language, and it holds a unique place in their culture. This special role their beloved language plays for them can sometimes make them seem displeased with individuals attempting to use it. In fact, the French do appreciate Americans attempting to speak French—so much so that they are quick to correct you when you do speak it wrongly. Like a firm, concerned teacher, they take pleasure in your earnest attempts and want you to do it right, so they will make the effort to correct you when necessary. This does not show displeasure; instead, it shows interest, but in a typically French way.

In countries where it is not expected that you speak the language, using a few basic words will open many doors. It will break down barriers of suspicion and indifference. It begins the relationship that often is so much more important in those societies than it is in ours. This is an activity not to be overlooked.

At the same time, there are dangers in using someone else's language. First, be careful about the few phrases you do learn. Perhaps it might be important to learn the phrase, "I am sorry, but I don't speak_____very well," first. In some cases, if you speak the few phrases you do learn very well, your listeners might think you speak the language fluently and immediately respond with five-hundred-mile-an-hour answers in their language that leave you in the dust. Be sure to indicate to your associates that you are a novice if you really are. You don't want to use their language to indicate that you speak it well if you don't. Good business and good negotiations are, after all, based on honest relationships.

Additionally, if you speak a foreign language very well, you have a tool that can be both misused and misinterpreted. I remember a case in which Americans and Japanese were negotiating. There was an American on the team who spoke Japanese. However, he did not indicate this to any of the Japanese. The Japanese assumed right from the beginning that none of the Americans spoke Japanese and were quite comfortable breaking into Japanese at the table whenever they wanted to discuss things among themselves. The Americans on the team thought that this would be a great advantage to them. While, in fact, they did learn things from their Japanese-speaking associate, much of what was discussed by the Japanese in Japanese was soon revealed to the Americans in English anyway. Most people will break into their native language at a negotiation simply because it is easier and more efficient to discuss things among themselves in their team's first language and not necessarily because they have something to hide from the other side. When you have to speak in a second language, it takes a great deal of time and energy to constantly rethink, translate, and repeat, etc. It's important for Americans not to allow their paranoia (based more, of course, on their own inability to speak the other's language than on anything else) to run away with them when their international associates start jabbering away in their own language. Unless you have evidence to the contrary, it is safer to assume that they are doing so not to hide things from you, but rather to get on with their efforts.

In the above example, though, there were a few things discussed by the Japanese in Japanese that did not come out later in translation. The Japanese-speaking American was able to pass on these items of information to his teammates, who found them very useful. This is a negotiation tactic that can, obviously, yield some information, perhaps even important information. However, sooner or later, if the negotiation is important and the relationship between the teams is important, I have found that such secrets come out. In this case, the Japanese were quite concerned when they learned that there was an American present who spoke Japanese. And their concern was not primarily because he might have heard some things he shouldn't have, but rather that it was kept a secret, that the Americans were using this as a ploy. It implied mistrust, a serious breach of mutual confidence. And in a culture like Japan's, where long-term relationships are the key to effective business, the Americans' ploy backfired. In the end, the game wasn't worth the candle. Serious damage was done.

I have heard of similar situations in reverse, in which the Japanese have tried to make their apparent lack of English work in their favor. By always and only speaking in Japanese and expressing ignorance of any English used, they lulled the Americans into speaking in English freely among themselves at the table. I suspect such cases are possible. More often than not, though, no matter which side is responsible for the deception, it *is* a deception and ultimately not worth the risk. Sooner or later, the facts will emerge about each other's language capabilities, and, if a relationship has been established, the facts can be damaging. If you play this kind of game, play it carefully, and only after considerable thought.

And then there are those strange, albeit rare, cases in which speaking someone else's language fluently can actually become a handicap. I am speaking primarily of Westerners speaking fluent Japanese. The Japanese, too, have a unique relationship with their language: It is a symbol of the uniqueness of Japanese culture. There is a central and deep belief that only those who are Japanese can truly understand the Japanese. Non-Japanese, therefore, who speak Japanese fluently are viewed as unusual. It is not the norm. In fact, for the Japanese, it is not "normal." They will be deeply curious about how one learned their language; nevertheless, they can be, at heart, suspicious about the *gaijin* (foreigner) who speaks their language so well. Speaking some Japanese and showing respect for the language and the people are all that is expected. The Westerner who does more, who goes "too far," is attempting to be something he or she cannot be. I have seen cases in which fluency in Japanese on the part of Americans has increased suspicion and delayed the development of a solid business relationship.

Interpreters, Translators, and Other Gods

In fact, in many cases, language go-betweens are indispensable and have access where mere mortals fear to tread. Should you use an interpreter or translator when negotiating with people who do not speak English? Will the other side have one? What's the difference between interpreters and translators? What should you know about working with them? These are some of the questions that naturally arise when negotiating with individuals whose first language is not English.

The first step is to determine the degree of language fluency you can anticipate on both sides before the negotiation begins. Remember that, although the level of fluency you'll need will vary with the specific topics to be negotiated (whether they are deeply scientific, technical, or industry-specific, for example), you should generally anticipate needing a fluency level higher than what you think either side's capability is. It is simply a fact that when people get into the depths of a negotiation, the nuances of someone else's language are often more than even the most ambitious novice's capabilities can handle. Therefore, if you suspect you will need a translator or interpreter, you probably do.

Translators do just that: they turn the words of one language into the words of another. They are most often used for documents. Interpreters, on the other hand, make the thoughts of a person speaking in one language intelligible to a person who speaks another. Interpreters are

most often used in face-to-face cross-language situations. Interpreting is
a difficult, exhausting job. Interpreters must be forever on the alert,
translating, evaluating, judging, weighing, and balancing. They must
make the thoughts of one language clear in another, while constantly
taking into account the context in which the interpretation is occurring
(the individuals, the negotiation, the setting, the requirements for information, the speed of the transaction, etc.). And they must consistently
judge the intent as well as the words actually spoken. These are sophisticated skills. Interpreters need to be treated as the high-level profes-
sionals they are. You should get to know them ahead of time and try to
share with them what your goals and expectations are. Try to have them
also understand who you are, both as a person and as a negotiator.
When your interpreter understands you and your needs, he or she can
more easily and accurately provide you with the information you are
seeking. Ask about specific skills if you need them. Some interpreters
are not comfortable with work that is highly technical or industry-
specific. Be very careful about numbers; confirm that the other side has
received the same number you said, and vice versa. Numbers can easily
be mistranslated in the course of negotiations; thousands get translated
into millions ("mille" means one thousand, not one million), etc. There
are too many horror stories in this area to disregard the need for con-
firmation. Make sure your interpreter is comfortable translating numbers if your negotiation will have a lot of technical and statistical information to deal with. Treat your interpreters and translators well. They
can be expensive. And they need to rest. The interpretation process is
exhausting, and you will wear your interpreter out if you expect him or
her to stay with you at the table for hours on end. Be sure to give your
interpreter frequent breaks; and if possible, have a backup interpreter
so that the two can tag-team each other.

   You can make maximum use of your interpreter if you remain sensitive to his or her presence but direct your remarks to the person to
whom you are speaking, and not to the interpreter. Additionally, break
up your speech into clauses, don't make your statements either too long
or too short, and give the interpreter time to speak to you. Many people
are apprehensive about working with interpreters at first, but then
come to rather enjoy the process. For one thing, working through an
interpreter gives you time to think—and time to observe your listeners'
reactions to your words, clause by clause, as you speak them. Americans
often have a tendency to ramble on and on, letting the words flow without too much careful concern. When you work with an interpreter, you
are more conscious of your words. They take on a greater meaning,
since you want to be sure you are understood clearly. And, as you wait
for your interpreter to translate your remarks, you can weigh your next

words more carefully in light of the other side's visible response to what you've already said.

If the other side provides an interpreter, should you bring your own? *Yes, yes, yes,* if you can afford it. Do not necessarily rely on the other team's interpreter to provide you with all the facts you need. The other interpreter is being paid by the other side, and his or her interests may not be as dispassionate as you would like. Remember, interpreters "interpret," and there is latitude here for misunderstanding, unintentional misrepresentation, errors of judgment and omission, etc. You want your interpreter to work *for* you, not against you.

One final thought about interpreters. Don't kill the messenger. It's not their fault if they tell you something you don't want to hear. They are extensions of you. You wouldn't hurt yourself, and you don't want to hurt them, either.

When They Speak English to You

If English is the language of the negotiation, you have a real advantage. It's important, therefore, to maximize this advantage. You can use your international associates' English language skills, no matter how limited, to your advantage by responding to their English language initiative in particular ways. Make their efforts work for you. Don't let their initial hesitancy dishearten you. ("Oh, no, they really *don't* speak English!") After all, you're lucky that they're willing to negotiate in English; they are doing you the favor, remember. And there are certain things you can do to make their efforts really pay off for both of you.

1. *Keep your English simple.* Use common, short, easily defined words and phrases. There's no law against monosyllabism, if you can say what you mean. Don't say "in a positive direction" if you mean "successful." And don't say "it's successful" if you mean "it works." There is a tendency in American business to garble-up the language with extraneous references, elongated words, and tortured syntax. Don't do it. It's not understood.

2. *Be aware of and avoid words that have more than ones meaning.* For example, *right* can mean "opposite of left," "correct," or "to redo something." Non-English speakers might have to guess at what you really mean.

3. *Speak slowly.* Speaking more slowly may not be something you're comfortable with, but it's essential. Your listeners will appreciate the extra time your slower delivery gives them to translate as you go. If you're concerned about sounding as if you are being condescending by

going too slowly, don't be. Your listener will probably tell you if you are, or indicate to you (probably by using some English phrase) that you can speed up. No harm done, if you speak slowly and with respect. Never, ever, however, shout in an effort to be understood. Your non-English-speaking associates are probably neither deaf nor stupid. Shouting at someone who does not speak English is like shouting in anger. And it's insulting.

4. *Use action words — verbs, etc. — to describe more specifically what you really mean.* For example, don't say, "make this happen" if you mean "sign here."

5. *Do not make nouns into verbs.* This is part of that tendency we've mentioned before to complicate things when there is no need to. Industry-specific jargon does this all the time (technolog-ese, military-ese, legal-ese, corporate-ese, psycholog-ese, etc. are all guilty of this), and it is often not understood by your foreign associates. What does "to Lebanonize" mean, anyway?

6. *Don't use words which you think might have a different meaning for your listener.* When an American says "check," as in "Let's run a check on this," a European hears the word "cheque" as in "Pay for it by cheque" (as they spell it in Britain). Similarly, when any American says "draught," as in "There's a draught in here," a Brit will hear "draft," as in "Let's get a draft (of beer)," or "Pay for it by draft" (as the British call a check). And, of course, there's the old story of the British maid "knocking the guest up for bangers in the morning." (It's not what you might think.)

7. *Avoid repeating yourself.* If you speak slowly and carefully and confirm mutual understanding often, repeating yourself only increases your margin for error and misunderstanding.

8. *Avoid metaphorical and colloquial references unless they are absolutely what you mean (which they probably aren't).* Non-English speakers are going to take your words much more literally than English speakers. They may not have the subtleties, the nuances, or the sense of play (double entendre, etc.), that come with real fluency. For example, don't say "Run that by me again," or "Walk me through that, please," since these phrases do not express to your listener what you really mean to say, which is, simply, "please repeat that."

9. *Avoid humor.* It doesn't translate well. What is funny in one culture may or may not be funny in another, and you run the risk of embarrassing either one or both of you. Keep the office jokes in the office. If you tell a joke to a Chinese, for example, you might get laughter in response, but chances are that it is more a typical Asian response of embarrassment since it might not understood as intentionally funny.

10. *Avoid all idioms and slang.* These are word pictures and are not understood. American business language has become infiltrated with American sports terms, and unless such sports also dominate in the country of your listener, they are probably not going to be understood. Baseball terms are notorious: "Can you pinch-hit for me?" "Here's a ballpark figure." "Let's make this one a home run." "That idea is out of left field." Don't use such expressions; they simply make no sense outside our borders.

11. *Begin on a formal note.* Since Americans are generally more informal than most other cultures, it's a good idea, unless you have information to the contrary, to start out a bit formally. This means using "Mr." or "Ms.," plus the title or last name. Never presume to use your associates' first names, even if you introduce yourself with only your first name. Remain formal until your opposite numbers tell you you may do otherwise, which they may or may not do. Being formal also implies being more courteous. We tend to "hang loose" where courtesies and formalities are concerned and let them go much sooner than most of our foreign associates are comfortable doing. I can't believe I am saying this, but *please* and *thank you* are absolute musts all the time.

12. *Being formal and courteous, however, does not always mean being impersonal or uninvolved.* On the contrary, formality for most other cultures is not necessarily a way of keeping you at a distance for distance's sake, but merely a way of building a relationship. Since relationship-building is a goal being pursued in these cases by respecting formality, your using a more formal style shows respect and will move things along toward the building of better relationships. Ironically, these same more formal cultures are often the ones that have a greater need for the development of relationships in business than do Americans. Therefore, the development of a relationship in all your communication should be a primary goal, despite the formality you may need to use to achieve it.

13. *Confirm understanding.* Language differences mean that there is a greater margin for error, misunderstanding, and miscommunication. We will talk about various positive behavioral skills later. Suffice it to say here that one of the most advantageous skills you can develop is that of confirming mutual understanding all along the way with your foreign associates. Sometimes this is known as active listening. Repeat back what you understand them to have meant after they have stated something important to you. This is a marvelous skill even between speakers of the same language; it is absolutely essential between speakers of different languages. What you think they meant by what they said and what they actually meant can often be two different things, as we'll see in many examples throughout this book. Confirming your under-

standing ensures accuracy of communication. Ask things like, "Let me see if I understand what you mean," and then repeat back your interpretation of what they've just said.

In addition to clarifying things for you, the technique of active listening also helps your non-English-speaking associates to feel that you are concerned about having heard them accurately, that you are interested in how they feel, in what they have to say, in what their needs and interests are. This helps develop real communication. One of the major reasons for breakdowns in communication, at the negotiating table and elsewhere, is that one side feels that it is not being "heard" by the other side. Active listening confirms the fact that you are listening, and the importance of this cannot be overemphasized.

It's Not *Always* Cultural

Cultural differences alone do not, of course, always explain why communications and negotiations fail, why your counterparts act as they do, or why you can't seem to get things done. There can be many reasons why things are or are not working out at the negotiating table, cultural differences being just one factor among them. Comprehending cultural differences, however, can provide an additional guide; understanding their impact on what you and your associates are doing will better arm and prepare you for what lies ahead and help you to move a situation in your favor. However, it is important to recognize the possibility that there are other factors at work, and to consider *their* impact as well.

We like to think of these factors as external to cultural considerations; each one is worthy of its own book, but let's briefly highlight them here.[2]

The Individual

Although our culture is a major player in determining who we are (and subsequently, how we will act in and respond to certain situations), each individual is the result of the interaction between culture and his or her genetic self. We come into this world with many aspects of who we are and what we are to be already predetermined (or, at least, predisposed to go in certain directions given certain cultural stimuli). This is the old story of nature versus nurture, of course, and the degree to which we are predetermined by nature or the degree to which culture (or environment) determines our fate is always in hot debate. Suffice it to say that the personalities of the individuals sitting opposite you are the re-

---

[2]ITAP, International assisted in the development of these concepts.

sult of a complex interaction of their culture and their genes. While cultural differences may explain why someone seems unreasonable, you may also want to look for clues to support the view that the individual is just plain difficult—with his or her own associates, as well as with you.

I recall a consultation program I worked on with a Latin American/Caribbean team. As an external consultant, one of the first things I needed to do was to learn about the needs of the team. And while most of the five team members were very willing to discuss their concerns with me, one particular individual from Jamaica was not. It seemed that nothing I did could elicit any real information from him. To the contrary, despite my efforts, this individual was derisive, petulant, uncooperative, and sometimes, downright rude. This was certainly a test of my people-skills, as well of my cross-cultural sensitivity. Not wanting to commit any of the errors we've been discussing in this chapter, such as attributing wrong motives or selecting out and misreading behavior from my own cultural filter, etc., I wanted to give this person the benefit of the doubt. Perhaps there were cultural differences at work here, I thought. Jamaicans, like Americans, have a strong sense of individuality. While this should create a synergy between the two, I have seen cases in which it results in mutual hostility, each side perceiving the other as a threat to his or her individualism. Perhaps this dynamic was at work here. Perhaps there were individual problems. Perhaps there were external factors I was still unaware of. I needed to keep trying, in order to find this out.

However, despite my best intentions, this man remained reticent, closed, and defensive. After the second meeting, I spoke with another member of his team about my difficulties. "Oh, don't worry about him," was the response I got. It seems that the person causing me so much grief was thought by all his team members to be basically surly and contentious and that he treated his colleagues in much the same way as he treated me. This wasn't a problem of cultural differences as much as it was one of personalities. Knowing this helped me adjust my behavior; it was one less thing I had to be concerned about.

Therefore, while culture certainly has a major effect on the behavior of the individuals sitting opposite you, factors such as their education, class, birth and family status, age, sex, ethnicity, upbringing, and early childhood experiences certainly, in combination with culture (and I'm not sure the degree to which any of these factors can be separated out from culture) also affect their personality and hence, their behavior.

The Environment

By *environment* here, we mean such factors as the political situation, the social conditions, the economy, even the climate and the weather. Of course, culture interacts with these factors, but they need to be considered as separate and apart from purely cultural differences if one wants to look fairly at a situation to understand it well. Certainly in business, these conditions can have a great impact on behavior at the negotiating table.

At a negotiation session a few years ago between Argentinians and Americans, the Americans were extremely frustrated with the Argentinians' refusal to commit to a timetable. Despite the repeated efforts of the Americans, the Argentinians would not commit to specific dates for deliveries, completion of certain tasks, etc. There was always a reason for not being able to make the decision that would commit them to these dates, and the Americans were mystified. I believe, in this case, that had the Americans and the Argentinians developed a closer relationship, communications between the two would have been more open, and the Argentinians might have been able to speak more truthfully. In fact, however, this negotiation was just at the beginning stages, and the two sides had not had the opportunity to really get to know each other yet. Under these conditions, Americans often feel they can still talk freely and openly (and therefore, expect the other side to do so as well). However, for many other cultures, including that of Argentina, free and open discussion is something that occurs only after the relationship is established. At this juncture, it was not possible for the Argentinians to explain truthfully to the Americans what their problem was.

In such situations, it is usually more productive to find an individual with whom you can discuss things off-line. I was developing a relationship with one of the Argentinians informally, and at dinner several days later, he spilled his troubles freely. "Look," he said, "you Americans are boxing us into a corner. There is no way I can make commitments on things five and six months from now. You don't understand how things are in Argentina today. It is very difficult to plan for anything, even for tomorrow, let alone for six months from now. I wake up in the morning and just try to get from 9 a.m. to the end of the day. I don't think about tomorrow. With a 1000-percent inflation rate, there's very little planning or management or decision-making one can do. I can sooner promise to deliver the moon to you than agree to a price or a delivery date six months from now. Every day is an emergency in Argentina."

The stalemate at the negotiating table had little to do with cultural differences. Rather, the external factors of politics and economics were playing a more significant role in what was occurring at the table. This possibility must never be overlooked. A war, a coup, a monsoon, or a 1000-percent rate of inflation are all real possibilities. Doing business internationally means dealing with external conditions that we, as Americans, are often protected from but that are very real problems in other countries. It is important not to discount such problems, and to take them into consideration as important possible motivating factors affecting the behavior of your opposite numbers.

Corporate Culture

The constraints of the corporation (or government or agency) for whom you and your counterparts work have a significant determining affect, often outside of culture's purview, on people's behavior. Policies, guidelines, and internal political considerations can determine to a significant degree the behavior of those across from you at the negotiating table, even in cross-cultural settings. Look at the following example:

By all accounts, it looked like today would be the final day of negotiations. At the end of yesterday's session, it appeared to Roger Greene, CEO of an American truck manufacturing company, that Boris Nabolovsky, head of the Russian licensing agency, was ready to agree on the final term: pricing. Greene put his first offer forward and got what he expected: an explanation of why it was unsatisfactory. Then he made his second offer, which he assumed would be accepted, since it was based on the price requirements the Russians had given him in the previous sessions: a lower price in exchange for reduced buy-back requirements. But Greene got no response from the Russians. Greene was puzzled. "According to the information I received from you the other day," he said, "this price is entirely appropriate and is based on an acceptance of the buy-back requirements you put forward." No response. Greene continued, "In order for us to be able to arrange for manufacturing in Russia, I have to feel sure that the pricing we agree upon is fair. I am sure you have the same need, and that is why I put forward this price, since it seems to reflect both of our needs." Nabolovsky finally replied, "This is true, but we still will have to meet again at a later date to discuss these issues further."[3]

There may be cultural considerations in this example, no doubt, but the primary difficulty has more to do with the external factor of Russian governmental, or more specifically in this case, agency, constraints. Nabolovsky simply could not make a decision regarding the new price put forward because he didn't have the power to do so. He was constrained by regulations that govern what he can and cannot do on his own at the table. The new price will have to be brought back to the appropriate authorities for their consideration and then responded to at another future meeting. Greene, for his part, was unable to see this ex-

[3]ERI contributed this example.

ternal political condition because of his cultural filter. "If the new price fits with the previously agreed-upon requirements, then why can't we just agree to it now and move on?" he reasoned. Americans value action and decision making based on logic and individual initiative, but that's not what determines most action and decision making in Russia.

Americans are often stymied in their negotiations with the Chinese, and, in addition to cultural differences, here, too, an explanation lies in the greater constraints placed on the Chinese by their political system. One must understand that when doing business with China, one is really doing business with a system that perhaps more nearly approaches the pure essence of bureaucracy than any other system on earth. The history of China, among many other things, is the history of the development of bureaucracy and all of its attendant efficiencies and inefficiencies. When negotiating with the Chinese, the fact that you are negotiating with a bureaucrat who needs to get approval, information, and sanction from others up and down the line must be considered a possible explanation for the interminable delays and insufferable indirectness and ambiguity of responses that most Americans endure when negotiating with the Chinese. You simply must give them time to work through the constraints their own system puts on their ability to respond to your offers, positions, and need for information.

Clearly culture has an impact on all three of these so-called external factors, and it is difficult to single out any of these factors as standing alone, one from another, or independent of a culture's effects. But it is important always to consider the possibility that these determinants can have a significant effect on why your counterparts do what they do on the other side of the table. Always check out these possibilities. Ask questions, seek answers, probe for information—in culturally appropriate ways, of course.

Some Perennial Words of Wisdom

Here are some final practical words about integrating all this information:

1. *Be rested and be ready.* Too many Americans, perhaps due to our unique notion of time, hit the ground running when they arrive overseas for a negotiation, only to find themselves running out of steam, thoughts, and patience, in the middle of the meeting. If the negotiation is worth the time and expense of a flight overseas, it's worth doing it right. Take an extra day if at all possible. Jet lag is a real drag. You are not superhuman, despite what your culture says and despite what your

boss expects. And you need to be extra sharp to succeed. You cannot run on half a tank. As you can see, cross-cultural skills require a lot of energy. Give yourself the break you need, and recover from your flight before you walk into the negotiation room. And because chances are your overseas associates operate at a different pace and with a different sense of time from you, and because things there will inevitably take more hours than you anticipate, a good rule of thumb is *not to schedule more than one meeting per day overseas.*

If your meeting is an important one (and it probably is, to have taken you abroad), you will want to schedule it in the morning. In many cultures this means you might not really get started until midmorning. The time your associate will want to spend with you will probably be considerable. There is a good chance that you won't get down to business immediately, and that business actually might not be discussed until several hours later. Lunch will intervene, and your associate, continuing his or her efforts to try to get to know you, will insist on taking you out to lunch, which can last anywhere from one to three hours (again, depending on the culture). In the afternoon, your host will need to go back to his or her own work for a few hours, and it would be useless for you to try to schedule a meeting with anyone else that late in the day, since late in the day is when work for the day needs to be caught up on. Besides, at this point, you are probably tired and want to get back to the hotel. You will need to anyway, since your host has probably arranged to take you out to dinner later that night. The moral of the story? Unless you have additional information that allows you to plan differently, schedule no more than one meeting per day, make it in the morning, and avoid Fridays. (Everyone wants to leave early if they work on Friday, and if your hosts are Muslim, the office will probably be closed anyway, because Friday is the Muslim sabbath.)

2. *Prepare, prepare, prepare.* Learn as much as you can ahead of time. Do your homework. Speak with people in your organization who have both figuratively and physically been there. Remember, your associates abroad probably know more about you than you know about them, and that's true whether they are coming to you or you are going to them. If you are going to see them, remember that you are going to a different culture and will experience both good and bad things there, just as there are good and bad things at home.

Don't compare the place you're visiting with the States: accept things as they are; there certainly isn't much you'll be able to do to change things there anyway.

3. *Keep a sense of humor and adventure.* Very few things in this world are that tragic. Discomfort, displeasure, unease, fatigue, and disorientation are all common international business side effects. Remem-

ber, nothing lasts forever, and experiencing the world beyond our shores can be a wonderful revelation. Despite the pressure, the requirements, the risks, and the costs, doing business with people from other cultures allows you the opportunity to really get to know another culture in a way few tourists can. It can be an enlightening, thrilling, exotic, glamorous and eye-opening experience whose benefits will last a lifetime. Enjoy yourself. We only go around once in this world.

PART 2

Americans at the International Negotiating Table

3
Individualism

The Lone Cowpuncher Syndrome at Work

"When in Rome do as the Romans." I like to call attention to the fact that this saying is not, "When in Rome, *be* a Roman." Therein lies all the difference. We cannot be who we are not. In fact, there is probably nothing more ridiculous, and certainly nothing more apt to fail, than an American trying to act French, Chinese, Arab, or whatever. Our cultural identity restricts us, yes, but in that restriction, also defines us. Remember the two sides to ethnocentrism. There is perhaps nothing more unnerving, or downright insulting, to a Mexican than an American trying to imitate his or her manners and mannerisms. In fact, in Japan, a non-Japanese will always, for all intents and purposes, remain a *gaijin*, or foreigner, no matter how well he or she may adapt to Japan or how many years the person lives there. That is not only accepted in Japan; it is expected.

There is a saying in Japan that if you are a *gaijin*, you need to learn how to do business in Japan "with an accent," meaning to keep to your own ways, to be true to yourself, but to bend a little, to adjust to the overall Japanese style. After all, you *are* in Japan. Note that the Japanese do *not* require non-Japanese to adopt the Japanese way, to become Japanese. For the Japanese, this would be an impossibility, for only Japanese can be Japanese. A Westerner who speaks Japanese "too well," as we have noted, can find that this asset is viewed as a liability. (Your Japanese hosts will probably be more comfortable with your inability to speak their language than they'd be if you were to walk into a negotiation in Osaka and begin speaking fluent Japanese. Not speaking Japanese supports their expectation of you as a *gaijin:* this they can work with; this they understand. There are no surprises. The Westerner who speaks perfect Japanese is a rarity, an unknown, something many Japanese will have difficulty figuring out.)

We cannot, and should not, therefore, try to "be" as our hosts. We can, however, "do" as our hosts—in the sense of taking our cues from them. The challenge in another country is to be yourself, to be American, while retaining a sensitivity and respect for the differences between yourself and your hosts. Remember, in another country, you are the one who is different, despite many Americans' tendency to view their hosts as the different ones. To think this way, of course, is an example of attribution, which we discussed in the previous chapter, and we must always be careful to remind ourselves that when abroad, *we* are the different ones.

What Is "American"?

When discussing what it means to be American, we are, by necessity, generalizing. Because the United States is so heterogeneous and because Americans have generally come from somewhere else, it can be a challenge to define particular "American" traits. What we describe here, therefore, as particularly "American" are characteristics that most Americans share, or that at least become more visible when they're abroad. It is the cultural baggage that we carry as a group no matter what our individual cultural heritages that is often most strongly identified by our international hosts as marking us as "Americans." In this sense, it doesn't matter whether we are male, female, Irish-American, Afro-American, Asian-American, or Hispanic-American. In the eyes of our overseas hosts, we all share certain characteristics that unite us as Americans and separate us, as a group, from the people of the country we are visiting. In this chapter, we will focus on those aspects of "being American" that are true for all groups in the United States, that subsume our multiculturalism under a broader band of behavior that is perhaps most keenly observed by outsiders when we are "out of our element."

As we have already noted, we are often unaware of our environment and its effects on us until we are removed from it and placed in a new environment. There are many characteristics that define all Americans, to varying degrees. But often, we, as Americans, do not see how we are similar to other Americans until we are outside our own cultural environment. Within our culture, we tend to notice our differences. Outside of it, we tend to band together. Perhaps for the United States and other heterogeneous societies; the overarching uniting characteristics are

more a matter of degrees. Certainly, one might say that for more homogeneous societies, such as Japan, a higher percentage of the population could be assumed to reveal similar characteristics than would be the
case for a heterogeneous culture. However, if we limit our investigation
to specific groups within each culture, such as businesspeople going
abroad, the disparity between individuals is reduced, whether the society is heterogeneous or homogeneous, so that statements about shared
characteristics within the group take on even greater validity.

A word of caution about generalizations: We are discussing norms.
The fact that we ascribe a particular characteristic to being American
does not mean that all Americans act that way. It does not mean that
you and I are the same. It means that, on a continuum, within a representative cross section, most of the Americans, under certain conditions,
could be counted on to exhibit certain behavior and attitudes, and to
subscribe to certain values. If this all sounds as though we're hedging
our bets, we are. People are slippery. It would be wrong to assume that
people will absolutely behave in a predictable fashion under XYZ circumstances. The miracle of human nature is that they probably won't
and are always full of surprises. If social scientists always knew for sure,
we would be able to control our world, for better or for worse, a lot better than we presently do. What we are able to do when we generalize is
make some statements about people's *tendencies*. We can say of a particular group that a percentage of them will have more or less of a tendency to do this or feel that.

It might be useful to imagine a bell curve, with the top of the curve
representing the norm. As we go down either side of the curve, we find
a smaller and smaller number of individuals who are similar to the
norm. On a curve representing the entire U.S. population's attitude toward individualism, the views of most Americans—and thus the norm
for this country—would be represented at the top of the curve, assuming that the top stands for "high value." As we move down and away
from the norm at the top, there would be fewer and fewer Americans
placing a strong value on individualism. If we were measuring individualism in another culture, we might have a differently shaped curve for
that country's norm, depending on how strongly the majority of its people valued individualism. If we slowly bring the two curves together,
there may be a point at which they overlap, and it is at this point where
some individuals from the United States and some individuals from the
other country may share similar attitudes toward individualism. There
are some people of the United States, no doubt, who place little importance on this value (they are a distinct minority). They would overlap on
these intersecting bell curves with those people of a different culture
whose norm devalues individualism.

The moral of this story? As an American, you might be very similar, in behavior, values, attitudes, etc. to a person in another country and still be very different from the norm of that country or the norm of your own country, for that matter. In fact, finding the "typical" American could be difficult, for he or she would have to be an individual who represents the exact norm for the United States for every characteristic studied. Therefore the individuals you are negotiating with overseas might, in fact, be more like you in a particular area of business behavior than they are when compared to their fellow citizens; or, they might, in fact, be even more "American" than you, or you might be more like the norm of their country than they are. The point of all this is this: It's important never to assume that your overseas associates will behave in a certain way just because you are able to identify certain characteristics of business behavior in their country. You yourself would not appreciate being pegged as predictably behaving in a certain way just because you are "American." Always give your associates time to inform you about who they are, how they operate, and what their values and attitudes are before you assume they will behave a certain way at the table. The statements we make about how different cultures behave in business are meant to serve only as guidelines for understanding, not standards of truth. From a distance, in the absence of other information, the most they can give us are some parameters by which we can begin to assess what is happening. And what makes us American is the similar set of parameters by which our non-American associates begin to judge us.

On Being "American"

Now we want to look at some very clear, broad aspects of being American, that have some very important meaning for international business negotiations. And, in keeping with this book's goals of self-learning, we'll start our examination of each of these areas with some self-assessment exercises. Let's begin with what is perhaps the most important aspect of "being American," the largest piece of cultural baggage we carry, at least in the eyes of many of our non-U.S. business associates — our unique American emphasis on "individualism."

For each of the scales following in this chapter, indicate:

1. Where you think the American value norm would be by writing "A" at the approximate position
2. Where your personal value would be by writing the first letter of your name at the approximate position

3. The first letter of a country you may be dealing with at the approximate position on the scale that you believe represents its norm (guessing is OK)

There should be three indications for each scale. For example:

1. Relationship to Work

Group worker   *Lone worker*

1	2	3	4	5	6	7	8	9	10

On this scale, I might put an "A" for the U.S. somewhere between 7 and 8, a "D" for Dean somewhere between 6 and 7, and a "J" for Japan (the target country I've chosen), relative to the U.S., on 2. There are no absolute right or wrong answers: we just want to look at tendencies and directions. While these scales may also be revealing of other important areas, fill them out keeping the notion of "individualism" in mind. Now try these:

2. Decision making

Consensus   *Majority*   *Individual*

1	2	3	4	5	6	7	8	9	10

3. Self-Assertion

Self-asserting   *Self-effacing*

1	2	3	4	5	6	7	8	9	10

4. Self-Image

Maker of regulations   *Follower of regulations*

1	2	3	4	5	6	7	8	9	10

5. Initiative

Self-initiating   *Leader-following*

1	2	3	4	5	6	7	8	9	10

6. Responsibility

Self   *Others*   *The system*   *Fate*

1	2	3	4	5	6	7	8	9	10

7. Power

Proactive is good   *Passive is good*

1	2	3	4	5	6	7	8	9	10

The extreme individualism of the United States is no doubt tied to values created out of our history. The United States after all was born out of revolution and pioneering. Individual ruggedness and self-sufficiency were required if pioneers, pushing the frontier while crossing a continent, taming nature, facing uncertainty, and overcoming adversity were to succeed. Ingenuity, self-initiative, and taking responsibility are all tied to our history and are highly respected personal traits. These traits, however, are not necessarily the fruits of other nation's histories, nor do they, in whole or in part, necessarily translate well in other countries. The transfer of certain aspects of Americanism, be it technology or pop culture, can be simultaneously admired, derided, loved, and hated in cultures abroad. Our "can-do" rugged individualism can be breathlessly refreshing at times, while at other times regarded as hopelessly naive.

The history of the United States is several hundred years old; the history of many European, African, and Asian civilizations is counted in millennia. These cultures have seen whole civilizations come and go. As a result, their people can exhibit an element of conservatism, a built-in doubting about people's ability to control their lives, an acceptance of the futility of planning, and a disbelief in an always-improving and inevitably-better future. And while these different histories have affected many different values, perhaps none comes across so clearly for the American doing business abroad as their notion of community, versus our own notion of individuality.

American children are taught at a very early age to be self-reliant. It is expected that they achieve on their own. Studies of kindergarten children in the United States and Japan reveal just how early cultural values can be instilled. When grouped around a table and provided with paper, paints, and brushes and then asked to make a painting, American nursery school children usually will each individually produce a painting and will keep a keen eye on the work of their colleagues at the table as they produce theirs. Often being the first one to produce a painting turns out to be a source of great pride. Japanese nursery school children, in the same setting, will usually, as a group, begin work on one painting per table. And while there is no competition internal to the group, there is great pride felt by each table as they complete their painting and compare it to the paintings made by the other tables. As these Japanese and American schoolchildren grow up, many will enter business. Someday they might actually sit opposite each other at the negotiating table. And when they do, the Americans will each make individual decisions at the table, will each ask his or her own questions, and will not be uncomfortable about displaying differences openly. The Japanese will show no open disagreement, will make no individual decisions at the table, and will assign only certain individuals to perform certain tasks at the negotiation.

"God Helps Those Who Help Themselves"

Let's look at an example of what happens when this uniquely American notion of individualism comes in contact with a culture where no such value exists; where traditionally, in fact, the valuing of individualism, as manifest in its many American forms, is actually discouraged.

Although she merely held a clerical position, Ms. Marku always approached her work with intelligence, diligence, and responsibility. It was a shame, thought Ms. Rogers (the American manager of the Indian subsidiary in Delhi where Marku worked), that because of the economic and social constraints in Indian society, Marku was stuck in this position. Rogers thought she could help. She began by offering more responsibility to Ms. Marku with the ultimate goal of turning her into her assistant. After all, it would benefit Marku and it would be a great help to Rogers to have a native Indian as her assistant. How disappointing it was, then, for Rogers to find Marku shirking any new responsibility, task, or challenge that Rogers offered. It seemed there was always a reason, excuse, or explanation for why she was unable to do the work, complete a task on time, or perform as instructed. Worse still, her usual clerical day-to-day duties were becoming shabby, and whatever relationship Rogers and Marku had had before Rogers' plan was now seemingly threatened. 'What went wrong?' Rogers wondered. She was very distressed.[3]

Cultural differences do not explain everything, as we have already noted. However, in the absence of any additional information, the above incident puts in bold relief the almost opposite attitudes held by an American (Ms. Rogers) and her Indian worker (Ms. Marku) in regard to the values of self-initiative, individual responsibility, and personal decision taking and decision making. In short, there is a significant difference between these two individuals in their values regarding individualism, especially, in this case, as it affects work.

It's useful to begin a discussion of American characteristics in busi-

[3]Example contributed by ITAP, International.

ness with this category because Americans, relative to most other cultures, are so extreme in the value they place on individualism. It is also striking to note how both cultures interpret God's will in almost opposite ways when it comes to personal responsibility, decision making, and self-initiative. If, in the West, "God helps those who help themselves," in India, there is very little one can do to alter God's will. My Indian friends, however, are quick to point out the requirement, in both Hinduism and Islam, to do all that one can, even if such effort is ultimately meaningless, because doing so is an unavoidable condition of the here and now. Without going into such subtleties, suffice it to say that there are distinctly different (if not directly opposite) attitudes in India and the United States regarding the value of attempting to exercise individual control over one's fate.

Proverbs and sayings can provide a quick introduction to a culture's values. In training programs for individuals attempting to learn about a culture in which they're preparing to live or work, we often provide a proverb from that culture with a key part missing, and ask the participants to fill in what they believe the missing words might be. Of course, most of the time what they tend to fill in is a reflection of their own culture and not of the one we are trying to examine. This exercise, therefore, does more than analyze the values of the other culture. It reveals the process of projecting our own culture onto that of the other, an example of the attribution process we discussed earlier.

One of the most startling contrasts in attributions or projections inevitably occurs when we ask people from other countries to fill in the blank for this United States proverb: "God helps those who_____."
In the main, Westerners are already familiar with this saying, and white, Anglo-Saxon Protestants in particular almost always get it right: "God helps those who help themselves." (After all, it *is* a reflection of the Protestant, individualist, hard-work ethic.) However, when this proverb is presented to Asians, they inevitably fill in the blanks quite differently, so that the proverb reads: "God helps those who help others." Clearly here, the individualist aspect of the proverb is put in bold relief, for in Asian cultures, group-orientation is much more the preferred value. In Asia, to help others, to support the group, is the way to salvation. In the West, to take care of oneself is primary, and we believe that if everyone did so, a better world would result. Furthermore, when we point out to Asians that their version of the proverb is not the standard one here, they are startled to find out how it is usually expressed in the United States. I remember one gentleman from Thailand who refused to believe that Westerners really thought this way. After all, he said, how can you help others if you are only helping yourself? Clearly, from the Asian point of view, the difference in the ending of the proverb re-

flected the fundamental difference between individualist and group orientation. Asians fail to see the uniquely Western connection, the causal step from taking care of oneself to then being able to take care of others, because their cultural history does not involve, in the same way as it does in the West, the idea of a struggle in the individual's relationship to God.

The Lone Cowpuncher Versus the Tribe

Geert Hofstede's studies indicate that the United States scores the highest among all cultures surveyed in the individualism category.[4] What do we mean when we talk about this as a characteristic of American business behavior? One Japanese negotiator summed it up this way: "Each one [of the Americans] had his or her own ideas to say....I was quite embarrassed for them, as the team could not decide which way they wanted to go. I was also quite surprised to see that they would willingly, almost with pride, display to us this lack of unity and cooperation on their part."

Clearly, for this Japanese, American individualism ran counter to the Japanese emphasis on group consensus and the Japanese devaluing of self-assertiveness. Using this example, on the above scales, one might locate the Japanese (in comparison with Americans) more toward the group-worker side of scale 1 (relationship to work) and more to the self-effacing side of scale 2 (self-assertion).

Values do not stand alone. They are often intertwined, creating a larger pattern of behavior, and cultures have the disturbing habit of creating unlikely (or, based on your particular cultural position, counterintuitive) combinations of values. Self-effacement, as represented in this example by the Japanese sublimation of the will of the individual to the greater will of the group, can be manifested in various ways—combined, if you will, with other Japanese values such as the requirement for formality, and revealed through behavior regarding seniority. The Japanese speaker in the above situation went on to discuss his team's confusion: "We didn't know who was in charge. We didn't say very much, because we didn't know whom to speak with."

The will of the group in Japan, the decision taken, the path to be followed, is often revealed by the senior negotiator. Each member of the team has a specific role to play in the negotiation, and the spokesperson for the group may well be the one senior individual present, often the one sitting in the center of his group. ("Spokes*man*" is most important here, since seniority in Japan is based primarily on sex and age, but

[4]Hofstede, Geert, *Culture's Consequences*, Sage Publications, London, 1984.

more on this in Part 3.) It can be confusing for Japanese when negotiating with Americans because the Japanese can have difficulty distinguishing clear-cut, individual roles among the American negotiators. In
turn, of course, Americans are often frustrated by the seniority, hierarchy, and formality of the roles in the Japanese team (again, more on
Japanese hierarchy and formality in Part 3). The point here is that seniority, formality, and notions of hierarchy, etc. all combine to form a
unified pattern of behavior, and that these notions are each, in varying
degrees, created out of certain values. In this case, we see that the particularly different Japanese and American attitudes toward individualism, as reflected in decision making and self-assertion, can play themselves out dramatically at the negotiating table.

In Latin America, the self-assertive aspect of individualism has a dual
nature that can cause misunderstandings among *Norte Americanos*.
In one sense, Latin men seek out opportunities that allow them to "assert" their individualism and can often feel threatened if their "self"
is challenged. Notions of machismo, power, and responsibility to family
and kin can often drive the Latin to what might be considered by
the *Norte Americano* as extreme, and sometimes inappropriate, self-
assertive behavior (i.e., making unreasonable demands or promises, taking inflexible positions in order to reaffirm or establish "power," making "outlandish" statements, grandiose plans, etc.). In this sense, self-
effacing behavior is generally inappropriate to Latin American business
(especially for Latin men). In contrast to *Norte Americanos*, however,
such "individualist" behavior in Latins is often done for what is perceived to be the betterment of the group, in order to satisfy group
needs, in order to achieve what the group deems necessary. Prideful,
individualist behavior is often engaged in so that the Latin man will look
good in the eyes of the group with which he identifies. Approval, support, and admiration from this group, be it work associates, friends or
family, provide the Latin man with his identity and his power. He is not
the loner, pursuing independent goals with little or no consideration
of what others think. On the contrary, his individualist efforts are undertaken specifically to engender the positive attention of important
others.

The importance of appearing powerful, decisive, and important in
the eyes of the significant group to which the Latin relates cannot be
overemphasized. This is often a mystery for *Norte Americanos*. American managers were incredulous at a negotiation when the Mexican negotiator suddenly refused to accept a delivery date that the Americans,
based on their past experience with this particular organization, had expected the Mexicans to have no trouble with. The Mexican negotiator
instead provided what appeared to the Americans to be an unsatisfac-

tory delivery date, and he provided little justification for why the delivery time had to be so extended. The Americans had been doing business with this group for several years and had established what they believed to be an effective working and social relationship with the Mexican hierarchy, including the negotiator. Why, all of a sudden, this apparent "power play"? What could the Mexicans want? The American team began preparing for some kind of hard bargaining over issues they thought had been previously resolved, researching alternate positions in regard to other terms of their business. All this was really unnecessary: the Mexicans were not looking for new terms, concessions, or any real substantive changes in the relationship. In fact, they viewed the relationship as so stable that they felt confident in being able to work out what were, in reality, their own internal issues, assuming, in effect, the implicit understanding, cooperation and support, of their *Norte Americano* associates.

What was really going on was that several new people had recently been hired on the Mexican side, and the hierarchy, in this hiring process, had been juggled around. The management felt a need to reassert its importance, to make its power clear, to appear strong to its new team members, in the face of the *Norte Americanos*. This need is not often discussed openly, of course, so the Americans had no real way of understanding what was really going on. Had they known, all they really would have needed to do was be willing to play the game a bit longer, help the Mexican managers maintain power and authority in the eyes of their hew hirees, and all would probably have been back to normal. In this case, fortunately, the Mexican and American negotiators had established such effective communications through their past business that they were able to discuss privately what the real concern was. There are other, similar cases in which Mexicans have put themselves in untenable, or irretrievable, positions with *Norte Americanos*, all because of some "second agenda" requirement to exhibit power and authority in the face of new internal or external pressures.

The importance of such posturing is reflected in the fact that this behavior occurs even as it may jeopardize the business at hand. Ironically, Mexicans can be aware of this predicament and can often feel themselves in a tremendous bind, drawn between the powerful need to assert or reassert authority, and an awareness, nevertheless, that such behavior could jeopardize the deal. Here is where the skillful, tactful, cross-culturally sensitive behavior of the American is critical, rather than simply reacting negatively to the Mexican posturing. In fact, it is at this moment that the American can turn a problem into an opportunity. It is a chance to help the Mexican in his quest for authority in the eyes of his people by cooperating to the degree possible, by helping the Mexican associate, in private, discuss his real issue, and by providing support and understanding for the Mexican's "internal agenda."

Individualism Versus Independence

We have seen that in order to maintain or achieve a positive image in the eyes of his all-important group, the Latin may actually appear individualistic, at least as that quality is valued by North Americans—that is, assertive in the extreme, perhaps aggressive, certainly not like the humble, self-effacing Asian. The difference here between the North American and the Latin American, however, has to do with the reasons, the values, behind the behavior. While the North American traditionally behaves individualistically in an effort to maintain independence from others, the Latin behaves individualistically in an effort to establish, reinforce, or reaffirm a positive dependence on others. The group is significantly important to the Latin. For the North American, the traditional Anglo, individualism is asserted by rejecting, or standing out from, the group.

The pull of the group for the Latin American explains the other side of the Latin's attitudes toward individualism, particularly toward such individualist notions as self-assertiveness, self-initiative, personal responsibility, and individual orientation to power and authority. Here we often see, not an embrace of individualism, but rather a kind of retreating from more aggressive, individualistic North American-type behavior. This can cause serious problems for North Americans, especially after they have been surprised (or downright pleased) to have witnessed assertive "North American" behavior on the part of their Latin associates previously. Then suddenly, and often inexplicably, the Latins seem to "retreat" into behavior that provides North Americans with opportunities for stereotyping their Latin associates as "lazy," "unmotivated," "unconcerned for the work needing to be done," etc. What's going on here?

A Lesson in Latin Individualism

Time and again throughout Latin America, I have consulted with U.S. managers frustrated and mystified by their Latin staff. What I hear from them inevitably sounds something like this:

"I cannot seem to get my message across...they say they understand, but nothing seems to get done when it is supposed to."

"I try to provide them with motivation, offering them opportunities for advancement, to make a name for themselves...they don't appreciate it."

"We're offering a lot of positives in this organization for them: there's work here they wouldn't have otherwise, and while they say they appreciate this, their actions certainly don't support their words. You should see them sometimes: They don't understand about promptness, they take days off whenever possible, there is always some family problem they're coming to me with. It's a wonder anything gets done around here!"

Then I speak with the South Americans and I hear something like this:

"We don't know what we are expected to do here. The confusion around this place makes us crazy! Nobody has told me exactly what I have to do, yet when something isn't done just the way they expect it, I get blamed."

"I'd get a lot more done and be more successful at my work, I know, if they'd tell me what they want and leave me alone to do it. Instead, they tell me nothing, but always want to be sure I am doing things their way."

"We want to cooperate. I am really grateful for the opportunities working here gives me, but frankly, it makes me angry to always try so hard to do things their way when they make no effort to understand why I want to do something differently."

In between these two groups is a yawning chasm, a gaping emptiness of misunderstanding, miscommunication, and a lack of effective work. And culturally this is due to two very opposite notions of individualism and two very conflicting sets of expectations. Let's take a closer look. The North American manager in this case is approaching work issues with a set of assumptions based on the North American work-ethic culture. Such assumptions involve values and attitudes concerning:

Self-initiative. This suggests the idea that people are always looking for a way to do better, to give themselves an edge in success and that, given such an opportunity, they will seize it in order to stand out as successful individuals, taking the credit and glory for their individual work. According to this idea, people always do better at working toward their goals when left alone to create on their own, to find solutions independently, and to reap the rewards of their hard work.

Personal responsibility.   The idea of personal responsibility is that individuals are primarily responsible to themselves and have only themselves to blame or applaud for what happens to them in their life. In business, this means that if you want to get something done, you have to make it happen yourself and that there are no external reasons why things don't happen. One must simply learn to do what one must do in order to get the right things to happen (no excuses, "just do it"). This also means that you work around or through the hierarchy in order to get to the individual you need, whether it is for information, a decision, or assistance. It is no coincidence that hierarchies are often less rigid and rules more flexible in cultures that subscribe to a more self-assertive, get-it-done kind of approach than they are in group-oriented cultures.

On the other side, the Latins subscribe to a more authoritarian, structured, community-centered, conservative culture. They wait for instructions, details, and information before taking any initiative in regard to accomplishing their tasks. Unlike North Americans they do not place the same emphasis on self-initiative and more readily ascribe responsibility for the way things happen to someone or something else (including fate, God, and the unexplained mysteries of life). Their priorities regarding the importance of time and family are often in direct conflict with North American assumptions about individual responsibility. In this sense, on scale 6, one might locate Americans very close to number one, but would place Latins (and Arabs, as well) floating somewhere along the line when it comes to ascribing responsibility to others, the system, God, or fate.

The Americans in the complaints quoted above are managing the South Americans as if they were North Americans. That is, they assume that the Latins are on the look-out for opportunities that will enable them to individually strike out on their own and compete for the goodies, that they work well independently of each other, and that they will take full personal responsibility for the accomplishment of their task. In fact, as a direct result of Latin values, the opposite is more or less the case. For their part, the Latins are responding to their North American managers as if they were South American managers. That is, they are expecting the managers to tell them what they can and cannot do, to know that they will have to find a way of working together in order to get any of the individual parts of the task accomplished, and to understand when other things (such as family emergencies, time crises) happen to get in the way of reaching a goal at the time originally stipulated. (In fact, they may even go to their managers with personal problems, expecting their assistance.) The Latins look to the Americans to provide authority, almost permission, and the Americans look to the Latins to take the initiative and to come up with their own individual solutions to problems. The Americans expect the Latins to consult with them freely; the Latins expect the Americans to provide them, basically, with detailed instructions. The Americans welcome, even expect, contributions, opinions, and suggestions. The Latins wouldn't think of contradicting a superior, let alone of making a suggestion that the superior hadn't already, in some fashion, suggested.

The conflicting expectations each side has of the other guarantee failure. The Americans perceive the Latins as not rising to the occasion, as not wanting to succeed, and, in this atmosphere of misunderstanding, might describe them stereotypically as lazy, slow, and "more concerned with other things." The Latins see the Americans as irresponsible and unable to manage effectively. They describe them stereotypically as ignorant, immature (or not ready for the responsibilities of their job), and unable to see the importance for doing things in their country their way. As far as they are concerned, the Americans are insensitive to the needs of the people they are depending on. The Latins, further, might find Americans obnoxiously informal, disrespectful of them, and insensitively insistent on an uncomfortable degree of informality. They might be very hard-pressed to speak up to a manager with such informality, as if they were equal. Certainly they might have great difficulty making suggestions or countering instructions or demands.

Individualism at the Negotiating Table

Cultural differences in regard to individualist notions of self-assertion, initiative, individual decision making, and action taking also reveal themselves in more structured negotiations. As we saw in our Mexican example earlier, the key Mexican negotiator needed to reaffirm his power to new members of the group, and used the negotiation with the *Norte Americanos* as an opportunity to do this—a dangerous, but not uncommon game. Often in negotiations, the group, whether at the table or behind the scenes, will determine the degree of risk taking the individual negotiator can embark on. The group acts as a qualifier to the personal impulses of the single Latin negotiator. In fact, in the negotiation, the group will almost always ensure that the action taken is conservative, that all decisions are carefully considered, and that nothing is done in haste.

This stands in direct contrast to the individual impulses of grand, assertive, almost impulsive risk taking that, as we saw, can also be common with the individual Latin. When there is a group at the negotiating table needing to make a decision, the power of the group mitigates independent individual efforts of self-assertion. In fact, a Latin negotiation is often an internal contest of the assertion of individual wills battling for position and power within the parameters allowed by those individuals with true authority. Often, such individual sparring will occur because it is allowed, tolerated, or unknown to the higher authority. When the higher authority makes a decision, whether after, during, or before such internal jockeying, the sparring usually ceases. In negotiations with Americans, most Latins will have conducted all their internal jockeying well before sitting down at the table. Sometimes, in the course of the negotiation, however, individuals will reveal individual differences. It would be wise for the North American to understand who the decision-makers really are at the table before expending a good bit of energy meeting, answering, persuading, and otherwise engaging with "individualists" from the other side who, in fact, may have no real authority (and who might just be using your involvement to advance their own cause within their group).

At a negotiation between two teams of Colombian businesspeople, for example, both sides engaged each other with great enthusiasm over a number of points. The negotiation appeared to be speeding off from the beginning at 90 miles per hour with individuals from both sides debating with other individuals over particular points. Without reaching conclusions about any of the issues raised, the negotiation would zoom off onto another point. There was definitely a "polychronic" attitude toward the topics open for discussion. To the outside observer, it seemed as if a hundred different things were being discussed at once, with different individuals responsible for different topics to be negotiated. Then, rather suddenly, after several caucuses, a spokesperson emerged from both sides and summarized a rather conservative position, from which both sides then proceeded to carefully, and rather more slowly, negotiate, as teams.

What was happening, in fact, was that apparently "individualistic" members of the teams were jockeying for positions of respect and power at the beginning of the negotiation. In fact, the real negotiation did not seriously begin until the jockeying ended, and the real person of authority in each group made some decisions regarding the key starting issues to be discussed. Subsequent negotiations continued to follow a similar pattern. And in all cases, the negotiation that started off with great gusto, indicating a lively, aggressive, individualistic approach to problem-solving, actually developed into a conservative, authoritarian, group-oriented quagmire that in two out of three scenarios yielded no final solutions.

One last comment regarding Latins and these particular aspects of individualism: it is different, of course, depending upon the Latin country one looks at. In Spain, for example, the difference between individualism and independence that we have already explored in South America can be even more significant. In fact, Spain provides us with an excellent example of the importance of making a distinction between these two subtle, yet profound, aspects of what the North American often fuses together. For the Spaniard—proud, fiercely individualistic in his thinking and behavior—his individualism is unquestioned. However, his dependence on the group, his need to justify action based on underlying group needs, is great. In fact, his individualism is often driven by the needs of the group that will benefit from his success, whether that group is at work or at home. This is similar to the Mexican example we were looking at, but more intense (and not surprisingly so, as might not the Latin Americans have gotten many of their attitudes from their former colonial masters?), and it is perhaps the best example of how individualism, in all its forms in many cultures, is still significantly different from the unique American fusion of independence and individualism. (It is this aspect of American individualism that makes Americans *so* "individualistic.")

A Spanish businessman had this complaint to make about an American associate:

Each time the American pushed his ideas forward, I felt I just had
to produce my own. It wasn't that his ideas were bad, just that I had
to have the opportunity to put mine forward. After all, he was in
my country. Besides, Americans are so pushy, you have to push
back almost automatically.

The American had a different take on what their first meeting was like:

Every time I had something to say, he negated it. Sometimes
directly, sometimes indirectly, but he denied it. It was like he wasn't
even listening. I found him rude and condescending. I don't
know why he wasted his time with me, and I certainly don't know
why I came all the way to Spain to meet with him.

Eventually, this negotiation did get going, and, after three trips by the American, he and the Spaniard were able to agree on a successful manufacturer-distributor relationship. On the second trip, the American found out what his distributor-to-be was actually looking for and capable of delivering, and there began the process of mutually satisfying needs. Here the very individualist American was at first getting equally individualist-type behavior back and was put off by such contrary behavior. However, he must have indicated a willingness to continue discussions, for by continuing, he encouraged the Spaniard to feel that he had a welcome ear in his American associate, and together they were able to begin building the all-important relationship. That probably began rather well in the second meeting, so that by the third meeting they were able to discuss issues seriously and in good faith.

The important thing to remember from this example is the need the Spaniard had at the beginning to assert his individualism, even if it meant "excessive contrariness" (or at least that's how the American took it). In fact, by the third meeting, if not the second, it should have become quite clear to the American that, while this Spaniard may have been making individual decisions in regard to the business at hand, he would not have agreed to the deal had the arrangement not satisfied some deeper, group-dependent needs. One might assume that such needs were family-, group-, or clan-oriented.

The French Twist

When we look at the French, we are looking at yet an additional twist to the issue of individualism as it compares with American traits, for the French require us to exercise a unique precision when using the terms *individualistic* and *individualism*. This is their contribution to the discussion, and it is in this distinction, forced on us by the French, that American behavior once again differs greatly from individualist behavior in many other cultures. Perhaps the most unflattering stereotypical traits Americans ascribe to the French are those of arrogance, self-congratulation, stubbornness, and unwillingness to compromise. Equally unflattering and stereotypical is the French view of Americans as naive, shallow, uninteresting, and unaware. (Both nationalities gleefully seek proof of these respective stereotypes in their encounters with each other.) In fact, there are many reasons for the two nationalities' ideas about each other, but the one that interests us here is the different interpretations that Americans and the French give to the concept of *individualism*.

When French and American ideas about individualism are compared, the American version takes on an almost political tone, while the French version is clearly more cultural. Americans speak of individualism as a guaranteed political right, a constitutionally protected condition of humanity. When the French speak of individualism, they refer to a more social and personal condition, certainly not a political one. For the French, individualism is an aspect of being, a way of defining oneself by setting oneself *in opposition to* someone or something else. When Americans speak of standing up for what they believe, of speaking their minds, or even of being original, it is always within the larger context of a greater, constitutionally guaranteed way of life. In fact, standing in opposition to the greater structure is not the way to make a stand for individualism in the United States. It would engender questions of why one can't get along, of decency, of common sense and generally accepted attitudes of right and wrong, good and bad. No such parameters exist for French men or women. For them, questioning is open-ended. Americans tend to base relationships on the mutual acknowledgment of similarities. The French (and many other Europeans as well, but the French in particular) tend to base relationships on the mutual acknowledgment of differences. (We will go into this in more detail in our discussions of relationship-building and American values.)

The French therefore may tend to see American individualism as the right to be like everyone else, while they see their own individualism as the right to be oneself, even if it means being substantially different from everyone else. Americans, on the other hand, see their own brand of individualism as standing up for American virtues and view French individualism as obstinacy and quirkiness. The French emphasize the individualist, the Americans emphasize individualism itself.

The French are a very specific variety of Latins, standing as a bulwark, in many ways, between Mediterranean Europe and the English to their north. The ideal French individualist (so different from the ideal American as the lone, shoot-from-the-hip cowpuncher) is a uniquely French combination of personal assertiveness and group concern. The respect shown by the French for the individualist is their version of Latin individual assertiveness. The French concern for the larger culture (that's Culture with a capital "C") and the uniquely French notion that society defines humanity (and not the other way around) is their version of Latin concern for the group. Society, as a concept, is extremely important to them, and French society sets the standards for civilized behavior. The French Revolution established the primacy of society over the individual, a reverse of the social evolution that was occurring across the channel in Protestant England. Perhaps it is this difference in emphasis on the role of the individual — valued in both societies but for different reasons — that explains the differences between the Americans and the French. It is a clash between individual interests determining society (American) and social interests determining the individual (French).

At bottom, it is a clash between two different paths to salvation: direct, one-on-one Protestantism versus Church-mediated Catholicism.

If all this sounds too far removed from the negotiating table, think again. Many other aspects of French behavior are ultimately grounded in this special "take" on the role of the individual. Many an American has been frustrated by the "unpredictable" and "erratic" (for which read "highly individualist") behavior of their French counterparts, only to be informed that it is they themselves who aren't acting in the best interests of all concerned. A recent negotiation held to organize a joint venture between a large American multinational and its Parisian partners-to-be provides a good illustration of this kind of standoff.

The U.S. multinational representatives went into the negotiation assuming that American technical and managerial expertise would be viewed as a positive asset: they assumed their expertise was a real bargaining chip. In fact, it turned out to be a bargaining "chop," because the French actually felt threatened by the expertise. For their part, the French had a much larger agenda than just the logistics of arranging the joint venture details. They wanted to back up considerably, look at the larger picture, and generate significant new concerns that the joint venture should address. Some of these concerns had to do with their fears of American expertise supplanting, or at least not respecting, the degree of French expertise already in existence at the Paris company. Others of these concerns had to do with ensuring that the Americans would respect French ways of doing business. The French were convinced that their well-established methods would be discarded, if not at least tampered with, by the new American management component. The French demands, in fact, seemed to the Americans to be endless, one almost geometrically generating others, while the American requirements (which seemed straightforward and task-related to the Americans) seemed insulting, demeaning, and threatening to the French.

The French responded indignantly to what the Americans quite matter-of-factly put forward, and protested that American demands did not address many of their larger concerns. The Americans, in turn, felt as if they had stepped into a black hole of problems. Instead of moving forward toward a light at the end of the tunnel, they were moving ever downward into an abyss of uncertainty. French individualism, supported by strong group identity and history, was being threatened — or at least the French, with their supersensitivity to such issues, perceived it that way. Meanwhile, American individualism, as manifested by a straightforward, task-oriented, and common-sensical approach, was, according to the Americans, being undermined at every turn by unexpected and unnecessary problems of French creation.

Individualism and Self-Determination

Earlier, when we looked at differing cultural notions of responsibility, we commented that blaming the system, others, fate, or God, in lieu of taking personal responsibility, was a trait common to both Latins and Arabs (and, I should add, to many other traditional cultures). In fact, it is a convenience so easy to employ that all cultures have recourse to it sometimes, under certain conditions, and in varying degrees. The point here is that there are some cultures that have institutionalized it to a greater degree than others and where, as a norm, one should expect the "passing of the buck" onto agents other than oneself. The Arab *insh'Allah* ("if God wills it") can excuse a multitude of human errors and explain insufferable delays. It can also justify the taking of great risk, for if we can never be sure of tomorrow, if only God knows what will happen, then we're not exactly liable if we decide to take chances, letting the chips fall where they may. If one has agreed to have the shipment arrive by Tuesday, but Tuesday comes and goes and it still has not arrived, it may have been God's will. Individual responsibility in these cultures goes only so far. In fact, planning too far ahead may be suspect, for only a fool believes he can change the future. In this sense, American individualist planning and concern for organization may reveal you to be, in the absence of other factors, of course, naive and simple, certainly not holy, and not worth an Arab's time. (There will be more on self-determination, risk taking, and control of destiny in Chapter 4.)

The Squeaky Wheel Gets the Oil

American individualism gives authority and value to the individual, pure and simple. No thing, no group, no institution, is more sacred. Within the individual lie all the solutions, all the creative power for the advancement of society. In a culture that enshrines the individual in such a position of power, it is not surprising to find that the individual is also given a very powerful voice.

Mr. Yakashima was reporting to Mr. Cannon, his American manager. He was describing difficulties he had had during the negotiation he recently conducted with an outside American client. Mr. Yakashima noted that Mr. Roberts, who represented the American side, seemed tired and frustrated at their last meeting. Yakashima stated that he didn't understand why, since he had been finding the meetings to date very informative. Yakashima admitted, however, that he found Roberts's insistence throughout all the meetings on decisions and answers that Yakashima could not provide disconcerting. "It was uncomfortable for me to always say that I had no answer for this or that now," Yakashima said to Cannon. "Several times in our discussions, Roberts expressed doubt over our sincerity, wondering why I wasn't working harder to get things done! But it was even more difficult for me when Roberts said, 'OK, I am willing to lower my price by $5000, but only if you will accept this right here and now; no more stalling, please.'" "What did you do?" Cannon asked. "Nothing," Yakashima answered. "I couldn't make that decision alone."[5]

In Japan the saying equivalent to our "squeaky wheel" is more like, "The bird that honks, gets shot." "Stand up and be counted," we say. The Japanese say, "The nail that sticks up gets hammered down." It's a central virtue of American individualism to be the one to make the loudest noise, to toot your own horn (for unless you do, no one else will), and to be the biggest kid on the block. This notion of standing up and announcing oneself to the world is the philosophical wellspring, if you will, for the entire broadcast and media industry in America, for advertising, and for show biz. Its roots go back to the biblical command, "Don't hide your light under a bushel," and is represented today in nationwide media-time, measured at $100,000 per 30 seconds.

Individualism and Competition

Of course, deeply connected with this highly individualist American notion of making more noise than the next guy is the way we praise the virtues of the competitive system. In the United States, the two fit hand in glove. We are speaking of the squeaky wheel being, in the case of Americans, an individual. Group-oriented (nonindividualistic) cultures, however, are not necessarily any less squeaky; it's just that the whole group will squeak together, and this can make a mighty noise, too. "Making noise" is not only about announcing one's needs or wants, though; it's also about seeking acknowledgment, praise, reward, or getting one's comeuppance. Credit for a task well or badly executed needs to be acknowledged. Those who shine get to stand up and take a bow, and those who screw up need to be corrected. The focus on individual recognition, reward and punishment, entails issues of motivation and incentive, especially in the business world. The singling out of an indi-

[5]This example was contributed by ITAP, International.

vidual for recognition in a U.S. business often serves as motivation. But, in less individual-oriented cultures, this kind of managerial action can be unproductive—if not downright destructive.

American businesspeople need to become aware of just how toxic this aspect of our extreme individualism can be in other, more group-oriented cultures around the world. We need to develop a sensitivity to the effects of our individualism for, as individual fish living quite naturally in the pool of individualism, we can be unaware of how different it is for many people around the world. In the example above, Roberts did not understand how his insistence that Yakashima make his own individual decision was asking Yakashima to do something that went deeply against his grain. In Japan, decisions are usually made by the group, and here we're not talking about majority vote; we mean full and total consensus. Since the group is all-important, issues are discussed until a complete understanding is reached regarding its position, which will often then be articulated by the most senior individual on the negotiating team. In contrast, Americans are often comfortable playing out their individual differences right at the negotiating table, as we saw in our previous example. Yakashima was doubly hurt by the American's implication that he was not trying hard enough, not going to whomever was necessary in order to get the job done, etc. It was an implication that Yakashima was shirking his responsibilities and not taking it upon himself to do whatever was necessary to make things happen.

This is very dangerous stuff in Japan. Yakashima was losing face in being asked to explain why he did not take personal responsibility for doing whatever was necessary, for pulling strings, for going after things on his own. Of course, in group-oriented societies, that's not the way to get things done; rather, that's the way to get oneself ostracized from the group. It is a bit like the ancient Greeks' notion of the worst possible punishment for a criminal: to be cast out of the community, to be made alien to the Greek city-state, to be denied a group to belong to. (In group-related societies, such isolation from the group can be equivalent to death, and, in fact, group-oriented cultures have often institutionalized suicide in extreme circumstances as an honorable alternative to ostracism, to no longer being allowed to belong to or to live in the larger society). To ask Yakashima to take it upon himself to make an important decision that was going clearly to affect members of his group, to ask him to do whatever was necessary to get the job done, and then to berate him and question his intentions when he said he could not do this is behavior about as destructive as one can get in Japan. There is no doubt that Yakashima will not want to do business with Roberts again.

From Roberts' perspective, however, Yakashima's behavior was mystifying. He appeared (and that's an all-important word) unwilling to extend himself to honor his commitments, to get things going when they needed to get going, to find the right person, no matter what, and to make a decision. Worse, the guy didn't seem to care, and when confronted with American displeasure over his "do-nothing" behavior became silent and passively resistant to anything else. Roberts felt that he couldn't break through to the guy and was left feeling very frustrated.

On the scales provided at the beginning of our discussion of individualism, one could place Americans nearer the 10 side (individualist) on the first scale measuring decision making, and the Japanese, in this case, closer to the 1 side, or consensus. Additionally, there is a complicating element of individualism that is reflected in scale number 7, which may be highlighted by looking at the Yakashima/Roberts problem.

Individualism and Action

To be a squeaky wheel, at least according to our proverb, implies "doing something." It requires action; it is, to use an overworked but, in this case, appropriately legitimate term, *proactive*. In order to be squeaky, to make a noise, to raise a stink, to shake things up, or get what you want from somebody or something, you've got to be doing something, and there is an implied value here in *doing*. We'll discuss this in more depth when we examine implications of the notion of time for Americans coming up in the next chapter. But for now, it is well worth noting the individualist aspect of this value: that while there are many action-oriented cultures that are also group-oriented (Japan being one of them), there is a distinct relationship between being in favor of action ("Why won't you just do whatever it takes to get the job done?") and individualism. Perhaps because an individual can act more easily than a group can (if only because it's logistically easier to get things done when working on one's own), the belief in doing, the faith in the future, the cult of progress, are all often associated with individualism.

Even in those group-oriented cultures that appear to be action-oriented (Singapore, Hong Kong, Japan, and the other Asian dragons), what we're really seeing is a unique application of activity not necessarily dependent on faith in the future or action itself. Rather, such activity is associated with an attempt to organize the group, or society, into a more harmonious, stable whole. Activity here is a means to an end, the end being a harmonious organization of the largest group of all: society. Activity in an individualist culture occurs as individuals attempt to make the future better for themselves than it is today. It is based on an inherent belief in the virtue of action and individual competition. No such belief exists in the action-oriented *group* cultures, and that is why as a value, action is associated more specifically with individualism. Some group-oriented cultures (such as India, China, Burma, and Indonesia) favor action as long as it is taken for the good of the group. Other group-oriented cultures, which might best be termed passive) place a minimal value on action, whatever the circumstances. But every individualist culture prizes action—the more so if it advances the fortunes of the individual.

Roberts was annoyed that Yakashima reacted to his anger and frustration with silence, with a passive resistance, with a quiet, yet solid, refusal to get in the ring with Roberts. Roberts pushed Yakashima so far that the relationship that originally bound them together was destroyed, and Yakashima no longer felt the obligation to engage. In many group-oriented cultures, passivity, the "not-doing," has power, and the Western orientation toward doing, pushing the envelope, making something more happen, is seen as weak and powerless. A kind of power resides in a group that is holding off on its final decision, even if it means doing nothing for the moment. And there's a kind of powerlessness about individuals expending a lot of energy vainly trying to persuade the other side to agree to something. In fact, this is sometimes what happens when the Japanese and Americans come together.

The Japanese might regard American activity as obsessive, rushed, confusing, and excessively individualist. From their point of view, it risks causing embarrassment and loss of face, and it can unsettle the all-important harmony of the negotiation. Americans, on the other hand, tend to regard apparent Japanese passivity: their concern for respect and harmony, their endless exchange of information without any at-the-table decision making, and their endless series of exclusive, behind-closed-doors meetings as obstructive, engendering suspicion, and generally an impediment to progress. These opposite attitudes can be interpreted as the result of opposite cultural views regarding passivity and activity and are grounded in deeply different concepts of the world.

"Passive" as "Active" in Asia

Being aware of each other's values in this regard can be beneficial at the negotiating table. The Japanese can attempt to use the Americans' energy to get what they want. In effect, they are turning it around passively and using our energy to further their own goals. One might call this "negotiation *ju-jitsu*," and the parallel to the martial arts only reinforces the connection between the Japanese notion of negotiating and deep-seated Japanese cultural values. Americans also can benefit from such techniques, as Roger Fisher has so aptly pointed out in his book, *Getting to Yes,*[6] but it means understanding how to use, and avoid, the other side's energy or activity to your advantage, without necessarily responding in kind with your own energy. Often, in training programs preparing Americans for work in Asia, we perform a small exercise that demonstrates the possibility of power in passivity, and the possible powerlessness of action.

I ask a participant (let's call him "John") to join me in the front of the group. (I often choose the brawniest fellow in the room.) I then ask him to stand facing me and place the palms of his hands up against mine. I state that the goal is for me to move toward John's side, and for John to move toward my side. We are clearly opposites, standing in each other's way. Then I ask him to push toward the direction he needs to go. But instead of pushing back, and making this a "push-of-war" (as opposed to a tug-of-war), I do not resist. I let go, carefully, and in a controlled way, so that John's energy does not push him over, but rather pushes me back. As John keeps pushing forward, I move backward through the room, winding among the desks and seated participants, taking my friend exactly wherever I want him to go, but using his energy to get there. Finally, I end up on the other side of the room from where I began. Then I ask the group, "Where is John?" The answer, of course, is that John is where *I* want him to be.

In the East, nothing is something, black is not just the absence of white, opposites together form a unified whole, what is not said or done may be more important than what is said or done, and passivity has power. This is not an easy thing for Westerners to automatically understand philosophically and is perhaps a harder concept to act on behaviorally, for it requires a fundamentally different world view than the traditional American one. The stories are legion of Americans in Japan losing patience, pushing too hard too fast, becoming nervous during those long silences at the negotiation table, and rushing in to fill that silence with poorly-thought-out proposals.

Westerners are quickly made very anxious by silence and seeming passivity. Forgetting, or not knowing that the Japanese negotiate with each other this way, too, they assume that they are getting some special treatment designed to make them uncomfortable. Americans in particular are known for their compulsion to fill up the space with words. In some cultures, the sign for "an American" is a hand motioning near the mouth as if words were spilling out. Here's some standard fare:

After lots of mutual stalling around, I finally put forward my price, and was met with silence. This made me very nervous. It must

[6]Fisher, Roger, and William Ury, *Getting to Yes,* Penguin Books, New York, 1981.

have gone on for at least three or four minutes, but it felt like an hour. Then I thought that maybe he realized I was bluffing and was waiting for me to make a better offer. So I did. I expected him to respond, say something like it was closer to what he expected, but he went silent on me again! Now I was really nervous, so I gave him the absolute lowest price I was willing to go. He takes in a big suck of air, pauses, says that the proposal needs further study, and thanks me for my time. Well, I was confused, but I felt like he was calling the meeting to an end, and, since the price was more than fair, I left feeling that we had a good shot. The funny thing was, we never heard from him again.

In fact, the American's anxiety over the silences probably did more damage than anything else. While the business facts at hand may have been negotiable (and to the degree that there are mutual interests needing to be satisfied at the table, these issues *are* negotiable), the cultural behavior at the table is not. During the first silent period, the Japanese negotiator was probably thinking, deciding, weighing, and judging the effect of this arrangement on the long-term development of a business relationship. No need to respond. By the second silent period, he was doubting the viability of such a long-term business relationship, since, from the Japanese perspective, it would be difficult to do business with someone who changed the price so quickly. By the third silent period, the Japanese was convinced that this Westerner could not be trusted and that he did not want to build a long-term relationship with him. The deal was dead. The American's insistent action guaranteed it.

Certainly the Japanese have learned to use this difference in orientation to action and passivity to their advantage, and there are, no doubt, many instances of Japanese making Americans uncomfortable in an effort to pressure them. This is not as common as it is thought to be (Japanese negotiating style is *not* designed to disturb harmony, but to develop it), or as successful (Americans will not negotiate for long under these conditions). But to the degree that it does happen, one could say that at least it proves, in a self-fulfilling-prophecy way, that passivity does have power. More probably, such exaggerated reports reflect Westerners' suspicion, and understandably subsequent fear, of behavior they simply do not understand.

Therefore, based on this example, on scale 7, power resides more exclusively in activity near 1 for the American, while for the Japanese, power may reside on both sides. In fact, effective negotiation techniques, as well as communication techniques, require a more balanced appreciation of where power truly resides and an acknowledgment of the sharing of power within passivity, as well as within activity. Good communicators and negotiators understand this, know when not to get in the ring with someone, know how to use their energy to supply them with information about the other side, and appreciate the power of listening (a relatively passive behavior) as opposed to speaking (a relatively active behavior). It is well to remember the truth of the proverb that goes something like this: God gave us two ears and one mouth that we could listen twice as much as we speak.

God Bless the Child Who Has "His" Own

Let's end this discussion of individualism with a Global Homecoming Exercise©. Remember, the purpose of these inward-looking exercises is to find the "foreigner" in you, the part that resonates in harmony with the non-American in the scenario. And since we have already been discussing such particular cultures as Spain, Japan, and France in this section, the critical incident below exemplifies a different one. Remember, whether or not you are familiar with the culture is unimportant for the purpose of the exercise, which is to increase your sensitivity to and empathy for the values inherent in it. Additionally, the *process* is the important thing, not the answers. Therefore, even if you know a better way of handling the following situation without going through the Global Homecoming© process, go through it anyway. It will help improve those global mind-set skills you need to use when faced with a situation in which you *won't* know a better way.

A Journey to Slovakia

You are eager to take advantage of the fact that a formerly state-run manufacturing company is privatizing in Bratislava, Czechoslovakia's second city and capital of the Slovak Republic. The company has expressed an interest in your proposal for a joint venture to manufacture quality products in Czechoslovakia. More specifically, the Czechoslovakian Chamber of Commerce has introduced you to the three appropriate managers of the company, and you have met twice with them and believe that you are close to finalizing all particulars. On this, your third trip, you hope to sign the deal. There have been some complicating considerations, such as the fact that privatization has not been completed and will take at least another six months, at which time "shares" of the formerly state-owned factory will be sold to private investors in Czechoslovakia. Additionally, the three managers represent different aspects of the former organization: one is a former floor manager, the second a Communist currently running for local office, and the third, a former agitator and organizer for reform. The third seems the most glad about all the changes.

The previous two meetings have gone very smoothly. You felt comfortable with the men, and details were brought forward quickly and were apparently ironed out. There seemed to be a general collaborative effort to express needs openly, and your associates' positions seemed reasonable. The negotiations have occurred over a period of about three months, and in that time, there has been great change in the economic conditions of the country, with new currency laws, a rise in inflation, etc. The situation appears to be more unstable now, but you don't believe this is serious enough to threaten the deal.

The meeting begins cordially. You say how eager you are to finalize the project; there is a sharing of the mutual woes and triumphs that have occurred to each of you since the last time you were together. Then the former floor manager raises a concern about a previously-agreed-upon percentage. You are a bit put off by this, since it was agreed on at an earlier meeting. His explanation is that the situation has changed, there is a lot more competition now, and the managers have learned that indeed they could get a better price. Nothing personal, they all assure you, but they would hope you would reconsider. They all profess great ignorance of the ways of capitalism and are appealing to your professionalism, friendship, and understanding in this special time for them.

The maverick former organizer raises a point about worker security in the face of privatization and the switch to a market economy, and he begins to list some requirements he would like to see put in place to make the transition easier for the workers. Again, the justification for this is the great insecurity that the people are currently facing.

The Communist adds on the side as you are walking to lunch that he will enlist the help of some of his associates in order to get some of the permits required, and that, since they are now doing business together, some special consideration needs to be made to him directly. This is disturbing to you, since you regard it as ethically, if not legally, improper. Besides, once again, you did not know this before. You mention this to him, and he agrees with you, sympathizing but adding that neither did he, but he is not surprised that these things happen. There could even be more surprises for all of them before everything is settled, he says, justifying his statement with a reminder that the country is still going through great change. In these unsettled times, it appears that everyone is seeking some security.

While you try to be sympathetic and give them all the benefit of the doubt, you are upset by what you are feeling to be a series of unexpected new demands. Not only are you unsure of how they affect your earlier understandings, but you are disappointed that this might mean a delay in the agreement you were counting on wrapping up on this trip. These added surprises also raise in you a disturbing concern about trust. You thought you had a good relationship, that they trusted you, and that you could trust them. Now you feel different. You feel that now you don't really know who they are or what they are after.

At the afternoon meeting, you decide to raise some of your original concerns without addressing their new demands. Mainly, you are concerned about getting some information from them on manufacturing requirements, standards, distribution, and quality control. However, when you ask for this information, it is not available, and when you press them, they say they are unable to get it or that they are unable to make those decisions. They promise to try soon but protest that these things are not important and should not hold up the deal. However, they are eager for agreement from you on the points they raised in the morning and are disappointed when you are unable to make a decision on them right then and there. In fact, you feel they don't really believe your reason for needing more time to think it all over. They vaguely indicate that they don't understand why someone in your position needs more time, and you hear this as a subtle implication that they are beginning to wonder what you're up to. It seems they truly don't understand why you can't respond immediately to their new demands.

The meeting ends in disappointment and a sense of mistrust on both sides. What seemed so promising now seems very doubtful.

Global Homecoming
Exercise© 1:
Individualism

1. *Recognize* differences: In regard to the-individual-versus-the-group dimension, how are the Americans and the Slovaks different?

Slovaks	**Americans**
The Slovaks expect	The Americans expect
_____	_____
_____	_____
_____	_____
_____	_____
_____	_____

2. *Retrace:* Spend one minute meditating quietly to help relax and clear your mind. Close your eyes. Spend the next few minutes visualizing yourself going back to an event in your early years (at home, with relatives, at school, at church, with friends) in which you were with people very close to you who *held similar values* to the Slovaks in regard to individualism. Describe the scene:

_____

_____

_____

_____

_____

_____

_____

_____

3. *Reclaim:* Who were the people in your scene? How would you describe their culture?

_____

_____

What is their country?_____ Ethnicity?_____

Religion?_____ Generation?_____ Sex?_____

Relation to you?_____

How did you feel about these people?_____

_____

_____

_____

4. *Reframe:* What factors in these people's culture do you think might have caused them to act the way they did with you?

_____

_____

_____

What cultural gifts have they brought you?

_____

What have you learned from them?

_____

Go back to this situation from your past now. You are there, but as the person you are now. What will you do differently?

_____

_____

_____

5. *Resurface: You are the American in the "Journey to Slovakia" Case.* What cultural gifts can you bring to this encounter?

_____

_____

_____

What cultural gifts do they bring to this encounter?

_____

_____

_____

What can you say or do to find a better way home (to reach a more satisfactory agreement or conclusion to this business situation)?

_____

_____

_____

_____

4
Time

The Amazing
Time Machine of
American Business

Time Is Money

Time—how we define it in our lives, how it affects our work, and what role it plays in our particular cultural worldview—is a profound universal aspect of all cultures. Inevitably it takes a particular form in the United States. The consequences of the way any society deals with time are felt in so many different and disparate areas of life that it merits a special chapter. And certainly our particularly American notion of time has a pronounced effect on a variety of important business concerns.

As we mentioned earlier, proverbs can be good indicators of deep cultural values; and in many of our cultural training programs we ask the participants to identify the underlying values of a culture by interpreting the proverbs of that culture. As an example of how proverbs can reflect a culture's deeper values, we begin by asking American participants to think of an American proverb that conveys an important aspect of American business life. Inevitably, "Time is money" comes to mind more quickly for Americans than any other. There's something very telling about the fact that the proverb chosen is about time. It's telling, too, that the chosen proverb equates time with wealth. The proverb's popularity indicates the highly significant role time plays in American business life—both its pervasiveness and its countless subtle but powerful influences.

Time's impact at the negotiating table can be direct or indirect: the two effects are equally profound. Do we expect to be able to make a decision quickly, or do we expect to need several meetings just to get to know each other? Do we go straight to the heart of the matter, or do we socialize, avoid confrontation, talk about secondary issues first? Is our negotiation conducted in an orderly and predefined manner, or does it take on an organic, as-we-go kind of development? All of these aspects, and many more, have differing cultural notions of time at their heart.

As you work through some of the scales below, it will be easy to identify those that are directly related to aspects of time. In the case of other scales, though, the relationship to time may not be so apparent. As with all cultural categories, the final form is a result of many intertwining values and traditions. No doubt all the scales below are affected by other cultural considerations as well as time. Nevertheless, how a culture looks at time has such a powerful effect on so many other aspects of life, especially in business that, often, first-glance appearances to the contrary, a culture's idea of time lies at the heart of how it conducts its business.

A culture's attitude toward time determines the importance placed on the development of personal relationships in business, for instance. It would be very difficult in a culture where everyone is always busy, where there never seems to be enough time to get everything done, to take the time necessary to build solid, long-term personal relationships. In such cultures, other business priorities would most likely lay claim to the limited available time. Looked at the other way round, in those cultures where time is less of a constraint, we might expect a certain valuing of personal relationships if for no other reason than there is time for them. We could look at the scales we've used in other chapters in this book and try to identify different cultures on them—this time, however, with the idea of time in our minds. In fact, a few of the scales we've used in other parts of the book have been included again here, specifically because time, in these areas perhaps more than in others, plays such an integral role. These are areas that tend to be of primary concern when we speak of culture and time and business.

Once again, for each of the following scales below, indicate:

1. Where you think the American value would be by writing "A" at the approximate position

2. Where your personal value would be by writing the first letter of your name at the appropriate position

3. Where you believe the country you're interested in would be by writing the first letter of its name at the approximate position you believe best represents its values

1. **Pace of Daily Business Life**

Rushed   *Relaxed*

| 1 | 2 | 3 | 4 | 5 | 6 | 7 | 8 | 9 | 10 |

2. **Orientation Toward Change**

Progress-oriented   *Status quo-oriented*

| 1 | 2 | 3 | 4 | 5 | 6 | 7 | 8 | 9 | 10 |

3. **Orientation to Work and Life**

Functional relationships   *Human relationships*

| 1 | 2 | 3 | 4 | 5 | 6 | 7 | 8 | 9 | 10 |

4. **Production Orientation**

Quality-conscious   *Output-conscious*

| 1 | 2 | 3 | 4 | 5 | 6 | 7 | 8 | 9 | 10 |

5. **Importance of Efficiency**

Primary   *Not valued*

| 1 | 2 | 3 | 4 | 5 | 6 | 7 | 8 | 9 | 10 |

6. **Valuing of Competition**

Functional   *Dysfunctional*

| 1 | 2 | 3 | 4 | 5 | 6 | 7 | 8 | 9 | 10 |

7. **Importance of Punctuality**

Inflexible clock   *Flexible clock*

| 1 | 2 | 3 | 4 | 5 | 6 | 7 | 8 | 9 | 10 |

8. **View of Business Relationships and Activities**

Long-term   *Short-term*

| 1 | 2 | 3 | 4 | 5 | 6 | 7 | 8 | 9 | 10 |

9. **Attitude Toward Risk**

Conservative   *Adventurous*

| 1 | 2 | 3 | 4 | 5 | 6 | 7 | 8 | 9 | 10 |

10. Definition of Functionality

One thing at a time								*Many things simultaneously*	
1	2	3	4	5	6	7	8	9	10

Timing Is Everything

Sometimes the whole world can be seen in a grain of sand, the poets remind us. Certainly, we've been trying to make the case that much international behavior can be found in our own American backyards if we merely choose to look there. Here's an example of the way a certain attitude toward time has a direct effect on business. It's as close to home as we can get and yet is just as representative of the kind of different approach to time (and business) that Americans encounter abroad:

I had a client in West Virginia who bought from me for several years. He had a family business that he'd started in a small town with his grandfather, and it had now grown to be the major employer in the town. We had developed quite a close relationship. Every few months, I would make a trip up from North Carolina to see him, knowing after a while that he would need to place an order with me as long as I spaced our visits out every few months. When we got together, at first we would talk about everything but business, catching up with each other. I would ask him about his life, the business, his family, the town, etc., and he would ask me about my work and the company and life in the big city in North Carolina where I lived and worked. Once we'd caught up with each other, we would get down to some business, and this was often after lunch. Each and every time, it would take a few hours of this and that, but I'd always leave with an order, and it was always a pleasant break, at least for me, from my usual hectic pace.

One day I phoned in preparation for my next trip, to see if he would be in, to arrange a convenient day, and he told me that he'd like me to meet a friend of his next time I was up there to visit him. His friend, he said, was interested in some of the things my company was selling, and he thought I should meet him. Of course I was delighted, and we arranged a convenient day for the three of us to meet.

When I arrived at my client's office, his friend, Carl, was already there. We were very casually introduced, and my client began explaining Carl's work, and how he thought what my company sold could be useful to him. Carl then took over and spoke a little about what he did, and I thought for a moment that we were going to go straight into business talk. However, in just a few moments, the conversation between the three of us quickly turned back to discussions of life in town, North Carolina, our respective families and personal interests. It turned out that Carl liked to hunt, and he and my client began regaling me with stories of their hunting adventures. I'd hunted a little, and shared my stories with them. One thing led to another, and soon we were talking about vacations, the economy, baseball—you name it.

Occasionally, we would make a brief journey back to the business at hand, but it always seemed to be in conjunction with the small talk, like how the tools we manufactured were or were not as precise as the mechanisms on the guns we used for hunting, things like that. I realized that quite a lot of information about our mutual work, my company, their needs, and their work, was being exchanged in all this, even though business was never directly addressed. I remember the first few meetings my client and I had had with each other many years ago—how we learned about each other this way then, too. I was struck with how quaint it felt now, how different it was from the way I usually had to sell, and yet how much I enjoyed working like this!

Well, our discussions went on this way through the rest of the morning, weaving some business back and forth through the larger context of informal chit-chat about each other and our lives. Just before lunch, my client leaned back and began what seemed to be a kind of informal summary of who I was and what I did, and how what I did seemed to him to be just the thing that Carl and his company could use. Carl agreed, and my client asked him, almost on my behalf, how much he wanted to order, and Carl thought for a moment and gave me the biggest order I ever got from West Virginia. "Now that that's done," my client said, "how about some lunch?" We all went to the same place we always go to when I'm in West Virginia, talking about life and things and some business. By midafternoon I said I had to be heading home. We all agreed to stay in touch. We've been in touch ever since, and now I've got two clients to visit whenever I'm in West Virginia.

Time Warps

Even in America, time can seem different from place to place, from culture to culture. The difference between rural and urban life, for example, is often described in terms of time, and in business, as the above example demonstrates, these differences set the pace for the larger context in which business, or the negotiation, is conducted. I am always struck by how time can be almost palpably different in different places. It can be stretched like a rubber band in some places or be as inflexible as a steel band in others. No matter how much rational thought one tries to give the feeling, it seems as if time is a living, breathing thing that changes as one moves across the geographic landscape.

Living in New York City, I am always running out of time; there is never enough of it. Sometimes it seems as if it will take the entire day to accomplish even the simplest chores. Then when I head off for the weekend to the country or the shore, there is suddenly more than enough time to do everything I need to do. The days drag on, the afternoons seem to last forever, dusk falls slowly, and the night seems endless. If I think of the same minute of time in the country and the city, that minute passes swiftly in the urban world; it is shallow and one-dimensional. But at the seashore, it is stretched and multidimensional, rich and deep.

As I travel for work, I notice how time takes on a different shape in the different cities and countries I go to. And one doesn't need to go very far; sometimes just crossing from Manhattan to New Jersey, I am struck by the different pace at which business is conducted. When I'm in the corporate parks of New Jersey, for example, there seems to be time allotted for moving from one place to another. Such "travel time" is rare in Manhattan; one is simply where one is, and getting to and from it is somehow supposed to be squeezed in between being in one place and the other. For me, the alien from New York, time appears to move more slowly in the suburban offices, and a day's work seems to be accomplished more smoothly and methodically within a larger, less distracting context. In New York, the workday no doubt moves equally slowly for many people, but the context is not smooth or methodical, but jagged, unpredictable, and sometimes very distracting. While a few hours in the afternoon might drag, the lunch hour is hectic, the travel to and from work a jangling experience of rushing and hurrying, an hour here or there, a manic attempt to beat a deadline. There is a constant background noise that sets a very different beat in the city. Clearly, the pace at which the business day goes by can be very different depending on the city, region or country. Certainly the beat or the pace of business can be different from country to country.

Our example above shows how difficult it might be to make a generalized statement about the American view of time. But in relation to the generalized norms of other countries' view of time, an American norm does emerge. Certainly in modern business life, as we have seen when attempting to gauge other cultural categories, the varieties are significantly reduced, so that we can say that when it comes to time's effect on international business, there is a definite American attitude. And it can be summed up in that proverb at the beginning of this chapter: "Time is money." On scale 1, relatively speaking, I would place an "A" around 1, 2, or 3, while, with a closer, more refined focus on the West Virginia subculture, I would put a "WV" around 7 or 8.

Time Waits for No American

Non-Americans often say that when they first come to the United States, they experience time as they never have before. It is controlling; it sets the pace of everything. In their countries, time may not be king; it doesn't set the pace of everything. There are other, more important considerations that determine activity. Americans in business are constantly "scheduling." Time is compartmentalized; there is a beginning and an end to each activity, and activities can be piled on top of one another, "slotted in," organized, arranged. Time moves very quickly: we say "the clock is *running*," not "the clock is *walking*." Time is a commodity, it must not be wasted, it must be maximized, it becomes our most precious possession—often the most important aspect of our work. If this is not new to the reader, it is because time's effects are so profound and so pronounced in America. The point is, all this might seem very odd to many people from other cultures. And the degree of difference can vary from one extreme to the other, with many subtle variations in between, around the world.

In more traditional societies, from southern Italy to Central America, sub-Saharan Africa, and upland Thailand, the daily pace of life is much slower than in the United States. The time shown on your watch does not rule your day. The more important determinants of activity might be the weather, the person sitting next to you, or your own personal needs and those of your family. This is not to say that time does not rule; in fact, in such societies, people are more controlled by time *in the long term* perhaps, than modern-day Americans. It is the *daily* pace that is different. Given their organization, traditional societies are often more dependent on nature, on the seasons, on the weather, and in that sense, are clearly tuned in to the way time affects these things. They define time, therefore, more in terms of the seasons, day and night, the discernible stages of personal life (childhood, puberty, adulthood, old age). They are controlled by the events of the world around them, by time itself. Our modern, developed societies are oriented in the opposite direction. They are based on the idea of controlling the world around us, of no longer being subject to nature's whims. In this system of control, people, not nature define time. The day, the month, the year, can be broken down into as many definite, discreet sections as one wants; there is no longer just morning, afternoon, and night; winter, spring, summer, and fall; rain or sun. Rather, no matter what the time, season, or weather, one can do whatever one wills at any particular moment. Time, in the modern business world, is controlled by people. And in this controllability, it moves as fast, as furiously as we, with our technology and our competitive wills, want it to.

Those societies that have a long tradition of rural life often have deeply ingrained values and behavior that govern their lives, including their business lives. These values and behavior developed over the millennium preceding the modern era. The Industrial Revolution, even for the West, occurred a mere two hundred years or so ago, and certainly the information and service revolutions are still going on. Most of the history of the United States—when the values, behavior, and traditions of our society were developing—occurred during the time of the Industrial Revolution. Our formative years as a society were, in a sense, posttraditional, at least in relation to much of the rest of the world. For European countries, for example, the two hundred years or so since the Industrial Revolution are just a small fraction of time in the full breadth of their development. Most of the history of these societies took place in a preindustrial and rural past. Many of the traditions, behaviors, and attitudes that define them, even today—in business as well as in social life—were formed during these preindustrial years.

We in the United States simply do not have the same length of history, and hence, the same traditions. And the older the civilization, the stronger and more defined these preindustrial traditions can be. In civilizations that have existed for thousands of years—in China and Japan, for example—there is a complex interrelationship between premodern and postmodern behavior, values, and traditions. This is not to say that historical weight and influence automatically increase with time. There is a great debate today, for example, over the power of modern posttechnology society and its ability to overwhelm more traditional forms, even though the traditional forms have been around so much longer, are so ingrained, and have such historical and cultural weight. Much concern today centers around the power of modern technology to solve problems previously unsolvable for much of the world, but only at the price of destroying land and culture that have existed for thousands of years.

However this turns out (and it is a central problem of the modern world), Americans abroad today often do business with people who, while living in modern cities, run their lives and conduct their business according to older, premodern rules that involve an older concept of time. The fact that we ourselves lack similar traditions can lead to real differences in the way we and they conduct business.

The modern business context of glass skyscrapers, computerized bureaucracies, and fast food tends to fit in with American expectations, values, and traditions; it is certainly compatible with our notion of time (time being money). So we, as Americans, tend not to notice that in many cultures, this modern business context is a new development, a sudden overlay on top of a preexisting culture that for perhaps thousands of years developed with a very different notion of time, in a world ruled by nature. The traditions of the individuals sitting opposite us at the negotiating table in that modern steel and glass skyscraper might dictate a very different view of business, specifically because it is embedded in a preindustrial culture thousands of years older than our own. Despite our international associates' contemporary intentions, their actual way of achieving their goals, their pace, the beat at which they go about their discussions with us, might be very different.

Those cultures that have escaped the modern world (and I suspect there are very few that Americans actually do business with) exhibit a sense of time that is distinctly different from, perhaps even opposite to, our own. More often than not, however, Americans abroad negotiate with individuals whose cultures combine the fast-paced timing of the modern, technology-dependent world with more traditional, nature-dependent histories. (In fact, the fast-paced efficiency of these societies, perhaps specifically because it is so often grafted on, can, in some cases, be even faster than what Americans are used to; I think of such dynamic Asian dragons as Hong Kong, Singapore, and Tokyo.) In these cases (the majority, in fact), fast-paced modern life occurs within a context of long-range, broad-view planning. It isn't the hectic, day-to-day part that Americans have trouble with, because that's compatible with their own lives and their own culture. Rather, it's the larger context in which this modern activity occurs that so often trips us up. This long-range, larger context is the modern-day heir of these societies' older, preindustrial traditions, and for this context there is no comparable parallel in American society. So while the pace of life in today's Tokyo, for example, is perhaps more frenetic than that in most major American cities, Americans, as they negotiate with Tokyo businesspeople, may still find them slow and indecisive, precisely because older traditions in Japan, such as group consensus, drive actual decision making in negotiations.

An Asian Time Capsule

The Japanese are certainly in a rush to embrace the modern world. But their more traditional, preindustrial experience also provides them with a very long-term view of things, enabling them to place the day-to-day frenetic pace of Tokyo within a larger context. America's much shorter historical tradition is one in which people are eager to embrace, as quickly as possible, a new, wide-open world and to get rich faster than the next guy. These critical differences of history are the reasons why Japan, for all its modern-day pace, is market-share-driven, and America is profit-driven; why the Japanese are committed for the long-term, and why Americans back out after two quarters of low profits. On scale 8, I would place a "J" for Japan at 2 or 3, while I would place an "A" at 7 or 8, yet both Japan and America could most assuredly be placed around 2, 3, or 4 on scale 1. Our histories explain the split in the scales.

Such historical differences also explain the dichotomy in Asia between such "Asian dragons" as Taiwan, Japan, Hong Kong, Singapore, and Korea, and the "docile dragons," such as the People's Republic of China (and those that may be changing from one mode to the other, such as Thailand and Malaysia). The dynamic dragons have, for various cultural reasons, been able to adopt Western notions of fast-paced time onto their traditional backdrops; the docile dragons still live only in their preindustrial world. Japan was able to graft modern-day time onto its traditional preindustrial backdrop; China was not. Japan has seized every moment to hurtle itself toward the future. But Mao Zedong, when asked what he thought of the French Revolution, tellingly revealed the Chinese long-range view when he replied (only somewhat in jest), "It is too soon to tell." I suspect the Japanese wouldn't even be able to provide an answer to the question since, for their agenda, it is probably irrelevant.

Here are some other examples: While the face of modern Brazil's São Paulo looks like Manhattan gone wild, Americans can still find communicating efficiently with Paulistas a frustrating experience precisely because older Latin traditions dictate a very different communication style. And while business in Frankfurt might appear to be as cut-and-dried as a deal on Wall Street, American-German business dealings can falter in the long term because Americans fail to grasp certain German traditions determining exactly how ongoing relationships are to be conducted, which responsibilities are to be carried out by whom, etc. In each of these cases, older, traditional values come into conflict with modern, American values. And at heart, the conflict can often revolve around the two different notions of time.

A Latin Time Capsule

I remember a particular negotiation in Mexico a few years back involving several days of meetings. Despite the time we would all agree to begin, each meeting would inevitably begin at least 10 to 30 minutes later. It wasn't merely that people who were to be there were arriving late. Many, in fact, would arrive on time. A few would even be a few minutes early. None, however, was prepared to begin business at the stated time.

While waiting for the ones who were actually late to arrive, those who were already there would take their coffee and use the time for social-izing or conducting other business on the phone or off to the side with their associates. Finally, once everyone had arrived, business would more or less begin.

Although an agenda was passed around and agreed on beforehand, the Mexicans would often introduce topics not previously discussed, while ignoring some that were slated to have been discussed at the meet-ing. Often the Americans I was with would become suspicious of the Mexicans when this happened, and the Mexicans, in turn, would either lose face or become suspicious of and hostile toward the Americans. In-evitably, we would not get to cover all the things the Americans were hoping to discuss within the time frame allocated in the agenda for the meeting, and just as inevitably, the Mexicans would be disappointed that their points, as well, were not covered sufficiently. However, the Mexicans were always content just to continue the discussions, especially when it was about their points, whether or not they had been previously set in the agenda — and even beyond the time allocated for the meeting if necessary. They often resented the Americans' need to end the meet-ing at the prescribed time in order to meet other commitments, con-cluding that the Americans were not really interested in what they, the Mexicans, considered important. At the beginning of one of our meet-ings, several days into the negotiation, it was I who was waiting to begin. One of the members of our team, a Mexican, had not arrived yet. It was not until 45 minutes later that she arrived. While I, and several others on our team, were quite distressed, none of the Mexicans, on either team, shared our anxiety, Later, during a break, I inquired what had happened to make her arrive so late during such an important meeting, and she calmly explained that she had gotten a phone call earlier that morning from her sister. There was some sort of problem, and she had to go over and help her. I was so astonished at the matter-of-factness of this answer that I remember feeling quite speechless, yet what I wanted to do was ask very angrily why she hadn't at least called us to let us know there was a problem. However, from the reaction of the other Mexi-cans, or, more specifically, from their lack of reaction, it became clear to me that she hadn't called precisely because, from the Mexican perspec-tive, there was no problem. I was the only one with a problem. While time is important in Mexico, it does not dictate punctuality, especially when other, more important, concerns, such as family issues, take pri-ority. There is also no need necessarily to inform others in such cases; they should simply assume something else more important has come up.

In addition to the Mexican disregard for promptness, one of the first things I had to adjust to during this negotiation was the pace of the day. Even when we all sat down, the business at hand was rarely what was addressed first. Sometimes we would get to it quickly, but then be distracted by a point someone would make, and when I or one of the other Americans on the team would try to get the negotiations back on track, the Mexicans would often not cooperate, as if preferring to stay off-course and finish discussing this secondary point. The problem for me was that I was having trouble maintaining priorities, with point A giving way to point sub-A, which in turn gave way to points sub-sub-A and perhaps B, then sub-B, and so on. To make matters worse, the Mexicans didn't seem to mind giving equal importance to any of the ancillary points being brought up, sometimes giving significant weight to them and not wanting to return to the main point. I found this extremely frustrating, time-consuming, hopelessly distracting, and inefficient. Yet, despite my best efforts to reroute the discussions, I failed time and time again.

Even the day's schedule was problematic. While we would get started somewhere between nine and ten o'clock in the morning, and have several breaks for coffee, lunch did not begin until around two o'clock. Invariably, the American tummies were growling by twelve, and American patience, given the other things at work, would wear increasingly thin. Noon to two was often a waste of time as far as the Americans were concerned, for hunger made them lose their attention, and anyway, all sorts of miscellaneous conversations would be going on. When we finally broke for lunch, we wouldn't return till about 4 p.m. — close to the end of the working day for most Americans, while the Mexicans were ready to return to the negotiating table for a few more hours.

By the afternoon session (which for the Americans was really early evening), the points of the morning were often up for bargaining and further discussion, making for some lively conversation. Just as my energies were flagging, particularly after a much heavier lunch than I'm used to in the States, the Mexicans seemed to gather steam. The style, as well as the content, of the conversation now was often confusing, with many people speaking at once, sometimes very emotionally. In addition to having trouble keeping track of the content, the other Americans and I would also be having trouble now following the content being discussed. Nor was the free-for-all style of the communication the end of our problems. While English was the agreed-upon language for our discussions, at this late stage in the day the Mexicans would often break into long statements in Spanish and certainly spoke Spanish among themselves. Most of the American negotiators spoke, or at least understood, some Spanish, although there were a few leading Americans on the team who neither spoke nor understood Spanish. At this point in the day, we were uncomfortable reminding the Mexicans that we needed them to return to English. They inevitably seemed to us somewhat resentful when we did press the point, and yet it was an absolute necessity in order for us to make any progress.

I remember one particular late afternoon session, when it seemed as if all of the above was taking place all at once, and tensions were rising. Clearly nothing was going to be resolved at this meeting, and what we all needed was a break in order to defuse, decompress, and redefine. I was just about to suggest something along these lines when a mariachi band came strolling out of the distance and struck up a wonderful rendition of what I later learned to be an old Mexican favorite right below our window. There was no way anyone could continue. The Americans were stopped dead in their tracks, and the Mexicans immediately wanted to stop and listen. One or two began to sing along. My Mexican opposite number leaned over to me, smiled and said, "Well, that's Mexico!" As the mariachis went from one song to another, conversation moved to dinner that night, a few nonproblematic minor points of business, and the setting of tomorrow's agenda (which we all knew would not be adhered to anyway). The negotiation for the day had come to an end.

As the meetings moved on, it became clear to us that there would still be many important points that were going to be unresolved by the time we had to return to the States. Additionally, the new points that the Mexicans were now raising were creating concerns that we didn't have answers for immediately so that they, too, were going to have to accept some unresolved problems by the end of our scheduled round of talks. In fact, the morning of the next-to-the-last day was spent trying to figure out ways to schedule additional meetings within the next two months. In this discussion, the Mexicans kept trying to reassure us that there was no need to schedule additional meetings to discuss the points for which *we* felt more meetings were necessary, while pushing for another meeting or two in order to discuss some points that we felt we *didn't* need additional meetings for. Clearly, what merited mutual attention was quite different for the two teams.

We found ourselves trying to convince the Mexicans that their concerns would either have to be taken care of over time or were not the most pressing issues of the moment, and that, once the more pressing issues were agreed on, their concerns would automatically be dealt with. Meanwhile, the Mexicans kept trying to reassure us that they would be able to follow through on the decisions we had already made and that everything would turn out just the way we wanted it to once the job was begun. In fact, we had experience with the Mexican team before and felt that, despite their reassurances, it was mainly well-intentioned rhetoric and that follow through, without clearly agreed-upon terms, was simply not going to happen.

By the end of the negotiation, of course, we had not covered the points *we* thought were really important in enough detail to ensure movement. Nor, in the eyes of the Mexicans, had we allowed enough time to discuss all the things *they* felt were important. Both sides walked away from this negotiation frustrated and somewhat confused, with little to show for the effort and with a less secure platform from which to move forward next time—should there be a next time.

I am, of necessity, of course, emphasizing the time-related aspects of this negotiation and deemphasizing many other aspects of the negotiation that, for our purposes here, are less time-related. Of course, every cross-cultural negotiation—this one included—is richer and more textured than this. But, in fact, many of the problems at this negotiation revolved around a difference in the central conceptions of time held by the North Americans and the Mexicans. The conflict revealed itself in many different aspects of the negotiation process, from scheduling to communication styles, relationship-building, etc. And, at heart, these differing notions of time existed because of the differences between the histories of the North American Anglo culture, on the one hand, and, on the other, the unique combination of ancient Indian and Latin culture that is Mexican culture today.

Monochronic Versus Polychronic Time

Culturally speaking, one can define time as either "monochronic" or "polychronic."[7] *Monochronic time* is linear. Things are done separately, one after another. Time is compartmentalized, organized, and controlled. It is a commodity that has value because of its scarcity and its usefulness in defining the context in which activity occurs. *Polychronic time,* on the other hand, is more circular. It is endless; there is plenty of it; it has no beginning or end. It exists beyond humanity, external to the control of human beings. It is therefore useless as a means of exchange, and it defines the context in which things occur only in the broadest sense: rather than setting limits (beginning and end times, for example), it simply sets the background for a set of events. Most important, since it is nonlinear, many things can happen at once. There is the simultaneous use of time as a backdrop for all sorts of events in life. If one were to cut out a slice of time in a polychronic culture, all sorts of events would be going on horizontally and simultaneously. Cut a slice of time out of a monochronic world, and we usually see one event occurring after another.

[7]Hall, Edward T., The Silent Language, Doubleday and Co., New York, 1973.

Remember that these are generalizations in the extreme. No one culture is either all monochronic or all polychronic. But some are more or less polychronic — or monochronic — than others.

In the above Mexican/American example, our American team was more monochronic, the Mexican one more polychronic, and these tendencies were revealed in many aspects of the negotiation. Generally, time is more polychronic in Latin cultures, while Western, Anglo-Saxon cultures tend to view time as monochronic. In this sense, Germans tend to be very monochronic about most aspects of business life; Americans tend to be somewhat monochronic in many aspects of business life. Traditional societies that have not experienced significant modernization, as represented by some of the nations of Africa, Central and South Asia, and Polynesia tend to be extremely polychronic in most aspects of life, business included. Countries or cultures that have significant traditional histories, yet are experiencing equally significant modernization, such as those in the Pacific Rim and the Arab world (in a sense, with one foot in the distant past, and another in the equally distant future), are often polychronic in certain aspects and monochronic in others.

In the Mexican/American example described above, the conflict between monochronism and polychronism touched literally every aspect of the negotiation. The Americans were most comfortable discussing things in an "orderly fashion" (for which read "linear fashion" here, though what is "orderly" for Latin Americans is "disorderly" for North Americans; the definitions as well as the content change as we cross borders). Not only was it acceptable for the Mexicans to discuss more than one point at the same time; the style of the discussion was more vertical than horizontal. People were speaking simultaneously, not willing to wait turns, often talking over and louder than one another when emotionally trying to emphasize a point. For the Americans at the table, this was terribly confusing and inefficient. As we had previously discussed, emotional expression differs from culture to culture, but here we see how conceptions of time also play a role in how different cultures get their points across.

Not only were ideas being discussed simultaneously, but other types of activity were occurring at the same time that business was being conducted. Not only was family more important than business, but family and other concerns could be dealt with simultaneously, or at least during the same time period, as business was to have been dealt with exclusively. From the Mexican perspective, discussions ancillary to the main issues, whether discussed formally at the table, or on the side by phone, or with a friend over coffee, could also take place within the time allotted to the business at hand.

For the Mexicans, time was not a set of parameters. It was just a backdrop for many simultaneously occurring things that did not necessarily take place at predetermined moments. In a more polychronic culture, there are too many things that cannot be controlled by people. Life is too unknowable, too unpredictable. Therefore, punctuality is not emphasized. There always can be an unexpected delay, an unanticipated problem, a higher priority, to alter one's intention to arrive on time or carry things out as planned. In traditional Arab cultures, stopping unexpectedly to have coffee at a café with a friend one has not seen for many years can be much more important than maintaining a previous business appointment — especially if the previously arranged business appointment is with someone not as close, relationship-wise, as the long-lost friend. It would be assumed that the person kept waiting would understand these things (certainly, once explained). Besides, the long-lost friend is where the real business is anyway, since relationships, in this culture, determine business. In the Mexican culture as well we see the powerful pull of other priorities. Certainly, the digital clock carries no weight against the needs of family and friends. And planning, the organization of task against time, can be suspect anyway, for who can explain all that might happen? In Mexico, it could be the unexpected arrival of an afternoon mariachi band. In a traditional Arab culture, only Allah knows the future. Therefore, to plan too much is foolish at best and presumes the right of human beings to interfere in a realm best left to Allah.

"Progress Is Our Most Important Product"*

In such a polychronic culture as Mexico, the future is part of the present, part of the larger backdrop of time. Therefore, things will work out; tomorrow is as good a time as today; and today should be lived for its own sake, not tomorrow's. Perhaps the stereotypically Mexican notion of *mañana* is a reflection of this polychronic "presentness." Monochronic cultures often view today as a means to tomorrow. There can be a built-in belief in the goodness of the future, an idea that the future is likely to be better than today. Polychronic cultures, often being older and more traditional, have experienced more of the world and realize that tomorrow is not necessarily going to be better than today, that progress is not an automatic component of the future, that in fact, the future can be more difficult than either today or our past. Americans are seen by many polychronic cultures as cheerily forging ahead

*Advertising slogan used by General Electric in the 1960s and 1970s.

into the future without too much concern for the present, armed with a powerful faith that tomorrow will *always* be better than today. Older cultures, which have witnessed great civilizations come and go, often see us as naive in our great rush toward tomorrow and wisely warn us that, despite our best intentions, our great technology, and our faith in it, we might not make tomorrow any better than today—that, in fact, there is a limit to what we can control.

This is often a very difficult idea for Americans to swallow. After all, we took control of a continent, reached the moon, and went beyond it. It is an inherent belief in America that people can take control of their lives, that change is possible, if not inevitable, and that change is inherently good. We value change and are changing all the time, and if something is not to our liking, well, we change it. The very idea of "America" is change. Here people have an opportunity to start anew. Here people believe in tomorrow. It hits us hard then when we run up against cultures that see tomorrow as never coming, as not necessarily bringing good, as being something to avoid perhaps—certainly as something that should never stand in the way of making the most of what we've got right now. Mexicans do not necessarily place their faith in tomorrow; rather, tomorrow is suspect. One must not rush too fast into it. "Getting on with the show" can be a dangerous thing. The phrase "conservative and risk-avoiding" describes many polychronic cultures, while "bold and risk-taking" defines many monochronic ones. (A note of contra-indication here: There can be a curious risk-taking aspect to poly-chronic cultures as well. After all, if God controls everything, we are free from responsibility if things don't turn out well and are equally free to take risks. This is the philosophical underpinning for, among many other things, the popularity of the national lottery in many Latin poly-chronic cultures.) The Mexicans in the negotiations described above were involved with the present, eager to discuss their simultaneous concerns of the here and now, unable to see the value of taking time today to plan for tomorrow. Yet that was exactly why the Americans in the same example were at the table.

Que Sera, Sera or, Let's Live for Today

If some cultures tend to be "future-suspicious" as opposed to "future-embracing," then they are also "present-embracing" as opposed to "present-denying." As we have seen, Americans are action-oriented and future-oriented, with an inherent belief in progress. Time moves swiftly for us because we are always hurtling toward a better tomorrow. But cultures that are not interested in rushing toward tomorrow are usually more interested in today. The Mexican needs to enjoy the here and now because he or she has no inherent belief in the virtues of tomorrow. The two-hour Latin lunches, whether in restaurants in Mexico City, Madrid, or Paris, and the traditional French five-week vacation have their cultural roots in a polychronic notion of time and in a conservative approach to tomorrow. If we cannot control tomorrow, let's make the best of today. Instead of making something new and different, let's make what we already have as good as possible. This results in lifestyles that are oriented around enjoying and making the best of the moment, in an emphasis on quality versus quantity, and in a work orientation to the precise and the technical as opposed to marketing and sales.

Conversely, the 30-minute American fast-food lunch at the desk is the result of our monochronic orientation toward progress and our future-embracing ethic. The United States was built by people eager to start again and forget the past, eager to get on with the future and their lives. As much as we might possess today, things could always be better. To believe this is the fulfillment of the American promise. Accepting the inevitable, seeing planning as futile and unnecessary, seeing reality as unchangeable, making the most of the present and leaving the future to someone or something else...these are not American traits. But they remain characteristic attitudes toward work among many of the people Americans do business with abroad. They are often the characteristics, too, of our grandparents, even of ourselves before we became Americans, for it was the hope of transforming these characteristics into American ones that brought so many of us to this country in the first place. If we don't hold to these characteristics today, it is because we have been remade. But we can still "know" this way of being when we see it now in others at the other side of the negotiating table by remembering our grandparents, our parents, perhaps even ourselves before the process of Americanization had been completed.

From the traditional roles expressed in the above example, I would place "M" for Mexico on scale 2 more in the middle, with "A" toward 2 or 3; and on scale 7, "M" nearer 7 and 8, with "A" nearer 2 or 3. On scale 9, I would place "M" closer to 2 or 3, and "A" nearer 7 or 8. Finally, on scale 10, I would put "M" nearer 7 and 8, and "A" nearer 3 or 4.

The Almighty Deadline

In discussing various future-oriented and present-oriented attitudes toward time, we have described some of the key areas of conflict between the United States and other cultures, focusing on Mexico in particular.

One area worth taking a closer look at is the American concern with the deadline, particularly when it comes in conflict with cultures in which the emphasis on the deadline is not as extreme.

Several years ago, I participated on the American side of a negotiation between a United States–based firm marketing high-tech equipment in France. I was asked to participate in a series of advance negotiation simulations designed to help the Americans better understand what they would be facing when negotiating with their French counterparts. As I understood some of the problems, the Americans were very frustrated with the delays they felt they were constantly enduring whenever they expected a decision, or sometimes just an answer to a response, from the French. In previous negotiations, one of the leaders of the American team told me, the French had constantly wasted his time by providing answers to questions he hadn't asked, not responding to his inquiries directly, but choosing, rather, to go off on their own as if his requests were irrelevant. He said it always seemed as if the two sides were talking beyond each other.

He was hoping to avoid a replay of this situation in the upcoming negotiations. But even in the agenda-setting preparations, he was starting to get the same set of signals, and he was worried that things were going to go the same way as before. He and several others were particularly annoyed that information the French had apparently agreed to give him by a certain date had not arrived. When I asked him what he had done about this, he told me that he had called them up and asked where the material was. According to my colleague, they were surprised that he was calling and a little indignant over being put on the spot about something they had already told him they were going to provide. He got the impression that they thought he was doubtful about their intention of keeping their word. And while he didn't think the French were really not going to give him the information, he *was* annoyed and more than a little puzzled that the deadline for the information had passed and he still did not have it. In turn, they must have sensed his concern and were equally put-off that he was nagging them. He told me that they had weakly agreed to send the material to him at the end of the week and that when he hung up the phone, he felt that some serious damage had been done to the relationship he was trying so hard to build with them.

He admitted that he was really disappointed, because he wanted very much to develop a successful relationship but felt that he was frustrated at every turn. To me, a fellow American, it seemed he was just plain angry. And he was fearful that the upcoming negotiations would not succeed, given the preceding events and his prior history with the French team.

Barring other factors, this situation appeared to contain some very juicy cross-cultural issues, mainly revolving around different conceptions of time and how these different conceptions play themselves out in business. I saw two conflicts at work here (not in any order of importance). First there was a difference in priorities regarding deadlines, and second, there was a difference in styles of communication used when negotiating.

Let's first look at the difference in priorities surrounding the deadline issue. While both the United States and France are generally monochronic, there are significant polychronic tendencies in France, and these can be located in the continuing Latin traditions of the French. Future-orientation in the States is often manifested in the emphasis Americans place on deadlines, on the importance of keeping to a schedule, of following through as planned, *despite unexpected developments*. While unexpected developments are accepted as a possibility, Americans believe that the basic plan should be realistic enough (i.e., well-designed and well-executed enough) to allow for completion given all reasonable contingencies. The deadline is usually a fairly hard-and-fast fact. It can take precedence over most other considerations, including external, unexpected contingencies. In this American view, having to make room for such developments should be the exception, not the rule. The emphasis on the deadline can relegate other considerations, such as quality, personal satisfaction, and so forth, to a secondary position. Being so monochronic and ruled by the clock, Americans place a high value on efficiency, and the deadline represents the importance we assign to this aspect of business.

The French, on the other hand, while certainly valuing efficiency, do not in general value it to the degree that Americans do, their culture being less monochronic than ours. They simply have other values that equal or occupy the high place of honor we Americans reserve for efficiency. For the French, traditionally the concern is less for time than for precision and quality. This means, in a pinch, that Americans will opt for the deadline, while the French will opt for taking what they consider a reasonable amount of extra time to get the product or project to the level of quality they view necessary. All other factors being equal, faced with a situation where a choice must be made between the two, the Americans will tend to see the deadline as a more important criterion to be met, while the French will see the quality of the product as the primary concern. The time concern simply does not preempt the quality issue for the French, while the time concern is often the preeminent issue for the Americans. Any French person not understanding this difference in priorities will take offense at the American preoccupation with the deadline, while any American not familiar with these variances will be furious at the French disregard for the deadline. The Americans think the French are at best inconsiderate of them and the project, or, at worst, up to no good. The French cannot understand why the Americans are so hung up on the deadline, or why, when the deadline is missed, Americans do not assume (as any other French businessperson might) that there were obviously still some important details to work on and that the work would be completed shortly. Missing a deadline does not need to imply irresponsibility. To the uninformed French businessperson, the American behavior implies a lack of concern for what the French see as primary: quality and precision. To the uninformed American, the French reaction (or lack of it) implies disinterest in what is most important to them: getting things done on time.

Before we go any further, I want to stress that in no way are Americans unconcerned with quality, nor are the French unconscious of efficiency and the importance of time. In fact, a curious aspect of this particular conflict was that it was French/American, since the two countries are certainly more similar in their conceptions of time than, say, the United States and Afghanistan, or France and Sri Lanka. They are not extreme opposites, and yet, perhaps that's what makes this example so important. It is possible, even likely, for cultures not strikingly dissimilar in many important aspects of business to still get hung up over differences. Subtlety can be profound; profound need not always be obvious.

And now for the differences in communicating styles between the French and the Americans and how time played a part in these differences. As the story was relayed to me, the Americans were frustrated about not getting answers to their questions, being told things they had never asked about, and being given the impression that the French were bogging down instead of moving things along. I assured my colleague that if my analysis was correct, the French were probably just as frustrated with the Americans. Their complaints, however, were probably that the Americans refused to cooperate by providing any substantiation or evidence for the claims and requirements they were making, that the Americans were always unrealistic about how quickly things could get done and were putting the French team under a lot of unnecessary pressure, and that the Americans had closed their minds when it came to any ideas, proposals, etc. that the French attempted to offer. While my colleague was incredulous that the French might be feeling this way, I was able to check out my hunches informally with several of the French participants on the other side, and the responses I got corroborated my suspicions. Once again, all other factors being equal, the conflict here was over a difference in communication styles of argument, persuasion, and negotiation. And while these differences were caused by a variety of factors, the differing conceptions of time were a central ingredient.

Americans get to the point. There is no time to waste. "Don't beat around the bush," we say. Not only are we extremely direct (a characteristic which we'll discuss in other chapters as well), but our concern for the maximum use of a minimum amount of time, in combination with other cultural factors, forces us to put the bottom line first, the conclusion up front, the summary at the beginning. How many American business proposals and articles begin with a short summary? How many American executive briefings sum up ahead of time the contents that brought the writers to their conclusion in the first place? We are driven to state our conclusions at the beginning, and only then (and often only if required to) to provide our reasons or rationalizations for having come to those conclusions. From a classical rhetorical perspective, this is *inductive reasoning,* and it is exactly the opposite style of thinking and communicating used by the French.

For a variety of reasons, the French are trained to think *deductively.* For one thing, their educational system traditionally emphasizes the development of logic skills. Most French students study philosophy throughout their entire university career. Descartes, the great French philosopher and mathematician, explored the system of deductive reasoning that bears his name, Cartesian logic, and it is formally taught in French schools. Primarily for this reason, the French businessperson across the table from you will tend to present the big picture first, and then carefully and skillfully take you from one "therefore" to another until every detail is logically considered and every consideration logically dissected, moving flawlessly to the final conclusion (which is, if properly reached, clearly foregone, and therefore unassailable). Details become critically important, for the conclusion one is moving toward is built on these bricks of rhetoric. For the French, argument is an admirable skill and mastery of logic an intellectual accomplishment worthy of great admiration. We will talk more about this when we discuss persuasion styles in Chapter 8. Suffice it to say here that when the French, with their emphasis on deductive, causal reasoning and the time they need to build a case from a masterly presentation of details, come in contact with the "here's what we think we should do" clock-watching Americans, the French feel that their intelligence has been insulted, while the Americans feel that everything but what they want to discuss is being brought into the picture.

My colleague regarded the French attempts to get him the information he wanted as digressions so far removed from the object of his questions that he thought they were actually discussing other topics (perhaps even, from his perspective, their own personal agenda—a misguided conclusion that only fueled the growing lack of trust between the two). The French, however, were "backing up"—trying to provide answers that not only supplied the *what* the Americans were looking for, but also the *why* that is so critical a part of any answer in France. For Americans to make their point with Europeans and with the French in particular, they must take time to address the French need for understanding the *why* as well as the *what*. And for the French to make their point with Americans, they need to appreciate American impatience (time, again) and the greater American concern to be given quickly-grasped facts. The way we Americans view time is related to our own cultural requirements and must be considered a "different," even problematic, approach under certain circumstances, when doing business with other cultures.

I remember being struck by the way time even determined the communication style I was to use when conducting one of my negotiation training programs in Europe. It was taking place in Brussels for a major American firm. Seated around the table were representatives from this company's European offices. The room, with each person's name and country written out in front of him or her, resembled what I imagined an European Community meeting might look like. As I had administered the program many times in the States, I was curious to see how it would "fly" in Europe, how it might be different, how the responses might vary among the different cultures present. Among the many things I quickly learned on this maiden voyage was the need to completely revise the schedule, pacing, and time segments allotted to various exercises and discussions. In fact, differences in time concepts affected almost every aspect of the program, starting with the most obvious—the scheduling—and moving on in a more subtle way, to the actual content. The differences mirrored many of those discussed in the example of the American and French negotiation above.

I came to realize that in almost all important aspects, the program had an American bias, and this was certainly true in relation to time. On the obvious level, I had expected to be able to begin and end punctually at certain points. This was not possible because several polychronic cultures were present. The Italian, Spanish, Greek, and Portuguese participants simply did not follow the prescribed starting, ending, and break times. There were relationship and socializing needs (like two-hour lunches) the American schedule had not allowed for, and individuals just took it upon themselves to make time to fulfill these needs. The time allotted for certain discussions was inevitably too short, and the pacing of the entire program appeared to be too fast. There was always more discussion, once it got going, on particular points, than there had been in the States, although getting the discussion going was always more difficult. (Differences in learning styles and in the student-teacher relationship accounted for this.) Above all, the Europeans were always seeking the *why* behind my statements to a degree I had never encountered in the States. And when I raised points relating to the States, there would be much inquiry in order to understand the exact rationale behind my statements. The point here is that without the *why*, the *what* is simply not enough for Europeans, while the *what* is often the central focus, to the exclusion of the *why* for Americans in business.

To return to the initial French-American negotiation scenario: I explained my analysis of the cultural differences at work in the conflict to my American colleagues. Then we formulated an action plan for the American team that included anticipation and practice in responding to the French need for quality, precision, and Cartesian "big-picture/little-detail" logic and presentation. Our goal was to ensure that our responses were authentic, appropriate, and constructive. In addition, we discussed how our most recent actions might have been received and misread by the French, and we outlined the steps we might take to reestablish a more cordial relationship in anticipation of the upcoming real negotiation. Several members of the team recommended a simultaneous acknowledgment of the French group's quality efforts with an explanation of the pressures that we Americans were under to get the information in a timely fashion. Others suggested that they had good relationships with their French associates and were going to put through a prenegotiation social call to them to shore up good feelings, ask if there was anything they needed in anticipation of their arrival once they got to the States, and reaffirm our good intentions. Reporting back after the first round of the negotiations, my colleague told me that they had made more real progress with less mutual confusion in this negotiation than he remembered their ever having made in any of their previous meetings.

We need to be particularly careful not to select out those qualities in individuals of a particular culture that reflect only what we have, from our own incomplete information and stereotypes, come to expect. As we discussed earlier in Chapter 2, selecting out is one of several dangerous cross-cultural processes that we need to identify whenever we can. In the case of the French, it is not only that we expect them to be cold and arrogant to Americans, but we tend to see only the behavior that reinforces this expectation. As we've seen in the above example, we Americans don't usually think of the French as having supremacy in precise, "hard," technical areas. Our stereotype of the French can tend instead to be one of a people excelling in such "soft" areas as quality-of-life concerns: good food, wine, art, etc. Given the additional American em-

phasis on "good enough within the time allotted," Americans are often
driven to select out only that behavior that reinforces our stereotypes.
We therefore miss their emphasis on technical precision because we do
not expect it from them and because (perhaps more important) it does
not exist in us to the degree that it does in them. Instead, we define
their unwillingness to compromise as obstinacy because we do not see
their emphasis on faultless logic. And we define their refusal to hold to
a deadline per se as uncooperative and inconsiderate because we do not
place the same value on precision and quality ourselves.

To return to our scales, on scale 4, therefore, I might place an "A"
between 7 and 8 and an "F" for France at around 2 or 3, while on scale
5, I would place an "A" at 2 and an "F" at 5 or 6.

An interesting example highlighting the differing French and American view of time, the differing emphasis the French place on logic, precision, *what*, and *why*, is the way the two nationalities determine the ages
of identical twins. In the U.S., the older twin is the first twin to be born,
for (so the reasoning goes) he or she came into the world first. In
France, traditionally the older twin is the second, the last to come into
the world, because he or she was the first to have been conceived. Because the second twin was formed out of the first (so the French de-
duce), he or she is therefore the younger. In America, however, that
same twin is considered the older, precisely because (according to inductive reasoning) he or she was presented first and took the least time
getting here. In France, truly, *conception* is first.

One Thing at a Time, Please

In the Mexican example earlier and in several other examples in other
chapters, we have illustrated the fact that polychronic cultures can be
comfortable with the idea of many things happening at once, while
monochronic cultures often have difficulty, at least in business, in dealing with several simultaneous developments. It might be useful to look
at other business situations where polychronic, vertical, "simultaneous-
ness" can be in conflict with the monochronic, horizontal, "one-thing-
after-another-ness."

At a negotiation in Rome, one of our goals was to get the Italian team
to buy an expensive piece of equipment on a more accelerated payment
schedule than they were used to paying for previous purchases they had
made from our company. Their previous purchases were not as expensive as the equipment we were hoping to sell them now; nor were we
sure that the Italians were going to be that interested in our new piece,
since they were merely looking to replace the older piece of equipment

they had purchased from us in the past. We were convinced that our new updated, and yes, more expensive, model was a better piece of equipment for them in the long run and that, also in the long run, it would be less expensive for them, given what they would be getting for their money. Convincing them of this was the problem.[8]

An agenda had been circulated and agreed to by both sides ahead of time. It was understood that the Italians wanted to replace an older piece of equipment and that the Americans wanted to talk to the Italians about the replacement. A good relationship had been built up between individuals on both sides from previous negotiations; everyone knew each other. When the negotiation began, it appeared as if the Italians were ready to get right down to work, and that pleased the Americans. However, it soon became clear that the Italians had several other issues on their agenda that we had been unaware of.

This was a lesson in agenda-setting, for one thing. Setting the agenda ahead of time, giving both sides an opportunity to contribute to it and agree on the other side's topics, can be an extremely useful way to avoid misconceptions and misunderstandings and can go along way toward speeding up the actual process of negotiation once you get face to face. This can be extremely important for Americans, given our usual lack of time and our desire to get straight down to business. It can be especially valuable considering our opposite numbers' sometimes opposite views of the purpose of the negotiation. (They might, for example, be simply hoping to spend the time you take to fly over there and get some business done just getting to know you better!) However, one must be careful to ensure that the agenda-setting process does not itself become another vehicle for miscommunication or misunderstanding. There is no guarantee that hidden agendas do not exist, that the other side will not suddenly want to discuss things not previously on the agreed-upon agenda, or that what one side thought they had agreed to was not what the other side meant. When misunderstandings like these arise, despite the effort to set a clear agenda, the result can be mistrust twice magnified, since it seems that it came despite everyone's best intentions. This is not to say agenda-setting should be avoided. On the contrary, it can be quite useful. It, too, however, is subject to cross-cultural misinterpretations and therefore must be carefully executed with full knowledge that cultural differences may affect it.

In the case of the Italians and the Americans above, misunderstandings regarding the agenda were exactly the source of the difficulties that arose. It became clear, for one thing, that despite our mutually stated goals, the Italians wanted to take the opportunity to discuss problems they were having servicing other pieces of equipment they had previously purchased (an

---

[8]This example was contributed by Cynthia Milani Associates.

issue we thought we had cleared up long distance via phone and fax several months before), some training needs they still had regarding another piece of equipment they had purchased from us, and miscellaneous other items. It appeared to the Americans that additional items kept popping up, some major, some minor, but all apparently not mentioned previously as issues to be negotiated when the agenda was set. And once we began to speak about what our concerns were, we realized that the Italians were perceiving us as having our own secret agendas, for they were surprised to learn that what we wanted to discuss was not the terms for their purchase of a replacement, but rather the terms for their purchase of a new, more expensive, piece of equipment to replace the old one—which involved an accelerated payment schedule, no less. Apparently, as far as the ostensible item on the table was concerned, the Italians were simply interested in trying to get it at a lower price than what they understood we were selling it for on the world market. Both sides became distressed that it seemed as if the other had come with a secret agenda.

In fact, the Americans did not think they were withholding anything from the Italians simply because they had not mentioned in the agenda that they wanted to discuss the purchase of a new piece of more expensive equipment; for them, this was just a detail to be hammered out at the negotiation itself. The Americans felt, in a fairly monochronic way, that once the situation was understood clearly and the facts presented in a logical fashion, the recommendation for the new equipment they were presenting at the negotiation would be considered and that to present it as an option without clarification in an agenda would be premature. More important, perhaps, the Americans had set a team goal that was understood by all the individuals on their side to be the purpose of the meeting. While Americans are very individualistic, and certainly each individual on the American team could be expected to act in his or her own way, such individual actions would be for the achieving of the stated team goal.

Nor did the Italians, for their part, feel they had withheld anything from the Americans when the agenda was set. For one thing, their sense of what information should be shared publicly in such a vehicle is quite different from the American view. From their perspective, detailed information regarding the other issues they wanted to bring forward should *not* be discussed publicly ahead of time. Each individual affected by these issues would bring them forward at the proper time in the negotiation. In fact, some of the issues that eventually surfaced on the Italian side had probably been withheld as much from the rest of the Italian team as from the Americans prior to the actual negotiations. Information, and personal agendas, are very private in Italy. Information is power, and individuals build their power by retaining and gathering information. It is generally not shared, and certainly an individual's particular concern regarding certain business issues will only be divulged in private to other appropriate individuals at the appropriate time – preferably face-to-face.

Where there are various individuals coming to the table with private agendas, where there is a difference in the sense of what information should be shared publicly and privately, and where there is a different sense as to how and when these issues should be brought forward and negotiated, the result can be one side negotiating many issues in a vertical, simultaneous way, with the other side wanting to negotiate one issue at a time. Once the Italian-American negotiation began, it very quickly devolved into several different Italians presenting what appeared to be individual private agendas around all sorts of issues, some of which the Americans thought had already been resolved. Meanwhile, the Americans, as a team, were struggling to put forward their case for a new piece of equipment. Since the individual private agendas of the Italians were of more importance to them than what they perceived to be the "hidden agenda" of the Americans (a new piece of equipment at a higher price with a faster payback), their willingness to listen to the American proposal was significantly diminished.

The style of the communication at the table was simultaneous on one side and linear on the other, and the procedure of the negotiation mirrored this polychronic/monochronic split. The Americans were eager to move linearly from point to point, checking to be sure that previous points had been understood before moving forward to the next. There appeared to be a concern for causality and a desire to be sure that the Italians were partners in the understanding of this causality. "We think this, therefore...," "We see the situation this way, therefore we recommend...." The Americans were not pleased, therefore, when the Italians would suddenly jump from one topic to another, often from what the Americans were discussing to what the Italians themselves had on their minds, without any concern for the resulting *non sequiturs* in the negotiation. Scheduling mirrored this as well. There appeared to be endless coffee breaks, either for coffee to be brought in or for members to go down to the coffee bar. The Americans inevitably saw these as intrusions, while the Italians apparently were easily able to integrate these activities into the procedures of the negotiation. Personal interruptions were fairly constant, with individual Italians always being called away for a moment from the negotiation for this reason or that.

At one point in the negotiation, a very elegant, well-dressed woman appeared in the room. All the Italians recognized her and showed her great respect. She was introduced as the wife of the president of the Italian company, and, in fact, she had arrived specifically to show her husband the new coat she had just bought. For the time being, the negotiation came to a complete halt while the Italians admired her coat, chatted a bit with her and her husband, and introduced her to all the Americans at the table. I was convinced that if she stayed just a few moments longer she would become part of the Italian team, but she excused herself gracefully and left.

Clearly, the polychronism of the Italians also includes the allowance for dealing not only with several business issues simultaneously, but with all of life's issues simultaneously. There is a less rigid, more flexible line between life and work than exists in the United States, where work is often clearly defined as a very separate activity from other aspects of life. In Italy, life and work intersect in different ways and at different points, and both can be dealt with simultaneously.

From this example we may also draw a conclusion regarding differences in time concepts and thought processes, much as we did with the French in the previous example. Monochronic cultures, with their emphasis on linear time, are concerned with causality. In such cultures, communication and argument are based on the need for logic. Polychronic cultures are concerned with equilibrium. In such cultures with their emphasis on simultaneous activity in time, communication and argument are based on the need for *balance*. That is, when time is viewed horizontally, understanding is achieved by one thing leading to the next; when time is viewed vertically, understanding is achieved by balancing the many things that occur at once. Therefore, for the Americans, only logic (defined here as linear causality) could produce agreement in the negotiation, while for the Italians, only balance, achieved over time by the simultaneous presentation of many, perhaps illogically associated, points, could produce agreement in the negotiation.

The American preference for linearity and logic (sometimes generalized by non-Westerners to include a preference for this approach by all Westerners) makes us appear one-dimensional and sterile to many non-Westerners. Meanwhile, Westerners in general (and Americans in particular) tend to find the non-Western reliance on simultaneous balancing of differences (or even opposites) extremely frustrating. While we monochronics view polychronism as illogical and therefore unproductive, polychronics see us as being without concern for human reality and applicability. This is also the mono/polychronic aspect of Eastern pragmatism and Western principlism that we will discuss further in the chapter on egalitarianism.

Suffice it to say that Americans need to learn how to "go with the flow" more often—no matter how illogical it might seem at the moment—when dealing with polychronic cultures. For their part, polychronic cultures need to fine-tune their linear-logic skills when dealing with Americans. This means, for the Americans, that achieving conclusion, closure, and agreement will perhaps take more time and will be achieved, not as the crow flies, but in a more up-and-down, two-steps-forward-one-step-back kind of motion. Again, in polychronic cultures, efficiency is not necessarily the primary value, although achieving the goal(s) is nevertheless very important.

And on a less lofty, less philosophical note, this example also shows us how integral one aspect of cultural behavior can be to another. In this case, I am speaking of the connection between time (this chapter's concern) and the issue of relationship building (Chapter 5). Here the Italian need is greater than the American. Italians break for coffee many times throughout the day—not only as a quick pick-me-up, but as an addendum to, rather than a break from, business. At the coffee bar Italians continue to talk business—more informally, perhaps, but all the more seriously because of the informality, and with a greater reliance on the relationships between the individuals to facilitate business. Additionally, Italians' day-to-day business dealings are intimately tied to their homes and their families. Business does not preempt family issues; in fact, it is often the other way around. Indeed, in Italy family *is* business, more often than not. Most companies, large and small, are family organizations or got their start as such. In Italy, the family is the port in the storm, the one true place one can turn to when all around one is an unsafe and unpredictable world. (In Japan, the corporation is the business; in America, the individual is the business.) In this sense, on scale 3, I would place "I" for Italy at around 7 or 8, and an "A" at around 2 to 4.

One final word about this aspect of monochronism versus polychronism: both are clearly different approaches to handling basically the same problem, which is making sense out of a senseless world, providing safety in an unsafe place, and making things that are inherently mysterious more knowable and predictable.

While monochronism attempts to achieve sense, safety, and familiarity by controlling phenomena and limiting flexibility, polychronism attempts to achieve them by accepting phenomena and increasing flexibility. Americans tend to *exclude*, as extraneous, a certain type of concern from their negotiations in order to accomplish the business at hand. Polychronics (the Italians included) tend to *include* these very same "extraneous" concerns (as defined by the Americans, *not* the Italians; such concerns are not extraneous from the Italian point of view) and for the very same reason: to accomplish the business at hand.

Causality and logic might ultimately be necessary in order to reach a specific conclusion, but conclusions, at least in international business, are not the sole determinants of agreement; there are many paths to agreement. Americans (and many other Westerners, such as the British,

Germans, Belgians, Dutch, French, and Canadians) need to recognize the necessity for flexibility in regard to causal, linear thinking. Such flexibility is critical when dealing with more polychronic cultures and perhaps worth considering as an additional, alternate way for us to achieve satisfactory solutions in our negotiations.

"Had We But World Enough, and Time"*

There's a joke about an American and a Japanese sitting on a park bench in Tokyo. Both are businessmen. The American is saying, "Well, you know I've been in Japan for my company for forty years. Forty years! And now they are sending me home back to the States in just a few days." The Japanese replies, "That's the problem with you Americans: here today and gone tomorrow."

Throughout the world, Americans are known for their speed in business. We often think nothing of hopping on an overnight flight to Europe, getting off the plane, checking into a hotel, and grabbing a taxi to the business meeting. This is not the way I suggest conducting business and not the way most people want to, but too often it is the only way possible, given the severe constraints on time and money involved in a business trip abroad. We place a great emphasis on efficiency, and we design technology to support and fulfill this need. But our accent on speed is curiously selective. While we jet back and forth across the ocean for a one-day business meeting, we can often be perceived by Europeans as wasting time on too many meetings. While we will work late into the night and take work home on weekends in order to accomplish a task "on time," we can seem to the French to be more "long-working" than "hard-working." Conversely, while we see ourselves as fast-moving, hard-working, and work-oriented, the Taiwanese can see us as fun-loving, easy-going, and pleasure-oriented. And while we complain about how long it takes for the Japanese to make a decision we're waiting for, they complain about how long it takes for us to implement the decision once it is made.

Clearly, the areas in which we choose to move quickly are selective. Many of the dynamic dragons in Asia move faster than Americans. The French are perhaps actually more efficient than Americans with their time during the working day. Americans seem to move too fast in some areas, too slow in others. In fact, our bursts of activity tend to take place at the beginning of a project; over the long haul, we often slow down.

*From the poem "To His Coy Mistress" by Andrew Marvell, 1621–1728.

We're like sprinters. Our notion of time is tied up with our notion of speed, and the time we give something is often limited by the energy and resources we have to move quickly. Once we stop moving quickly, we often can seem to drop right out of the picture.

As the joke about the American and the Japanese indicates, Americans are perceived, at least in comparison with many other cultures, to be working for the immediate present, for the short term, for the quick buck. We're in and then out. As soon as there's a problem, we cut our losses and go. As soon as a relationship gets too deep, as soon as the unexpected gets too unmanageable, as soon as profits dip, we close shop and move on. Traditionally, the American company has been interested in short-term profits and good-looking quarterly reports at the expense of long-range strategic planning, the development of market share, and the long-range development of a market. This has often meant quick hits, emphasis on volume, not quality, and a stress on marketing and sales expertise, rather than on technical expertise.

Take even just a cursory look at the annual report of an average large American company, and then compare it with the annual report of, say, an equally large average Japanese company. The American company, no matter what problems it may be facing, inevitably publishes a report that faces the future with glowing optimism. In fact, it is often filled with statistical analyses that show how things are looking up. The Japanese corporate report, however, will often reveal very little financial data. And while it will present the company in a positive light, the company ethos it reflects is one based not so much on a faith in the future as on a nose-to-the-grindstone conservative work ethic driven by fear of what the unknown tomorrow might bring. The American annual report is a marketing piece written for the shareholder; the concern in American companies is to maximize shareholder return. The constituency is the stockholder. However, the concern in Japan is to grow profitably in order to meet salaries and other obligations, maintain and increase employment, and give meaning to the corporate mission as an integral part of the Japanese worker's life. The traditional orientation of the Japanese company is not first to maximize profits for the shareholder. And the annual report is not written for, nor are any of the functions of the company — marketing, operations, R&D, finance, human resources, etc. — designed to meet, primary stockholder criteria (quarterly profits). The Japanese worker is the primary constituency. And Japanese society, not the stock owner, is the recipient of the profitability of the Japanese company. The Japanese worker is traditionally with his company for life. Both he and the company are in it for the long haul.

Japanese companies make a commitment to a decision, often no matter how the implementation of that decision needs to change over time. The plan for implementing the decision may not be as clearly defined as the American plan, but once made, it is difficult to abandon. While the decision may be based on many factors, it is supported until accomplished. Whatever needs to be done, whatever changes need to be made, whatever new plans need to be drawn up, are usually arranged in order to accomplish the original decision, the original goal. Therefore, there is a flexibility in their long-range strategic planning that is often in conflict with inflexible American short-term planning.

Americans will often not make a decision unless and until they have a well-constructed plan by which they can carry out the decision. Since, in fact, we are all limited in the control we can exercise over the future (and suffer diminishing control over increasing time), Americans tend to make decisions for the future only as far as they can plan into the future in order to "guarantee" those decisions. The Japanese do not need an up-front plan to be sure that their decision will be put into effect because they are committed to doing whatever is necessary at any point down the road to implement the decision they make now. Today's decision is not dependent on a plan for all future contingencies. But since we Americans are limited to making only those decisions that can be planned for now—whose reach into the future is dependent on the contingencies we can anticipate and control from our present position—our decision making and hence our strategic planning, are of necessity limited in scope and distance.

In this sense, Americans, so often used to seeing themselves as pragmatic, down-to-earth, and practical, are less able to accommodate change and respond appropriately and creatively to new and unplanned-for situations than are the Asians (in this case, the Japanese) who practice a more flexible form of pragmatism.

Seen from this perspective, Americans move quickly, but only in response to the immediately knowable future. We move slowly in response to the long-range unknowable future. We take risks and seize opportunities within the parameters of what we can control, plan for, and organize, with the result, more often than not, being a commitment only to the here and now. We are flexible during the sprint, but our commitment over the long-distance run is questionable. Why are Americans unwilling to let go of the here-and-now planning, which, by its very nature limits the degree to which we can commit to long-term projects? And how are the Japanese able to feel secure without having to know today how to handle every possible development in the faraway future, thereby enabling themselves to make longer-term strategic commitments?

I believe the answer lies again in the differing approaches of polychronism and monochronism—in the different conceptions of time.

The two make sense of the world in opposite ways. The polychronistic approach balances opposites, accepts change, and recognizes the inter-relationship among possibly illogical phenomena. The monochronistic approach controls, separates out, and limits the effects of opposite and illogical phenomena. Monochronistic *planning for the goal* implies limits and inflexibility ("Stick with the plan, no matter what"). Poly-chronistic *commitment to the goal* implies open-endedness and fluidity ("We'll cross that bridge when we come to it").

Planning, in this monochronic sense, can have a limiting effect, while the polychronic acceptance of the vagaries and disparities of human existence (in a sense, the "world of people" as opposed to the "world of words") is more inclusive. It is interesting to note that in certain extremely polychronic cultures, such as those of Latin America, whatever orientation there is toward the future is based on an acceptance of the unpredictability of people and things. I have often heard business-people in these countries lamenting over the need for such skills as planning, organization, and goal-setting in their respective organiza-tions. In certain extremely monochronic cultures, such as Germany and, to a lesser extent, the United States, where future-orientation is significant but based primarily on planning for what is immediately con-trollable, I hear businesspeople lament the need for skills that empower, that enhance creativity, that improve effectiveness and employee satis-faction. Each has what the other offers. And it is in those cultures whose traditions are deep and complex enough to apply both a polychronic and monochronic interpretation that we see the ability to plan effec-tively integrated into a view of the future flexible enough to allow com-mitment to that which cannot be controlled. In the East, the flexible wil-low is the stronger tree. In the West, it is the mighty oak.

Time to Put Time to Work

Now that we understand intellectually some of the differences in the way time is conceptualized by Americans and others, let's try to *apply* this information behaviorally in our international work. You have al-ready been able to identify some very key characteristics of American notions of time and spot their impact on the international business scene. Also, you have been able to unpack a good deal of our own cul-tural baggage as it relates to the concept of time and to being American in the global context.

Now, in order to better understand and succeed with our associates abroad, it's time to dig through that cultural baggage a little more care-fully and, before we throw the baby out with the bathwater, practice a little reclaiming. This is the moment when we need to go beyond handy generalizations. There may be many characteristics of your own *individual* time-related concepts and behavior that are different from the average American norm we've been focusing on. In fact, true to the central thesis of this book, I suspect that you have experienced or encountered many attitudes regarding time and its use in business that are similar to some of the non-American attitudes we've been describing. The reason is simple: many of these attitudes were brought here from "there." If you've experienced them—and it's likely that you have—it's because you are an American living in a multicultural society.

Below, once again, is a Global Homecoming Exercise© that presents a conflict between an American and his foreign associate abroad. The conflict, for our purposes, has been highlighted to reflect mainly differences in perceptions of time. Once again, your job is to come up with alternate ways for the American to behave that are *authentic, appropriate* and *constructive*. In order for the American behavior to meet these criteria, you need to apply a combination of the cross-cultural information about time that we've been discussing in this chapter with an empathic understanding of how the non-Americans—in this case Spaniards—might be viewing time differently. And in order to do that, we're once again suggesting that you dig into your own experiences to find those reactions in yourself. Remember also that our concern here is to come up with positive, preemptive behavior. We're not interested in damage control as much as we're interested in successful planning. One final note: Try to maintain as much focus as you can on the internal processes of the exercise. While you may have sufficient cross-cultural information specific to Spain to enable you to come up with the answers to this exercise, the larger goal is the development of a global mindset—the skill that will enable you to deal more effectively with any culture, even one for which you may not have specific information.

A Time Traveler[9]

This was Jim Louden's first trip to Madrid for the company, and while he expected things to be a little different, he did not expect to encounter any real difficulties. After all, he said to himself, Spain is a Western country, really very modern these days. Besides, Jim felt confident about being able to establish relationships quickly with his Spanish associates because he planned to use his Spanish. While he'd never had the opportunity to speak with any Spaniards before, he felt sure that now he could finally put the Spanish he'd picked up from his Mexican friends while growing up in Southern California to some good use.

However, once he'd arrived at the meeting, things were beginning to annoy him. Deep down inside, he was feeling agitated,

[9]Ellen Raider International, Inc. and ITAP, International contributed to this example.

a little angry, and very frustrated. In fact, despite Jim's Spanish, the meeting was not going so well, and Jim had begun to admit this to himself even though he couldn't figure out why. At a break during the meeting, Jim used the excuse of having to make a phone call to leave the room and quietly reassess things. Looking back over the earlier part of the day, one of the first things that had really bothered him was the fact that the Spaniards seemed to be a basically very uncooperative lot, even though they appeared extremely gracious and concerned for all of his needs. For one thing, he had wanted the meeting to begin at 1 p.m., a perfectly reasonable time in his mind, since it gave everyone the morning to take care of office business, thereby freeing up the afternoon for the negotiation. When he arrived at his hotel, however, despite the fact that his secretary had sent a fax to Madrid setting the meeting at 1 p.m., he'd received a call from the secretary of the director of the Madrid office the day before he left to say that the meeting had been rescheduled to begin at 4 p.m. "Four o'clock!", Jim thought to himself at the hotel. "I didn't fly all the way over to Spain to attend at meeting at the end of the day." Besides, this would mean that he would certainly need to schedule an additional meeting the following day to continue. This was something that was going to set his business schedule back, as well as cut into the few precious hours of sightseeing he was looking forward to. When he asked the secretary why the meeting had been pushed back to 4 p.m., she expressed her boss's apologies for having to take care of some sudden unexpected details.

"OK," Jim thought to himself. But to make matters worse, when he arrived at 4 p.m., none of the Spaniards were there. As a matter of fact, they kept him waiting for 45 minutes. Slowly, one by one, they showed up, introduced themselves to him, and then ignored him while they went around chatting about this and that with each other. Jim felt very ostracized, but a little smug, too, because he was able to understand some of what they were saying, and he thought they didn't realize he knew some Spanish. However, nothing they were talking about had anything to do with the business at hand or with the purpose of the meeting. In fact, it seemed that everyone already knew each other and that the meeting was more or less a great excuse to socialize and catch up. There was much joke-telling, coffee-serving, coffee-drinking, and smoking. Jim had to admit that, under the circumstances, even this got to him since he didn't smoke and really didn't enjoy that thick, mudlike coffee he was finding in Spain. Finally, after a long wait, the director of the Madrid office arrived and gathered everyone together to start the meeting. Jim felt sure that now they were going to get down to some business.

He was wrong, however. Topics that he was sure they had agreed in advance to discuss he was having a difficult time even getting on the table. Instead, the conversation flowed back and forth among the Spaniards. It was mostly social talk, interspersed with some internal business issues that more often than not did not have anything to do with the meeting. When they did speak to him, it was to ask polite questions about him and the American company in general. Did he like being in Spain? Had he been there before? Where did he plan to visit? Too bad he had to leave so soon, etc. Then, when it appeared the Spaniards were finally getting down to business, they began to ask him all sorts of general questions about his company, his life back in the States, and his job responsibilities. What did the company think about the changes in Spain today? What were his company's strategies for Europe in general? Did he have any specific information regarding the company's strategic response to the European Community and the future?, etc. He felt overwhelmed by these questions on things he knew nothing about and things he was not interested in. And yet he couldn't get the meeting around to anything that was of concern to him.

At one point he tried to cut through the morass of conversation that seemed to be going on everywhere at once by simply pushing forward the back-up materials he had brought along with him. These materials were part of the larger presentation he had hoped to conduct. However, this attempt to bring the participants around backfired, for instead of enabling him to make his presentation, the Spanish were delighted to see that he had all the information for them written down in individual packets for them, so that there was no need for him to make a presentation. The director thanked him for his advance planning and thorough consideration and assured him that the information would be carefully studied. In fact, while Jim felt completely deflated, he noticed that his Spanish associates were quite pleased. Actually, Jim was getting the feeling that maybe this was really working out in his favor, although he couldn't quite imagine how. It was as if the Spaniards preferred to digest the information later anyway, on their own. With that out of the way, they felt free to turn their attention to what was clearly an important concern at this time of day—dinner. It seemed as if the Spaniards were more concerned in hosting Jim properly than in doing business with him, and this was absolutely mystifying to him. Try as he might, he had a hard time convincing himself that he should take all this as a compliment.

By this time, maybe it was for the best that no work was getting done, Jim thought, for he was tired, hungry, the Spaniards' attention, and not a little disgruntled. Not the best combination for effective negotiations, he thought to himself. So at the end of the break, he pulled himself together and returned to the table, having assessed the damage so far and hoping that what remained of the afternoon and the dinner could be salvaged.

When Jim returned to the table, he became aware of something else that might have contributed to his awkwardness earlier. He noted that his Madrileños associates were very formally dressed, and he was not. As he took his seat, he was suddenly aware of the way some of the men at the table were looking at him, and this made him very uncomfortable. He suddenly felt embarrassed because of the difference in the way he was dressed in comparison to the other people at the table. Obviously, he had made a mistake, but he'd decided to dress down (open collar, slip ons, sport jacket) because he had heard from a friend who had vacationed on the Costa Brava once that Spain was a warm and friendly culture. This was not, however, Jim's experience so far.

It was decided then to meet for dinner later that evening. Jim made up his mind to upgrade his wardrobe for that event by wearing a more formal business suit, white shirt, and tie. Dinner time was set for 9 p.m. Jim felt that that was a little late because he was already tired, but everyone seemed to praise the restaurant they had selected, and so, when they asked him if that was a good time, he assumed the reservations had already been set, and agreed to meet them at 9.

When Jim met everyone later that evening, he was very hungry and somewhat exhausted. He was also further confused, since the address he'd been given turned out to be a stand-up bar. While there were some tables in the back, there weren't many people there, and most of the crowd was up front snacking on this and that and drinking. When he arrived, he realized he made another mistake in his choice of clothes. While his associates were still quite nattily dressed, they were not in their daytime business suits. However, Jim chalked this up to his simply not knowing the customs, and nobody said anything about it, so he felt that it was either unnoticed or unimportant. At least he wasn't getting the stares he had received earlier in the office when he returned to the table.

Jim's main concern now was simply getting some dinner, since it was late and he was famished. He made several attempts to direct the group to tables in the back, but to no avail. Finally, he thought for a few moments and then, using his best Spanish, suggested to everyone, as he attempted to lead the director toward the back of the restaurant, that they take their seats. A frigid silence descended on the group. Someone asked him to repeat his words...slowly. More silence, then a little laughter. The director reassured Jim that they were not dining in this restaurant. They had just met there because they wanted him to sample the wonderful *tapas* — appetizers — of Spain before going to dinner. Actually dinner was already arranged at another restaurant on the other side of town for around 11 p.m. Jim was aghast, and it probably showed, since this time the silence was practically audible.

Everyone headed over to the restaurant a little after ten, earlier than the Spaniards had anticipated, but they didn't want to offend their guest. When they got there, they had to wait for a table — not because it was crowded, but rather because the dining room, having been prearranged, wasn't yet ready for them. Dinner was not the pleasant experience Jim had hoped it would be. It seemed rather to be an appropriately flat finish to an otherwise exhausting and disagreeable day.

Global Homecoming Exercise© 2:
Time

1. *Recognize* differences: In regard to the dimension of time, how are the Spaniards and the Americans different?

Spaniards	Americans
The Spaniards expect	The Americans expect
_____	_____
_____	_____
_____	_____
_____	_____

2. *Retrace:* Spend one minute meditating quietly to help relax and clear your mind. Close your eyes. Spend the next few minutes visualizing yourself going back to an event in your early years (at home, with relatives, at school, at church, with friends) in which you were with people very close to you who *held similar values* to the Spaniards in regard to time. Describe the scene:

_____

_____

_____

_____

_____

3. *Reclaim:* Who were the people in your scene? How would you describe their culture?

_____

_____

_____

What is their country?_____ Ethnicity?_____

Religion?_____ Generation?_____ Sex?_____

Relation to you?_____

How did you feel about these people?_____

_____

_____

_____

4. *Reframe:* What factors in these people's culture do you think might have caused them to act the way they did with you?

_____

_____

_____

What cultural gifts have they brought you?_____

_____

What have you learned from them?_____

_____

Go back to this situation now. You are there, but as the person you are now. What will you do differently?

_____

_____

_____

5. *Resurface: You are the American in the "Time Traveler" Case.* What cultural gifts can you bring to this encounter?

_____

_____

_____

What cultural gifts do they bring to this encounter?

_____

_____

_____

What can you say or do to find a better way home (to reach a more satisfactory agreement or conclusion to this business situation)?

_____

_____

_____

_____

5
Americans, Love, and Money at the Negotiating Table

Now Be Sure to Stop by Whenever You're in the Neighborhood

A German manager, expatriated with his family to the States, tells the story now with good-humored self-consciousness about how surprised he was when he first got here to find Americans so friendly. After meeting a colleague at work just once, he and his family were invited to stop by his colleague's home whenever "they were in the neighborhood." Although the German found this surprising, he was also thrilled by his swift acceptance into American society and by this American's eagerness to get to know him. No one in Germany would ever be so open, so trusting, so friendly, as to make this kind of offer after just one meeting, he thought to himself. Here was a real America living up to the myth! Today, he laughs about how embarrassed he felt when he *did* show up unannounced on his colleague's doorstep one day for a visit, just because he "was in the neighborhood."

Over and over, in interviews with foreign nationals expatriated to the United States, I hear this common refrain: "Americans were so friendly, I thought I was really going to have a lot of friends here...but it hasn't happened." Or, "I feel disappointed...just as I thought I was getting to know her, she seemed to pull back. I hope I didn't do anything to upset her. Doesn't she want to be friends?" Coming to work in the United States for the first time, foreign nationals often feel welcomed at first, and then disregarded, lost, left alone without direction. "I didn't know what I was supposed to do." "I didn't want to ask anyone to help me, since nobody seemed interested in whether I needed help or not." "I'm not used to working by myself." Encouraged by their initial acceptance and happy about being able to feel that what they are doing, who they are, is just fine, they are doubly disappointed when suddenly, after the initial welcome, they are left feeling stranded, sometimes even abandoned. Then they question how they are really fitting in and become self-conscious and withdrawn, just at a time when they should be working hard and getting on with their colleagues. It can be a difficult transition for foreign nationals coming to work in America.

Our Special Relationship with Relationships

We Americans have a special attitude toward relationships, toward the way we relate to each other, that people from many other cultures can find difficult to understand. This view of relationships, of course, is grounded in many of our values and forms an important part of our view of the world. Every culture has its own world view, its own set of beliefs about the way people are bound to each other, the role that human beings play in the larger world, the links to be forged between a person's life, work, and even the natural and spiritual worlds. In this chapter we're going to look at the unique American world view as it compares with other cultures in this regard. We'll try to see ourselves as others see us in an effort to anticipate the differences in world views that stand between us, particularly as they affect our ability to do business with each other. The American view of relationships in business has traditionally been quite different from the view held in the rest of the world. When it comes to business, we Americans like to do business first and only then establish relationships. For much of the rest of the world, it has traditionally been the other way round: one must first establish relationships, and only then can we do business.

We'll be emphasizing this point over and over again throughout the book: In international business, to the degree the circumstances permit, *it is always preferable to go for the relationship, not the deal.* However, the way one goes about building relationships differs from culture to culture and, as we saw with our German friend, American openness and informality mean something different to the American than they do to the German. There are, then, two important issues for Americans to consider here when doing business across borders: the degree to which other cultures require relationships in order to do business and the way in which people in those cultures form relationships. In both cases, there can be real differences between their approach and the American's.

Let's begin then, with some self-assessment exercises that look at attitudinal differences regarding work, life, and relationships. What is the purpose of work? How does it fit into the larger world? How do you feel about friendships at work? What place does work have in your perception of the world? How are work relationships formed? Are they important to accomplishing your goals? How does all this play itself out at the international negotiating table? Once again, for each of the following scales below, indicate:

1. Where you think the American value would be by writing "A" at the approximate position
2. Where your personal value would be by writing the first letter of your name at the appropriate position
3. Where you believe the country you're interested in would be by writing the first letter of its name at the approximate position you believe best represents its value.

1. Importance of Personal Relationships in Business
Essential   *Unimportant*

1	2	3	4	5	6	7	8	9	10

2. Style of Friendship at Work
Reserved   *Outgoing*

1	2	3	4	5	6	7	8	9	10

3. Form of Relationships at Work
Functional relationships   *Human relationships*

1	2	3	4	5	6	7	8	9	10

4. Display of Feelings
Emotional   *Unemotional*

1	2	3	4	5	6	7	8	9	10

5. Personal Self at Work
Serious,   *Fun-loving,*
businesslike   *joking*

1	2	3	4	5	6	7	8	9	10

6. Pessimistic/Optimistic

Pessimistic   *Realistic*   *Optimistic*

1	2	3	4	5	6	7	8	9	10

7. Negotiating Style

Diplomatic, collaborative   *Debating, competitive*

1	2	3	4	5	6	7	8	9	10

8. Work Orientation

Quality conscious   *Quantity conscious*

1	2	3	4	5	6	7	8	9	10

9. Orientation to Life/Work

Work to live   *Live to work*

1	2	3	4	5	6	7	8	9	10

10. Responsibility

Self-deterministic   *Fatalistic*

1	2	3	4	5	6	7	8	9	10

Let's begin with a look at how differing perceptions in these important areas can affect international business.

For five years, Señor Gomez had been doing business successfully with his U.S. manufacturer, U.S. Fabrics, Inc. More specifically, he had been doing business with U.S. Fabrics' main Mexican representative, Charlie Moss. Each time Moss and Gomez would get together (which would be about four or five times a year), it was always as if old friends were meeting again for the first time. There would be much drinking, eating, and socializing. An outsider might almost wonder whether any business was being conducted at all, and yet Gomez always sent Moss back to his company in North Carolina with a big new order. How disorienting, then, for Gomez to learn one day, in a letter from U.S. Fabrics, that, in part because of Moss's success in Mexico and the company's need to beef up sales in a sagging Asian market, Moss was being reassigned to sales in the Pacific Rim region. The letter went on to say that Ms. Harris, a "promising new sales professional" from the Boston office, was going to become U.S. Fabrics' new representative for Mexico. Gomez met her once in Mexico City, but didn't feel comfortable about placing any orders right away. After seven months, U.S. Fabrics is still waiting for an order from Mexico.[10]

---

[10]ITAP, International contributed to this example.

In fact, this may not be the best example of how concepts of relationships can differ, because the American and the Mexican in this example were very much in sync with each other. However, Moss had learned over the course of five years how to do business with Mexico, and one of the key points he'd learned was to build a solid personal relationship with the individual he did business with. In the example above, the point is made that for five years Gomez had been doing business, not with U.S. Fabrics really, but with its representative, Charlie Moss. As a company, however, U.S. Fabrics does not see this. The company does not recognize that, in Mexico, the people you do business with may be more important than their company, that the quality of the personal relationship plays a vital role in the business relationship. In this example, it's the failure of the company's policy makers to consider cultural requirements that causes U.S. Fabrics to lose its Mexican business.

This is an example of a scenario that is played out over and over in business. If American businesspeople stay in the international arena long enough (or get a solid grounding in cross-cultural work before they begin), they learn the importance of building relationships, of developing the big picture, of committing not just to the immediate deal at the table, but rather, to a long-term, perhaps even lifetime and multigenerational, business relationship. The difficulty arises when they try to pass this information on to their organization back in the States. Too often, the management in the domestic organization, detached from the realities the foreign troops are facing, tend to administer, organize, and revamp as if the rest of the world were a chess board. Whenever someone new joins the team, management can tend to replace whole cadres of people and move things around without any consideration for the impact on the hard-fought-for relationships already established.

In the above example, someone in the domestic organization made a decision, based on misguided information or more likely on no information at all, to move someone who had spent years cultivating a successful business in Latin America to a thoroughly unrelated region. The logic, of course, is irrefutable. Moss was successful in one region, so let's turn him loose in another region requiring his skills. The mistake, of course, is twofold: Moss's skills may have worked in Latin America, but they may not work in Asia; and the personal relationship that Moss has carefully nurtured in Mexico has been the primary reason for his success. The home office has compounded the mistake by announcing this change via a faceless letter. In a society like Mexico's, where personal relationships are critical, such an announcement needs to be made face to face to those affected by it. Certainly Moss should have been the one to inform Gomez of this change in person.

Management has compounded its mistake still further. Again, based no doubt on the bloodless logic of the corporation, they are replacing Moss with someone they feel could benefit from the assignment in Mexico: a new, talented employee, needing the experience of working in an already established market—a young woman from New England.

The value we place on egalitarianism sometimes blinds Americans to the difficulties they may be creating for their associates from other cultures. There is, in fact, a lot to praise in'this kind of decision, for it represents a belief, among other things, in the equal treatment of men and women. On the other hand, one would hope that simple ignorance of the repercussions of such a decision is the real motivating factor here, and not the other way around. Knowing full well the problems a woman will face in doing business in Saudi Arabia, Japan, or Mexico should never be the reason for sending her there. The sad truth is that while such decisions may reflect a belief in the equality of men and women, they often result in women being treated very unequally. Making the decision to send a woman to Mexico or Japan or Saudi Arabia (or a Jew to Syria, or an African-American to South Africa, or a Hindu to Pakistan, etc., ad culturum!) must be made with everyone's eyes open. And any such decision must be made with full knowledge of the possible (and I stress the range here from highly probable to maybe occasional) difficulties it can create for all concerned.

In the case of Ms. Harris and Mr. Gomez—assuming that both represent extreme stereotypes of their regions—there could be no greater mismatch between traditional Anglo and Hispanic values. A hardworking, let's-get-down-to-business woman from New England trying to do business with a machismo, let's-get-to-know-each-other male from Mexico? It would be the stuff of a hit movie. In all fairness to both Mexico and the United States, however, we must emphasize that this example, based on an assumption of exaggerated type-casting, is offered only to make a point. In real life, U.S. Fabrics might well have been very successful with Ms. Harris had the announcement been made in person, and had Moss brought Ms. Harris along on his final trip and introduced her to Gomez himself.

We can see clearly from our example that business dealings in Mexico require the development and maintenance of personal relationships in order to be successful. This fact conflicts with the general American belief in getting straight down to business and only later, when business is finished, becoming friends if both parties want to. Most other cultures seem to require the establishment of a cordial personal relationships *before* getting down to business. On scale 1, then, I would place an "A" beginning at 7 and going upward, with an "M" for Mexico somewhere around 4 and going downward. Why any particular culture has this re-quirement can be answered by looking at its individual history. Why the United States is not relationship-oriented when it comes to business may be answered by looking at U.S. history.

The "Unimportance" of Relationship Building in American Business

In addition to values, such as egalitarianism and individualism, the age and geography of our country play a part in our minimizing relationship-building as a prerequisite to success in business. Compared, for example, to many other cultures, the United States is very young, and its lifetime has been during that moment in history that has seen the reign, not of kings and queens, but of technology and the mass society that results from technology. In combination with so many other aspects and values in its history, the U.S. business experience has primarily been one of the industrial, technological, and now informational revolutions. Technological advancement, whether in the twentieth-century form of computers and telecommunications, or in the nineteenth-century form of steel and machines, can obviate the need for human relationships by superseding them. In order to improve upon one's abilities (enabling speech, sight, or travel to extend over miles instead of feet and in seconds instead of years, etc.), it replaces the human with the technological. I might be able to pay my bills by computer today, but I am known only by my number. Or I might want to speak with someone thousands of miles away but can converse only with an automated answering system. Or I might desire to fix my car myself, but only my mechanic, trained to operate a diagnostic auto computer, has the skills to do what my car needs done.

The concern over the social benefits and price of such technology are the stuff of great debates, not to be repeated here. The point of raising this issue is to emphasize that technology has enabled us to do business by superseding the human relationship. In combination with (and, no doubt, in response to) the American values we have been looking at, such as efficiency and the need to make the most out of the time available, technology allows us to accomplish things faster and more efficiently than any combination of human beings can. If the best of human relationships can take us just so far in business, technology can take us further. (I no longer have to wait five days for the mail carrier to physically deliver the document you have sent me, since our fax machines can deliver it instantly.) Certainly, by superseding the human, we not only can improve on the best we mere mortals can do, but we can avoid the worst—misunderstandings, emotional interruptions, mistakes, errors, laziness, the whole gamut of human frailties that slow things down and muck up the works, despite our best intentions.

Much of U.S. history was one of filling a continent, of a rich and opportune land waiting to be populated, fed, put to work. Technology enabled that to happen: the railroads tied the coasts together, the machines kept people and things moving, kept the harvest on time, kept the lights on and the furnaces powered. Science was revered for its abilities to rise above human limits and provide for human concerns on a growing mass scale. In an egalitarian, competitive, individualist society, those who moved fastest with the best for the most and produced at the least cost were the most successful, and science and technology allowed for this. For much of U.S. history, business has relied on technology and science to provide the means for validating our values and our ways of life.

This is not the history of many other cultures. Older societies have histories, heritages, and traditions (hence, values) that reduce the recent technological developments of the last two hundred years to a mere 5 percent or 10 percent of their history. Most of their history is pretechnological, prenineteenth and twentieth century, and consequently, many of their attitudes and values predate those of modern America. These countries' values were based on preindustrial life, where "business" was not a rationalized endeavor providing for masses of people, but rather a day-to-day struggle for individual and community existence. In such a struggle, individuals relied on friends and family and protected themselves as best they could against foe and nature.

In the preindustrial world, work was based on human relationships: yourself, friends, family, and kin. Technology did not exist to enhance (or obviate) your involvement in your work; nor did the nature of work go beyond providing for yourself and your own. (Note: We are discussing pretechnology as if it were in the past, but only where the United States is concerned. Pretechnology is a condition that is quite a part of the here and now in much of the rest of the world today.) In pretechnological countries today and in countries that may now be going through the technological revolution, we must consider that the older values based solely on human relationships play a much greater role in business. While the content of business may be as up to date as the purchasing of computer chips, the form of the business transaction may be dictated by behavior based on values and traditions from a pretechnological time.

While we live in a high-tech world today, we are not far removed from the world of business based on human relationships. Indeed, a central thesis of this book is that in reaching out globally, Americans are rediscovering a kind of world they have left behind. Business in the international arena, for one, is more likely to be based on human relationships. However, the grandparents of first- and second-generation Americans and in all likelihood, the lives of immigrant Americans today are still oriented very much around human relationships, usually with immediate family and friends. Today's new Americans, in fact, shore up what have traditionally been known as "American family values," but what were, in fact, pretechnological values. They bring with them today a human relationship basis for work, social life, and traditions that will eventually be integrated into the posttechnological society currently being built. In order to succeed in the international business world where human relations are key, we need to rediscover and refine those human-relationship skills that new Americans, in concert with our grandparents, bring to this country today. We need only look to our new neighbors or remember our grandparents. Fortunately, it is not a difficult or unpleasant skill to master. But it takes practice and time.

Geography has also contributed to making Americans less dependent on human relationships to accomplish tasks. The size of the country is vast. It took a century to tame the wilderness, to decimate the existent native North American civilization, to go from the Atlantic to the Pacific. This tradition of the frontier, of always pushing on farther, of growth and change and newness, has had a profound effect on the American psyche. We will discuss many of the ways the frontier mentality has affected American business throughout this chapter. Here, however, I want to focus our attention on the specifically geographical aspects of this phenomenon.

Americans are perhaps the most mobile people on earth. The statistics say that, on average, Americans change homes every seven years. They change jobs. They make midlife career changes. They change spouses. They are relocated from one city to another. They have an ongoing love affair with personal, private transportation, the car, specifically because they are so mobile. Geography has cooperated with the values of individualism, change, egalitarianism, and independence to create an incredibly physically dynamic society. As individuals, we are devoted to activity, and as a society, we are devoted to movement. In such a world, it can be difficult to sustain deep, long-lasting relationships. If my job might take me to another city tomorrow, if my life might force me to pack up and move to the other side of the continent, if my car can open up new possibilities, if the media can make me aware of new opportunities elsewhere, and if I have the right to seek those opportunities, the energy, time, and inclination I have to invest in deep, committed relationships are reduced.

Americans are simply more comfortable, if not socially, then certainly in business, with casual relationships that do not require deep commitment. This is not to say that Americans do not appreciate such relationships. In fact, we decry the loss of them in our lives and constantly seek solace for the price we are willing to pay for our values. The society as a whole, however, appears to provide more opportunity for those able and willing to "stay loose," and the pressure to do so increases as the United States becomes more and more technological and more and more a mass society. As time becomes compressed, as technology moves things along at a faster and faster pace, mobility is increased, society becomes more and more complex, people tend to get more and more atomized, and there is less and less time and fewer resources available to invest in the development of long-term traditional personal relationships.

The American notion of relationship, then, can be quite different from the way other, more "relationship-oriented" cultures, view it. From the American's point of view, relationships are often casual, on the surface, easy to get into and out of. They often do not require a deep commitment. Americans do not have the time or necessarily the inclination to devote to the one-on-one learning about each other that is necessary in the formation of deep friendships. Americans, in their breezy in-and-out style, are very informal, very friendly. But we have difficulty becoming friends — friends, that is, as defined by cultures with opposite traditions, where deep, long-lasting relationships are required, and where, by necessity, they take time.

A Difference in Form as Well as Content

So we see a difference not only in the need for relationships, but in the way those relationships are built. Let's compare both aspects by looking at the following example of British-American business. It is important to emphasize again, here, that the degree to which differences exist, in any comparison, vary from country to country, from individual to individual, and from industry to industry; we are speaking of general tendencies formed by cultural values. In fact, the British can be as highly motivated by a good one-time business deal without the prerequisite of established personal relationships as the American; it is just that the tradition of personal relationships in business is more a part of the way business is done in Britain than it is in the United States. While the British would never walk away from a good opportunity at the negotiating table, they would tend, in general, to have a longer-term outlook, an outlook, in turn, ultimately dependent on the successful development of a close relationship between the individuals and the firms involved.

Tom Loftis, the expansive and outgoing leader of the American negotiating team, was now trying some of his famous humor to break through the wall put up by the British across the table. The Americans wanted to seem as friendly and warm as possible, since they heard that the British could be icily defiant in negotiations. However, this was the beginning of the first day of negotiations, and the Americans also wanted to open up with a tough position from which they would, of course, bargain. Therefore, they insisted on a close working relationship throughout the talks. Loftis immediately introduced his team by first names only. At the beginning of the conversation, in response to an inquiry by a member of the British team, he mentioned that this was his first business trip to London and that he would really like to see how the British live. In fact, he went on to suggest that they show him the town, and the next time they were in the States, they'd be invited over to his house for an old-fashioned American barbecue.

He anticipated that some of the initial U.S. demands would be rejected, but he assumed that the British, being cousins, so to speak, of the Americans, would understand that this was just the beginning of a bargaining process. He recalled a joke about Americans and English needing to work together since at least they spoke the same language, unlike the rest of Europe. Then he joked again about how the Americans didn't come to London to finish the revolution, just to negotiate a deal. Loftis continued a strategy of juggling jokes and friendliness with hard-nosed positions and demands. At one particularly tense point after lunch, Loftis suggested that everyone take a break and go out and play some football to relieve the pressure. Jason Peters, leader of the English team, responded: "We thank you for your suggestions. However, we will have to take your proposals back to HQ and review them there with the appropriate personnel."

While Americans may not require personal relationships, when they perceive or acknowledge the need for developing one, they go about building a relationship in their own particular American way: with informality, cheeriness, a playful disrespect for status and position, breezy hospitality, and an expectation that everyone will find this charming and hospitable. Should the relationship-building need to proceed further, this light and easy openness, however, becomes less and less inviting. In fact, as the American continues the relationship-building process, the seriousness of opening up on a deeper level and the commitment required for honest and true communication and sharing can become difficult, troublesome, or a game not worth the candle. As the friendship-building becomes more serious and committed and the American is expected to truly open up and share deeply, he or she is more and more likely to question the benefits of investing in such a cumbersome and sometimes difficult process. After all, there is so much to be gained by just keeping it "lite." Without going into a socio-psychological analysis of loneliness in America, suffice it to say that Americans in business, too, prefer for a whole variety of reasons to keep it easy and on the surface, and they seem to drag their feet when pressed into deeper personal relationships. It is for this reason that non-Americans, trying and failing to form relationships with Americans, often accuse us of being shallow.

From the perspective of the foreign national, and in this case let us use the West European as an example, Americans are embarrassingly easy to get to know, but very difficult to get close to. Not necessarily any more difficult to get close to than anyone else, however, for becoming friends with anyone takes time and commitment—two things that Americans may not be willing to make available for this activity. From the perspective of most foreign nationals (with the exception, perhaps, of Australians), the American is easy to penetrate, initially. The big smile, the informality, the warm handshake, all seem to invite you in, seem to say, "Let's be friends," "Let's get to know each other." West Europeans, delighted at this reception (although slightly perplexed as to why someone who doesn't know them should be so eager to be their friend), now expect to be able to get to know the American very well. They are inevitably disappointed when they push very hard toward the center of the American, and the walls come up.

Friendliness Versus Friendship

From the perspective of the American, friendliness is not an invitation to friendship, or even to a relationship of any real depth, although this might come in the future, once business has been established or is finished. Friendliness for the American is merely an expression of egalitarianism, a way to emphasize similarities, to dismiss time-wasting formalities, to clear the decks to enable us both to get down to the business at hand. In fact, Americans are often put off by what they see to be a distinct lack of friendliness on the part of Europeans. The Europeans are simply not as open at first. There is no equivalent emphasis on friendliness, although there is greater long-term emphasis on friendship. Europeans believe that in order to get to know each other, we need to take the time to pierce through the tough, protective outer shell. Once that shell is pierced, however, the European will often move much faster toward the center and will in turn allow movement much more quickly toward his or her center. In fact, this process of building relationships is diametrically opposite in Europeans and Americans. Europeans will expect to build a relationship based on the acknowledgment of differences, on respect for status, on deference to title. Americans want relationships based on equality and similarity. It is not coincidental that this parallels the major historical themes of both societies.

In the American-British negotiation scenario described earlier, the British were not amused. It is worth noting that humor, in general, does not translate well across language barriers, and this is true even from one English-speaking country to another. But in a deeper way, it isn't what the American said that was unfunny, but rather that the American's attempt to build rapport, establish a relationship, stood in direct contradiction to the British way of relationship-building. (It is ironic that this should be so often the case between Americans and other cultures, when it is in fact the other cultures that so often place a greater importance on establishing a relationship.)

The British, while perhaps anticipating, and maybe even being a bit charmed by, the American's informality, were also a bit put off and insulted by it. There was no acknowledgment by Tom Loftis, in his efforts to establish a rapport, of the status and position of his opposite numbers in a society where class is critical. The jokes were witless and egalitarian, vaguely insulting to British history and pride. And under the circumstances, Tom's efforts to create an aura of good feeling smacked of ingenuousness, for, from the British perspective, this was neither the place nor the time for direct relationship-building; the British do that, in a conscious way, at the club. The Americans, being egalitarian, open, and sharing, wanted to be invited to their homes and were willing to do the same when the British came to America. There was no acknowledgment on the part of the Americans of the European requirement for strict separation between home and professional life. The suggestion to go out and play American football in the middle of a business meeting was outrageous from the British point of view and revealed an American ignorance about the national sports of rugby and soccer in Britain. But perhaps most of all, the British were put-off by the direct, hardnosed straight-talking kind of bargaining tactics the Americans were using. "How could the Americans be serious about building a relationship when the next minute they were out to get as much as possible from us?" the British asked themselves. On scale 2, I would place the British closer to 2, and the Americans, in relation to the British, at 8 or 9.

Seeking Similarities Versus Emphasizing Differences

The American notion of establishing relationships based on what we have in common, what we share, what is similar, comes directly out of our egalitarian ethic and stands in contrast to the European notion of establishing relationships based on how we differ, which derives from their aristocratic, hierarchical ethic. This can be evident even in the kind of rapport-building communication both parties usually enter into at the beginning of a negotiation. In the case above, the American is seeking, and assuming, similarities of interests ranging from sightseeing to barbecues to football. As Americans, we often feel we can build a relationship more successfully with people we have something in common with. In fact, in more hierarchical societies, such as Western Europe, relationships, at least in business, are often based more on differences and whether there can be a mutual respect for the differences that stand between us.

The French are a good example, for from the American perspective, their insistence on emphasizing how we differ from them as opposed to how we might be similar is often taken as contentiousness. In fact, they build relationships by valuing a good tangle, a rich debate, a well-expressed difference. For them, similarities might be comfortable, but often boring. An American at his first business dinner in Paris complained afterward:

I tried everything to start up a friendly relationship. I'd heard how difficult the French could be, so I made every effort to put my best foot forward and to avoid saying anything that might annoy or offend them. But it seems nothing I did was right. From the start, I felt they were not trying to be friendly to me, although I was certainly making every effort. There was a certain coldness that I couldn't break through. And it only got worse. If I agreed with anything they said, they became arrogant, and pressed me to admit they were right. When I said anything even slightly contrary, they jumped on me and questioned me, almost grilling me. I felt I was being baited. By the end of the evening, despite all the smiles and good intentions, I was exhausted and angry, and I didn't feel like I'd accomplished anything in the way of establishing a closer relationship.

The American was trying to be friendly the American way: seeking similarities, looking for common interests, trying to smooth over differences. The French, however, were trying to become friends by admitting and respecting differences, by seeking interesting and differentiating points of view that would make the American stand out. If Americans value individualism, the French *individuate*. They will invite you into the ring to test and be tested; this is the way to establish a relationship. (More on this in Chapter 8.)

Display of Emotion

There is another aspect of American relationship-building that was highlighted in our British-American example above that we should mention here: the range of emotion displayed by the American. As compared to his British associates, the American was far more emotional; that is, he expressed his feelings along with his thoughts in a variety of ways, some of which were beyond the behavior usually considered appropriate in a business setting in Britain. Every society has its own implied rules regarding the range of emotional expression considered appropriate under different circumstances. During negotiations at an upper managerial level between individuals just getting to know each other, the range of emotional expression considered acceptable is greater for Americans than it is for the British. It is greater still for Latin Americans. For the Japanese and most Asians, it is more restricted than it is for the British. If the circumstances change, the range of emotional expression often changes, too. Once the British go out to the pubs, once the Japanese go out to the *karaoge* bars, then the range expands considerably.

It is important to note here that we are speaking of a range of emotional *expression*, not merely whether or not a particular society is emotional. All people experience the same feelings, some emphasized or deemphasized more than others, but we all feel basic human emotions. It is the *display* of these emotions, particularly in a business context as part of the relationship-building process, that can be considerably different. Americans unfamiliar with Asia in general and with Japan in particular often attribute a lack of what they perceive to be emotional expression in public as meaning that the Japanese are cold. A Japanese friend of mine once expressed great dismay to me, quite emotionally, that Americans do not understand the Japanese this way. "We are quite a passionate people," he said. "We are just not emotional."

Looked at from the Latin perspective, however, the overenthusiastic, back-slapping, emotional American suddenly becomes a chilly, reserved *Norte Americano*, a "dead corpse" with no color, no life. Latin Americans have often referred to *Norte Americanos* as cold, too serious in business, unable to loosen up and enjoy themselves. In the Latin business world, the range of emotional expression is considerably greater, and in contrast, therefore, we Americans seem limited in the emotions we have, and less expressive in the emotions we show. In general, Latins might permit the display of affection, warmth, anger, frustration, sadness, disappointment, and joy at the negotiating table to a greater degree than would be considered appropriate for Americans. Going in the other direction, Asians consider Americans much too free, in business settings, with such emotions as anger, frustration, disappointment, and friendliness.

Steve Reynolds, credit manager for a U.S. bank, was trying to get a word in edgewise at a meeting in São Paulo with the bank's Brazilian clients. The Brazilians were not happy that the bank was unwilling to renegotiate their outstanding debt. From Reynolds' point of view, the bank was already out on a limb with the Brazilian firm, an exporter of timber, and now they wanted to borrow another $3.5 million. His mind had been made up long before the meeting started, and now all he wanted to do was to get out of there. "Look," Reynolds tried to say, "the bank will have to review this request at the next regularly scheduled meeting of its Latin American investment group..."
The Brazilian firm's financial manager cut in abruptly and denounced this as just buying time, while the manager's assistant informed other members of the Brazilian team at the table that this meeting Reynolds was talking about wasn't scheduled for at least another six months. The press relations officer of the Brazilian firm simultaneously started reading aloud a press release he had prepared in case the meeting had turned out this way, while the press officer's assistant was also reading a list of the names of the various media the announcement was being sent out to. Reynolds was silent. He was the only one silent.

Not only is the range of permissible emotional expression different for Brazilians and Americans at the negotiating table, but the style of expression is also different. The American is attempting to provide rational information as a support for his feelings about lending the Brazilians more money. The Brazilians are expressing their feelings of anger at being put on hold and then providing rational information to support their emotions. The primacy of feeling over fact, or fact over feeling, varies from culture to culture and, in negotiations, can be a source of great confusion. Americans and Europeans tend to provide facts first. The next layer to be revealed is usually beliefs, attitudes, and values. As discussions continue and should more justifications or explanations be required, intuitive thoughts are revealed, and finally feelings may be expressed. In many Latin American, Arab, and African cultures, however, feelings constitute the first level of information provided in a negotiation, the next level being intuitive thoughts, and the next level, beliefs and values, with the revelation of facts saved for last. Clearly what is expressed first, and the order in which information is revealed, should have been considered by Reynolds when negotiating with his Brazilian associates in order for him to have been better prepared for what he was about to face at the meeting.

Additionally, the Brazilians' spectrum of emotions was displayed in a way many Americans (and, curiously, many Latins, as well) find disconcerting: everyone expressing their feelings all at once. This simultaneous style of speaking is tied in to the range of emotional display permitted and is directly related to different notions of time, as well, which were discussed in the last chapter. I asked a Venezuelan friend of mine if this particularly Latin way of communicating was confusing or frustrating for him. "Of course," was his reply. "But we feel that we must always fight to make our points, or else the other people will make theirs over yours, and then you are nowhere." Studies of various speech patterns have revealed wide variations from culture to culture. In the United States, for example, there may be some overlap between the individuals speaking, but, in general, one speaks, then another, then another. It is the result, perhaps, of egalitarianism — which ensures that everyone gets a turn, as long as everyone is equally willing to wait for it — and the result of a differing business pace. In Japan, one person speaks, there may be a pause, then a short acknowledgment, then another pause, then another speaks, then a pause, then a mutually expressed acknowledgment, then another pause, and so on. Such variations are tied up with the many values of the culture being examined. Suffice it to say that when attempting to build relationships at the negotiating table, the pattern of speech, the emotions permitted to be revealed, the degree to which they are revealed, and the order in which feelings, in contrast to thoughts and facts, are revealed, can be very different for Americans and their international associates.

Permissible and
Impermissible Emotions

Sally Marks, an American, was invited by a university to teach English in China for a year. This was the first time Sally had ever been to Asia, and she wanted very much for everything to go smoothly. She had always dreamed of going to China although she admitted that she did not know very much about the Chinese. But she was fascinated by the prospect and the opportunities it offered and eager to make this a rewarding experience. She was very excited the day she arrived in Beijing. She was met at the airport, as had been arranged, and taken to the university. On the drive from the airport, she was struck by how poor the country seemed to be, and once in Beijing, she was saddened that the city appeared less attractive, more run-down, than she had imagined. On the ride to the university, she was also informed that unfortunately, the room that had been arranged for her was not ready. Her hosts apologized for this and explained that temporary arrangements had been made for her behind the kitchen of the dormitory. Sally was concerned about this, since the living arrangements had been clearly outlined in her many preparations before the trip. However, she was going to be as understanding as she could and try to accommodate herself to the circumstances, not knowing her hosts' problems and in an effort to be a good guest. After all, they had invited her.

Several weeks went by, and there was no word about when Sally's room would be ready. Whenever she inquired, she was told that they were working on it and doing everything they could to get it ready as soon as possible. Several more weeks went by, and Sally was determined to resolve this problem, but not to appear upset. However, sleeping behind the kitchen was becoming an increasingly unpleasant lifestyle. Each time she inquired, however, she got the same answer. Finally, her frustration overtook her best intentions. Upon getting the same response to her questions, she finally expressed how disappointed she was, how hard it was for her to believe that they were really trying to treat her well, or even really caring for her well-being. She told them that she was angry, tired, very frustrated, and at the end of her rope. Several days later, she was asked to leave Beijing and was presented with the necessary papers to return to the States.[11]

In Asia, there is a distinct split between one's personal self and one's private self that minimizes the amount of emotion permitted to be displayed in public. It is considered immature to display emotion. One keeps one's thoughts and feelings to oneself. A display of anger is particularly destructive. One simply should not display anger in any form in Asia. Anger disturbs harmony, and the maintenance of harmony, primarily by avoiding confrontation, is perhaps the most fundamental value at the heart of most Asian (business and social) behavior. Sally, in

[11]From *Encountering the Chinese: A Guide for Americans* by Hu Wenzhong and Cornelius Grove, International Press, Yarmouth, Maine, 1991. Copyright 1991 Hu Wenzhong and Cornelius Grove. Used with permission.

the above example, violated this basic rule. It's not that she shouldn't have been upset, it's just that she should not have displayed it in anger. There is a difference between feeling something and acting on it, and nowhere is this distinction made more clearly than in Asia.

From the Chinese point of view, Sally accepted the living conditions and the situation as presented to her when she first arrived; she was, therefore, buying into the Chinese way of doing things. Since she did not insist on having the problem rectified when she first arrived, she was apparently choosing to avoid a confrontation. Why then, from the Chinese perspective, did she blow up? And why, *we* might well ask, was a room for her unavailable? Perhaps it was because of a lack of resources. (China is a developing nation, it has been said that China is actually a civilization in search of a nation. Just because as a civilization it has existed for 5000 years does not mean it is as advanced as a modern, industrialized nation.) Perhaps it was due to the usual complicated bureaucratic requirements. (China is a bureaucracy par excellence. Its history of dynastic rule from Beijing made the social ground fertile for the twentieth-century communist version of bureaucratic dominance over all aspects of people's lives, including where and when and how they live.) Perhaps it was simply the different notion of time in China. (Suffice it to say that "soon" or "as quickly as possible" have a very different meaning in a society that has been around for 5000 years.) But whatever the reason or combination of reasons, this is the way things are done in China, and in dealing with it, the one thing you don't want to do is *express* your anger and frustration over it. The Chinese, in this case, were insulted at Sally's behavior, probably lost a great deal of respect for her (which called into question, no doubt, her qualifications for the job), and, most importantly, could do very little else but send her home given the loss of face they had suffered from her public outburst about being mistreated by them.

Doing Business in Asia Equals
Building Relationships

Wa in Japanese means "harmony." It is the value one must be most concerned with when doing business in Japan. One's behavior is judged according to whether or not it promotes *wa*. Negotiations, therefore, are opportunities, first and foremost, not for making decisions (a very American idea) but for building relationships based on such principles of harmony as mutual understanding, mutual respect for each other's needs and positions, and mutual appreciation for each other and each other's firms. It is an opportunity for mutual probing, politely and with respect, to locate those areas where mutual needs meet and for ways in which both parties can satisfy each other's needs. This is why Japanese negotiations often take the form of questions and answers: they are venues for the gathering of information about the deal at hand, about the venture that both sides are considering entering into.

More important, until solid relationships are established, this information gathering is an attempt to find out as much as possible about the negotiating team on the other side of the table and about its firm, in an effort to know how close the "fit" can be, how each can help the other, if and how *wa* can be established. For the Japanese (and for many other Asians) negotiation is an exploration undertaken to determine whether or not the other side can be a trustworthy business *partner*. In this sense, *wa*, as a value, requires that the negotiation be a collaborative process of learning about each other, establishing a balanced harmony, and finding ways in which mutual needs can be satisfied. The resulting deal is simply one expression of the newly formed relationship, based on *wa*. The relationship, in fact, stands above the actual, immediate deal. And ideally, the deal is expected to be just the first of many deals, each one reinforcing and maintaining the larger harmonious business relationship. Negotiating in Japan is a relationship-building process, first and foremost.

Once the initial relationship has been established, subsequent negotiations are usually easier, and each deal becomes an opportunity to validate the harmonious, mutually satisfactory partnership. Each new negotiation becomes an opportunity for each party to prove its value and worth to the other and to deepen their mutual respect. Should trust break down, should *wa* become unbalanced, should either party ever not return the respect and favor of the other or do anything to cause harm or loss of face to the other, the relationship will be seriously jeopardized, and future negotiations will be difficult. Building this kind of relationship takes time, patience, and effort. But well maintained, it can last a business lifetime. And, more important, it is what the Japanese look for in order to do business, both with each other and with other nationalities.

The importance of *wa* as a fundamental value for building relationships cannot be overemphasized in Asia. A well-balanced relationship does not imply passivity; rather, it requires trust and an ability to work very closely together in order to constantly reestablish balance in the face of inevitable change. Nor does *wa* imply an absence of competition. As we know, Japan and the other dragons of Asia (Taiwan, Korea, Singapore, Hong Kong) are highly competitive. Rather, a relationship based on *wa* means that we both will get as much as we can from each other without harming each other. *Wa* establishes a larger context in which competition and dynamic business can take place; it provides the rules of the game.

The Importance of Harmony

The importance of *wa* and its effect on the way people relate to each other, especially in comparison with the West, is brought home strikingly to me as I think about the 1984 Olympics in Los Angeles and the 1988 Olympics in Seoul, Korea. Both were highly competitive sports events. As is certainly the case in the United States, sports events provide many parallel metaphors for business. So it was particularly interesting to see how the two different venues gave the concepts of "competition" and "winning" two completely different contexts, one Western and the other Eastern. The contexts mirrored, not merely Korea or the United States as societies, but quite specifically, the differences in the way relationships are built at the negotiation table in the East and in the West. At both Olympics, the crowds in the stands were provided with placards that they would flip over at specified times. When the cards were flipped over, they spelled out a message. In Los Angeles, the cards usually spelled out the name of a particular country in competition; in Seoul, when the crowd flipped the cards over, it spelled out, in English, H-A-R-M-O-N-Y. I think that the two different messages accurately reflected deep cultural values. In L.A., the competition was being conducted within a larger context of such values as egalitarianism (may the best country win, everyone has an equal chance, etc.), individualism (different names for different competitors), objective rules (relationships between players are not important; rather, observance and acceptance of overarching rules as they apply individually are). In Seoul, the competition was being carried out within the larger framework of harmony, a framework that emphasized the importance of the larger Olympic goals as one group venture, rather than the individuals' goals as ends in themselves. The two different messages are part and parcel of the underlying values that guide business dealings in the East and in the West.

Too many Americans have gone to Japan ill-prepared with information about themselves and the Japanese. And too many have shown themselves unwilling to make the kind of long-term, time and money commitment to relationship-building that's ultimately required in order to succeed with the Japanese. Many Americans get sidetracked by the questioning to which they are usually subjected when beginning negotiations with the Japanese. In the Americans' haste to get the bottom line signed, sealed, and delivered, they miss what the Japanese see as the whole point of the negotiation. Especially at the beginning of a new relationship, the Japanese concern is not necessarily the deal on the table, but rather the gathering of as much information as possible about the people on the other side of the table in order to decide whether or not they feel comfortable about entering into a business relationship with them.

Additionally, because the Japanese are generally more conservative in risk taking than Americans (again, based on certain value differences which we will discuss shortly), their need for information is much greater in order to come to a decision about whether or not to do business with Americans. This is why Americans often feel as if they are being grilled by the Japanese at a negotiation. The Japanese need lots and lots of information (not only because of their general conservatism, but also because there are usually many more people involved in the decision-making process, and there must be enough information to satisfy all the decision makers). In order to develop a sense of trust they will, very politely but very energetically, pump you for as much information as possible, while being hesitant to reveal much about themselves at first. Often we Americans don't ask for information — either because we have less of a need for information in order to make a decision, or because we do not know how to ask the Japanese for the kind of information we want. So the information-gathering stage seems one-sided. Once some trust is established, however and the Japanese begin feeling comfortable with the Americans, they are usually very willing to provide any appropriate information to the Americans because, at this point, they have decided to move a little closer toward building that all-important relationship.

It is very important for Americans, then, when planning for a negotiation with the Japanese, to come prepared with as much information as is appropriate about the company and the business at hand and to understand that the point of the negotiation, in the Japanese view, is not to make a deal, but rather to begin an exploratory process of discovering whether or not the two of you can be trustworthy business partners over the long haul. If you're not prepared to invest time and money in this relationship-building process, it will be difficult to do business in Japan.

Information as Proof of Relationship

It is important to make the point here about distinguishing between what information is appropriate to divulge to the Japanese and what is not. From the American side, since we generally require less information to make a decision, it usually appears to us that the Japanese are asking for a whole lot more information than they really need. Certainly, depending on the stage of the negotiation, there are decisions to be made about divulging certain types and amounts of information. This is why trust is so important. If you think the Japanese are asking for more than they need, they probably are—but only if you're thinking what their needs would be if they were Americans. But that's just the point: they're not, they're Japanese, and, for the reasons outlined above, they require more information than we do in order to make their decisions.

As Americans, this might make us feel uncomfortable, but that's because we're attributing certain meanings to their need for so much information. As Americans, we look with some suspicion on someone asking so many probing questions. However, it's important to avoid attributing our meanings to others' behavior, so unless you're being asked to divulge proprietary information that needs to remain proprietary or have additional information that substantiates your concern, you should consider the Japanese requirements and provide the additional information whenever possible.

Given what we've been saying about the display of feelings and relationship-building, if we were measuring Japan and the United States, on scale 4 I would place the States at 4 or 5, with Japan at 8 or 9. However, if we were measuring the United States and Brazil, I would put the States at 8 or 9, and Brazil at 2 or 3. If we wanted to compare all three cultures, I would put the States around 5 or 6, with Brazil at 1 or 2, and Japan at 8 or 9. In fact, Gary Weiderspahn, a cross-cultural researcher, conducted a study* wherein a survey of Taiwanese and Mexicans asked each group to rate certain American characteristics. In the categories reported, the Taiwanese and Mexicans saw Americans as complete opposites, for from their respective points of view, Americans were quite different. The Mexicans, for example, saw Americans as reserved and unemotional, while the Taiwanese saw us as emotional, friendly, and outgoing. Truth is in the eye of the beholder. (Additionally, on scale 7, in relation to Japan, the United States would be closer to 6 or 7, and Japan would be closer to 3 or 4.)

Bargaining as Relationship Building

I was involved in helping several local government phone companies in the South Asia region improve their service, build better

*Gary Weiderspahn, *The Bridge* (summer 1981).

customer relations, etc. One of my tasks, really, was also to help
them collect on overdue phone bills, which were a critical problem
since people simply didn't pay on time and would complain bitterly
when their service was shut off. They truly did not understand
why the phone company would do that to them. In one area where
I worked for a few months, we were able to solve the problem by
simply expanding the size of the office and office hours and
changing the ambience of our offices. Now it wasn't that the office
couldn't accommodate the customers, it was just that the company
was trying to sell the idea of paying the bill by mail and had
reduced the public access to the office. However, it turned out that
people were not used to paying bills by mail, did not trust it, did not
understand that they could perform transactions without having to
go down to the office in person.

No matter how hard we tried to emphasize the convenience of
paying by mail or the importance of paying on time, people insisted
on coming in person to pay their bills. They would spend time in
the office, they would meet other people there, there would be
much discussion. It turned out that the office was an important
public meeting place in their lives, and people simply insisted
on taking care of their payment this way in order to meet and catch
up with each other. The most curious aspect was the fact that
customers would come in and try to *negotiate* their phone bill. They
would try to engage the office personnel in negotiations over the
size of the bill, when calls were made, the length of calls, the
legitimacy of the charges, etc. At first I was shocked. Then I came
to realize that the negotiation, too, was a way of connecting, face to
face, in order to be able to pay their bill.

It is true that in many countries people are unused to technology and
therefore unwilling to trust in it. It is also true that people in poorer
countries are hesitant to spend money on postage when bills can be
paid, and possibly negotiated, with cash in person. However, the point
here is that *in addition to* these reasons, the face-to-face bargaining was
an important cultural requirement for people — even for those sophisticated and well-off enough to own telephones and pay for them by
mail — in order for them to establish and maintain relationships. A similar story was recounted by an American recently expatriated to a Caribbean island nation to do consulting for the local phone company
there:

The phone company was trying all sorts of marketing campaigns to
get the populace to sign up for long-distance services. Nothing the
company tried seemed to work. Direct mail, bill stuffers, ads on
radio and TV announcing the new service — none of it generated
significant sign-ups. However, when the company started opening
up minibooths at key junctions, such as on a corner in downtown or

at the crossroads of two main highways outside of town, people started signing up. So they started advertising the minibooths on radio and TV instead of the service itself. The booths became meeting places. People congregated there and could ask face-to-face questions about the service. The phone company, in its determination to be high-tech, to move into the modern world, had overlooked the fact that these people, many of whom could not read, were interested in the service only if it could be explained to them by friendly, helpful assistants, people whom they often already knew as neighbors, relatives, or friends. The booths also served as places where people could meet and socialize, giving added value to the phone company in the eyes of these customers.

These may be exaggerated examples of some cultures' needs for the involvement of human relationships in business, but I suggest that they are perhaps more exotic than exaggerated. Only in comparison with the extremely rationalized Western approach do they perhaps seem extreme.

In both of the above cases, individuals required the creation of human relations in order to conduct their business, and they could not conduct their business unless and until such conditions were met. The notion of negotiating a phone bill might seem odd in rationalized modern Western society, but it is an attempt to establish the all-important human relationship in order to be able to conduct business. In fact, bargaining, that stage in the negotiation where we attempt to compromise and find a middle ground over an issue at hand, isn't always the cut-and-dried process of settling for something mutually expedient. Sometimes underneath the back-and-forth lies the greater need for trust, for getting to know the other person, for taking the time necessary in order to develop some form of personal relationship.

In traditional Arab culture, the bargaining, the haggling, the give-and-take, whether at the souk or the negotiating table, serves many functions, not the least being the opportunity for both sides to get to know each other as individuals. Both parties are saying many things to each other: that I respect your needs, but I expect you to make certain adjustments in order to respect mine; that I need to know who you are as a person in order to do business with you and will make judgments based on your response to what I say and do. The bargaining is often conducted with much entertaining and serving of refreshments, in a setting where both parties take the necessary time to learn about each other, their backgrounds, their activities. Their respective status, family, and friends are also revealed through the other interactions that can often occur at the same time that the bargaining is going on.

Traditional Arab society was a culture of tradesmen and merchants acting as brokers and middlemen at the crossroads of trade between East and West. For Arab and European trader alike in pretechnological times, success in crossing the vast and often harsh land they served meant having the resources (people, connections, and power) necessary to obtain vital assistance, protection, water, and supplies. The core of the culture became reliance on and honor of the family, hospitality, reputation, and pride.

The value placed on an individual's honor, reputation, word, and commitment holds a very high place in Arab culture, for in the past, the lack of such personal characteristics could literally mean the difference between life and death in crossing Arab lands. Not only were distances great between water sources, but under such conditions, no overarching enforcement of generalized rules and regulations was possible. For centuries, in this sense, Arabia was comparable to the Wild West of nineteenth-century America. Those with power in a particular area needed to be respected, have tribute paid to them, have honor bestowed on them, in return for the privilege of safe passage, locating the next safe oasis, getting the supplies and information necessary to continue in the right direction. For centuries, individual human attributes determined, in a very direct and profound way, the business interactions between Arab and Arab and between Arab and non-Arab. In today's Arab culture, such centuries-old traditions still play out in the modern, posttechnological world, a new world not yet fully integrated into the world of the past. Bargaining is a negotiation metaphor for the significant need for human relationships and opportunities to demonstrate friendship and honor when negotiating in the Arab world.

The Relationship Imperative in the Face of Technology

Americans then, will need to rely more heavily on their interpersonal communication skills in international business than they probably do domestically. Certainly "whom you know," "connections," and "networking" are crucial in the domestic environment, and perhaps—even in the United States—these are ultimately the true determinants of long-term business. In this sense, we are not very different from the rest of the world. However, there is a certain reliance at first on technology, on the ability to conduct effective business impersonally, in the United States that still does not exist in much of the rest of the world. We must not let our enthusiasm for technological efficiency dull our interpersonal skills, for it will be some time—if ever—before the rest of the world adopts our reverence for nonpersonal, technology-based deal making. There are simply too many values deeply embedded in other cultures that militate against this style of business being embraced as fully as it is in America today. And we do not have to look only to more traditional cultures to see this difference at work.

I am reminded of the research I was conducting recently in preparation for a cross-cultural communication program I was planning between American and French managers for a large U.S. multinational. I was asking questions of the French managers as to what their major concerns were when doing business with their American counterparts. I was surprised to learn from more than two-thirds of them that what irritated them most about doing business with Americans were the answering machines they always had to leave their messages on. One after the other, they complained bitterly about how they hated to talk to a machine, how disagreeable it was for them to call the States, only to be asked to press a series of numbers in order to get to a department where they could leave their message. They were all, every single one of them, united in their belief that, rather than making communication more efficient, such answering systems were used as an excuse by Americans not to answer their phones and to avoid contact. For the French, it made work cumbersome. It was difficult for any of the complainers to understand how people talking to machines could promote better communications.

Of course, this is not to say that answering systems do not exist in Europe. Of course they do, and they will increase in use to a point where I am sure there will eventually be little difference between Europe and the United States in regard to the use of automated answering systems at work. Nor do many Americans find this latest technological wizardry perfectly satisfying. Many find it annoying. But at bottom, the elimination of the human factor is not decried in the United States as a price to be paid in order to do business. Americans are simply neutral on this issue, while Europeans see the human relationship element as a positive, if not downright necessary, factor in accomplishing the business at hand.

The fax machine, for example, has revolutionized the speed and efficiency of business; however, we see a greater acceptance of this device throughout the world's cultures because the fax machine achieves its goals without eliminating or interfering with human relationships. This is not the case with telephone answering systems. Americans in general calmly accept the replacement in business of the human relationships by technology. Many other cultures, however, are particularly sensitive to this development and recoil from it.

We have been emphasizing the need at the negotiating table and at work, for personal relationships around the world and the variety of ways in which this need is expressed, emotional expression being just one. It is easy for Americans to recognize such a need when it is as openly expressed as it is, say in Latin America. It can be more difficult to recognize when its expression is guarded, as it is in Asia, or when the need for such a relationship is hidden behind a facade of formality, as in Western Europe. In these cases, Americans have difficulty recognizing such a need because it is expressed differently from the way Americans might express such a need. To make matters worse, we simply do not *have* such a need and often, therefore, have difficulty responding to it—let alone recognizing it—in all its various forms. This is a wonderful example of the selecting-out process and the attribution processes at work. Western Europe, as we have seen, can especially trip us up, for the formality and seriousness with which business is approached there can appear to Americans to be a form of valuing efficiency above all else. We have examined examples of the way Americans can be in conflict over just such an issue in Britain and France. Germany provides another good example.

Formality and Relationship Building

In Germany, we see the expression of emotion in business as having all the color, spice, and variety of the most conservative Japanese, yet (as with the Japanese), the Germans too require personal relationships for long-term business. Because they also typically have a longer-term view of business associations than Americans do, their need for personal relationships is greater, even though they are less emotionally expressive in business than Americans are. (It appears there is a relationship between long-term expectations of a business association and the need for a parallel personal relationship. As a corollary, when the expected term of a business relationship is shortened, so the need for—and of course the opportunity for—a personal relationship is also diminished.)

Americans tend to attribute to Germans even less of a need for personal relationships in business than they themselves have because they see only the Germans' emphasis on task and their less emotional behavior. In fact, because the human relationship is necessary for long-term associations in Germany and is not dependent on emotional expression at work, it is unseen from the American point of view. (The American point of view requires more emotional expression and a shorter-term view of work.) Americans would be wise to anticipate a serious, thorough, and unemotional approach to work when negotiating with the Germans: they will be prompt, prepared, and prescribing, for they have done their homework thoroughly—both on you and on the business at hand. However, Americans would be wrong to assume that the Germans are uninterested in building a long-term relationship. Much like the Japanese, the Germans will be judging the Americans as business partners for the long term. However, the judgments will be made according to the German world view and German values — not on emotional expressiveness, but rather on the basis of qualifications, power, and authority. (There will be more on German values in Chapter 8.)

On scale 6, the Germans might place themselves at 2 or 3 and place the American at 7 or 8; if they were measuring the Mexicans, they might place them at 8 to 10. The Taiwanese might put the American at 9 or 10, while the Mexican would place the American at 2 or 3. Once again, it all depends on who is doing the judging, what values they hold, and the degree to which they attribute these values to the business behavior of the other culture.

An American director of marketing for a U.S. multinational provides us with the following experience:

We were trying to develop a European-wide marketing strategy. It was to be a comprehensive strategy for dealing with sales within the European region (we have manufacturing and sales sites in five major European countries) as well as between the European offices and other worldwide regions of our company. There were many points to consider in developing such a strategy, and we had had one all-European manager's conference already. At the last meeting, each European office had agreed to prepare a report on its present marketing plans to be given at the next meeting. The purpose of these reports was to clarify each country's marketing goals, strategies, and activities for the others. The hope was to be able to leave the meeting with an idea of where each country saw the company needed to go in order to synthesize the goals into a pan-European strategy we could all agree on. Now we were all together at the next meeting, and I was eager to hear the reports. Since Germany was our largest European office, we were sure that the Germans' report would be critical. They had, as we expected, outlined a very comprehensive and detailed analysis of the European situation from their perspective and went on to present a thoroughly researched plan of action.

What we did not expect was the dogmatic inflexibility of the Germans about considering any other plan if it did not meet the terms and criteria of theirs. At every turn, once all the plans were presented, the Germans were adamant that anything that disagreed with what they were saying was flawed, biased, unworkable, etc. It was as if, once they had determined their plan, their minds were closed to the possibility of anything else, and that was directly in conflict with the whole purpose of the conference as far as I was concerned. The concept was an airing and sharing of views, at least from my point of view. I learned too late that, for the Germans, it was an opportunity to present their way as the prescribed way.

Worse still, each time there was discussion over the points being made by others, the Germans would say things like, "You are wrong," "You will do it this way," "There is only one answer to this question," etc. Frankly, just hearing them speak this way made me see red. Nobody ever tells *me* what to do. I don't know if anyone else in the room was as upset over this as I was, and I had a hard time controlling my anger. Boy, that really pressed my buttons.

This is a misreading by an American of German communication style (i.e., emotional expression, or the lack of it) in comparison with American expectations. Communication styles can be a particularly sensitive issue for extremely informal Americans. In addition, we see here an example of a classic German/American cross-cultural misunderstanding: American individualism coming in conflict with the German need for authority, directness, and organization. For the German, there is nothing inherently disrespectful, abrasive, or incorrect about stating facts as givens: "You will do it this way," "You are wrong." From the German point of view, if there is a clearly prescribed method that you need to follow and if you are not doing something correctly, there is no room for qualifications: they call it as they see it. For Americans, such statements might be true (i.e., they might, in fact, be doing something incorrectly), but first they will react to the *way* the statement is made. If it sounds like a challenge to their authority as individuals to make their own decisions, they will take it as an affront.

It is interesting that Americans hear first a challenge to their individualism and only then, secondarily, a factual statement. They may even go so far as to admit that the Germans are right but will still insist that they should not have prescribed or commanded in the way they did. Americans are supersensitive, because of their extreme individualism, to the blunt and direct German way of stating a fact. Americans, making the same statement, would be more likely to employ qualifications like "There is another way to look at this," "I see your point, but this is how I see it," etc., acknowledging individual variances. German directness and seriousness in business, along with a lack of emotional expressiveness, are interpreted through the American value filter as cold, authoritative, self-important, and challenging. If the American director in the above example had been more aware of the classic cross-cultural German-American interaction he was finding himself in, his buttons might not have been pressed so hard.

Additionally, there is a difference in the way organization, a priority for both Germans and Americans, is expressed and achieved. For Americans, organization is achieved through the relatively free expression of individuals working together as a team to accomplish a task. For

Germans, organization is achieved by the agreed-upon exercise of authority by some individuals over others. The American was frustrated that the German did not want to be a "team player" in the development of European-wide goals with the other Europeans. In fact, the Germans, after careful consideration, concluded that their own way was the most effective, and therefore saw a clear legitimacy in attempting to prescribe this decision for the others. Organization meant doing it the German way, but to the American, this smacked of authoritarianism and riding roughshod over individual rights. For the Americans, this called up the mythic power of the individual, the pioneer. Our culture has a strong tradition of rooting for the underdog and the powerless, against their oppressors, as long as the underdog and the powerless fight fiercely for what they individually believe in. In Germany, the underdog, the powerless, are not necessarily admired; they might instead be pitied.

Human Relationships in Inhuman Systems

We have seen how the need for human relationships can powerfully affect business relations in various important countries. I'd like to note here that this is particularly true in those countries where there is an oppressive system imposed from above. In many places—from the countries of Eastern Europe, the former Soviet Union and the People's Republic of China, to many African and some Latin American nations—the structures of government have been so oppressive, inefficient, dysfunctional, and self-serving that they have clearly inhibited the day-to-day lives of the people, as opposed to enhancing them. In these circumstances, people's goals are to carry on, in business and in life, despite the obstacles imposed from above. In effect, there develops both a formal and an informal way of doing business. As mentioned in our discussions of egalitarianism, people learn to rely heavily, if not primarily, on the informal human relations they can establish (friends, family, community connections) and not on the system that fails and oppresses them while ostensibly existing to serve them.

I was recently conducting a communications training seminar in Budapest, Hungary, and was introduced to an associate's friend. I learned that this man could help me locate some local art. I found this surprising since I had only incidentally mentioned to my associate, almost in passing, that I was interested in Eastern European art. Suddenly, here was someone before me who was ready, willing, and able to help me buy some art. Of course, there would be a fee involved. Of course, I was sure he was going to steer me to those objects and paintings in which he already had an interest in some form. But that was to be expected. Unrequested assistance is common as a way of soliciting work in many societies.

What I found unusual here was the style in which this was occurring. This helpful gentleman kept showing up unannounced at various times with suggestions, offers to take me to see important pieces, offers to go out for drinks, and so forth. I became aware of my own reaction: at first, I was annoyed at this kind of solicitation, especially annoyed at having him show up to speak with me without appointments, without a previous acknowledgment of my availability. As I stayed on in Budapest, however, I came to understand that it was just such unannounced human contacts that made things work. The *system* didn't work. The usual ways of getting things done did not work. Things only happened when one could rely on another person. From the American perspective, I felt put upon, intruded on, obliged to have to accommodate my schedule to his. During·the training session, for example, he would show up at lunchtime without any prior notice, fully expecting to be able to speak with me and hoping to drive off somewhere for an hour to show me yet another find of his.

But from the Hungarian perspective, the human relationship established between two people looking to do business with each other was the key to the business: telephones, appointments, planning, were all unreliable or useless in the face of a system that was breaking down. The only thing one could count on was the human contact that could be established in order to make things work. I began to learn that nothing on the outside, nothing stated, nothing from above, was to be taken as fact, counted on, or even considered in the process of getting things done. What made the wheels go round each day were the one-on-one human moments, the favor one could ask for, the help one could get, the information one could in turn pass on. These human relationships, sometimes formed quietly and surreptitiously, were what put bread on the table, what gave life some real meaning. I came to welcome such moments, for they became the only thing that was real and alive; everything else was false and useless. A few weeks later, by the end of my stay in Budapest, I no longer resented what I had first seen as unpredictable intrusions, thoughtless selfishness, impossible self-importance. Now I welcomed it all as the breath of life itself.

The challenge for the American businessperson in Eastern Europe is to understand that the people there, after a generation of living this way, expect to have to do things around and in spite of a system or predetermined way, that includes forms, regulations, clocks, procedures — anything that precludes one-on-one human relationships. It is perhaps one of the most extreme examples of the need for establishing a personal relationship in order to do business I can think of. For a long time there, *nothing* has happened without it.

I recall speaking about this with my associate one evening over some brandy. He was able to distinguish, very clearly, the "old way" of doing business from the "new way." He said the old way was having to rely on family, friends, contacts, connections, in order to get anything done. He said the new way was being able to deal with a system that hopefully provided the things you needed, a system that worked. Since such a system in his experience had never worked and could never be trusted, he doubted if it really works anywhere. His experience was that you cannot make a system work for you. You learn to avoid it, go around it, and count on your friends to make things happen for you. This, he said, he knew how to do. This he was comfortable with; he did not like the new way, and frankly doubted whether it would ever succeed.

This, in fact, might be the most serious issue in Eastern and Central Europe today. The one-on-one approach that everyone once relied on has been shaken; the authority-from-above system that, in its previous incarnation, was surely uncertain and illegitimate is now, in its new form, to be considered dependable. Americans, on the other hand, have learned to believe in the system, to make it work for them. They trust in it as a dependable way to get from here to there; it is designed to dispense, to more or less acceptable degrees, equal opportunity and justice for all. In Eastern Europe, Americans are working with people who do not trust the system but depend only on what they can do as individuals for each other *in spite of it*. Procedures, plans, strategies, are all questionable. Personal commitments are the only things that count. On scale 10, pre-1989 Eastern European governments might have listed themselves at 2 or 3; in fact, I suspect the people would have listed themselves at 8 or 9.

Where There's a Will, There's a Way

If personal relationships are a major consideration in international business, their importance, style, and form are reflections of the even deeper attitudes and values that make up a culture's world view. The attitude that we as Americans have toward work in relation to life can be similar or different from that of other cultures and affects our ability to do business with them. When we discuss such issues as our attitude toward private time, the separation of personal and professional life, the importance of personal relationships, the degree to which we take risks, the degree to which we believe we can control the outcome of our efforts, we are inevitably also discussing the values we hold about life and work. As with all aspects of culture and work, we cannot look at an aspect of work as the result of one value only, but rather as the result of the interaction of all the values and attitudes in our particular culture. What shape does work take in our lives? Do we work to live or live to work? Do we emphasize quality or quantity? Are we a marketing or technical work culture? And why are we these ways? Answers to these questions and others can be found by examining the values that shape our general view of the relationship between life and work.

Central to American work values is the belief that if you want to do something badly enough, you can. Underlying this notion is an implied faith in hard work and the freedom to dare, a respect for the individual who does, and a belief in the ability of the individual to exercise significant control over his or her destiny. As we have seen, these are not universal givens. There are many other cultures that do not share these values, whose histories have given them quite different world views. We have looked at the aspect of individualism; let's look now at the American world view of fate and hard work, two other essential values that affect how we conduct business with the rest of the world.

American "Can-Do"

I was conducting a training program recently on negotiating with Americans for international businesspeople looking to export into the United States. I particularly remember Ahmed, the Jordanian because, in everything he said and did, he appeared more like the stereotypical American wheeler-dealer than any American I had ever met. He said he'd had several businesses in his young life already, most of them export businesses, and that he'd dealt a lot with Americans. He admitted that he liked Americans, that he just "knew how to speak with them." He also added that he does a lot of business with West European countries and that he doesn't have too many problems with them, either. His recent venture was trying to export a product natural to his country as a cosmetic for women; he was sure it would have great appeal for Americans, and he said he was already getting a good response from Europe. But, he revealed at one point, one American he had been negotiating with recently was giving him problems.

Ahmed said that he'd had a few conversations with this American and he could not get him to talk price. Ahmed said he was very frustrated and at first thought the American really wasn't interested in negotiating a deal. But then, several days later, the American called Ahmed, and the negotiations were on again. But then again, once they started talking, Ahmed said he had the feeling that the American was backing away from bargaining about the price. In fact, Ahmed recalled, what the American seemed most interested in talking about was the quality of the product. Ahmed said he could appreciate this concern but that he had already more than answered all the questions about quality in their first conversation. In fact, Ahmed said, he felt hurt that the American kept questioning him about the quality of the product. The American's insistence on going over this quality issue so many times made Ahmed suspicious that maybe the American was going to try to use this as a bargaining chip to lower the price, and this would certainly have been very insulting.

There was an additional problem, Ahmed went on. The American was also pressuring him for information on delivery quantity and dates. It was as if the American, Ahmed said, wanted to know everything about the shipments for the next two years, even though the first order hadn't even been placed yet. Ahmed said he found this made him feel very uncomfortable, because how could anyone expect answers to these kinds of questions? As strange as the American's behavior appeared to Ahmed, he was still having conversations with him, even though it was now almost two months since the initial contact had been made. Ahmed was feeling frustrated at the state of the talks, since, even with all the energy both sides were putting into the negotiation, he was still not sure that it was going to be fruitful. "What's the problem with this American?" this expert on Americans asked me. "Do you have any ideas?" "Do you have any thoughts for Ahmed?" I in turn asked the other participants in the group.

After some conversation, the group decided that there were some very major cultural communication problems between Ahmed and his American associate, despite the fact that Ahmed felt he was so U.S.-savvy. I agreed that there was a very real possibility that this American was not an anomaly and that some serious conflicts in values were driving the two very different sets of needs at the negotiating table.

Ahmed had not experienced resistance before in Americans to his bargaining over price, and this had probably conditioned him to expect to meet little resistance this time as well. In fact, Americans can be bargainers, too, although the tradition of bargaining is not as deep or multifaceted for the American as it is for the Arab. Since Ahmed himself was probably tempered by his past experiences with Americans, I suspect he had learned how to adjust his bargaining style so that Americans generally found it agreeable. And the aggressiveness of Americans probably did fit with Ahmed's personality, so that he expected Americans to perceive his entrepreneurial, aggressive spirit as positive, too.

It's not that this American was unwilling to bargain; rather, it was that Ahmed's view of the negotiation was primarily as an occasion to bargain over price, while this particular American was apparently interested in other things first. And one of the things he was apparently most interested in was the quality of Ahmed's merchandise. This concern, expressed over and over by the American, was insulting to Ahmed because it implied that the relationship he thought he was developing with him was not important. After all, if there were a relationship, it would be based on trust and mutual honor, and Ahmed would never sell shoddy material to a trusted business partner. It was humiliating for Ahmed even to think that this American might feel that way about him; and it was mystifying to Ahmed that the man would not engage in lively bargaining over price.

The result of these two misfitting sets of values and expectations was a standoff at the negotiating table. Ahmed was assuming that he was addressing the American's main need by bargaining aggressively over price and was not seeing the greater needs the American really had, while the American was unaware of how, by pressing those other needs forward, he was putting the critical (from Ahmed's point of view) personal relationship in jeopardy. Not only did Ahmed's value on price bargaining blind him to the American's real needs, but his reliance on the personal relationship, which made him disinclined to admit issues of quality into a negotiation between two honorable men, also prevented him from seeing the American's need for a rational, dependable business plan, one that the American could use to strategize delivery dates, quantities of shipments, and retail pricing to his buyers over long periods of time. Looking more deeply at the value differences between them, there were some key issues in traditional Arab culture regarding planning, taking risks, and taking control that stood in direct contrast to the American's, despite the fact that Ahmed thought he knew all about working with Americans.

I went on to explain to Ahmed that there was a very good chance the American was simply not going to enter into this relationship until he knew some very basic facts about how, when, and where Ahmed was going to export to him in the future. While Ahmed was content to build a relationship and to allow that relationship to determine the future course of events between the two of them, the American, while perhaps finding the relationship an interesting development, was going to make the deal on the basis of hard information he could get right now about how much of what could be delivered by when, for how long, and for how much. The American was not just less dependent on that all-important personal relationship; he was also much more calculating, rationalistic, eager to plan, and dependent upon statistical information. He was operating from a set of values that supported a belief in being able to control the future, to plan for certain outcomes at certain times, and to take risks based on those plans. Ahmed was operating from a set of values that supported a belief in developing a personal relationship so that partners might continue to trust in each other and do business even when the unpredictable, the uncontrollable, occurred (which it surely would) to threaten their arrangements. From the American cultural point of view, we can plan to overcome whatever obstacles may come our way in order for both of us to expect this shipment to take place in six months. From Ahmed's cultural point of view, it is useless to plan so far ahead, since there is so little human beings can do to affect the inevitable events of the world. Such things are determined by Allah, and it is foolish, perhaps slightly sinful, for people to try to do the same. On scale 10, we might place Ahmed at a 7 or 8, the American at 1–3.

If Ahmed was conservative out of fear of inevitable, uncontrollable change, the American was conservative, too; it was this that drove his compulsion for statistical verifiability. If Ahmed was a risk-taker, it was because he was not ultimately in control; therefore nothing he did, risk-taking or not, would have any real effect on what would ultimately happen. If the American was a risk-taker it was because he believed in his individuality and his power to control his destiny. In fact, both Ahmed and the American were risk-takers *and* conservative, depending upon how you looked at their respective societies. The point here was that, for Ahmed, acting conservatively or in a risk-taking fashion was determined by a deep belief that one is ultimately not in control of what will happen, while acting conservatively or in a risk-taking fashion for his American associate was determined by a deep belief that one is ultimately the master of one's fate.

The American's Destiny Is to Control It

This notion of being in control, of making what you will of your life, of creating your own destiny, is a central value in American life. It is so central to American thinking and so foreign to the traditional Arab world view that Ahmed and his American associate were unable to see the true needs of the other and, therefore, were unable to move the negotiation along. We suggested that Ahmed try to address the American's real needs, which were not issues of price, but rather issues of quantity, reliability of delivery times, and, yes, quality (not a personal affront, just a business need, Ahmed). Then, as a group, we explored how a negotiation around these issues might look. Here, too, cultural differences arose.

To start with, discussing things beyond price bargaining, such as assurances of quality (take-back and return policies, for example) was unfamiliar to Ahmed. Connecting price to some of these issues (such as a lower price given guarantees of larger orders, or orders in quantity over a certain period of time) was also something Ahmed hadn't thought of, and he realized that there might be advantages for him built into the formerly unrecognizable American needs that he had not seen. Several months later, I received a letter from Ahmed telling me that he and the American had arranged an export deal, and that his first shipment was being made the following month. In the letter he made a point of letting me know that the negotiation had moved quickly once Ahmed began solving some of the concerns the American had for dependable shipment dates and quality assurances. He added that by being able to meet these requirements, he was able to ask a higher price and get a commitment to long-term orders from the American.

The American value of asserting control over circumstances in order to direct their outcome is a product of our history. It is the result of the confluence of many historical factors, not the least of which are the frontier and the Protestant work ethic. To understand the American mind, one must understand the effect these two factors have on it.

Unlike many countries with vast geographical areas of untamed wilderness, the American frontier was knowable, conquerable. It was temperate. It was not the great Arabian desert, the harsh Australian outback, the frigid Siberian plains, or even the frozen shield of northern Canada. When harnessed, it yielded, whether for the Native Americans or for the newcomers from Europe, the necessities of life for those who lived off of it. And, unlike the frontiers that are harnessable only through the extreme and technologically advanced applications of today, the American frontier was controllable in the nineteenth century and before. It provided, in fact, just enough challenge, yet more than enough reward, to ensure its own demise.

The people came and came and came. Not only was the land fruitful, but it could be sown and harvested through one's own individual efforts. Maintaining one's life was difficult, but not impossible; challenging, but fulfilling. Nature could be controlled, the unknowable known, the unpredictable dealt with. And the context in which this temperate challenge existed was one of free choice, unfettered by traditions, by aristocracy, by oppression. It was indeed possible to take charge of one's life, in very immediate, day-to-day terms. In the simplest terms of life on the frontier, every moment alive, in fact, was an immediate validation of one's control over one's life, over one's destiny.

As the continent grew, as a new country required the full spectrum of civilization, opportunities abounded for certain individuals to meet these requirements. Stories abounded of people who were not necessarily more skilled, well connected, or naturally endowed than their neighbors, suddenly taking charge of their lives in great and wonderful ways, simply by putting their backs into it. It seemed as if men and women who simply *wanted* to, worked hard, and dreamed a little, could truly change the course of their lives.

The frontier, and the accompanying vast psychic, as well as geographic, freedom available there, also served to vindicate the great Protestant work ethic in its uniquely American form. What began as an effort by fundamentalist Protestants to find a safe place where they could discover a more direct, pure, and personal connection to their God was transubstantiated in the developing secular society into a way of ensuring a glorious life in the here and now. If the original Puritans could only be sure of their salvation through the demonstration of good works, then those who could demonstrate more good works were clearly those more likely to be saved. What determined the saved man or woman, the good man or woman, the righteous, then, was the evidence of his work: the rewards of labor. And hard work in the developing country often provided immediate rewards. It was a short leap, then, to the valuing of hard work, in and of itself—not only as a sometimes disagreeable means to an end, but also an ennobling thing, with an inherent value bestowed by God, in and of itself. If today we still value hard work because of the possibility for great reward, it is because at its heart lies the Puritan valuing of the work itself: that "doingness" is holy.

This is a particularly and uniquely American idea. Even in Britain, where the Puritans came from, where the Protestant ethic had its birth, there is considerably less valuing of work for its own sake. (Indeed, this fact is often bemoaned as one of Britain's great problems. It is also an area in which Americans constantly misread their English cousins when it comes to doing business with them. Perhaps it is a legacy bestowed on Britain by the aristocracy, who were always a bit loath to get their hands dirty, but former Prime Minister Margaret Thatcher notwithstanding, the Brits can have a terrible time with the amazingly enthusiastic American penchant for "making things happen." The Brits are often quite content simply "making things do.") Neither is there, to the great degree found in America, the remarkable transubstantiation of religious belief (hard work yields salvation in the hereafter) into secular zeal (hard work yields the most toys in the here and now). The idea that there is great value in "doing," that change is inherently good, that tomorrow can be better than today, is a modern, secularized form of the Puritan's hard work in an effort to please God. The process is the same today. It's just the god that's changed.

There are many cultures where "doingness" is not valued, where keeping things as they are is, in fact, good enough, thank you. In such cultures we do not see a valuing of change, we do not see an eagerness for tomorrow. Instead, we see a general conservatism, a skepticism about newness, a requirement for a good deal more information before decisions are taken, before new things are tried. In these cultures, "new and better" is dangerous. The future is to be stepped into carefully. Traditions are powerful. One spends energy protecting what one already has, rather than wasting resources in efforts to produce an unknown tomorrow. Certainly such differences are deeply involved in another critical cultural dimension, time, which we looked at closely in the last chapter. Suffice it to say here that many cultures value the passive, "nondoing" approach, and Americans doing business with such cultures often find themselves frustrated at what feels like a disabling reticence on the part of their associates across the table to really get anything done. It may be because "doingness" is not central to their culture. Its absence is felt keenly by Americans precisely because "doingness" is so central to theirs.

This uniquely American belief that one can do anything one sets one's mind to is often seen by non-Americans as an optimism bordering on the irrational, if not downright silly. It is over this particular American value that non-Americans often voice their ambivalence. Our fresh optimistic expectation that things *can* happen, the assumption that what we plan *will* get done, is often both admired and derided. This American breeziness, this built-in assumption that one can control the outcome of whatever one plans, our faith in the pragmatic, is the source of admiration and sometimes wonder; it is also the reason why Europeans, for example, can find us naive, unrealistic, or just plain unreasonable. On scale 10, an American might put a European somewhere around 8 or 9, while the European might place the American around 2 or 3. It was an American President, Woodrow Wilson, who said, "Sometimes people call me an idealist. Well, that's how I know I'm an American."

Enthusiasm and Ethnocentrism

Our enthusiasm feeds a particular stereotype that non-Americans often have of us: Americans think that just because it works in the United States, it's the best way to do things everywhere else, too, and that, given half a chance, we'll march around the world ignorantly ramming the American way down everyone else's throat whenever we can. Unfortunately, this kind of stereotype has all too often been justified. The Americans who choose to see Europe merely as a mirror on the other side of the Atlantic, who don't understand why "they" can't do it the way it's done in the States, who assure their European associates that there's no need to test it in their country since the product's already been tested in the States...These and countless other examples reinforce the stereotype of the enthusiastically ethnocentric American specifically because *this kind of behavior negates the value of the other country*. If American gusto is to be more easily accepted, if we are to elicit delight in response to this unique American trait instead of disgust, we need to adjust our enthusiasm so that it embraces, instead of denies, the uniqueness of the foreign cultures where we do business.

Unfortunately, because of their negative experiences, many non-Americans may admire America but express dismay, if not downright disappointment, with actual Americans. It's no wonder, really, when so many Americans have in the past tramped across their countries loudly calling attention to their own ignorance about why the people they meet there might prefer to do things differently from "the way we do it back home." We must carefully disassemble the stereotype that has been built by the "ugly American" of the past. At the very least, we must be careful not to become, through our own behavior, a reason for the maintenance of the stereotype.

This means several things. First, it means understanding how powerful this "can-do" value is in ourselves, recognizing the ways in which we, as individuals conducting our business with non-Americans tend to express it, and appreciating that this value might not be shared by those with whom we are doing business. Second, it means understanding the values of the other and valuing the differences, particularly in regard to this "can-do" baggage we carry. Third, it means understanding that others (depending on their sensitivity to this issue in the light of their own past experiences with Americans) may still choose to see us as ramming our ways down their throats at every possible opportunity. Hence, if we are dealing with people who are particularly sensitive to this issue, it would not be unreasonable to expect a certain defensiveness on their part to any American initiative.

The "Not-Invented-Here" Syndrome over There

The "not-invented-here" syndrome—the apparent automatic rejection of any American suggestion simply because it originates from an American and not a country national—is a perfect example of the kind of defensiveness Americans can run into abroad. (It is not exclusively directed at Americans, by the way. All cultures are ethnocentric, as we saw earlier, and, in varying degrees, we are all guilty of practicing this syndrome. Additionally, it is not only a response to an expected behavior; external factors, such as real economic concern, policies of protectionism, labor requirements, etc., can also be the source of defensiveness.) Since this resistance is sometimes unexplained, Americans have been mystified by it, for there appears to be no justifiable reason for it. Local pride, it seems, can be stronger than what appears to be the sensible, reasonable, or simply profitable thing to do. Sometimes explanations are given for a rejection that seem logical but that really do not explain it. Sometimes the proposal is merely rejected out of hand with no explanation.

Americans need to be aware that their reputation precedes them in some countries and that because of this reputation, they may be operating at a distinct disadvantage. They first must overcome their international counterparts' possible expectation that they are going to have the American way forced down their throats. This means communicating respect for the ways of those opposite you, building personal relationships based on mutual trust, taking the time to understand their culture, and delighting in its differentness. All of this occurs *before* you address your business initiative. If you are doing business in a country where you need to overcome this handicap, it is essential to anticipate this need and to devote the time and energy necessary to dispel the stereotype. This can make the negotiations longer and more costly but, in the end, will allow you to begin as equals. Under these circumstances, without taking these measures, you may be starting out on a long, uphill battle, with little chance for success.

The French have a particular reputation, at least among Americans, for behaving defensively. The French are extremely proud of their culture; to be French is to speak of culture with a capital "C." They are sensitive, for historical and cultural reasons, to Americans, who often appear to be the antithesis of all that the French hold dear, culturally speaking. The French are formal, reserved, respectful, discreet, precise, technical, quality-conscious. In contrast, the Americans appear brash, informal, casual, loud, too gregarious, and quantity-conscious.

In business, this often takes the form of the "not-invented-here" syndrome. Until I established a personal relationship with the training director of a French organization, it was impossible to overcome this automatic response. Despite the fact that I was keenly aware of controlling what might seem to be my American "enthusiasm," I was either not doing a good enough job, or my French associates were simply not willing to relinquish their stereotype of me as an American. The response to any initiative I made was rejected out of hand with such explanations as, "the research had no basis in France," and "in reviewing the material, it was decided that too many adjustments would have to be made in order to make it appropriate for the French participants."

Instead of attempting to prove that such statements were false (as I believed they were), I worked hard at building a personal relationship based on everything *but* business with the appropriate training personnel (often long distance; one does not have to be on-site in order to build and maintain relationships). My goal was to make it impossible for them to continue to stereotype me as yet another too-ambitious, French-ignorant American, which I believed to be the real reason behind their behavior. Once I had broken through the assumptions they initially had about me, I learned that there was really great interest in the materials, that they had actually found them novel and exciting, that the video-tapes really represented a unique perspective that could be shared among the staff, etc. Instead of pushing my position or defending my-self against their judgments, I applied my American tenacity to embrac-ing their uniqueness, thereby defusing the source of their defensive-ness. Ultimately I was able to help them get excited about the true nature of my work...even to appreciate my uniquely American eager-ness and excitement to be working with the troublesome, glorious French.

Put Your Nose to the Grindstone, Roll Up Your Sleeves, and Get to Work

If the Puritan ethic provides Americans with the philosophical justifica-tions for hard work, such valuing of work for its own sake can be in direct conflict with the world view of those societies where no such philosophical valuing exists. For example:

John Williams, manager of personnel programs for his Chicago-based company, walked into the office of Peter van Dam, the personnel manager of the company's Dutch subsidiary in Amsterdam, on a Friday afternoon at 3 p.m. Williams' plane from Chicago had been due in at 10 a.m., and he had scheduled his visit for 11:30 a.m., asking Van Dam to keep the rest of the day free. However, the plane had been grounded before takeoff for almost four hours.
  "You must be dead with fatigue, flying against the clock and with the extra delay," Van Dam said. "We can postpone our meeting till Monday, if you'd like. That's no problem," he added. Williams said he really felt fine, and started discussing business right away. At 5 p.m., Van Dam showed some unease, asked to be excused for a moment, and grabbed the telephone, chatting away in Dutch. "I called home to tell my wife I will be somewhat late," he explained as he hung up. "But no problem. I've got until 6 p.m. Then I'll have to leave. I've got to put the kids to bed tonight."
  At five minutes to six, Peter Van Dam started to unpack his briefcase and put on his coat. "Shall I drop you off at your hotel?" he said. In the car, Williams proposed to continue the discussion on Saturday morning. "So sorry," Van Dam said, "but I promised to take the kids to the zoo. Would you like to join us? My wife has a

meeting tomorrow. She's in politics, so it's my turn with the kids."
Williams muttered something about a presentation to the general
manager he still wanted to prepare, and Van Dam added that he'd
arranged to keep Monday and Tuesday available to continue
working with Williams. Van Dam was surprised when Williams
responded that he expected to be back in the States on Tuesday for
that presentation. Van Dam said, "You would make such a long trip
just for such a few days...no time even to enjoy yourself in
Amsterdam!" The two men parted in silence at Williams's hotel.[13]

Americans push themselves hard. They seem to be driven by an energy
that much of the rest of the world hasn't tapped into. Many an American
has touched down in Europe, jumped into a cab, and headed off to the
meeting. Not only in their work, but in their play, Americans are
schedulized, organized, compartmentalized. "If it's Tuesday, it must be
Belgium," is not only the cry of the American tourist but also the theme of
many a lonely international business traveler. Such business travelers have
day planners, some more appropriately called day *runners*. They are
proud of a tradition of working hard and playing hard. They pack as
much as they can into a day. Forgetting the more traditional rule followed
much of the rest of the world of planning only one or two meetings per
day, Americans will schedule themselves so tightly and rigidly that they
compress several meetings into one day. As we've indicated in the preceding chapter, this reveals a particular way of viewing time. But it also reveals
a particular view of the role of work as it relates to life—a view that in
many ways is quite uniquely American and that can be in conflict, as the
example above demonstrates, with the values of other cultures.

There are some cultures that work to live; others that live to work. An
Australian was once quoted as saying that "You Yanks are always re-
hearsing for life; we Aussies live it." We work today in order to retire
tomorrow; we fill our time with a task in order to accomplish it efficiently, and then we move on to another task as soon as it is done. All of
this, of course, is in an effort to move into the future, which is always
better than today, as quickly as possible. If the Mexicans appreciate
mañana because it never comes, we are in an eternal race to catch up
with it. In the above example, Williams's view of work was in conflict
with Van Dam's in several areas. Williams managed his time very differently from Van Dam, although both, interestingly enough, had similar views of the value of time. It's just that for Williams, time was for
the purpose of accomplishing a task (or series of tasks), while for Van

[13]This example was contributed by ITAP, International.

Dam, time was for the purpose of living life, beyond mere task accomplishment. (In discussing the relationship between work and life, discussing differing notions of time becomes almost unavoidable.)

Van Dam viewed life as considerably larger than work; certainly most Americans probably do the same, but the important point here is the degree to which the balance is struck. For Van Dam, home life had a special meaning. It was important enough for him to feel that he could end the meeting even though Williams had just flown in and clearly wanted to continue working. The degree of importance Van Dam's life beyond work had for him was also revealed by his surprise that Williams was returning to the States so soon, without giving himself enough time to enjoy even a little of Amsterdam. (Williams's degree of task orientation was revealed by the fact that he hoped he could wrap up his work the same day he had flown in.) For Van Dam, his relationships in life — with his children, his wife, and even with Williams (whom he invited to join him at the zoo the next day) — were all more important than the accomplishment of the task within the very constrained limits that clearly were a part of Williams's expectations.

Quality of Life

Americans pride themselves in being task-oriented, in getting the job done, in rolling up their sleeves and tackling it. ("It's a nasty job, but somebody's got to do it.") In fact, there are other cultures that are significantly more task-oriented and efficient and perhaps even more productive. The Japanese are especially task-oriented. They spend more labor hours at work than Americans; the government has had to develop a campaign to encourage Japanese workers to take their vacation time; and they are generally extremely efficient. The French understand that Americans are naturally frustrated at the five weeks' vacation French workers are given each year, but a French associate of mine observed, not unlike the Aussie above, "You Americans will fill up whatever time you have with work. If you worked as hard and efficiently as we do, you'd have time to take a five-week vacation, too." Europeans might not stay in their offices after hours as Americans might (remember, office hours can be different, so what is "after hours" in one country may not be so in another). They may not take work home with them as naturally as Americans do or give out their home number in order for work associates to be able to reach them after hours. But they will insist that all this is simply not necessary, for while they are *at* work they are much more focused, more serious, and more productive than Americans tend to be. They will say that they balance life and work, and make time for

both in the proper proportions. They view Americans as too preoccu-
pied with work, as having lives that are often empty and friendless, so
that we rush to fill up the time with activity and work.

In traditional Asia, personal friendships are simply valued more than
work. Work, after all, is what one does to survive day to day. It is the task
of living, but living is more than a task. Traditionally, in Thailand, there is
the notion of *senuke*, that things need to be "fun" (a rough translation),
challenging, stimulating, fulfilling, and enjoyable, in order for people to be
motivated to work at them. The supervisor of a project in rural Thailand
complained bitterly of workers simply walking off their jobs when relatives
from nearby villages would show up. Then they would go off and visit the
children, catch up on family matters, solve personal problems, and expect
to return to work after the personal tasks were handled. In Bangkok, a
maintenance supervisor at a construction project complained that the
Thais were extremely hardworking when putting up the building, but it
was very difficult to motivate them to do even the simplest tasks when it
came to maintaining the building once it was up. Apparently, constructing
the building was challenging, fun, rewarding, requiring the mutual efforts
of all concerned. But maintaining the building was dull, boring work.
Money, for rural folks used to working by living off what was immediately
produced, was of course important, but not central to life. And work done
solely for money, without consideration for whether it also contained other
valuable ingredients, such as *senuke*, was also unimportant. Clearly, work
was a means to a greater end and was only a part of the larger spectrum of
life.

This difference in orientation between life and work, or at least, in
the balance between life and work, is revealed in the way people manage time, value the importance of relationships, and relate with each
other, as men and women of different ages and ethnicities, at work. It
reflects the degree to which people value quality of life over work, and
it reveals their world view of work: Is it a means to an end, or is it an
end in itself? For the American, chiefly because of the influence of the
Protestant ethic and the Puritan heritage, hard work has had a value in
and of itself, and our actions in business often reveal this deeper belief.
On scale 9, most Latins, rural Asians, Europeans, and Africans would
put Americans closer to the right, while Americans would put most of
these people closer to the left (although some Americans might also put
themselves closer to the left since sometimes our image of ourselves is
different from the image others have of us). This is not to say that
Americans do not appreciate their free time, their personal time, their
vacation time. Nor do we mean to imply that Americans believe the only
honest money is earned money. (A brokerage house during the Reagan
years sponsored an ad campaign, obviously geared to maximizing sen-

timent for old-fashioned American virtues regarding hard work and Puritanism by associating the earning of money with old-fashioned values. In fact, it was doubly ironic, since the slogan was trading off the traditional Puritan American value of hard labor, when in fact the brokerage house itself had made its money by speculating and investing.) After all, a quick buck is as American as apple pie, too.

Remember, though, we are speaking of values, of what people believe to be the way the world should work, rather than the way they know it works, and in America, the value is commensurate reward for good, hard work. That's why the high-roller is entertainment, lucky but insubstantial; why the underdog who pulls himself up by the bootstraps is a hero, and why the poor deserve to stay poor, if that's what they really want. Clearly in this view, both the poor and the very wealthy prefer not to work, a fact that, for the American, is antithetical to the way the world should work. That is why both are essentially scorned in America.

Relating to Relationship Building

We have been looking in this chapter at particularly American views of the relationship between work and life, the relationships between individuals and their work. Let's put some of this awareness, once again, to work in an international business scenario, by applying the Global Homecoming skills we've been developing. Remember, the purpose of this exercise is to develop an understanding of the way the other person is behaving by rediscovering that part of ourselves that resonates with his or her circumstances. Culture-specific information is, of course, important, and under certain controlled circumstances it may be possible for you, an outsider, to learn all the facts necessary to understand everything that your foreign associate is experiencing. But we're stressing here, through the Global Homecoming Exercise©, the development of what we believe to be a more useful skill: that of a global mind-set that leads to empathic understanding. And the best way for Americans to develop a global mind-set is to rediscover those aspects of their own roots that resonate with those of their associates abroad. So, with this as our goal, let's try to understand and resolve the problems arising in the following scenario.

Bargaining in the Sun

While enjoying the lunch hosted for him by his Italian associate, the American sales manager, Paul Stoneworthy, confided to Signor Conti that although he enjoyed all this hospitality, he really didn't see why so much time had to be taken up socializing on every trip he made to Napoli. "After all," he said, "we're close enough to be able to meet and just do some business without partying all the time, right? I mean, isn't your time more valuable than that?" he added with a grin.

Conti replied that it was important to meet for lunch today because a friend of his, Signor Mondavi, was going to join them. Conti wanted to introduce Mondavi to Stoneworthy because Mondavi would be joining them in future negotiations representing the Italian company. When Mondavi joined them at the table a few minutes later, the discussion moved quickly to business, although not exclusively. However, after coffee was served, Mondavi skillfully maneuvered the conversation into a hard negotiation over price. Mondavi began with what Conti perceived to be an extremely high, almost ridiculous price. Stoneworthy looked uncomfortably at Conti. Almost as an aside, Conti apologized profusely, insisting that he was unaware that Mondavi would behave this way.

Conti continued to whisper that he had very little control over what the company was doing, that Mondavi was management's choice, and that he, Conti, had had no idea Mondavi would be acting this way. He said he was a little embarrassed. Mondavi kept the pressure on, while Conti played mediator, alternately seeming to implore Mondavi to be reasonable and then asking for Stoneworthy's understanding. At one point, Conti even mentioned that, because of his personal relationship with Stoneworthy, he had always managed to keep the prices lower than the market but that it was obvious now, with Mondavi's involvement, that management was eager to bring the price up to what they felt they could really get on the market. Conti expressed the "deep fear" he'd had all along that sooner or later this would happen. He had been trying to protect Stoneworthy, he said, because of their relationship.

Stoneworthy, meanwhile, was incredulous that all this was happening. When he said that he felt Conti's company was taking advantage of their relationship, Conti reminded him that it was he who had kept the price so low for so long, because of what he viewed to be their important friendship. Conti seemed a little hurt, which made Stoneworthy nervous, since he needed Conti in his corner at this difficult time. Conti also feigned surprise at Stoneworthy's remark by stating that he thought the socializing and personal relationships were not important to Americans, after all. Perhaps, but that was why Mondavi's outrageous price offer was so disconcerting for Stoneworthy. Stoneworthy thought to himself: "This man cannot be serious. I simply will not negotiate with him." But despite Stoneworthy's efforts to negotiate directly with Conti, Mondavi successfully insisted on focusing the negotiation on his demands. The lunch ended coolly, with an agreement to meet again the next morning in Mondavi's office at 10 a.m. Conti smiled and assured Stoneworthy that he would be there and that he was sure things were going to work out. Stoneworthy left the cafe not looking forward to the next morning.

Global Homecoming Exercise© 3:
Relationship Building

1. *Recognize* Differences: Keeping the importance of business and relationships in mind, how are the Americans and the Italians different?

Americans	**Italians**
The Americans expect	The Italians expect
_____	_____
_____	_____
_____	_____
_____	_____

2. *Retrace:* Spend one minute meditating quietly to help relax and clear your mind. Close your eyes. Spend the next few minutes visualizing yourself going back to an event in your early years (at home, with relatives, at school, at church, with friends), in which you were with people very close to you who *held similar values* to the Italians in regard to relationship-building. Describe the scene:

_____

_____

_____

_____

3. *Reclaim:* Who were the people in your scene? How would you describe their culture?

_____

_____

What is their country?_____ Ethnicity?_____

Religion?_____Generation?_____Sex?_____

Relation to you?_____

How did you feel about these people?_____

_____

_____

_____

_____

4. *Reframe:* What factors in these people's culture do you think might have caused them to act the way they did with you?

_____

_____

_____

What cultural gifts have they brought to you?_____

_____

_____

What have you learned from them?_____

_____

_____

Go back to this situation now. You are there, but as the person you are now. What will you do differently?_____

_____

_____

_____

_____

5. *Resurface: You are the American in the "Bargaining in the Sun" case.* What cultural gifts can you bring to this encounter?

_____

_____

_____

What cultural gifts do they bring to this encounter?

_____

_____

_____

What can you say or do to find a better way home (to reach a more satisfactory agreement or conclusion to this business situation)?

_____

_____

_____

_____

6
Egalitarianism

Hi! My Name's _____!
Nice to Meet You. What
Do You Do?

Some version of this greeting is repeated thousands of times every day
in America, at business luncheons, cocktail parties, on long-distance
telephone calls, in the corporate cafeteria, on line at the post office. It is
light, simple, informal, to the point, and task-oriented. There are many
aspects of the American psyche, of American behaviors and values that
are revealed here, but perhaps underlying them all, at the very heart of
this statement, is the pervasive and powerful sense of American "egalitarianism." As a value, it is as ubiquitous in the American persona as
individualism, and certainly the two are bound to each other in unique
and special ways. As with any cultural attribute, our egalitarianism becomes more recognizably "American" as we move about in different cultures. In fact, very few other cultures hold (or at least translate) this notion of egalitarianism as powerfully in their lifestyles, business and
social, as the American culture does.

Egalitarianism, as a cultural value, means, of course, that "all men are
created equal," and if that sounds familiar, that's an example of how
profoundly deep this value goes in the American mind. It *is* a value,
however, and this means that in reality, as we all know, all men and
women are not equal. It is the work of a nation to create a society that
meets the standards it sets for itself. In this sense, we Americans admit

195

that the work is not over and take pride in the struggle. However, we hold this idea of the equality of all people (extended as a value, if not as a reality, since the eighteenth century, to both sexes and all races) as just that: a value, sacred and important, and a standard by which we measure our success as a society.

The Roots of Egalitarianism

For Americans, egalitarianism is intertwined with and dependent on many other traditional values. And, as is the case with all values, it has its roots deep in the history of the United States. First and foremost, of course, it is inscribed in the Declaration of Independence. In this sense, egalitarianism began in America as a reflection of eighteenth-century European history: revolutions against aristocracy, the tearing down of the last forms of feudalism, the rising up of free and independent individuals, in charge of their own lives, in charge of their own fate, in control of their own government. But the great migrations of the next century, which ultimately populated the country, added a new dimension of meaning to the original, constitutionally enshrined notions of political equality. Now egalitarianism became a deeply embedded vision of how individuals should behave in regard to each other.

For the most part, immigrants coming to the United States arrived here looking for a new opportunity, a second chance, a better way. They were all, for the most part, escaping something dreadful, be it famine, oppression, or war. In this sense, they all shared a common background, a common dream, and a sense of a common opportunity. In this, they were all equal. (We are speaking here primarily of eighteenth- and nineteenth-century European immigrants. Nineteenth-century Asian immigrants may have shared similar backgrounds and dreams, but had their opportunities considerably circumscribed, and most African-Americans, due to their forced enslavement, were excluded from this opportunity completely.) Within these parameters, a growing country did provide millions with the opportunity to better their lives, to rise up past boundaries that were immovable in their previous homelands. As a growing nation, the limits were sometimes nothing more than the strength of their backs and the frontier. Supported by the value of individualism, with no turning back possible, and brand-new opportunities in front of them, the revolutionary notion of all people being equal took on a new dimension. Subsequent frontiers—whether the Pacific Ocean or the moon, and subsequent challenges, whether two world wars or the Great Depression—all served as tools for the entrenchment of egalitarianism. Each national crisis provided an equal opportunity for those willing to take the plunge or a chance for all to work shoulder to shoulder to get a dirty job done. Bit by bit and event by event, these values gelled into a shared vision of America as a place where everyone is supposed to get an even shot.

In our social and business lives today, egalitarianism is translated into our behavior in myriad ways. The effects of the greeting quoted above are perhaps most visible in the day-to-day behavior that is so clearly identifiable as "American"—especially when encountered abroad: friendliness, informality, directness.

Measuring Our Equalness

Let's look more closely at some of the important behavior and versions of egalitarianism in comparison with important other cultures. As before, below are several different scales designed to measure variations of such attitudes and beliefs. For each of the scales, indicate,

1. Where you think the American value would be by writing "A" at the approximate position
2. Where your personal value would be by writing the first letter of your name at the approximate position
3. Where you believe the country you're interested in would be by writing the first letter of its name at the approximate position that you believe best represents its values (guessing is OK)

As before, there should be three indicators on each scale. For example,

1. **Importance of Hierarchy**

Status-respecting   *Egalitarian*

1	2	3	4	5	6	7	8	9	10

On this scale, I might put an "A" for the United States somewhere around 8 to 10, a "D" for Dean somewhere around 7, and a "B" for Britain (the target culture I've chosen) relative to the United States at around 2 to 4. Again, there are no absolute right or wrong answers: each indicator should be relative to the others. We just want to discover tendencies and directions. While you may have lots of other thoughts in regard to the categories these scales cover, please answer with egalitarianism in mind. And remember, it *is* a value. The scales do not ask how successful you think the societies have been in actually becoming egalitarian. Rather, they offer a way to discover how important egalitarianism is as a value. (In fact, an argument can be made that it is an especially important value in those cultures that are far from being egalitarian…that the lack of real egalitarianism there is also why it may be so highly valued there.) Now try these:

2. Importance of Seniority

Age is the criterion for recognition   *Competence is the criterion for advancement and recognition*

1	2	3	4	5	6	7	8	9	10

3. Management Style

Consultative   *Paternalistic*

1	2	3	4	5	6	7	8	9	10

4. Communication Style

Direct   *Indirect*

1	2	3	4	5	6	7	8	9	10

5. Criteria for Judgment

Based on morality, principles, precedent   *Determined by situation*

1	2	3	4	5	6	7	8	9	10

6. Sex Roles in Business

Rigidly defined   *Overlapping roles*

1	2	3	4	5	6	7	8	9	10

7. Criteria for Appraisal and Reward

Personal judgment   *Professional, objective requirements*

1	2	3	4	5	6	7	8	9	10

8. Socializing in Business

Informal   *Formal*

1	2	3	4	5	6	7	8	9	10

Telling It Like It Is

Americans in international business are often too blunt. We talk too much. We get straight to the heart of the matter. We say, "Don't beat around the bush," "Let's cut to the bottom line," "Look, we're friends, so I'm going to tell you the truth, even if it hurts." We hold "plain speaking" to be a positive value, and the plain truth is that much of the rest of the world does not. It's not that truth isn't as great a commodity elsewhere (although in some places, a case might be made for this, too). It's just that the process of getting to the truth is different. The paths taken are more serpentine. The journey to the bottom line is more circuitous. And this roundabout procedure is not necessarily followed with an intent to deceive, avoid, evade, or confuse, as many Americans caught in this mire often suspect. Rather, the importance other cultures place on ambiguity (often in direct contrast to the emphasis Americans place on clarity), often represents their equally strong need to maintain harmonious relationships, something Americans do not necessarily value. In America, because we are all equal, because I am as good as the next person, we can speak directly and plainly with each other. No one is so elevated that I cannot speak my mind, that I must qualify, elaborate, justify, or mystify to the degree we often find happening in other cultures. Egalitarianism makes the hierarchy "jumpable," the red-tape "cuttable," the CEO approachable, and plain speaking preferable.

However, in cultures where egalitarianism is not as strong a value, American directness is often simply too harsh. It is too impersonal. It is considered vulgar. For any number of reasons, depending on the culture we are negotiating with, directness can stand in conflict with such values as the need to save face, to maintain harmony, to elaborate and decorate, to preserve softness in human relationships, to spare feelings, to confirm the importance of the human over the functional, to respect status. Let's take a closer look at how these differences in communication styles reveal themselves in negotiations and business.

We'd been negotiating for some time. This was, I think, the third or fourth meeting in several weeks, and we had developed quite a rapport with each other. So I was really disappointed when the Italian side came back to us with what I considered a seriously half-baked set of numbers. I thought that our information requirements had been made quite clear at the previous meeting, and I expected a more thorough response from them. Without this information, we were looking at another few rounds of meetings in Rome that I didn't have the desire, time, or money for. It was especially irritating, because more meetings were unnecessary and could have been avoided if the Italians had just done their homework. So I told them, point blank, that I thought they were all wrong, that I was disappointed, that this was going to set us back, etc. I was so frustrated, I also questioned their sincerity about the deal and wondered aloud if they weren't trying to put something over on us.

The Italians seemed shocked and assured us that they were in

earnest, that they would certainly review their report again, and that
they were sorry for the added inconvenience it was causing. I
calmed down a little, said I looked forward to putting this all behind
us soon, and, since it was late in the morning, suggested that we all
go out to lunch. I'm trying to smooth some ruffled feathers here,
eating my words, working hard, I'm not sure why, to "make nice"
over *their* mistake. And, guess what: They act indignant! Marco says
they have a previous engagement and won't be joining me for
lunch. I'm insulted, he's clearly upset, and I wonder at this point if
we'll ever regain the relationship we had.

   The American in this example was just doing "what came naturally,"
especially in light of the fact that he has established what he considers to
be a close enough relationship with his Italian associates to enable him
to speak honestly and directly. Never mind that the relationship he assumes he has may, in fact, not be as close as he thinks it is. It is real
enough for him to be able to feel comfortable about expressing himself
in business in that most typical of American ways: directly, even when
the information communicated is clearly negative in nature. Marco,
however — and the rest of the team, no doubt — was probably shocked.
Romans would not speak to each other so directly, so bluntly, especially
when having to convey news that would cause the other side embarrassment and loss of face. In a negotiation where both sides are clearly
working collaboratively with each other in the search for mutually satisfying solutions to the problems at hand, the Italians would not want to
hurt the feelings or openly invalidate the position of the other side. The
Americans, no doubt, would want to avoid this, too, but do not recognize that directness carries this meaning in Italy. In America, directness
is valued and appreciated, and Americans, working collaboratively with
each other, will often use directness not as a club, but as a way to continue the discussions, honestly, forthrightly, etc.
   However, with Italians, such directness is sometimes simply too harsh.
It attacks the competency of their efforts; in fact, it is a direct attack on
them as individuals. Americans tend to separate the personal from the
professional: we can critique the performance but still maintain a relationship with the person. In Italy, if you critique the performance, you
are critiquing the individual, the heart and soul of the performer. While
there is a clearly drawn distinction between the professional and the
personal in the United States, that line is finely drawn in Italy (and in
many other countries). That is why Marco could not go out to lunch after the "chewing-out" he received from the American.

American values emphasize honesty, truthfulness, directness. When thoughts and feelings are communicated this way in America, they may hurt, they may be uncomfortable, but they are understood, and the accompanying forthrightness may even be appreciated. In a culture such as Italy's, forthrightness and honesty may be appreciated in themselves, but—as in the above example—communicating forthrightly and honestly can cause great harm to an individual and can severely damage a relationship. In America, a relationship may become even stronger as a result of heart-to-heart, albeit negative, communication. In Italy, a relationship will be stronger only if the individuals involved help each other save face and take pains not to injure the other's egos. It would have been much more useful if the American had taken a less direct, less confrontational, less personally challenging approach. Here, American egalitarianism allowed the American to speak plainly and forthrightly to his Italian associate. But in Italy, egalitarianism is not as important a value as *fare bella figura*—saving face, maintaining one's dignity, appearing always to be in control and performing well. The American's egalitarianism challenged the Italian's notion of *bella figura*.

The American needed to find a way to express his disappointment about the Italian report in a way that did not directly challenge the dignity of his Italian associates. Of course, as we have stated earlier, cross-cultural awareness is often a case of preemptive action. Once a cross-cultural problem has developed, it's sometimes too late. At that point, damage control may be more pressing than learning what you did wrong. However, with cross-cultural knowledge up front, the American in this case might have taken some preemptive steps to reduce the possibility both of Italian error and of his own frustration. For example, he might have anticipated that the report would not answer all his questions, given the nature of the flow of information in Italy (poor: information is power there and is closely guarded and protected). He should not have anticipated moving as quickly in the negotiation as he did. Second, he should have prepared a response to the situation that was not damaging to the *bella figura* of his Italian associates, such as praising those areas of the report that were valuable, while asking for their help in showing him how their information answered all his questions. (Clearly it did not, but this approach puts the responsibility for that shortfall on them, where it belongs, *without* causing them to lose face.) Finally, being unable to do any of these, he should have known that they would never go out to lunch with him after his response. But then, if he had known that, he would never have reacted the way he did in the first place.

Straight to the Heart Versus
Straight from the Heart

In addition to the importance of *bella figura* in Italy, another issue affecting the direct/indirect component of communication is worth mentioning here, and that is the degree to which some cultures (Italy certainly included) place a value on felicity, elaborateness, and beauty of expression. This somewhat baroque notion of communication can often stand in direct contrast to the American bottom-line, plain-spoken, technically-oriented mode of communication. We will discuss this more in Chapter 8, but it is worth noting here that the American in Italy would be wise to appreciate (and, if possible, practice) the art of what might be best described in one word: eloquence.

In many older civilizations (represented in Western Europe by France, Italy, Spain, and Germany; in Asia by China, Japan, and India) a high value is placed on a special quality of expressiveness, on the high art of communication, on a grand style of speaking and writing (indeed, even of listening) that transcends common day-to-day speech. Americans are not completely unaware or incapable of this kind of communication. We are familiar with the differences between speaking to a large, formal gathering and speaking with friends around the dinner table. We are aware of certain phrasings we use when speaking with higher-ups; we "watch our language" when in the presence of certain individuals. However, in some older civilizations, even everyday "business speak" employs elevated language. The particular use of formality, whether in face-to-face or written communications, is more common (titles and last names are offered, given names are not). The complexity of the language used to convey certain thoughts, concepts, and ideas; the infiltration of written style into spoken style; and the sophisticated manipulation of subtleties and variations to convey many meanings are all techniques that represent a concern for language and its complexities that goes far beyond the average American say-what-you-mean style of communication.

Formality Versus Informality

In Italy, nearly all those with a university degree are referred to as *dottore*, "doctor," whether or not they have obtained a Ph.D. An individual in Germany may be referred to as *"Herr Schmidt"* by his co-worker in the office for as long as they work together, whether or not a personal relationship develops between them (only something of a possibility). French associates will greet each other every morning with *"Bonjour, Monsieur LeGrand"* and a handshake. They shake hands when they return from lunch, and they wish each other a pleasant evening with another handshake at the end of each day. This ritual may continue unchanged for as long as they work together. The Japanese regard business cards almost as extensions of the individual and treat them (and expect them to be treated) with respect and honor. Americans, on the other hand, are notoriously informal in their communication style. They rush into the use of first names, avoid using their titles or respecting the titles of others, make all sorts of jottings on business cards, then stick them in their back pants pockets, and sit on them. When excusing themselves from a group, Americans often casually wave and make a mass announcement of their exit. In Europe, one would normally be sure to shake hands and make several comments of farewell individually to all present in the group. When receiving individuals at the beginning of a business meeting in Japan, each and every member must be greeted and introduced individually, and in order of rank and position.

Clearly, there are many varieties of this formal/informal dimension, and we will be discussing some of them in further chapters. Our point here is that the American style of communication, supported as it is by the philosophical base of egalitarianism, is, in comparison with much of the world, uniquely informal. In developing effective communication with other, more formal, cultures, we would often be better served by learning about and practicing our own more formal styles of communication.

Plain Speaking Versus Grandiloquent Effusion

The more formal cultures have developed an appreciation of the "art" of speaking, whether informally at the café table, or more formally at the negotiating table. The skillful use of ambiguity, the intentional obfuscation, the baroque, convoluted interpretation of concepts, the artful employment of prevarication, or simply the grandiloquent application of semantic brocades—in other words, the art of saying less, or more, or even something different from what you mean. Diplomacy, if you will, is an art well developed throughout the centuries in many civilizations. It stands in direct contrast to the plain spokenness of Americans and can trip up the plain-speaking American beyond redemption.

It was the third round of beers and Jack Roberts, the American director of international operations, was trying to convince his Australian counterpart, Tim Smith (better known as Smitty by all who did business with him), that the Americans were extremely concerned about the productivity of the operations in Sydney.

Basically, Roberts was trying, as diplomatically as he could, to let Smith know that the Americans were no longer willing to sit by and watch the problems mount and that they viewed the heart of the problem to be the inability of Smith and his team to handle some thorny labor-management issues successfully. Roberts added, as gently as he could, "You know, Smitty, we Yanks have had a lot of experience with this kind of thing, and we're suggesting that perhaps it's time we took a whack at things here, maybe come up with some solutions you've perhaps unintentionally overlooked." "Really, mate?" Smith answered. "Well, then, perhaps it's also time to report back to HQ that what they regard as problems are the way we do things down here. By the way...the next shout's on you, mate. Cheers."

Americans are identified throughout the world by their plain-speaking, direct style of communication. However, put an American and Australian together, and the game can become one of who can out-"direct speak" the other. It has been said that Australians can give Americans a taste of what the rest of the world feels like when communicating with Americans. Aussies have developed a particular kind of egalitarianism that sometimes makes the American version look tame. If American egalitarianism is a built-in, *a priori,* silent but solid given of the American mind, Australian egalitarianism is an active statement, a challenge to all, a value that's "out there" and reaffirmed by every Australian every day, in countless numbers of ways. Americans assume we all start out the same but that as we work hard, we earn our rewards and move up the social ladder. A higher rung on this social ladder is part of the reward. For the Australian, the assumption is also that we all start out the same, but that as we work (not necessarily so hard), we have a nice life, and moving up the social ladder is simply not a major consideration. For the American, everyone is created equal, but it's certainly important to make ourselves more important than the next person. For the Australian, everyone is created equal and had better stay that way. If the American strives to get an invitation to lunch with the "big cheese," the Australian dismisses the importance with "Jack's as good as his master." This is a central aspect of Australian egalitarianism: that no one acts or is better than anyone else, despite money, rank, social class, or position.

How Those Outback Outdo the Americans

If Australians take pains to remind each other of this central value of Australian life (disdain for formal titles and hierarchy, acute sensitivity to anything smacking of authority, stress on an easygoing lifestyle) they take even greater pains to remind an American. To the Australian, someone possessing American self-assurance invites being knocked off one's pedestal. To the Australian, our American determination presents a challenge to prove us wrong. To the Australians, our American directness is a signal that we are willing to get in the ring with them over just about anything. And, in the above example, the American's exercise of authority almost automatically pressed Smitty's buttons.

By being even more direct than the American, by taking egalitarianism to even greater extremes, Smitty is engaging in the process of "levelling," of communicating that no one here is better than anyone else. This means redefining authority, knocking people off their pedestals, cutting them down to size. To Americans like Roberts, such Australian behavior can appear disrespectful, uncompromising, obstinate. Americans report that, for no apparent reason they can come up with, Australians keep pushing them, taunting them, teasing them, chiding them into a debate, a fight, a test of authority, credibility, earnestness. Under positive circumstances, this play-fighting can take the form of good-natured jokes, of comfortable informality and familiarity. Under stress, this play-fighting is not so gentle. It can become very important for an Australian like Smitty to let an American like Roberts know, often in no uncertain terms, that he will not be told what to do, especially by someone who does not know how things are done in Australia. Roberts is actually adding to his problems by trying to be diplomatic. Australians are particularly sensitive to being talked down to, to individuals taking extra pains not to hurt their feelings. This can be very quickly interpreted as condescension, an implication that they are being tolerated, coddled, or manipulated by those more powerful. Nothing will raise their anger faster. What might, in Italy, be carefully worded language in the hopes of moving things along more collaboratively can backfire with Australians if they detect, or even think they detect, *noblesse oblige*. And their nose for *noblesse oblige* is very, very keen.

Much of this, as with all cultures, of course, can be explained by the history of the country. It should be remembered that Australia was, at first, a penal colony for mother England and that most of the settlers who followed were often looking for the freedom, escape, and second-chance opportunities of the pioneer. That Australia and the United States share a pioneer heritage, a frontier spirit, and, perhaps, the strongest sense of egalitarianism in the world is not coincidental. However, Australia is an even newer country than the United States. And its frontier is much more extensive. Geographically, it is much farther removed from its European source. And geographically, its frontier is not to be conquered. Rather, like Canada, its frontier is to be understood, respected, accepted. There is, accordingly, an acceptance of things as they are, of nobody being better able than anyone else. And while there is an increasing immigrant population in Australia, as in the United States, the interplay between the immigrant cultures and the Australian national culture is not as dynamic as it is in the United States, precisely because of the differences between the two basic cultures. On scale 4 then, if the United States lies around 2 or 3, Australia would lie nearer 1. And on scale 8, if we put the United States near 3 or 4, Australia, again, would lie closer to 1 or 2.

The Shortest Distance
between Two Points in Asia

Asians have stereotypically been portrayed as grand masters in the use of ambiguity in business language. It has become a common and well-known confusion for Americans doing business with the Japanese that it is difficult (to pun on a well-worn Japanese phrase) to know just when the Japanese agree or disagree. In a culture where *hai* ("yes") doesn't necessarily mean yes, and where "no" is not used, it can be difficult for Americans to know where they stand. And in China, the use of metaphors, proverbs, slogans, and symbolic speech is so pervasive that it has become a symbol here—in the form of trivialized Confucianisms and fortune cookie aphorisms—of the way the Chinese communicate. This valuing of ambiguity stands in direct contrast to the American notion of clear thinking and has traditionally been a source of much misunderstanding between American and Asian businesspeople.

For Asians, ambiguous communication can be a positive force. It can extract information as the other side seeks clarification; it can evade sensitive issues; it buys time for further consideration and/or manipulation; but, perhaps most importantly and most positively, it works to maintain harmonious relationships by helping both partners avoid loss of face. The Japanese will be evasive about saying "no" directly, because to thwart someone's wishes, to stand in someone's way, drives a wedge between the two individuals (more likely, the two teams), creating an imbalance in the harmonious relationship that is the sought-after state of relations between two sides doing business. The Japanese negotiation, therefore, is not necessarily one of at-the-table decision making, not one of providing "yes" or "no" answers on the spot, not one of direct give and take. Instead it is an opportunity for the exchange of information in a larger context of building a relationship based on the mutual gains to be had by what both sides can offer each other. Saying "no" to the people on the other side causes them to lose face because it implies that their needs, their desires, are not to be considered. It means that you either cannot, or will not, help them achieve their goals. It implies that their goals are not your concern.

This valuing of harmony, relationships, and face-saving, therefore, leads to a vocabulary of softness. Instead of, "No, it can't be done," the response is, "It is difficult, but we will try." Instead of "I don't think we'll have much interest in this," the response is, "We are eager to study your proposal more thoroughly and are pleased that you have given us the opportunity to do so." American egalitarianism requires a no-nonsense, give-and-take-between-equals approach to negotiation. The Japanese require a respectful, indirect avoidance of difficulties in an effort to establish a larger frame of reference within which two parties can explore the possibilities of becoming trustworthy partners.

The other aspect of the "yes or no" dilemma in Japan is the *hai*. While the literal translation is "yes," it is most used as the equivalent of the American "uh-huh." It does not represent agreement (although technically it could, if your Japanese associates commonly made such decisions at the negotiating table, which would be rare). Rather, it represents, "I hear you, please continue." It is an acknowledgment of your thoughts, an active listening response to what you have just said. Americans have returned from meetings with the Japanese believing that they have reached agreement simply because, at the table, the Japanese were saying *"hai"* to what they presented. In fact, no such agreement exists. *Hai* in this case simply means, "I acknowledge what you say. Keep talking."

How should Americans avoid falling into this "yes" or "no" trap in Asia? One way is simply not to ask questions requiring "yes or no" answers. Instead of asking, "Can you make this delivery by May 15?" ask, "When can this delivery be made?" Of course, we should consider the issue of directness/indirectness and soften the request so that it is not so direct. Now the proper question form becomes, "If we are to be able to continue to honor our customer's requests with the high quality goods that your organization has become so well known for, it is important for us to learn which month you will be able to supply us with your goods." Silence.

Egalitarianism in America is a way to get something done quickly, to strike at the heart of the matter, to quickly establish the ground rules of a business association in order to get business done. It is efficient. It is quick. It allows for business, just business. However, in Asia, the quickest route is not necessarily the most direct.

Truth Is Relative

I would periodically call down to the office in Mexico to see how things were going. According to the negotiations we had completed about six months ago, the plant should have been operating at about 80 percent. However, over the last few months, every time I looked at the figures, I could see that the plant was not even near the 80-percent mark. I would call down and ask how things were going, ask if the decisions we'd made at the negotiation were being implemented without problems, and I would always get reassurances from everyone. What more could I do? But when the figures actually started to slip, I thought it prudent to go down there myself.

When I got there I was shocked, to say the least. Some of the more responsible people had left, and I hadn't even been told! There were serious management-worker problems developing that no one had called to my attention. Apparently, there was a lot of internal fighting and unresolved turf issues among several of the higher-ups, and communication throughout the Mexican organization was at a virtual standstill. Worse than just being distressed at what I found was the feeling I got that I'd been deceived all along. *Why?* If they had just told me the facts, I could have helped. Now we're in a real mess.

Egalitarianism can result in direct, "tell-it-like-it-is" communication. In nonegalitarian cultures the preferred style is sometimes "telling-it-like-it-isn't." For reasons ranging from respect for status to a deep-seated cultural inferiority complex, there are many cultures where the prime emphasis is on telling the Americans what they feel the Americans want to hear — true or not. Unaware that this directly collides with the Americans' expectations of clear, direct, honest talk, they feel they're doing something positive, when in fact, they're doing something very negative from the Americans' point of view. When Americans learn they were not told the truth, they are bewildered and often angry. They become mistrustful and lose regard for their foreign associates. When they find out they were only being told what the other side thought would please them, most Americans are incredulous. "Why put yourself in that position?" they ask.

Mexicans, for example, can draw up the grandest of plans, will guarantee that something will, of course, be done by a certain date in a certain way, will wax philosophic on the merits of doing business between honorable men, etc. However, for reasons ranging from inability (which they do not want to admit), to powerlessness over external situations (which they will ultimately use to explain the delays), to misunderstandings (attributable to a lack of understanding, different styles of education, or external distractions), the project does not move easily from the conceptual to the actual, and, if it does, moves fitfully, and with difficulty all along the way. The American expectation of clear, honest, direct, and factual planning and reporting comes into conflict with several cultural requirements in Mexico that will inevitably take priority. It can simply be more important to "tell-it-like-it-should-be" than to "tell-it-like-it-is," if telling it like it is brings bad news, causes loss of face, and/or highlights the inabilities, powerlessness, or any assortment of indignities faced by the Mexican associate and/or organization. These concerns are very real, especially in the face of U.S. technology and advanced business practices, and in the face of Mexican pride. Coupled with a less-emphasized egalitarianism (Mexico retains much of its original Spanish class-system tradition), Mexican business communication can stand in direct contrast to the plain-speaking of the *Norte Americano*.

All Are Equal in the Eyes of the Law

If egalitarianism implies that all are created equal, then all should also have equal opportunity, equal access, and equal treatment. Such assumptions, however, are not valid in cultures that do not value egalitarianism as a cultural tradition in quite the same way it is defined and valued in America. Here's an example of how these differences might look when business brings two cultures together:

Walters had spent a considerable amount of time and money getting to this point. His company had finally got the senior government official responsible for approving the final contract to agree on the contract as it had been drafted after so many meetings with lower-level assistants. Today, Walters was waiting for information confirming the project go-ahead. This multimillion-dollar project had been in the works for over 18 months, and it looked like it was about to get off the ground at last.

However, the information Walters received was not exactly what he was hoping for. The commissioner's assistant called to say that there was a serious problem developing. Apparently, the "fee" for servicing the application through the government had not been paid. The assistant apologized that this had not been discovered earlier. Surely it was an oversight due to the eagerness of the government to get on with the project and a lack of information on the part of Walters's company regarding government regulations, etc. However, in order for the commissioner's office to review the final application, this fee had to be paid. Walters was furious.

He felt that this amounted to bribery, that there was in fact no such "fee," yet how could he risk the project after all this time?

   Americans doing business internationally can sometimes find themselves in circumstances where they feel their ethics are being compromised. Requests for special favors or arrangements, such as the fee mentioned in the above example, are not uncommon in many parts of the world. Whole societies seem to operate on graft or nepotism, and entire industries spring up to help the unknowing wend their way (at a fee, of course) through massive bureaucracies. Stories are legion of Americans who, after putting in years negotiating important contracts with the Chinese, find their Chinese associates seeming to break the terms of the agreement, almost as soon as it is signed. In these cases, Americans ask, "Were my opposite numbers negotiating in bad faith? Were they out to deceive me intentionally? Is lying a value in this culture? Must I cooperate with graft? When is doing a favor a bribe?" These kinds of questions raise thorny issues, and in following chapters we will look at some ways to handle them. Right now, however, in keeping with our exploration of egalitarianism, let's take a closer look at why Americans, perhaps more often than other nationalities, find themselves in conflict in this area. Not surprisingly, the conflict revolves around how particular aspects of American egalitarianism clash with important values of these other cultures.

   There are many kinds of truth in the world, and while cultural relativism is not meant to excuse unethical or deceptive behavior, one must be sure to examine all cultural parameters before calling behavior unethical. There can be serious, important cultural explanations for discrepancies in the expectations we mutually have of each other, and part of the explanation lies in acknowledging that what is "truth" for Americans may not be "truth" for our associates abroad. The fact is, Americans apply these notions of fact and truth in a particular manner that many non-Americans find questionable, or at least, entrapping and out of context. Criteria defining truth, honesty, and fact are affected by culture, and what might be true in one culture may not be true in another.

   At one time, all evidence pointed to the fact that the world was flat, that disease was caused by demons, that kings were divine representatives of God, and that fire, water, earth, and air were the only elements in the universe. For a variety of reasons, all of these "facts" have changed. There is a clear connection between beliefs in what is true and factual and the conditions and circumstances of the culture at the moment of such beliefs. Facts (or at least any single culture's notion of "facts") can be relative. Given this, it is not unreasonable to assume that cultures can also hold different views as to what is right and wrong, good and bad, expected or unexpected. If "hard facts," such as the shape of the earth, can change over time, certainly the criteria for goodness, ethical behavior, and correct assumptions can vary, not only over time, but also across borders.

Egalitarianism, at least in the United States, presumes that citizens subscribe to a system that provides equal opportunity for all in place of a system that provides privilege and rank to a few. It is further presumed that the giving up of one system for the other can only take place if there are set guarantees that all people in this egalitarian system will be treated the same—i.e., equally. Therefore, in order for a system based on this value of egalitarianism to work, there needs to be a set of rules, regulations, and standards, that can be applied equally. This standard (or more correctly, sets of standards including laws, norms, formal and informal behavior, etc.) stands outside of and above society as an objective by which all can measure and be measured. The key word here, I think, is "objective." In exchange for the right of equality, all must be subsumed under a banner of objectively determined principles, of a morality determined to be applicable to all. Right and wrong, good and bad, in an egalitarian culture, must be defined in terms applicable to all and must take on a universal meaning. If criteria for good and bad, right and wrong, must be applicable to all, then good and bad, right and wrong, become universals. They are determined as absolutes and take on a quality that stands above us. They become Platonic ideals, sometimes unattainable, but forever the standards by which we measure such things as good and bad and right and wrong, in all circumstances, for all time.

What I am saying here is that, in a curious twist, egalitarianism can promote absolutism, for it requires that the answers a culture provides to those troubling questions life raises in regard to morality, ethics, metaphysics, and philosophy be precedents by which *all* human beings, at *any time,* are to be judged. This means that these standards must become universals, ideals that are removed from the circumstances being judged, and that are, in fact, due to their separateness from the circumstances being judged, curiously unaffected by it. The Western legal system is a perfect example of the idealization (or "Platonization") of criteria that result from democratic, if not egalitarian, traditions. Our notions of "blind justice" or the "long arm of the law" represent our belief in a system that stands above us all, that treats us all equally. The law does not—indeed *must* not—change, regardless of who the participants are, regardless of the circumstances. In fact, those cases of greatest interest, of profoundest concern to us, are so precisely because they revolve around the "weighing of objective fact," the equal meting out of justice, usually in the face of profoundly challenging circumstantial conditions.

Western Idealism Versus Eastern Pragmatism

We need to recognize that this process of developing "universal standards," of searching for and relying on objectifiable fact is *not* universal, that it is, in part, a uniquely Western process and that many other cultures neither subscribe to this world view of ethics nor have histories and traditions supportive of it. In fact, it is precisely because of the profoundly opposite world view held by traditional Asian cultures in this regard that Americans find themselves in the mystifying position of having Chinese associates "change" contract terms on them right after they've signed the deal.

Not only is China nonegalitarian in its present condition and its historical traditions, but the resulting answers the Chinese culture provides to those unanswerable questions of life are distinctly non-Western, at least in the terms outlined above. If the West encourages the development of superstructures of universals and ideals in order to judge right and wrong, applicable to all at any time, the East, in contrast, tends to make few generalizations that stand above earthly conditions. In the East, right and wrong, good and bad, are *intimately connected with the circumstances* out of which they develop. It must be emphasized that this does not mean that there are no standards of morality or that "anything goes." Rather, the elevation of criteria for right and wrong to an idealized objective position severed from the circumstances being judged, by which all people and circumstances are measured equally, is simply not the traditional Eastern way.

In Asia, right and wrong, good and bad, are determined according to the conditions that apply. The question is not, as it is in the West, one of the moral nature or right and wrong. It is not a philosophical investigation into the nature of good and evil, but rather an exploration of what constitutes virtuous behavior. Virtuous behavior, by definition, implies a connection with the circumstances out of which the dilemma arises. "What is the *proper* way to behave *under these circumstances?*" In the West, we search for *morality,* we base our actions on and get our answers from previously established principles and precedents which always stand above us to guide us. There are universal (or at least, universally accepted) definitions for right and wrong behavior. In the East, they search for *virtue,* and they choose their actions according to the requirements of the situation. Right and wrong behavior can vary according to the circumstances.

The roots of these differences can be traced back to certain fundamental thinkers who have shaped East and West: Moses, Plato, and Aristotle on the one hand; Confucius, Laotze, and Buddha on the other. While Plato conceived of an earthly world that is merely the unclear mirror of the unknowable higher world of perfect ideals, while Aristotle provided a system of scientific observation and generalization, and while Moses gave us "the word," tablets of truth that literally came from above, Confucius discussed the honorable way for people to act under changing sets of circumstances, and the Buddha explored paths to enlightenment by transcending material circumstances completely. These ancient sources set the paths from which both East and West would travel, and most of the philosophical work done since in both worlds has been variations on a theme. In the West, the tradition of philosophy has been the attempt to employ self-consciousness and critical understanding in an effort to understand ourselves and our world. The tradition of philosophy in the East, however, has been one of overcoming, not employing, man's self-consciousness, in an effort to understand the world.

Believe it or not, there is a direct application to business for this quick review of Philosophy 101. Let's recall some of those ethical dilemmas American businesspeople were facing, and let's take a closer look at the problem many Americans run into in China, where the contract seems to be ignored or changed, even though the terms have already been agreed upon.

From the American (Western) perspective, there is no reason other than bad faith or intentional deception for an individual to sign on the dotted line agreeing to one thing and then insist, after the signing, on something else. From the American perspective, a contract represents the culmination of a series of negotiations, the end result of an arrangement, the development and delineation of procedures, rules, regulations, standards, by which we agree to behave with each other from this point forward.

Sound familiar? In fact, the contract will serve as an objective standard of behavior which we hold each other to and which we use to justify our actions should either party in this relationship act differently from the way we state we will behave toward each other in the contract. It is the Western objectified standard, universal under all circumstances that might develop (acts of God, death, and transferability) for as long as we so shall choose to work together (up to the termination date). Within the terms of the contract, there can be no variation, no modification (unless so agreed). That is why American contracts can be notoriously lengthy; every contingency must be carefully anticipated and thought through ahead of time, for the contract becomes a document of universal, objectively verifiable, and predictable action between two parties.

From the perspective of the Chinese, however, the contract is not the end result of a negotiation; in fact, it usually just represents the beginning. The Chinese will negotiate to agree to do business with each other, often leaving the specific terms, and certainly their immutability, to be determined in the future based on the circumstances of the moment. (Hang on, we will discuss this further when we discuss forms of agreement in Chapter 8.) Of course, the Chinese (and there are a wealth of horror stories to support this) have become masters at exploiting this tradition for their own benefit. But by and large, it must be remembered that we are talking about patterns of business behavior that are also engaged in with other Chinese. The Westerner is not necessarily singled out for such treatment just because he or she might be more mystified by it. The contract for the Chinese is not a document that simply represents the terms of a specific business arrangement. More traditionally, it is a protean statement of partnership, an agreement that both sides recognize each other as someone they can, with trust and confidence, do business with, that both sides acknowledge that the other will act with virtue in regard to them and their interests.

For the Chinese, the negotiations (and I caution here that they are not always so clearly well-intentioned) are an attempt to determine whether or not there are gains to be made by associating with you, and if you will pursue your interests honorably by also protecting theirs. Therefore, should your Chinese partners suddenly find themselves in a situation where honoring a particular term in the contract will be difficult, they may turn to their trusted Western business partner, expecting not only understanding, but support and help in getting them out of their dilemma by changing the terms in the agreement. At this point Americans usually respond with emotions that range from disbelief to horror. In response, the Chinese feel abandoned and deceived by a trusted business partner who, they are now discovering, is unwilling to help them in their hour of need. This only reinforces the suspicion they had had all along about Westerners (but were willing to put aside for a "special friend" like you) and justifies in their mind any action to protect themselves. While it is not inevitable, there is often a point in the relationship between Americans and Chinese where the ties that bind are sorely tested and the reactions by each merely serve to justify the original impressions, expectations, and stereotypes that each had of the other to begin with. What results is that both sides, wounded, retreat even deeper into their original misperceptions about the other, and the next time, either between themselves and Americans or between other Chinese and Americans, is even more difficult.

Looking at scale 5 now, it is easy to locate the United States closer to numbers 2, 3, 4, etc., and Asian cultures closer to numbers 8, 9, 10. There is clearly a relationship between egalitarianism and principle-based decision making (as contrasted with nonegalitarianism and situation-based decision making) that affects many aspects of business between American businesspeople and their colleagues abroad, not the least being negotiating a contract. Americans must expect to check their philosophical assumptions at the door when sitting down at the negotiating table with people from very different philosophical traditions.

Up the System!

Differences in how egalitarianism is valued are directly related to the stress on the hierarchy. Let's look at yet another conflict in values as they play out in business — this time as they are reflected in attitudes toward hierarchy.

Nick Stevens, the director of training for a U.S. manufacturing company that had recently bought out a French firm, was making a trip to the Paris office. Stevens wanted to discuss the implementation of the company's training-evaluation and progress-reporting forms for the French office. Through several phone calls and faxes prior to the trip, he was able to introduce himself, long distance at least, to the training director in France, M. LeBlanc, and his assistant, Mme. Bernard. Since the purpose of his meeting was discussed in these premeeting conversations, he believed the agenda was clear: to introduce the French office to the forms and arrange with them for the implementation of these forms throughout the training process in France.

Two hours into the first meeting, it became clear to Stevens that there were some major obstacles to achieving his goals. After the initial pleasantries, LeBlanc raised serious concerns about Stevens' timetable. "There simply is no way we could have this form implemented throughout all five French offices within the time given. You must understand that we need to discuss this with the responsible individuals in each office. There will have to be several meetings, individually, and then together, to determine an effective strategy for each office, and then we'll need to be sure that the strategy is integrated into corporate's overall human resource policies. This means, of course, that the director of operations and his superior, the vice president of human resources, must evaluate the effectiveness of the forms and our plans for implementation.

The five officers from each of the five offices will have to create a report, and submit it to the director of operations and the vice president of human resources, and we will have to await their approval."

Stevens was speechless for a moment. "Look, we've been using this form in the States for the last five years, and there's never been a problem. The form's been thoroughly tested and needs to be put in place as soon as possible. Besides, if all these other people are involved in this, why aren't they here with us now? When can I speak with them?" Bernard jumped in, slightly embarrassed for her boss. "I'm afraid that both directors are out of town just now, but they asked M. LeBlanc and myself to meet with you since you wanted to move quickly and we certainly wanted to cooperate with this effort."

Stevens persisted, "Then you do have authority in these matters?" "Yes" answered LeBlanc. "Then why don't you just call your boss and let him know what you're doing? We could arrange it all here, and you can roll it out. I'm sure when they understand all the details as you'll describe it to them, they'll see how it makes sense, and there'll be no problem. That way, we can move ahead right now." LeBlanc and Bernard looked pained. Slowly, they began to explain in detail the steps that needed to be followed when putting a new procedure in place throughout France.

If there is anything that will bring out the egalitarian in the average American businessperson, it's bureaucracy. Give Americans a task, set them in front of the hierarchy, and let them go. It is a sight that can leave much of the rest of the world gasping. No superior is too high in rank to be contacted, no middle manager too self-important not to be jumped over if necessary. For the American, the system ideally exists in order to allow the organization, and the individuals in the organization, to function efficiently, to "get their jobs done." "Efficiently" is the key word here (as it is when we examine many manifestations of American values in business). If the system does not promote efficiency, then something is wrong with it and it needs to be changed. And until it is fixed, Americans presume they have the right to do whatever and see whoever is necessary in order to accomplish their task. From the American viewpoint, the system is not meant to stand in the way, to make things problematic, to clog things up; it is supposed to make things work. The American respects the system, works within it because, for the most part (grumblings about inevitable bureaucratic hassles aside), it helps him or her achieve his or her goals, accomplish his or her task. It is a means to an end. It can be worked, climbed through, manipulated; Americans truly believe it exists to serve them. And if it doesn't work?

Until it can be made to work, Americans will avoid it, find ways to go around it, try to get it fixed, and complain that this is not the way things are supposed to be in America.

Bureaucracy and the American Gladiator

Americans, therefore, are often surprised to learn that in other cultures— in much of the rest of the world, in fact—bureaucracies and hierarchies exist primarily for their own sake. Many sociologists have made the observation that institutions, despite their stated goals, develop a *raison d'être* to maintain themselves first and foremost. They become their own self-fulfilling prophecies; after a certain amount of time, a bureaucracy's first priority becomes the maintenance and expansion of its own existence. On this principle, hospitals support sickness instead of health, schools support ignorance instead of enlightenment, and governments, in a similar fashion, promote fear instead of security, poverty instead of plenty, and oppression instead of freedom. If for no other reason than that they have simply been around longer, bureaucracies in many other cultures are well-entrenched, multiheaded hydras with lives of their own. Many will all but come out and admit that there is no other useful purpose for grinding you through their mills except for the fact that they can.

Of course, there are also other reasons. The famous Latin American bureaucracies, both formal (government agencies) and informal (graft and connections), exist because they serve several useful social functions. For one thing, they offer employment where it would otherwise not exist. Whole networks of informal advisers, people with the necessary contacts, people you simply must learn about and deal with, exist in many South American countries, for example, to do nothing more than collect a fee for taking care of something which you ostensibly either didn't need to have taken care of or theoretically could have done yourself. However, if you don't go through these people and try to do it yourself, you quickly find yourself in a labyrinth full of "catch-22s," double-backs, and never-ending treadmills.

In addition to serving a social function, these informal bureaucratic networks often fit the communication and organization styles of the nonegalitarian culture. Each contact is a step up a hierarchical ladder of power; each person is able to provide the appropriate introduction to the next person with the authority to help you with your problem. There is a great respect for status, hierarchy, and power, and power is specifically located within individuals to whom access is granted at a price. There is a verticality to the organization of this kind of bureaucracy (not limited, by the way, only to informal or extralegal organizations, but also to the formal, legal ones) and a compartmentalization of responsibilities that is severe and rigid. Individuals have specific roles; they must not be asked to perform outside their specified sphere. Of course, they may be completely capable of doing so, but this would, no doubt, invade and challenge the authority of the next one. The system guarantees work for as many as possible by keeping authority and responsibility limited, and the system remains discreet, rigid, and centralized by parceling power out to individuals at different levels. This system has the added advantages of making a commodity out of granting access to those loci of power, providing in turn whole new entrepreneurial opportunities for others outside the formal structure.

From Latin America to Africa to China, bureaucrats serve the same purpose: to protect themselves from the wrath of those above them by preventing problems from getting up to them. The eternal, irrational, mind-boggling regulations exist as a way of justifying certain courses of action that serve, in effect, to keep the higher-ups from having to deal with the lower-downs, thus, in a self-fulfilling way, preserving the higher-ups' power. The formal bureaucracies, therefore, are objectified vertical ladders of power, with responsibilities and authority held discreetly by individuals, and the communication style being one of deference from below and paternalistic *noblesse oblige* from above.

Bureaucracies and hierarchies, in *fact*, are not that different in America. But egalitarianism in America, as a fact and as a value, "softens" the official line. Our bureaucracies do certainly employ vast numbers of people, but also certainly not to the same degree as in developing nations. There is definitely a shadowy informal bureaucracy here, too, that exists either to help one through the formal one or to bypass it. But it, too, is probably not as significant as in less egalitarian societies. Egalitarianism helps Americans view the bureaucracy as a necessary evil (unlike the Italians, for example, who would question its very necessity but not its inevitability). All are created equal, but, in order to get things done, unfortunately some have to be in charge of others. In egalitarian cultures, we want to cut through the red tape. In the name of efficiency, we can go straight to the top, if necessary, in order to get the decision we need or the information we've been waiting for. No one is too powerful, no one too high, no one too petty, to stand in the way of our accomplishing the task. Titles, rank, and position have power only if such power is based on efficacy, competency. The hierarchy itself is deemphasized. That is, egalitarianism plays down the value of rank and privilege and localized power. To the outsider, the ladder may not be clear, power holders may not be obvious, status is not announced. The hierarchy, in fact, in egalitarian cultures like the United States, may actually seem fuzzy to the outsider. It's as if it is something we regrettably have to live with (that "necessary evil"), as if we're really not too proud of it. Americans take an almost apologetic position about their hierarchy. It's necessary, it helps get things done, but we're not going to make a big deal of it. After all, nobody is really better than anybody else.

The Importance of Rank, Status, and Position

In nonegalitarian cultures by contrast, the red tape is honored. One must wait one's turn respectfully; one must not intrude on others' responsibilities or authority; status and rank are important; and the etiquette and protocol that accompany rank must be followed. Position is based on age, seniority, sex, family, schooling, competency, perhaps, connections, more likely. The hierarchy exists not for the smooth and efficient accomplishment of tasks, but rather for itself. The formal hierarchy is often quite clear; in fact, it is proclaimed. To the outsider, responsibilities and individual authority, rules and regulations, are obvious and transparent. The logic of the bureaucracy may be unknowable, the rationale for those holding power untenable, but the rules and the power are for all to behold. The hierarchy is to be reckoned with and, in this sense, respected.

This is all something of a mystery to Americans, for unless there is a practical reason for all the hoopla over titles, position, and the like, there isn't much reason to defer to Mr. Upthere if he's standing in the way of getting the job done. The American CEO will be introduced by his first name and will make a point of rolling up his sleeves with the rest of the team in order to get the task accomplished. The American is frustrated and angry when he or she doesn't get the cooperation of higher-ups who he or she feels are there to serve his or her needs. Americans appreciate the clarity of the formal, nonegalitarian organization, but intensely dislike the stagnation and self-servingness of the operation. They recoil from the idea of having to *pay* (a tax, fine, or graft) to get done what "they're already getting paid to do." (Never mind that the bureaucrats they deal with in most cases are themselves overworked, underpaid, trying to get by on far less than is possible, and suffering the system, from their side of the desk, as much as the Americans are on their side of the desk.)

Many non-Americans find themselves lost in the murky, half-lit, world of the American hierarchy. It's not that the hierarchy isn't rational or clear: Americans are masters at rationality, and there is probably a handy organizational chart available for anyone who asks. Non-Americans working for U.S. companies in the States, however, complain that despite the road maps, Americans drive differently. It is difficult for non-Americans to "read" the American hierarchy because, coming from a less egalitarianistic culture in most cases, they are uncomfortable making decisions like who and when to pass in the hierarchy in order to get something accomplished. Americans have learned to "read" their hierarchy, and they know when to speed ahead, which curves to avoid, and whom they can detour around. In the hierarchical, nonegalitarian world, the orderly procession through the hierarchy is very important. In the egalitarian American world, supported by other values such as individualism and concern for time, one can drive through the hierarchy with a free-spirited assertiveness that would leave many an official bleeding in a more nonegalitarian culture.

That's what happened in the above scenario between the American and his French associates. The American is eager to get on with what he perceives to be the simple task of implementing a form. It has been done successfully in the States, and he sees no reason for its not being put in place quickly in France. Many other problems are inherent in Stevens' thinking. He is ignoring (or ignorant of) different notions of time and quality, and he is guilty of rampant ethnocentrism (he believes that what works in the States will therefore work everywhere, and mistakenly assumes that U.S.-style technology and implementation systems are in place in France). But perhaps Stevens' most glaring problem is being caused by the clash between his American egalitarianism and his French associates' respect for hierarchy, order, arrangement. Stevens simply cannot believe that the French have made things "so complicated" when, from his perspective, they're so easy. Additionally, he does not understand that it would be extremely difficult for the French to make decisions that are the province of others, particularly when they are the province of their superiors. Finally, he fails to understand why they don't see that their way of doing things is inefficient and cumbersome. If he were in charge, he would cut through all the barriers, take care of things himself, and "just do what had to be done." And he would be mystified if anyone objected. After all, he would only be doing what he had to do to get the job done.

As presented, this example is a bit of an exaggeration. It is based, however, on a real situation, and I suspect it's representative of the real clash, at heart, between two world views. One is the view of the John Wayne individualist and egalitarian, the take-charge, out-'a-my-way, nobody's-gonna-tell-me-what-I-can-do wrangler. The other is the view of the formal, status-respecting, aristocratic, conservative, nonegalitarian

West European. In fact, there are few areas in which Europeans and Americans are more dissimilar. On scales 1 and 2, it would be easy now to locate the United States toward the right side, while nonegalitarian target cultures, like France and Germany, would be more toward the left side.

Of Kings and Queens and Presidents and Things

European history is one of nearly a thousand years of feudalism — of kings and queens, dukes and princes, of rigid class systems with peasants down here, burgers here, Church officials up here, and kings and queens on top. In business, as in life, it would be foolish to expect there to be no residual influence of such stratification. And when examined, country by country, one can see the history of each nation reflected in the way business there deals with these issues of hierarchy, status, and formality. America, on the other hand, was born in a revolution against class, status, and aristocracy. There have never been kings and queens here, and this is a very important reason for the strength of egalitarianism in the United States. Americans have a keen nose (like the Australians) for anyone seeking to "put on airs" or "set themselves above others." As a corollary, we are very fascinated by aristocracy, but only when it is emasculated and close enough culturally to enable us to understand it, as is the case with the British monarchy. Equally fascinated are the Europeans by American egalitarianism: They find it spirited, annoyingly naive, and charmingly refreshing.

Perhaps nowhere else is this clash between egalitarianism and European aristocratic tradition more apparent than in business dealings between U.S. and British firms. Americans, lulled into complacency by the similarity of the language, assume there are few or no differences between the way business is done here and in the United Kingdom. But while the two countries have much in common, they are grounded in two fundamentally opposite value systems. Americans are anti-aristocracy, and the British are extremely class-conscious. In the United Kingdom, one's dialect, dress, the cut of one's hair, and one's manners at table all inform as to one's rank, schooling, origins of birth, and family breeding — important facts for the English when getting a fix on who you are. (Curiously, there is one area of British social and business life where all are leveled, where egalitarianism is maintained with stalwart intent, and that is the British pub. There, laborers and lords may stand shoulder to shoulder, and each is as good as the other. However, the lords have their own pubs — actually, private clubs — and the workers usually keep to their own around the corner. It is in a sense, as vertical a society as it ever was. However, it is in the pub where the American businessperson probably feels most comfortable with his or her British associates, precisely because the British, in that setting, are acting more egalitarian.) Privacy is automatically created and maintained within very limited amounts of personal space. The English have a stereotypical knack of publicly shutting out everything and everyone around them when needing to retain their privacy. And in British business, no one seems to be more private than the manager.

Dave Greene, from Chicago, was daily becoming more and more frustrated in his work in London. His team needed the advice and input of his business unit's director in order to complete the project satisfactorily, but the director was never available. Several times over the last few weeks, Dave had expressed his need for critical input from Mr. Spinder, the director, to the rest of his British coworkers. All apparently agreed at their weekly meetings that this would help move things along considerably. However, after each meeting, it appeared that no one would take the initiative to request Mr. Spinder's involvement in the project. Dave felt uncomfortable about approaching Spinder himself at first, assuming that such a request would be better received by Spinder if it came directly from one of the British staff members who had been working with him for so long prior to Dave's assignment from the States. It just seemed to Dave more natural that the British, who he assumed had known Spinder so much longer and better, be the ones to approach him.

However, after several weeks of no action, Dave approached Spinder himself with a request for his involvement. Dave presented him with a plan that required direct action from Spinder in several areas, as well as information that Dave felt was in Spinder's area of expertise. Dave was received politely and thanked for his thoughts and recommendations.

Another week passed, and Dave found himself becoming increasingly isolated from his coworkers. In fact, the small social interactions that used to occur at work throughout the day had suddenly become noticeably less frequent. A coldness now surrounded the team, and even less progress than before was being made. Then, one day in the hallway, Dave overheard Spinder chatting with one of his associates in the company, a member, in fact, of the team working on Dave's project. They were, however, not talking about the project, as Dave had hoped, but rather talking about Dave. He was shocked to learn that Spinder was annoyed at what he saw as Dave's "pushiness," and that he felt really "put-upon" at having to "answer to the American at all." "Typical!" was the term used by Spinder, and it was delivered with indignation. Dave was recalling the event later that evening to an American friend at his flat. Dave was incredulous. "It seems that the more responsibility the Brits have at work, the less responsible they individually become. And the Brits on my team don't even seem to mind!"

Americans negotiating with the British need to be keenly aware of the inherent conflict between American egalitarianism and British class tradition. Status, protocol, rank—all are important considerations. The British still retain their monarchy it must be remembered, and while this does not have a direct bearing on business, it reflects a value system very different from that of Americans, who pride themselves on having thrown out the king and his troops. In the above example, the American had not built an appropriate relationship (based, first and foremost, on respect for position and authority) with the British manager. He had acted according to his egalitarian instincts (the American subordinate inviting his superior to join the group in order to get the job done faster) and had imposed all this on his coworkers as well (who, not being as egalitarian-oriented as he, felt no requirement to bring their boss into the project).

The British are very aware, by the way, of their management issues, and there has been some intentional breaking down of the barriers that have traditionally kept the manager unavailable and the workers unwelcoming. However, it is interesting to note how strongly the traditional depiction of British managers as isolated from their workers and their work and the workers as not wanting their managers' input or intrusion still resembles the hierarchy of the British class system.

In the United Kingdom, managers and workers are not only stratified, but isolated from each other. In France, they are equally stratified, but not nearly as isolated. The French manager may indeed be removed from his or her workers, but is in constant communication with them through the bureaucratic channels. In Germany, managers and workers are also stratified, and communication occurs along the lines of the hierarchy. But the larger issue in Germany is the compartmentalization of individual managers and their teams and the difficulty of communication between such compartments.[14] While the British organization may resemble the organization development chart of an American company, the responsibilities and authorities, the "thickness" of the categories, and the requirements for passing upward between areas is much more rigid and defined. Americans need to be extremely sensitive when dealing with Europeans in general and should not assume they have reached the appropriate person just because a job in title or description is similar to the one they know or because if they were that person, they

[14]Hall, Edward T. and Mildred Reed Hall, *Understanding Cultural Differences: Germans, French and Americans*, Intercultural Press, Yarmouth, Maine, 1990.

would take on the responsibility they are hoping their opposite number will assume. In a rigid, nonegalitarian structure, roles are firmly defined. It is wise to be sure that the person you are speaking with has the authority to decide, implement, or whatever, before you sit down with him or her at the table.

In France, the organization does not resemble the vertical British ladder as much as it does a wheel, with the spokes of the wheel emanating out from a central authority. Here, too, is a modern-day business representation of French aristocratic traditions, for in France, authority is highly centralized. Louis XIV was the "Sun King," the divine center of the universe, from which all light emanated. France is central to civilization, and in the center of France is Paris. Even the organization of streets reflects this notion of centralization, with boulevards radiating out from central locations in different directions to form *étoiles*. All coordinated government activities in France have traditionally occurred simultaneously at any given moment anywhere in France. At any time of day, all the schoolchildren in a given grade are all learning the same thing at the same moment all over France. French territories abroad were (and those that remain, still are) never colonies in the traditional British sense, but rather were technically simply another *département* of France—a bit further away, perhaps, but revealing the strength of confidence in the centralized approach to organization.

Now while not all French managers would put themselves up there with Louis, there is a strong belief in the importance in French business of centralized command and decision making. Like the architecture of the city, the French office often is structured to allow the managers to have their office in the center of a large room, around which can be found the desks and smaller offices of their subordinates. They may be as personally unapproachable as their British associates, but their commands and decisions flow smoothly down to the subordinates through the communication process rationally instituted throughout the hierarchy.

The German model is neither a ladder nor a wheel, but perhaps many separate wheels, organized into a ladderlike hierarchy. Within each wheel, the central managers make fairly autocratic decisions, and the communication down to their subordinates is clear, rational and orderly. The problem comes in the communication between wheels, for here there is often a need for an integrating authority, order, bureaucracy, that is sometimes not there. The parallel with some of the central issues in German history is there: Germany was the last great European power to organize itself into a nation-state (and, in fact, only achieved final integration in 1990). This contrasts strongly with England and France, which constituted themselves into republics one and two centuries earlier (respectively).

Prior to German nationalization, what was to become the German state was an assemblage of principalities and fiefdoms. Within each fiefdom, the ruling prince reigned supreme, but between the fiefdoms, there was little coordination of effort and much dispute. German business faces the same challenge. The American would be wise to remember that the German manager sitting across the table is fully in charge of his or her "fiefdom," whatever realm of responsibility that entails. This provides the German with a self-assured security and a strong-willed conviction that how he or she does things is the right way to do them. Americans will be hard-pressed to challenge the will of German managers since their decisions are so intimately connected with the notion of their power in their realm of authority. Americans stand a better chance of convincing their German associates of their requirements if the Germans perceive the American requirements as also enhancing, maintaining, or securing the managers' power within their organization as well.

All three of these Western European cultures rely on an inherent set of values based on *non*egalitarianism and come out of European historical aristocratic traditions. Compare this to the American management organization, which, naturally enough, reflects the deep-seated American value of egalitarianism. Americans, in their tendency to *de*emphasize the importance of status and rank, are comfortable taking a consultative approach to management and negotiation. They approach their opposite numbers with a "we-are-all-equals-here" approach. When responded to in kind (which is the expected result in the United States), the outcome can be a dynamic and positive interplay of ideas, brainstorming, and problem solving. The manager or superior, despite his or her title and authority, expects to be able to talk equally in regard to the task at hand with whosoever has responsibility in the project.

At the negotiating table, Americans don't wish to be burdened with concerns about showing deference, respect, protocol, or any nonwork-related behavior. To them, such concerns only slow down the negotiation process. Americans will often be (next to Australians) the first to suggest dropping any formalities, rolling up shirtsleeves, and informally getting down to the task at hand.

The American model of organization might be visualized as many small ladders within larger ones, within even larger ones. In the American model, hierarchy exists, of course, within and between departments, but communication can easily move in all directions—both upward and downward, within and across departments, units, and divisions.

The MBO Example of
Egalitarian Management

MBO, or Management by Objective, is a very successful management style used throughout the United States. It is also an interesting example of how egalitarianism can run into trouble when Americans try to take a prototypically American idea and transplant it to foreign soil. MBO was first developed here, so it is not surprising that inherent in the MBO theory are many traditional American values that may or may not be shared outside the United States. Integral to the success of MBO is the specific assumption that all the participating individuals—managers and subordinates alike—share the ideal of egalitarianism. In MBO, managers and subordinates must consult with one another in developing a plan of action for task accomplishment. Then, periodically, they consult with each other again to keep the progress on track. In between consultations, the subordinates are expected to work on their own, or with the appropriate people, toward the accomplishment of their tasks. Ideally, the all-important consultations are collaborative. They are supposed to be an opportunity for both subordinates and managers to interact with each other as equals, share information, bounce ideas off one another, and come up with effective solutions together. The degree to which MBO is successful often depends on the degree to which all parties view one another as equals. Egalitarianism is central to the success of MBO.

In those countries where egalitarianism is not a central value, MBO often does not work. The degree to which it doesn't work is usually proportional to the degree that the country involved is nonegalitarian. In South Asia (India, Pakistan, and Sri Lanka, among others) and Southeast Asia (particularly Malaysia, Indonesia, and Thailand), where extremely nonegalitarian traditions prevail, subordinates expect their managers to tell them what to do and are quite unprepared to communicate honestly and openly with them. In such circumstances, subordinates will only tell western managers what they think they want to hear, whether it is true or not, will agree to unrealistic or impossible expectations, will refuse to take the initiative to discuss or suggest their own ideas, might withhold raising problems or asking for guidance, and can often leave the meetings with a notion that their superiors are actually showing their stupidity by seeking their advice and input on decisions they should in fact be making themselves and handing down to them.

We can extend this picture to the negotiating table as well. Where there is any possibility of an inequity of power in nonegalitarian cultures, those with power will appear to Americans to be dogmatic, authoritarian, and closed to new ideas, while those without power will appear to Americans to be submissive, passive, and unresponsive. Either position seems uncomfortable from the American perspective, and makes an unsatisfactory opposite number with whom to negotiate.

In the countries of Western Europe, nonegalitarianism may not be as extreme as it is in South or Southeast Asia, but it is nevertheless evident in various ideas to do with class, hierarchy, pecking order, etc. And here again, MBO fails to translate successfully. Traditionally, French managers are uncomfortable sharing information with staff members, for to do so runs the risk of diminishing one's power and authority. German managers are not eager to receive suggestions from below. And British managers do not gleefully anticipate rubbing shoulders with their subordinates at the next opportunity. Therefore, on scale 3, the egalitarian American culture would be closer to 1, while traditionally nonegalitarian cultures would be located more toward the right. Remember, the two opposite sides represent the most extreme versions of the scale; it would be unfair to say that Europeans expect their managers, superiors, or more powerful associates to act paternalistically toward them. However, combined with other important values, such as ideas regarding individualism versus group-orientation, Latin Europeans — and certainly Latin Americans as well as some extreme nonegalitarian Asian cultures — will tend to expect a paternalistic relationship between the power-holders and those who work under them.

Ascribed Versus Achieved Position

It would be difficult to leave a discussion of egalitarianism without mentioning the criteria used to determine status at various levels within different cultural hierarchies — particularly in connection with comparable American criteria. Egalitarianism tells us that here in the United States there is to be only one criterion: competency. Perhaps the fact that I have left this topic to the end of the chapter is itself a representation of my own American egalitarianism. I do not, however, mean to imply it is least important. In America, everyone is supposed to have equal access within the organization to move as far and as fast as he or she can, so any criterion external to that of competency is *supposed* to be nonexistent.

Why talk about additional criteria then? Well, for one thing, because other cultures don't see it quite the same way and, in comparison to the United States, often have a significant additional number of criteria for moving into (or even speaking with) various positions. But more important for Americans, whether at home or abroad, is the realization that these additional criteria have reality in the States as well. In fact, we know that, in addition to competency, there are other, very real, external criteria for moving upward through the American organization. Among these additional criteria are gender, ethnicity, race, age, schooling, and connections. In fact, the struggle in the American workplace has always been the attempt to bring reality into line with the egalitarian ideal—which, as represented here, is competency. But we Americans want to believe in egalitarianism so strongly that we save the mention of this nasty fact of life for the end, just as we tend to blur the lines of authority up and down the ladder for the sake of expediency and deemphasize the importance to the individual of the entire underlying structure.

The acknowledgment of these additional criteria in America is important to their demystification and hoped-for eventual disappearance. Meanwhile, it would help the American businessperson internationally to recognize these criteria as they really are at home in order to better recognize their more obvious existence abroad. Once again, central to our premise while seeing the clear stratification of work in other countries (whether based on gender, class, age, race, religion, ethnicity, or schooling), it can be dealt with more effectively by Americans if we seek parallels in our own multicultural experience at home. These noncompetency-based criteria, unfortunately, are not foreign to America.

The fact is, gender, race, age, physical condition, education, connections, sexual preference, etc. all—in both obvious and subtle ways, and to greater and lesser degrees in all cultures—influence the individual's ability to achieve positions within the hierarchy and even to be given access to other individuals within the hierarchy. Many of these criteria are ascribed (i.e., are a person's "luck of the draw" at birth); others are achieved. In more egalitarian cultures, ascribed criteria are supposed to be less important, less compelling than achieved ones; competency (measured in terms of quantifiable skills) is key.

In less egalitarian cultures, ascribed criteria are more important than achieved ones, with some being more critical than others. (In other words, one simply cannot become king unless first born a prince. Translated into business terms, this means that it is extremely difficult for someone not born of the right family or sex to become CEO of a major Japanese industrial corporation, for example.) Competency is simply not a major consideration.

An American businesswoman, or a younger (than his Japanese counterparts) American businessman in Japan might be mystified as to why, as they continue negotiations, they keep getting the feeling that the Japanese are backing away from the negotiation, hesitating. The Americans sense that "it" is not happening, somehow, and wonder why. The reason is simple: age and sex are very important criteria in Japan for determining who speaks with whom. In fact, what is going on should not altogether come as a surprise to either American, for such criteria also exist to some extent in the United States. Once recognized as a Japanese version of age and sex discrimination, both of which Americans have probably had some experience with back home, the Americans should be able to reach into their respective past experiences and develop authentic, appropriate, and constructive plans of action. (Ideally, of course, knowing this fact of life in Japan ahead of time is preferable, for it allows for effective preemptive action. Realizing this afterward is something like trying to put the tiger back in the bag as we've said.)

In the United States, too, all the criteria listed above play a role in allowing individuals access to higher levels. Such issues as discrimination based on race, gender, ethnicity, physical condition, sexual orientation, the "right" schooling, etc. do have their effect here. However, we view such criteria as problematic, as "shouldn't be's," and we legislate and fight against them. In other, less egalitarian-oriented, cultures these facts can be more or less accepted, expected, or even valued. (Many Latins, for example, have difficulty understanding the logic behind antinepotism regulations. Why is it wrong to want to take care of your family? There is an entire literature, still quite alive—upon which, I might add, Reaganomics founded its philosophical justification—about the practical and philosophical benefits to society of aristocracy and class; it is not coincidental that Anglo-American ties were so strong during the Reagan-Thatcher years.) Egalitarian cultures tend to deemphasize the importance of external, noncompetency criteria. Nonegalitarian cultures tend to rely heavily on these criteria.

We have been saying that Americans, because of similar domestic parallels, should not necessarily find the use of such criteria as age, sex, and race all that unfamiliar. As Americans abroad, we need to be careful not to let our heightened self-definitions (often helped along by the stereotypes foisted on us) blind us to similarities in patterns, say, of discrimination. For by recognizing such similarities, we are better able to respond constructively to them. And while Americans, being egalitarians abroad, might find it easy to identify cultures where sex, age and race, for example, are used more openly as criteria in business, it is important to note that there are also other nationalities who view Americans as more sex, race, and age conscious than they themselves are when it comes to business. In these cases, we egalitarian Americans can find ourselves in the curious position of negotiating with individuals who are more egalitarian than we are.

Americans and Socially Designed Egalitarianism

In certain Nordic cultures and in some socialist societies, egalitarianism is based not on a concept of all individuals sharing the right to get an equal place at the starting line, but rather on a concept of all individuals sharing equally in the abundance of society throughout the race. It is an egalitarianism based on valuing the group as opposed to valuing the individual. (The corollary is not necessarily true, by the way. Japan, as we saw, is group-oriented too, but it is not egalitarian.) In Sweden, and in several of the Central European (formerly Eastern bloc) countries, egalitarianism is visibly translated into an equality at work that goes beyond American individualist notions. For example, gender roles in business for men and women are typically much less differentiated. There can be women CEOs as easily as there can be men who stay home with the babies. For American businesswomen and men negotiating in Stockholm or Prague, it is important to know this, to be ready to encounter a different response (and, indeed, quite possibly a different sex) from what you will encounter in Tokyo. When we are in Tokyo, the Japanese might be the sexists, but in Stockholm, it is often our turn to wear the label. Egalitarianism, like all values, cuts both ways, and in international business, we are often confronted with the naked truth about our values by negotiating with people who not only hold opposite views, but who sometimes believe in the same values even more strongly than we do.

Let's put our awareness, at least in regard to egalitarianism, to work for us in an international business scenario. And let's use the opportunity to develop more global mind-set skills by applying the Global Homecoming© skills we have been developing to the following Global Homecoming Exercise©. Remember, the goal is to reach into your own experiences as an American with a rich multicultural heritage in order to find real, "do-able" (for which, read *authentic*) responses that are constructive and appropriate to the problem at hand. And remember, we are focusing here on differences in values surrounding egalitarianism.

Banking in Buenos Aires

You (the senior vice president for international operations and planning) and your three-member American team have already met with the Argentine bank representatives (all men: five bank representatives and two outside advisers) once before. That was about two months ago, when you outlined the basic terms of the arrangement you were looking for. As representatives of a major U.S. firm, you felt you could realistically expect the Argentineans to welcome your company's investment in Argentina and to accommodate you to whatever degree that they could, given the current changing state of the country's economy. Today, you are back in Buenos Aires hoping to wrap up the negotiations. During the first meeting, the Argentines seemed a little distant, but you felt they were merely being businesslike and didn't attribute anything special or important to what you perceived as a bit of distance on their part.

However, when you left the first meeting, in addition to feeling confident about their reception to the plan, you were pleased that one member of their team, Juan, the senior international vice president of the Americas region, and your equal, distinguished himself from the aloofness of the others by being warm and friendly to you. Perhaps it was merely because he was the best English-speaking member of the team. But, for whatever reason, you remember that when the first meeting began, you and your teammates were fidgeting a bit, having been kept waiting for about 20 minutes until the Argentines arrived. When they finally entered the room, Juan immediately introduced you and your team to his boss, Mr. Vienetti, and to the rest of his team. Juan seemed to take a particular interest in making sure that everyone was introduced properly and in turn to everyone else, and placed a special emphasis on making sure that you shook hands with everyone on his team. Unfortunately, your side was caught off guard by the delay and then the sudden formalities. Your colleagues did not have their business cards ready and were already seated in their shirtsleeves when the Argentines arrived. Everyone returned to their original seats as the Argentines were taking their places, despite the fact that Juan and you realized once everyone was seated that opposite numbers were not sitting opposite each other.

Anyway, Juan seemed to make light of it, and your team didn't make much of it either. They just wanted to get on with things. Additionally, although Juan was the first one to speak when you were first all introduced, he made a comment about appreciating being referred to by his first name, since his last name was so long for Americans to say and that it always took too much time. You liked that, since using first names all around made things a lot easier for you and your team. From your perspective, the first meeting was a success, with the exception of the minor confusion at the very beginning, but you felt certain that that was no big deal.

In the interim, between the first meeting and now, Juan has contacted you requesting that your boss be present, if this is possible. Apparently, this request came from Juan's superior. This was not possible, however, as your boss's schedule did not allow for it, and this project was specifically your responsibility. In fact, you would not have wanted to have had your boss present even if he could have come with you. But you did take the opportunity to inform Juan that you were bringing along Susan Lopez from your office. Susan is in charge of some important global accounting procedures, and you feel she might be able to contribute to the meeting, not only because of her professional expertise, but also because she is well versed in Latin-Anglo relations, being Mexican-American.

Now the second meeting begins. Juan is as warm and cordial as before, while the other Argentines are as businesslike and formal as before. Mr. Vienetti appears pleased to meet Ms. Lopez and immediately breaks into Spanish with her while the rest of the American team waits in silence. It seems like a nice exchange, although Susan ends the conversation by simply not responding to the last comment and sitting down. You ask Juan curiously what they were talking about, and he answers with a smile that Vienetti was asking her about her children at home, and he said that if she'd like, he could arrange for her to go out shopping later with his wife, etc. With such cordiality being expressed, you are feeling more confident that things are going well, and you feel encouraged to speak freely with the Argentines.

However, once the meeting gets going, it appears that things are not in sync. For one thing, the bankers are expecting a lot of new information that you do not remember them asking you for at the last meeting. You are having to respond that you either don't have the information, will have to send it later after you speak with your boss and appropriate others, or feel it is not relevant to the discussions. The Argentines, in turn, are frustrated, and act slightly put off. During a short break, Juan comes over to tell you that Mr. Vienetti is going to have to take care of some small emergency that just came up and has asked him to continue in his place. Juan says Vienetti apologizes for this.

Juan continues, "I see you are not as pleased with our discussions today as you were when we first met. I want you to know that I want this project to happen very much. I think it will be a good thing for our bank and a very good thing for Argentina. In addition, I like you, and I want good things to happen for you and your company, as well as here in my country." You are pleased to hear somebody on the other side being helpful, at least. Juan continues, "I am very eagerly looking forward to the day when your company is in Buenos Aires. You know, you must let me help. There are some things I can say. This information they need, for example. It is just a formality. A very important formality, of course, but nothing that should create such problems. Anyway, when your company is finally here and working in Buenos Aires, there are many things I can do then, too, to help make it successful. You know, you will need someone then to run things, to make sure no one is making problems behind your back, either at the bank or the government. You know the way things can be here in Latin America. I am sure Ms. Lopez has told you. Truly," Juan goes on, "if you and I can have an understanding now about how I can help you when the operations are set up in Buenos Aires, I am sure I can say a few things now to Vienetti to help that happen. We could probably have our assurances by the end of the day."

You were not expecting anything like this, and the situation is apparently a lot more complex than you have imagined. This is much more than you bargained for and something that you certainly need more time to think about. You ask Juan to ask his group if they would consider a long break, in order for you and your team to discuss some additional matters. Juan assures you that he feels this would not be a problem.

Global Homecoming Exercise© 4: Egalitarianism

1. *Recognize* Differences: In regard to the egalitarian dimension, now are the Americans and the Argentines different?

Argentines	**Americans**
The Argentines expect	The Americans expect
_____	_____
_____	_____
_____	_____

2. *Retrace*: Spend one minute meditating quietly to help relax and clear your mind. Close your eyes. Spend the next few minutes visualizing yourself going back to an event in your early years (at home, with relatives, at school, at church, with friends) in which you were with people very close to you who *held similar values* to the Argentines in regard to egalitarianism. Describe the scene:

_____

_____

_____

_____

3. *Reclaim:* Who were the people in your scene? How would you describe their culture?

_____

_____

What is their country?_____Ethnicity?_____

Religion?_____Generation?_____Sex?_____

Relation to you?_____

How did you feel about these people?_____

_____

_____

4. *Reframe:* What factors in these people's culture do you think might have caused them to act the way they did with you?

_____

_____

_____

What cultural gifts have they brought you?_____

_____

What have you learned from them?_____

_____

Go back to this situation now. You are there, but as the person you are now. What will you do differently?

_____

_____

5. *Resurface: You are the American in the "Banking in Buenos Aires" Case.* What cultural gifts can you bring to this encounter?

_____

_____

_____

What cultural gifts do they bring to this encounter?_____

_____

_____

What can you say or do to find a better way home (to reach a more satisfactory agreement or conclusion to this business situation)?

_____

_____

_____

PART 3

Successful International Communication

7
The Effective International Negotiator

Negotiation as Communication

We are all experienced negotiators. In almost every aspect of life, we are negotiating, attempting to resolve conflict, seeking the best advantage we can find in any given situation. We negotiate with our spouses, our children, our parents, our coworkers, our bosses, our teachers, our friends. Like many other basic skills in life, however, negotiating is a skill most of us have never really been taught anything about, except perhaps through the experiential school of hard knocks. Like parenting, teaching, and learning to be a good friend or lover, negotiating is something we all do all the time and have developed a certain individual style in doing, yet it remains something we don't really know that much about.

In fact, though, there has been much research in the field of negotiation, and there is fortunately now a good deal of information around that can guide us in our quest to become better negotiators. Most likely, as with many of the other skills mentioned above, we have had to learn how to negotiate through trial and error. Most likely, we have developed particular individual styles that we are comfortable with. However, research has shown that there are certain ways of negotiating that are simply more productive than others. If we take a look at some of this information and then take a look at ourselves and the ways we've come to negotiate, we have the opportunity to reevaluate our behavior, our previously established ways, and try some new behavior that might be more effective.

Negotiating internationally, of course, poses some additional concerns — primarily cultural — which we are addressing in this book. Some interesting points can be made about preferable styles of negotiation based on the research that may have an impact on our own preferred individual styles. For one thing, many of the ways that Americans "naturally" negotiate are really based on a series of assumptions that are closely, and not surprisingly, tied to our cultural values. Therefore, how we behave in a negotiation is not actually "natural," but culturally determined, and the same can be said of other cultures' negotiation styles. It is when two cultures come together that we see most vividly how "unnatural," or culturally determined, some of the styles really are.

Most important to us here, perhaps, is the fact that the research on effective versus less effective international negotiation styles seems to support certain aspects of the way some cultures negotiate, while discouraging other aspects. That is, a model can be developed that can serve as a guide to the behavior, techniques, strategies, and tactics that are more productive than others, and then we can compare such a model to how different cultures, including our own, stack up. It's a way of evaluating those areas where we can stand a little revamping and those areas that should be emphasized. It's also a way of anticipating the kind of negotiating styles that other cultures might use, and it enables us to make some decisions about how we can anticipate, adapt, and maneuver the negotiation, given the information about our counterpart's style, so that we can still succeed.

This chapter, then, will look first at some of the information now available about effective negotiating styles. When looking at this information, we'll also look at how today's effective international negotiators use some of these "best practices" in their work. Finally, we'll try to identify some of the most effective, proven techniques and styles in ourselves, in the way we negotiate today, or perhaps, in the "foreigner" within. We will discover that many of the attributes of the effective international negotiator are also elements of the "global mind-set" were discussing earlier in the book.

Then, in chapter eight, we'll look at the information that highlights the negotiation styles of various key cultures around the world, including the United States. This will enable us not only to compare ourselves with the ways other countries negotiate, but also to measure ourselves against some proven techniques. Again, we'll try to find the better ways in ourselves, in our present techniques, in the "foreigner" within, and in our own developing global mind-set.

If You Go for the Relationship, the Deal Will Come

Let's say it right up front: Good negotiating is not about outsmarting, out-maneuvering, or outmanipulating the other side. It's not about hitting your international associates over the head and running off with the good-ies before they know what hit them. It's not about deception, omission, or getting away with something. And most of the time, it's not about one side having to give something up it needs in order for the other side to get what it wants. The research seems to indicate that the better negotiators—i.e., those that get more of what they want—do so in a collaborative climate, where relationships are established, where needs are met, where both sides walk away winners. The fact is that you get more of what you want, more of the time, if the negotiation looks win-win, rather than win-lose. And the kicker is that if this is true when it comes to negotiations in general, then it is even more true when it comes to international negotiation.

If the evidence isn't convincing enough, there is a basic fact of life about international business that should put any argument about which path to follow (win-win or win-lose) to rest for good. And that fact is that, *in international business, the relationship is perhaps the single most important aspect to consider,* and you simply cannot build a relationship if you're going to hit the other person over the head and run away with the goodies. In most other cultures, a relationship must be established as a prerequisite to doing business, to negotiating. In the United States, this prerequisite is an anomaly. For various reasons, including our reli-ance on the wizardry of technology, our comparative youth (and inno-cence) as a culture, and our go-get-'em values, we tend to do business first and then, if appropriate, build relationships later (if we have the time). Since for the rest of the world, building relationships is such a critical requirement of doing business, it would be difficult to build re-lationships if one were to set about negotiating in a competitive, all-or-nothing mode. However, aggressive, cutthroat approaches to negotia-tion have not been uncommon in American business practices. The point here is that, if building relationships is critical in the international arena, you're not going to suceed in negotiating without them. The other side simply isn't going to want to sit down with you again. And, in international business, you're going to need them to.

Effective international negotiators recognize this requirement. They understand that the negotiation, first and foremost, is not about the numbers or the terms or the dates. It's about the developing personal relationship of trust and mutual respect between the individuals at the table. This means, among other things, that you should take the time to get to know each other. And while this might be a difficult requirement for Americans, in terms of their values, time, and resources, it will probably be the first main goal of your associate abroad.

There are various stages that negotiations pass through. And there is a timing that needs to be followed regarding these stages. Once again, different cultures emphasize some of these stages and deemphasize others and tend to move more quickly or more slowly from one to the other. But, inevitably, all follow the similar pattern. In moving from one stage to the other, the process should be smooth; negotiating in this sense is like a dance, and the partners should both move at the same tempo and speed, with the same rhythm. If one is dancing faster than the other, if one moves from one stage to another before the other is ready, the negotiation dance struggles along. In some cases, the partners trip over each other, and though the music goes on, the dancing stops.

Our world views all negotiations as passing through three stages. The basic stages of negotiation can broadly be outlined as: (1) ritual sharing, (2) positioning, and (3) problem solving.[15] The ritual-sharing stage is the getting-to-know-each-other stage. It's the time spent on learning about each other, on revealing information, feelings, thoughts, etc. It is an attempt to establish a relationship, or at least, the minimal amount of trust necessary in order to proceed to Stage 2. If the need for relationship building is different on the two sides, the dance can begin to break down even before it gets started. Ritual sharing usually begins the negotiation. Americans generally have a ritual-sharing period that extends for a few minutes. Then we're ready to move on to the "business at hand." We separate that business at hand from the "schmoozing". But in many other cultures, the socializing *is* the business at hand, or at least certainly more important to it than Americans usually consider it. Before negotiations can proceed in many cultures, the ritual sharing must be quite elaborate.

"Grow" Your Relationship

An associate of mine tells the story of her time spent in Togo, where, before any business discussions could be conducted, all parties had to inquire about the health and well-being of each other...and each other's family and wives...and brothers and sisters, aunts and uncles, cousins, nieces and nephews, close friends, dead ancestors, cattle, and other livestock. The ritual sharing would consume most of the morning. Then tales would be told of the latest domestic misadventures, food and drink would be served, and, at some point after lunch, some substantial matters of business might then be considered.[16]

---

[15] The conceptual model was developed by Ellen Raider International, Inc.
[16] This anecdote was contributed by Ellen Raider.

All of this elaborate ritual sharing is an effort to establish, define, and maintain the relationship. In many cultures abroad, if a relationship has not been defined, the most important issue to be negotiated, right from the start, is your involvement with the local culture. You will be asked to join your associates on tours of the city, the local monuments, restaurants, etc. You will be hosted until you drop. And while you are dying to get down to some serious nitty-gritty work before you fly home, your associates/hosts will seem more concerned about making sure you are enjoying your stay in their country. The point here is that the relationship is more critical for them than it is for you. The more effective international negotiators recognize this and try, within their parameters and constraints, to adapt to this need. In the long run, it will get you more of what you want. Your competitors will realize this, even if you don't.

For reasons already discussed, Americans can have a tough time with this. Our values, our time, and our resources often limit us. We don't want—or simply cannot—run halfway around the globe, to be simplistic about it, just to say "Hi." However, there are some things we can do to help ourselves in this dilemma. For one thing, while relationships are solidified and significantly helped along by face-to-face encounters, they can also be built, nurtured, and maintained through long-distance communications. Fortunately, despite our view of the negotiation as being an activity usually consisting of how much business you can do within three meetings in three days, your associates abroad will often view the negotiation as your entire association with them over a period of time that begins and ends much beyond the immediate parameters. It is imperative to "grow" your relationship. Having a contact with someone abroad with whom you are doing business is a precious asset. You must guard it, nurture it, and protect it. An associate of mine finds an occasion to write and call all his overseas associates religiously every few months, even if there is no apparent occasion. He keeps a log and finds reasons to stay constantly in touch. It is essential. Your associates abroad more than likely see each meeting with you as just another part of a much larger process of negotiation. Americans tend to get in and out quickly, forgetting the most important aspect of doing business abroad: keeping in touch, before, during, and after the particular meetings of the moment.

There are immediate advantages for you in operating this way. Since the relationship with you is what is important, what one person can or cannot do for you today may change tomorrow. A friend (or enemy) today can be the opposite tomorrow. Over long distances, information about conditions and competition abroad is essential and difficult to obtain, and therefore, valuable. All of this is made easier through constant relationships. All of this is harder when you just get in and get out.

Take the time, up front if possible, to build the association. Make the time throughout, to nurture it. The deals will come when the relationship is solid. And until it is solid, any deal will be difficult.

This is not to say that foreign associates won't sit down and negotiate a deal if it's staring them in the face, whether or not they have a relationship with you. Of course they will, if it's to their advantage. But the long-range relationship will ensure more and better deals to come. They want to feel as if they can rely on you again in the future. This means your negotiating with them in good faith and fairly right up front. And the advantage to you is that if your associates are worth negotiating with in the first place, they are worth holding on to. You don't want to have to start this long-distance search all over again in a few months or years with someone new. If you think investing time and money in relationship building is costly on the front end, try having to do it over and over again each time you need to step out there simply because the relationship wasn't maintained, or worse yet, was damaged because of "win-lose" negotiating.

Focus on Interests and Needs, Not Positions

The second stage of negotiating usually moves us from the ritual-sharing stage to the positioning stage. This is where both sides put forward their positions, what they think is the best they can get out of the situation. There's nothing inherently wrong with positions in the sense that they do serve to inform us and each other of some of the needs, thoughts, desires, and wishes of the other side. And as a first step toward mutually sharing important information, this is not a bad start. But it must be recognized as only that: a start. The better negotiators do not focus on positions. Instead, they look to the underlying needs that are often below the surface that are the *raison d'être* for the position in the first place. And, once again, if this is true of successful negotiating in general, it is even more true of successful negotiating internationally.

The position is merely one way of stating how a need might be fulfilled. The position is one side's perception of how to best meet its underlying needs. Needs underlie positions, and while the position might be a restatement of an underlying need, it is often a statement of just one way to get the unstated, underlying need fulfilled. It may not be the only way, but it is the way that one side decides is best for accomplishing its goals, i.e., fulfilling its needs. Roger Fisher and William Ury, in their work with the Harvard Negotiation Project, talk about the importance of separating needs (or interests) from positions in their wonderful book, *Getting to Yes.** The fact is, the better negotiators are able to distinguish positions from underlying needs and put their energy into focusing on the needs that both sides bring to the table, rather than into fighting over positions. Admittedly this is easier said than done. But as a general theoretical approach, it has been shown to lead to more successful negotiations.

The trouble here is that people don't put forward their underlying needs easily. Most often, we indicate our positions instead and hear positions, not needs, from the other side, as well. Talking on the needs level often requires trust and certain other cultural preconditions that, in certain cultures, may not exist. Making a demand regarding what you perceive to be your need presents you as having already made a decision about what you want. Discussing your underlying needs, however, presents a problem only, without a solution. A position is our one perception of a solution for meeting our deeper needs.

A position, therefore, is one ready-made or prepackaged solution to what might be a set of underlying needs. It keeps the other side at bay and out of your territory. It merely makes a demand to the people on the other side. It does not implicate them in your problem. Traditional negotiating has been based on each side putting forward its position to the other. Then, once the positions are clear, the negotiation becomes a process of concession making, whereby each side bargains with the other and compromises as little as possible in order to retain as much of its position as it can. Since traditional negotiation in this form does not implicate the other side in your efforts, it permits either side to use all sorts of techniques, clean and dirty, in the achievement of its goals, which is to retain as much of its position as possible. The use of power, manipulations, dirty tricks, as well as legitimate compromising becomes possible in these circumstances.

The result of this kind of negotiating, of course, is often win-lose. Should the positions be so far apart, should power be so unequal, should one side be able to manipulate much more effectively or hold more powerful cards, then that side gets what it wants (or most of it), while the other side gets little of what it wants (or none of it). Traditional negotiating of this kind allows for the expectation of a winner and loser. The sharing of mutual needs is minimal, and the style of the negotiation is competitive: who can best get away with what, often at the expense of the other.

When negotiation is focused on position, as this kind of traditional negotiating is, the most one side can get is its position met, since that is

*Fisher, Roger, and William Ury, *Getting to Yes*, Penguin Books, New York, 1983.

all it is asking for. Of course, most of the time, it must settle for much less, having to give away certain things in order to get some things in return, so that the other side can get *some* of its position met as well. The negotiation takes the form of give-backs and compromise. In fact, if power is equal in a competitive, win-lose negotiation, often the best you can do is to settle for less than what you have stated in your position: you compromise.

This of course, explains the reason why people often start out with inflated positions, expecting to have to give things away, expecting to have to compromise. The idea being that if you start out asking for twice what you really want, you'll be able to compromise down to what you really want. This also explains why, in the process of compromising or concession-making, people misrepresent what they can really do or really have, in order to be able to give something away, to justify, in turn, their own demands. These techniques and others are the result of having to negotiate positionally. They result, at best, in compromise, in both sides having to settle for less than what they really want, or, on the other hand, in their having to play games with each other about what they really want and what they are willing to give away in order to settle for what they get. At worst, these techniques can result in no agreement at all, in a deadlock whereby both sides are stuck with their positions, unable to meet each other's positional demands, unable to move, unable to succeed.

However, when negotiation takes the form of needs-based negotiating, when negotiators focus on their mutual underlying needs instead of digging into their own positions, then both sides become party to satisfying each other's needs. This represents moving to the third stage — the *problem-solving* stage of the negotiation process. No longer is one side providing a prepackaged, one-sided solution to the satisfaction of its own needs only. Now, both sides set out to explore ways to satisfy each other's mutual needs.

Positional negotiating can be so ingrained that people often do not recognize their own underlying needs. In planning for a negotiation, people often jump directly to the formulation of a position without considering deeply what their true needs are. Both sides come to the table, in many cases, with shadowy ideas of what they really need, but with very definite ideas of one particular "must" or "want." By negotiating collaboratively, you try to enlist the other side's help in finding satisfactory solutions to deeper needs. The result, in many cases, is that you may walk away with more than what you went into the negotiation expecting to get. Positions may seem to provide us with the ultimate pie. But the ultimate pie, as we see it initially, is only based on our own limited view. When the other side gets involved in helping us get what we want, we can sometimes see how much more there is to be gained for both of us.

Once again, international negotiating provides us with a unique opportunity to find even more effective ways to fulfill our underlying needs. By virtue of the fact that all individuals and groups are limited in their ability to conceptualize alternate solutions, the position we arrive at and finally put forward is a representation of what only we have been able to think of. It has been determined, or at least shaped in great part, by the limits of our own intelligence, creativity, and the cultural, political, corporate, and environmental constraints we negotiate under. When we bring other people into the picture, especially people who have different points of view, we are giving ourselves an opportunity to look at the fulfillment of our needs from a fresh and new perspective. Admittedly, the views and positions of the other side might not provide us with alternate solutions for meeting our own needs. But, in sharing mutual concerns, we begin the process of looking at both sides' real needs and the possibility of providing each other with additional, fresh input toward finding solutions. It is the old story of two heads being better than one. In fact, in international negotiations, we often have the opportunity to more than double the brainpower at the table. If you can turn the negotiation into a fact-finding, information-sharing, and trust-building collaborative effort for the satisfaction of mutual needs, you are using the other side's brainpower, creativity, energy, and fresh perspective, as well as your own. This can geometrically increase your chances of coming up with more and better solutions.

Of course, the problem in negotiating with a needs-based focus, as opposed to a position-based one, is that it requires approaching the negotiation from a win-win perspective. The other side is simply not going to help you satisfy your needs unless its needs are also taken care of. The result can be a richer solution for both, but it requires that each side get involved in the deeper needs of the other. It means that, instead of wearing the other side down in an effort to try to hold onto what you believe you must demand, you open the other side up to reveal its true needs in order to find areas where you can help. In return, you can expect assistance from the other side in meeting your side's own deeper needs when you reveal them to the other.

This process requires trust, a willingness to collaborate, and a repudiation of power-based negotiation in favor of negotiations based on a mutually respectful association. Coincidentally, these are the same preferred conditions for negotiating internationally. Once again, we see that, in general, the international context can actually favor collaborative, needs-based, relationship-oriented negotiating as opposed to more traditional position-based, competitive, compromise-oriented negotiating. Effective international negotiators are the ones who focus their efforts on the underlying interests and needs, and not on the positions, of their side, as well as of the other.

Getting the other side to reveal its true needs to you and feeling comfortable enough to reveal your side's underlying needs to the other is the goal of the more effective international negotiator. It is not an easy task. It certainly is not as easy as simply presenting a position and then fighting for it. But, as we have seen, the rewards can be much greater. And in international negotiating, as we've also seen, since relationships are so critical, needs-based solutions that satisfy both sides are better solutions than either compromise or deadlock. Moreover, they are the only solutions that ensure that the other side will keep coming back to the table, since they provide real needs satisfaction, and in so doing, deepen and strengthen the relationship. In opposite fashion, competitive, traditional positional, negotiation results in limited needs-satisfaction, risks deadlock, and certainly can weaken and sometimes destroy the relationship that is so important in international negotiations.

I recently attended a negotiation between manufacturers and distributors from various Caribbean and African nations attempting to sell their goods to U.S. buyers. The goods consisted primarily of certain natural resources, spices, foodstuffs, and native crafts. Once the ritual-sharing stage had been completed, both sides moved into positioning rather quickly. The manufacturers and distributors (the sellers) wanted to nail down prices right away, while the U.S. buyers seemed to be more concerned with providing the sellers with all sorts of information, like their required shipping and delivery dates, customer refund policies, corporate insurance requirements, etc. The sellers were frustrated in their efforts to confirm prices, while not having much luck in understanding what the buyers were really aiming for. During a break in the negotiation, some of the sellers complained to me that the U.S. buyers were avoiding giving them firm commitments on their price positions.

This was a case of traditional positional bargaining, in which neither side was meeting the position of the other. At this point, both sides were merely stating their positions to each other. With luck, there might be some meeting of the minds, someplace where the positions might "fit." In the real world, however, this is rarely the case. It certainly was not the case here. The sellers were putting price forward as their primary positional concern and were unable to grasp what the other side wanted. The buyers were putting forward corporate requirements regarding the prospective deal as their primary position; no doubt price was part of this package, but not as the up-front concern it was for the sellers.

As the negotiation continued, it became clear that the buyers were not even willing to discuss price issues until they felt comfortable that the sellers had a clear understanding of their other corporate requirements. For the buyers, this was a necessary parameter. But the sellers didn't understand how such details could be of primary concern and were not interested in looking at them until they felt comfortable that the negotiations were worthwhile—i.e., that the price issue was settled. This negotiation was headed for a deadlock before it had actually begun. In fact, that is what happened. As the sellers pushed their price concerns harder, the U.S. buyers simply backed off. The buyers became convinced that their ground rules were not going to be agreed to by the sellers, and without such understanding, the buyers simply could not proceed. The sellers, on the other hand, felt that the buyers were insincere about wanting to negotiate, since they wouldn't discuss price.

Had the focus of the negotiation been on the underlying needs of both parties and not solely on the expression of each side's respective position, this negotiation need not have collapsed. In fact, the underlying needs of both parties, I believe, were not that different. The sellers needed to generate revenue. While they thought they needed to focus on getting the best price for their items as quickly as possible in order to do this, they were using price as their position. But their real underlying need was the development of a profitable business relationship with the U.S. buyers that would satisfy their revenue requirements. In turn, the U.S. buyers also had as their underlying need the development of a profitable business relationship with the sellers. But they were focusing on getting agreement on operational details first as the way to achieve this. This became their position. At the positional level, the two sides' demands were very different. At the needs level, however, their concerns were very similar: the establishment of an ongoing, profitable business relationship. In fact, both sides' positions would have had to have been considered sooner or later. After all, price, delivery schedules, insurance terms, refund policies, and the like are all important concerns in building a business relationship. But in the absence of a mutual sharing of needs, these issues became stumbling blocks to the achievement of the bigger picture instead of issues to have been collaboratively discussed once both sides recognized that their mutual interests were the same.

Had such recognition occurred, a timetable or agenda could perhaps have been devised whereby the points within the positions of both parties could be discussed. In a collaborative climate, where mutual needs would have already been revealed, both sides' rigid adherence to their positions might have melted away. Once deeper underlying needs are revealed and addressed, the initial positions often *do* fall away. There simply is no need to hang onto a position when the real needs are being taken care of.

In this case, there might have been no need for the sellers to hold onto their starting price positions. One possible scenario that might have developed in a more needs-based negotiation would have been the sellers settling for a lower price in exchange for the guarantee of long-term contracts, contracts that would meet the operational requirements of the buyers. Again, the sellers might have been willing to lower the price if the buyers would guarantee volume purchases over significant periods of time. The sellers simply did not see the possible alternate solutions inherent in this situation because they were stuck on their price position as the way to satisfy their needs. Alternately, the buyers were blinded to alternate solutions in achieving their underlying needs because of their determination to meet their operational requirements. Had real needs been revealed and addressed, both sides might have been able to see that they could help each other achieve true needs satisfaction. The more effective international negotiators try to work at this level.

Probe, Question, and Communicate Cooperation

Admittedly, getting down to the needs level is difficult, and that's one of the reasons why the better international negotiators are highly skilled and practiced in the "art of communication." Getting the other side to reveal its real needs to you and safely revealing your needs to the other side takes time, patience, trust, skill, and a well-tuned sensitivity to human behavior and communication.

In a sense, collaborative, needs-based negotiating is similar to needs-based selling, which has, interestingly enough, become a major tool for marketing in the United States. Rather than push the sale (or, in negotiation terms, "push your position"), you elicit information from the customers about what *they* need, what *their* problem is. (In negotiation terms, you get the other side to open up to tell you what the problem is, what is wanted from the negotiation.) Then you check out your stock to see what you've got that satisfies those needs. (In negotiation terms, you see what kind of bargaining chips you can offer.) In needs-based selling, your reward for this is the sale. In needs-based negotiation, your reward for this is that the other side does the same for you and meets your needs as well.

This kind of negotiation means that you need to share lots of information. You need to build a relationship. You need to respect each other as equals at the table. This kind of negotiation can look more like a cordial meeting to gather information. And this kind of negotiation can take time. The ultimate goal of your negotiation is the establishment of a mutually trustworthy business partnership with the individuals on the other side of the table. This kind of negotiation seeks to deemphasize power differences while emphasizing the substantive values that each side can provide the other and the principles each side uses as standards of judgment and decision making. It looks, in fact, very different from the traditional competitive negotiation but very similar to many of the situations that we find ourselves in when negotiating abroad.

The effective international negotiator knows how to probe, how to ask questions, and how to listen. These behavioral skills are also adapted to the cultural requirements of the participants at the table. Without probing, seeking information, and revealing information, there can be no understanding of underlying needs.

At first, the effective international negotiator is looking for areas where needs are mutual. Mutual needs, certainly, are the easiest to satisfy, since if I satisfy yours, you can easily satisfy mine; for they are the same. This should be the first step: identifying mutual underlying needs, if any. It also goes a long way toward establishing trust and encouraging the all-important relationship. Build from one victory to the next. Once mutual needs are established, meeting individual needs, inherently more difficult, can be easier precisely because there is now a spirit of cooperation and willingness that energizes both sides toward finding solutions for one another. Seek the satisfaction of small, mutual needs at first. Then expand the exploration of each other's needs to include as many as possible, as deeply as you both care to go. The more information, the better. Once mutual needs are satisfied, go onto the next step: getting other needs on the table. One-sided needs might still require fulfillment. For example, you might have a need that I do not share. But I may still be able to fulfill your need, and in so doing, I obligate you to try to fulfill mine, even if, in turn, my need is also not yours. However, it is important to start first by trying to locate mutual needs. It is then easier to move on to individually different needs.

This is precisely why the sharing of information is so important. If I do not know what your needs are, I cannot know if I can satisfy them for you. And if I cannot satisfy them, then there is no obligation for you to satisfy mine. Once information is exchanged, I can decide how what I have to offer, my bargaining chips, might "fit" with what your needs are. In turn, until you know what I need, you do not know how your bargaining chips can fit with my needs. People bring positions to the table easily; however, they do not reveal their bargaining chips easily. What we can offer each other is often kept very close to the vest, for chips are power. But when I find out what you need, I know what chips I have that might fit those needs; I can use my power.

In fact, a "chip-satisfier" proposed too soon — that is, before the other side has had the opportunity to reveal its needs — will sometimes be rejected, even if it *can* satisfy an underlying need. Remember, negotiation is a dance, and timing is important. If a chip is thrown out before the need it is intended to satisfy is expressed, it might not even be seen, or if seen, not recognized and valued. This is another reason why the better international negotiators work at questioning, probing, and listening, rather than positioning, manipulating, and bargaining.

Some words about questioning and listening skills: if we are going to be concerned about revealing and eliciting information, we need to question and listen well. What people say, and how they say it, is an entire field of social science research in and of itself. Suffice it for us to offer just a few pointers here.

As mentioned earlier, confirming understanding is critically important, not just because of cultural and language problems, but also as a way of moving the negotiation along in your efforts to pull information from the other side. When you test your understanding of what your international counterparts are saying through active listening techniques, summarizing back, etc., you are not necessarily agreeing, but merely letting the individuals on other side know that they have been heard and that their point of view is being considered.

(This is, by the way, very much what the Japanese implicitly do in their negotiations. The *hai* is an acknowledgment to the other side that its statements have been heard; it is not necessarily the agreement that too many Americans have in the past mistaken it to be. As noted, in fact, the Japanese negotiating style is more similar to the information exchange we have been discussing above, and this can explain why many Americans feel so uncomfortable negotiating with the Japanese. We often hear the complaint that the Japanese are unrelenting in their quest for information from Americans at the negotiation table. While Americans often are put off by this, it should be understood that, all other things being equal, the Japanese are in the information-gathering mode in order to understand what our needs are and how best to deal with us. In fact, once trust is established, Americans should expect to be able to ask many questions of the Japanese, in a similar effort. Unfortunately, one of the initial purposes of all the questioning at the outset by the Japanese at the beginning of a Japanese-American negotiation is to gather enough information about you to enable them to trust and do business with you, and until they do, there can be an unwillingness on their part to provide you with information in kind. Again, though, once the relationship is established, Americans should feel comfortable about eliciting as much information as they feel they need from the Japanese. Unfortunately, American-Japanese negotiations can fall apart before this relationship has been achieved in part because the Americans feel suspicious about having been required to reveal so much without reciprocal behavior from the other side.)

Questions that put the other side on the defensive—that attack, that are threatening, derisive, patronizing, insulting, demeaning, disrespectful, challenging, stereotyping, or criticizing—should all be avoided. These kinds of questions do not help the other side open up. Rather, they force the other side to defend itself against such attacks, usually by attacking back. This soon degenerates into an attack-defend cycle of behavior that gets nobody anywhere.

Equally unproductive is questioning or communicating that personalizes the problem. If you are trying to build a collaborative environment in which real needs are expressed, the last thing you want to do is make someone feel as if he or she is the cause of the impasse or disagreement. If there is a problem at the table, it is important to establish a tone that says, this is "our" problem, not "your" problem and not "my" problem. And while you do not make the problem theirs, you also do not accept it solely as your own. Together, both must own the problem. It sits between the two sides in the middle of the table. It belongs to both sides and is the responsibility of both sides to solve. Questions must be asked nonjudgmentally. It is nobody's fault for the way things are, nor do individuals or teams need to justify their needs. Keep the discussions and the questioning, professional not personal.

Sometimes people make themselves feel stronger by using some of the unproductive behavior listed above, or by playing dirty tricks, or by employing manipulative power games. These same people often feel insecure and vulnerable when revealing underlying needs or attempting to respond constructively (with real bargaining chips) to the needs of others. While some behavior might "feel" good, it reveals weakness. In fact, people appearing powerful this way are often masking an underlying powerlessness. Positional bargaining is weak, and needs-based negotiating is powerful. A position can be shot down, alternatives can be offered (indeed, that is what we want), holes can be poked in the reasons for the position, justifications can legitimately be challenged. Needs cannot. No one can challenge what you need. It does not require justification and cannot be undermined. There can be no requirement to change, relinquish, or justify your true needs, ever, to anyone. There can be no compromising of needs. Positions, on the other hand, are specifically designed to be compromised. Needs-based negotiating is strong, firm, and legitimate. You may not agree, like, or accept the other side's needs, but you can understand them and you cannot deny them. The best you can do is try to find a way to satisfy them. Needs-based communication is powerful and assertive. Positional communication is weak and consequently aggressive.

Remain Culturally Sensitive

It is well to remember culture's role in the use and interpretation of behavior. If we are probing, questioning, responding, listening, we must remember that the more effective international negotiators do so in ways that are culturally appropriate.

For example, what might be viewed as aggressive, attacking behavior in one culture might be seen as an acceptable way to seek information in another. The French, for example, as well as the Chinese, can be extremely direct in their questioning—for quite different cultural reasons. (The Chinese are also expert at being ambiguous and vague. This, again, is one of the dichotomies, the balance and acceptance of opposites, that defines Asian culture.) Direct questioning of the French variety can be interpreted by Americans as threatening. It is usually not meant to be. Equally, we Americans do not mean to threaten when we ask direct, personal questions of the Thais or Italians, yet these cultures, for their own distinct reasons, can find our style threatening.

In some cultures, it is appropriate not to respond. Yet it may seem to us as if the other side is avoiding an issue, an answer, a decision. In America, evasive behavior is usually not appreciated and, in a negotiation, therefore, would not be viewed as helping the collaborative process along. Nevertheless, in those cultures where silence, aversion of eye contact, or the avoidance of conflict is important, such behavior is considered very constructive in the development of a mutually collaborative atmosphere. (And, it must be acknowledged, there are times, even for Americans, when evasive action can be useful: for example, when you might need time to consider or to caucus, or when you need to avoid getting into subjects where you do not have the authority to respond.) We have also seen cases where two cultures' interpretation of evasive behavior can be different. For example, while a Latin or Asian might be more concerned about hosting you properly, an American might see endless hosting behavior as evasive, as an attempt to avoid substantive issues. In fact, the American might be failing to see that, for the Latin or the Asian, relationship building *is* the substantive issue at the negotiating table.

How we provide information, in addition to how it is elicited, is also culturally determined. Some cultures are comfortable providing facts, statistics, numbers; some will reveal their interests and positions more philosophically; still others will talk about their feelings first. What information is revealed, and the order in which it is revealed, can vary from culture to culture. If Americans are expecting a team of Mexicans to respond to their immediate launching into statistics and graphs, they may be much mistaken. Conversely, the Americans would be wise to tease out the vital information embedded within the possibly emotional discourse of their Mexican associates. And remember, this is all relative. The kind of information we value and the way we relate it might look very different to one culture from the way it looks to another. The American impatience with the display of Mexican "feelings" is matched for example, by the German impatience with our American talk of "feelings" at the table. While we ourselves often talk about how we feel and expect others to do so in turn as a sign of good faith, the Germans can find it a bit naive and off the mark.

Consideration also needs to be given to the style used when probing and seeking information, particularly with cultures where status and rank is important. Questioning, particularly the direct, pointed type of questioning that Americans are comfortable with, can be much too provocative, indiscreet, and even irreverent for many more conservative cultures. Deference, humility, and concern for saving the other's face take priority in these cultures, and we need to adjust our questioning style accordingly.

Stay Flexible, Stay Calm, Stay Creative, Just Stay

Effective international negotiators have staying power. They recognize that things take longer to communicate across cultures, that relationship building can be a time-consuming process, that collaborative negotiating requires a long-term perspective. The better negotiators are ultimately pragmatic. They are not oaks; rather, they are more like willows. Unable to predict every situation, every twist and turn, even in a domestic situation, they know that it is nearly impossible to do so in a cross-cultural one.

The global mind-set insists that one:

- Remain calm
- Not lose sight of the ultimate objectives of the negotiation

- Be willing to accept new conditions if credible and productive (even if they are unpredictable and difficult to plan for)
- Remain on the creative lookout for needs and accompanying possible chip-satisfiers
- Communicate, above all, a commitment to the negotiation and the collaborative satisfaction of mutual needs

An American associate tells the story of looking forward to a meeting with his Indian associate. It was a meeting that had been very difficult to arrange, and the American was thrilled to be finally scheduled to see the man. The American was hoping to be able to sell some sophisticated data-processing equipment to this fairly high-level Indian government official. Finally, the American felt that he had an "in." At least a meeting was arranged, and he would have his chance to begin a negotiation regarding the sale of his equipment. He was especially eager for the meeting because, as the months had dragged on while he was trying to arrange it, he had learned that several of his competitors were also trying to arrange to see this Indian fellow. Certainly the American wanted to have first shot.

He prepared as much as he possibly could for the meeting. He learned all he could about who his counterpart was, what his responsibilities were, the work he had done in the government, and the situation that the government was facing. This enabled him to prepare a presentation that, the American felt, took into account many of the possible objections the man might have. He spoke with several associates who had had dealings with the official before. All in all, he felt as prepared as he possibly could for the meeting.

The important morning arrived. He cleared his entire calendar for the day. He confirmed the meeting several days before. He arrived on time. But he was not prepared for what greeted him as he was escorted into his associate's office.

In the office was a comfortable couch along a side wall. And seated on the couch was another gentleman. The American was escorted into the office by a secretary and introduced to the Indian official he had come to see. He was offered a chair. The two men sat down. The American found it odd that he was not introduced to the man sitting on the couch, but he did not comment. His Indian host acted as if the man on the couch actually wasn't there. This "ghost person" was simply ignored. He wasn't introduced, nor was he spoken to. The American attempted to follow his cues and also pretended not to notice the ghost-man, and, of course, he did not speak to him. It all felt quite odd and began to be even more disconcerting as the two men's conversation turned to some very specific points. In fact, the American started to feel a bit paranoid. "Here I was," he said, "discussing some very proprietary information that was not for anybody else's ears, and yet there was this third individual in the room with us! I didn't know who he was. For all I knew, he could have been from my competition!" As the meeting proceeded, the American felt more and more uncomfortable, until, he admitted to me later, his concentration and his ability to focus on the negotiation suffered. Today he remembers vividly the face of that ghost-man on the couch, but not much more of that ultimately painful meeting. He was so unable to respond flexibly to what he perceived to be an unusual and mysterious situation that he lost his ability to negotiate effectively. He never got the sale. And he wonders if the ghost-man did.

There really is nothing unusual about what happened...within the Indian cultural context. But such a context was not what the American was expecting, and, being inflexible, he was unable to adapt to something strange and different. In fact, within the Indian context, there can often be a "third person" present, sometimes several people, who may be friends, family, or close business associates. Their role is to listen, perhaps to analyze, and afterward, to provide counsel and advice based on their fresh perspective. Rarely do they intrude and rarely are they spies or "plants" from the competition. But not knowing this, and being wholly unfamiliar with the custom, the American expended all his energy imagining the worst.

The better international negotiators *stay calm.* They keep their emotions in check. In many cultures, the outward display of anger, displeasure, or frustration is not considered constructive. It can negatively affect the negotiation. In fact, the better negotiators, instead of reacting negatively, get quiet. They use silence constructively. In many cultures, silence is, indeed, golden. As Americans, we are often uncomfortable with silence. We value speech, we value time and action and doingness. Therefore, to have the clock tick by (and time is money) with nothing being said is generally very anxiety provoking for Americans. Try this little experiment: In a conversation with a friend, spouse, or partner, the next time a question is asked of you, or the next time you feel that a comment is expected of you, simply do not respond. Experience how long the silent time feels. And watch the reaction of the other. Then be ready to explain what you were doing and why. The point is, in many other cultures, silence is a form of communication and is *not* "doing nothing." The better international negotiators take advantage of this. They use silence in order to defuse tension, to rest, to think, to mull things over, to consider. It is an effective way to actively communicate—

not disinterest, but on the contrary—real concern. Take advantage of the pauses in the negotiation; take advantage of the time to interpret, take advantage of the silences. Make these new situations work for you.

Flexibility is not only important in the face of new and unexpected cultural conditions. Responding flexibly to the negotiation process allows for creative alternatives to traditional compromises. That is, in collaborative negotiations, we want underlying needs to come out on the table in order to explore ways in which both sides can creatively help fulfill them. What kind of bargaining chips do I have that can help meet your needs? What kind of bargaining chips do you have that can meet my needs? In this kind of climate, we brainstorm alternatives, options, possibilities. This requires creativity and flexibility. Brainstorming means looking for other ways in which we can see the problem and try to meet each other's needs.

The Benefits of Brainstorming

Brainstorming is best done in a collaborative, nonjudgmental atmosphere, in which both parties are free to explore what they have to offer each other. Much of what will be brought to the table will no doubt be discarded ultimately. But some of it will be useful, and what *is* useful will promote more thought and more possibilities. Once both sides are freed from the box of having to defend themselves against each other, they'll be free to use each other's talents, putting twice the brainpower and twice the resources toward solving their problem.

In some of our international negotiation training programs, we have a simple brainstorming exercise involving, of all innocuous things, the cap of a ballpoint pen. Holding the cap up in front of the class, we ask everyone in the room to come up with as many uses for the cap as possible within the course of two minutes. In the true spirit of brainstorming, no suggestion is discarded, derided, or minimized; in brainstorming, everything is (or at least, should be) possible. To pass judgment during brainstorming dissuades people from thinking further and from putting their ideas forward, and the same is true at the real-life negotiating table. You don't want to put the "quietus" on anything that's possible just because your limits prevent you from seeing more. Let the contributions flow. In our classroom exercise, each time someone comes up with a suggestion for the possible use of the ballpoint pen cap, we put one stroke on the flip chart. At the end of two minutes, we count the number of strokes. I am always astonished at the sheer volume of possibilities. Most, of course, are impractical. Some are silly. Some are merely entertaining. But there are always some that have merit. And the sum total of possible uses is always greater than any one single person could have come up with on his or her own. In fact, it takes the entire roomful of people to come up with all the wonderful possibilities, useful and useless, that we generate.

It's the same at the negotiating table. Brainstorm possibilities. The more brains the better. Once we move beyond the positioning stage, once we establish a collaborative, needs-based environment, we are moving onto the third stage of negotiation: problem-solving. Here we are looking at alternatives, options, and hitherto-unthought-of possibilities based on both sides' bargaining chips, creativity, ingenuity, and energy that this kind of environment releases.

One final note on flexibility. It is not only essential to the collaborative process and useful in the face of cultural differences; it is also necessary when dealing with the curveballs (there's that American baseball phraseology again) of counterintuitive situations. A counterintuitive situation is one that turns out differently from the way you might assume it would given the information available. A significant and growing number of Japanese businesspeople do not fit the mold of the traditional Japanese worker who stays with one company for a lifetime, for example. These people are often highly responsive to individual merit, too, which also goes against traditional Japanese values. If we find ourselves negotiating with Japanese who are individually responsive to entrepreneurial ventures that could promote their own individual positions, we might view this as counterintuitive. International negotiators should be able to spot these things. They must not only know what is predictable, but also be able to recognize the validity of what is *un*predictable when it arises in order to adapt flexibly to it.

In such cases, it is information that sorts out the mystery. Where the Japanese are concerned, for example, it's vital to know that Japan today is really two Japans: an over-forty Japan and an under-forty Japan. The over-forty Japan still subscribes, in the main, to many of the traditional Japanese values, but the under-forty Japan questions a great many of them and is attempting to integrate many traditionally non-Japanese values into its everyday life. This can be a useful explanation for why, at the negotiating table, your Japanese counterparts may be acting unpredictably like Westerners. Beware of being jarred by counterintuitive experiences. In this rapidly shrinking world, it is important to expect them, and when they occur, to try to find a reason for them.

Stay Professional

Finally, the better international negotiators stay professional. They avoid personalizing the problem. They do not blame; they do not seek to point fingers. The problem is always something they share with others, something that is the responsibility of both sides.

Expert negotiators base their work on principles. Negotiation isn't about being kind, being nice, or being liked. It's generally not about seeking favors. It's best when your side is presented in terms of its needs, for, as we said, needs are, in a very basic sense, nonnegotiable; they can't be bargained away. What such negotiators ask in return is responses based on principles—on established and agreed-upon ways of behaving, on what both sides accept as right and fair. Experienced negotiators do not make personal obligations outside the principles of the negotiation in order to get things done. While their personal involvement is crucial, while they personally might be responsible for the follow-through or implementation of some or all of the items negotiated, the negotiation itself is not about personal promises to do this or that in order to get the larger thing done. Decisions to do things must be based on principles—what is mutually assumed to be right—and not on what can be done on the side to move things along. Dealing on an individual basis outside the parameters of the negotiation is a dangerous precedent to set, and effective international negotiators stay clear of it.

Deal with Destructive Behavior

Being professional also means reacting constructively to potentially destructive situations. Dysfunctional or destructive behavior from the other side needs to be addressed, and, if possible, turned around. Perhaps the one most effective weapon against destructive behavior is constructive, professional behavior on your part. If you are not attacking or blaming the negotiators on the other side, if you are attempting to put yourself in their shoes in order to better understand their position, if you are earnestly trying to respect their true needs as legitimate, you have every right to demand that they do the same for you. Therefore, if they are blaming, attacking, or criticizing, you need to explicitly identify this behavior as unproductive to the solution of the problem both sides are facing. Again, this should be done respectfully and with sensitivity to cultural differences and requirements. For example, you could question the other side about whether or not they think such personal attacks are constructive to the solution of the problem that you are both there to solve. If you acknowledge the legitimacy of their needs, you can demand that the other side do the same for you. If you operate, decide, and behave according to independent principles, you can legitimately demand that the other side does likewise. You have a responsibility for setting the standards by which you and your counterparts will operate. You can determine those standards together if there needs to be such a discussion, but certainly, you need not negotiate under circumstances that violate such principles. If you find yourself in such a situation, you must identify it as you would any other negative or destructive behavior. Call the other side on it, stop the larger negotiation, and conduct a "mininegotiation" around the issue at hand.

In negotiations where power is unequally distributed, destructive behavior from the other side can take the form of pressure. In circumstances where the other side is in a politically advantageous situation relative to your own, it is essential to clearly define the ground rules by which the negotiation will be conducted *before* any substantive business issues are discussed Specifically, you want a clear agreement that decisions will be made according to principles of right and wrong as they apply to the issues under discussion and that fact and reason in regard to those issues will be the only determining factors. This will enable you to refuse to give in to pressure or irrational demands based on a power position later in the negotiation. Never yield to pressure—only to reason. Again, if this situation does arise in the negotiation, it is important to stop the negotiation, discuss the fact that pressure or power is being used to force a decision that may not be reasonable in view of the facts at hand, and point out that this is not the way both sides have earlier agreed to conduct the negotiation.

Acting professionally also means being true to yourself, your beliefs, and the larger picture beyond the negotiation itself. Sometimes things simply cannot be negotiated. Sometimes values are so incompatible that you cannot sit down with the people opposite you. Sometimes certain possible outcomes are unacceptable. Effective international negotiators determine these things ahead of time. They know in advance what outcomes are unacceptable and at what point they will negotiate no further. This gives you power, for it frames the discussion for you and keeps you focused on finding ways (possible options, alternatives, chips available on both sides) to get what you want within well-defined possibility limits.

Being professional also means being able to defuse potentially explosive situations. Again, here is where remaining calm and professional is all-important. If your opposite numbers are reacting unconstructively (too emotionally, irrationally, threateningly, etc.), defuse the atmosphere by asking for their help. Ask, "What would you suggest?" Involve them in your process. They are probably reacting this way because they haven't been able to get all their needs on the table yet and are not pleased with what you are suggesting. To the extent that you can, you need to take responsibility for their behavior. Perhaps you haven't dug deep enough yet to find out what their needs are. Perhaps you need to assure them that you really are hearing their concerns and trying to help them get those concerns out on the table. Effective international negotiators keep digging. If your opposite numbers react irrationally, if they don't play at all, if they dig their heels in, they may be indicating that more of their needs need to come out. Dig, dig, dig, and involve them in this exploration. Remember that, while it may appear that they are refusing to cooperate, they *are* at the table. They came. There has to be some reason why they are there. It's your job to find it out. If you cannot meet their position and they are angry about it, be sure to acknowledge their position (remember, acknowledgment does not have to mean acceptance). Then look for their underlying needs, reveal them, and brainstorm together to find alternative ways of meeting those needs.

Unconstructive behavior can also take the form of manipulation and unpleasant, even unethical, behavior. Once again, the effective international negotiator is ready to respond, first by not retaliating in kind, and second, by halting the larger negotiation and addressing the unacceptable behavior itself immediately in the form of a "mininegotiation." Reveal the use of the tactic; don't just sit there and allow it to get in your way. Some commonly used but unacceptable tactics are:

- Intimidating you by creating physical or emotional discomfort (providing insufficient heat, light, ventilation, or air-conditioning; seating you facing blinding sunlight; permitting constant and inconsequential interruptions; setting aside no time for lunch; and so forth).

- Claiming to have (or lack) the authority to reach a decision.

- Putting (or using) last-minute time constraints on the negotiation to extract last-minute concessions. (The Chinese have a reputation, well founded or not, for doing this. Knowing that you have traveled a great distance and that Americans' time is often very limited, they may virtually wait until you have to get back on the plane before giving you the answer you've been sweating for. Inevitably it's less than what you want…but at least you've got something, so you take out it of desperation…)

In all these cases, the effective international negotiator "calls" them, insists that they be discussed openly as unconstructive to the achievement of the goals both sides have come together to achieve, and points out that such behavior violates good principles of negotiating and forms no basis for which you or they should have to make decisions. It is important, however, to be sure that what you perceive to be destructive behavior really is intended that way. Be sure that you are not merely misunderstanding differences in cultural values. For example, no air-conditioning might truly be a condition of the country, or lunch may simply not begin in that country until 2 or 3 p.m.

In traditional Arab cultures, an American might find himself (and mostly likely it *would* be *him*self) attempting to negotiate with one individual, while that individual's attention is constantly being interrupted by visitors, phone calls, etc. He might be called away several times in the course of the meeting. To an American, this kind of behavior could be considered rude and insulting. After all, according to American values, you and he have scheduled a specific time in order to meet, so he should hold all his calls, and not accept visits from others. In fact, the American would be wrong to be offended and should he stop everything and call the Arab's attention to this fact, it might cause the Arab to lose face which could jeopardize the relationship and further negotiations. In Arab culture, an important man has many people seeking his counsel. He is at the center of a great network of friends and family who, because of their close, formal relationships, call upon him, seek his advice, and, in this process, are constantly reinforcing the network of relations that form the basis of traditional Arab society and business. An American, by tolerating and appreciating this process, is slowly being integrated into the Arab "family." By questioning it or objecting to it as unproductive behavior, he would be isolating himself from this new family, from this inherently Arab way of doing business, and would find further negotiations difficult. The moral of the story here: Unacceptable behavior can be considered unacceptable only within culturally understood (and accepted) parameters.

Be Prepared

In addition to "calling" unproductive behavior or tactics when they occur, experienced international negotiators try to protect against the possibility of their arising by preempting them as well. A clearly defined agenda, agreed upon in advance, does wonders to help avoid the last-minute-concessions ploy. And confirming the authority and responsibility of the other side's players *ahead of time* can preempt the use of the "I-don't-have-the-authority" trap. Remember, positions and titles are often not parallel across oceans. Don't assume that the individuals on the other side have the same authority as you to negotiate. It is vital to check this out discreetly ahead of time.

Effective international negotiators do their homework. They anticipate or find out ahead of time the kind of information their associates abroad expect them to have. By so doing, they avoid giving the impression of being unknowledgeable, of having no real power, or of not caring about the negotiation. In many cultures, possessing the information is a very important asset. It means more than just knowing the answers; it means you are a powerful individual. Obviously this can be very important at the negotiating table. Americans are often casual about information. When we don't have the answers, we aren't usually distressed to inform others that we don't have that information now, but will get it for them shortly. In cultures where power is judged by the information you have, this kind of admission can reduce your foreign associates' respect for your authority at the table. They may even wonder why you've been sent to negotiate with them at all, if you don't have the answers they seek. For Americans, not knowing may not be a problem, but, in combination with the fact that lacking certain information is an important admission of lower status in other cultures, it can result in a negative, but unintended, situation for you at the table. The better international negotiators preempt this possibility by anticipating the informational needs of their associates. (This does not mean that they give away the store just because it is asked for.) Proprietary information and the degree to which it is valued in the West is something that many other cultures do not understand. You need to be sure you know ahead of time how much of what you know you will be able to divulge. Just be sure to be able to justify your decision and, where appropriate, have the necessary information to reveal, in order to avoid the situation outlined above.

Experienced international negotiators create agendas in advance and try to get a buy-in from the other side before the negotiation. (The other side appreciates the opportunity to contribute to the input of the meeting in the form of an agenda. However people on the other side choose to use their time and however different it might be from our own priorities, they are busy people too, and their time — however they choose to allot it, is valuable.) Effective international negotiators also take notes during and after the negotiation so that they always have a clear picture of where they have been, where they are, and where they are going. This allows them to plan effectively along the way. They also establish, maintain, and nurture contacts. They have a solid, secure sense of themselves, in order to maintain concentration and focus, even in unpredictable and strange circumstances. They have a strong sense of right and wrong that can steer them through trying situations in which differences in cultural attitudes and a pervasive sense of cultural relativity can sometimes challenge one's own sense of ethics and propriety.

The more effective international negotiators are resilient, creative, flexible, and tenacious. They are positive, energized, and open. They are determined, and, above all, accepting and celebrating of the almost fathomless possibilities that are hidden in human interactions. Effective international negotiators make the differences in people work *for* them, not against them. They recognize that international negotiating, almost by its very nature, requires the flowering of differences in order to achieve maximum results — results that can often be far more rewarding than those that can be achieved in a domestic context.

8

International Negotiating Styles

Recent research into the processes of negotiation has revealed key aspects of negotiation in which cultures tend to differ. Among others, Geert Hofstede[18] has done much research into culture's effects on business attitudes, for example (which has important implications for negotiations), while Stephen Weiss[19] has done significant studies on culture's effects on the negotiation process proper. In this chapter, we'll look at the important research in the field in an effort to compare important different international negotiating styles. We'll first separate the process of negotiation into its important components, then examine the ways in which various cultures approach these components. Throughout, it will be important to remember that values in one area will, of course, interact with values in another, resulting in a behavior that represents an individual's approach to negotiation.

Let's begin by taking the negotiation process apart and looking at its component parts. Some of the components result in very obvious differences, such as those we discussed when we examined the way various cultures view time. Other components, however, point to even deeper, more subtle, and more profound differences, such as variations in patterns of thought. These differences, while not as clearly manifest in overt behavior, can affect the relationship of the negotiators even more

---

[18]Hofstede, Geert, *Culture's Consequences*, Sage Publications, London, 1980.
[19]Weiss, Stephen E., with William Strip, *Negotiations with Foreign Businesspersons: An Introduction for Americans with Propositions for Six Cultures*, New York University Graduate School Business Administration, International Business Department, Edition 2/85.

significantly in the long run. What we're looking at when we look at these variations are not culture's effects on business in general, but culture's effects on negotiation in particular. These are the ways in which culture determines negotiating table manners and how our own manners differ from those who join us at the table.

Geert Hofstede is one of the leading researchers in the field of culture and work, and, based on studies that he began in the late 1960s, he has provided significant data identifying the work attitudes in critical areas of thousands of individuals surveyed worldwide in over fifty countries. From this data, he has identified four broad areas in which cultures differ in their attitudes toward work. The cultures he has studied can be ranked according to their attitudes in these four areas, so that comparisons of norms may be made indicating possible tendencies and preferences at work in those cultures. As you will see, each of these areas has particular importance for us when we negotiate across cultures.

Four Major Areas of Cultural Difference in Work Attitudes

1. Power-Distance

This dimension measures the way individuals relate to authority at work in different cultures. What Hofstede discovered was that in some cultures, those who hold power and those who are affected by power at work are significantly far apart (high power-distance) in many ways, while in other cultures, the powerholders and those affected by the powerholders are significantly closer (low power-distance). High power-distance, for example, usually mandates respect for age and seniority. The style of management by the powerholder can be paternalistic. Status is often ascribed, and the outward forms of status, such as protocol, formality, and rigid hierarchy, are regarded as important. In addition, decisions regarding appraisal, reward, and redress of grievances are usually based on personal judgments made by powerholders or by those connected to powerholders. If working in this environment sounds as though it would feel just a bit uncomfortable, that's because, relative to many other cultures in the world, the United States has a fairly low power-distance rating (along with New Zealand, Australia, Nordic cultures, and, interestingly, Germanic cultures), compared to the high power-distance cultures of Latin American, South Asia (Malaysia has the highest in the world), and certain Arab cultures. A low power-distance culture like the United States would value competence over seniority and the style of management would be more consultative (the subordinate, for example, would probably feel entitled to provide some feedback to superiors if the information were useful or important to both parties). Status would be more or less achievable, and the tone of communication would be much less formal, with an overt disregard, or at least a questioning, of the importance of symbols of status, rank, and hierarchy. In addition, systems of redress, appraisal, and reward would be based on professional criteria and not personal judgment or connections.

A note of interest: it seems counterintuitive that Germanic cultures would rank low on power-distance. After all, isn't there a great respect for authority, rank, and power in Germany? In fact, there is, but it exists in order for everyone to operate effectively in an organized fashion; it does not exist for its own sake. Perhaps this example points up the difference:

Chuck Simon, American manager, was walking to the U-bahn train station in Vienna with the manager of the company's Austrian subsidiary, Dietrich Bauer. As usual, they passed through the entry gates without having to get their tickets punched. "You know," Chuck said, "I was sure the workers were going to strike; I was ready to prepare for some big losses from Austria. But you surprised me, the way you got the workers not to strike. As their boss, you must really know how to get them to listen to you!" "Oh, no!" Dietrich laughed. "I said nothing to them. We Austrians just wouldn't think of handling the situation that way." Dietrich bent down and took a newspaper out of the dispensing machine as they approached the train platform, without having put his money in first. "Would you happen to have an extra shilling?" he asked Simon. "I've run out of change." "Sure, sure," Simon said, as he gave the machine the needed shilling, even though Bauer already had his newspaper.[20]

In Germanic cultures in general, there is an internalized consensus on the importance of following societal norms that can obviate the need for externally imposed enforcement. In general, you put a shilling in the machine, even though it is possible to get your newspaper for free. You pay for your ticket even though the chances of it being checked are small. The workers will not strike, for that would be too disrupting to the general condition of the country, even though they seek important labor-management changes. In Germany, you wait till the light turns green before crossing the street even if there is no traffic coming. If your car has a dent, you'd better fix it, or you'll hear about it from the

---

[20]This example was contributed by ITAP, International.

neighbors and the police. And if you let your grass grow too long or play your music too loud late into the night, your neighbors will feel no compunction about reprimanding you sharply for it the next day. Compare this kind of behavior with attitudes in the United States, where regulations need to be more externalized, more enforced, and therefore, more apparent. Or, for an even more dramatic contrast, compare these German attitudes with those in Mexico where, even when regulations are fully externalized and enforceable, no self-respecting driver would stop at a red light if there is clearly no traffic coming the other way.

2. Individualism Versus Collectivism

These terms are cultural, not economic, and they refer to the orientation that people in different cultures have toward their work. Do we work for our own individual benefit, or do we work for the benefit of the greater group, the family, the clan, the company, the country? Those cultures that are more individualistic subscribe to self-interest-oriented theories of work and economics. Individuals in these cultures are self-actualized and self-motivated, and their relationships with colleagues are based on self-interest. They are generally task-oriented, have a high comfort level with anonymity, and seek individual reward and appraisal. In contrast, those cultures that are more collectivist subscribe to group-oriented theories of work and economics. People there are motivated by the desire to advance the interests of the group. Their relationships with colleagues are based on mutual self-interest, they are emotionally dependent on the success of the group, and they seek reward for the group.

At the negotiating table, differences in this dimension can clearly cause serious conflict. Individual responsibility for making decisions is easy in individualist cultures; in group-oriented cultures this can be difficult. Americans too often expect their Japanese counterparts to make decisions right at the negotiating table, and the Japanese are constantly surprised to find individual members of the American team promoting their own positions, decisions, and ideas, sometimes openly contradicting one another.

When we look at the rankings of various countries on this dimension, the United States comes out as the most individualistic culture surveyed, with the United Kingdom, the Netherlands, France, and the Nordic countries not far behind. Examples of more collectivist cultures include Asian and Latin American countries, with Guatemala being the most group-oriented culture surveyed (Guatemala's demographic is primarily Mayan Indian, with a strong group orientation that is almost tribal in nature). It's interesting to note that, while Japan popularly epitomizes the group-oriented culture for the United States, its ranking relative to the rest of the world surveyed is somewhere in the middle—an indication not so much of Japan's strong group orientation but rather of the United States' extreme individualism.

Americans, subscribing in general to the value of individualism, are often unaware of how extreme and powerful a value it is here and of how much it permeates all aspects of our work. While we have discussed this at length in an earlier chapter, it bears noting again the way many non-Americans react to being transferred for a year or so to work in the United States. Despite their initial enthusiasm, time and time again we have heard the same refrain after a few weeks: "I feel lost," "There is no one to tell me what to do," "I thought I would have such good friends here, but that is not the case," "I really find it very difficult to work all alone all the time." Americans value independence and self-initiative, and while many of these expatriates do also, they are coming from countries where these values are not as strongly translated into the work environment as they are here. Contrast the non-American's complaints about working here to the typical American's complaints when working in group-oriented Asia: "They wouldn't leave me alone," "I couldn't even retreat into my hotel room," "It's as if it's a sin to be left alone." (In fact, in much of Asia, culturally-speaking, it is.)

3. Uncertainty-Avoidance

This dimension measures the comfort or discomfort people in different cultures feel in the presence of uncertainty. In some cultures, people commonly seek to avoid ambiguous, uncertain, unpredictable, or risky (high uncertainty-avoidance) situations, while in other cultures, people can be generally more comfortable with ambiguous, unpredictable, uncertain situations and seek out risk (low uncertainty-avoidance). High avoidance of uncertainty can mean that decisions are made slowly and carefully, after much consideration of all possible details, often by many people. Low avoidance of uncertainty means there is a lot more shooting from the hip, a lot more "gut-level" decision making, with fewer people involved and less information required; low risk-avoidance moves fast, takes risks, and bounces back. High-risk-avoidance cultures need lots of formal bureaucratic rules in order to feel comfortable; they rely on rituals, standards, and formulas; they trust only those closest and most reliable (often family and inner circles). There is a sense that planning is very essential, for fate is unpredictable and the world is forever a dangerous place. For people in these cultures, the rules are meant to be followed; there is often an accompanyingly low tolerance for differences and ambiguity and a tendency to reveal thoughts, feelings, and emotions only carefully, if at all.

In contrast, people in low-uncertainty-avoidance cultures can dislike hierarchy — they find it inefficient and destructive. They rely on principles that guarantee safe actions and view planning less as a way to avoid inevitable catastrophe than as a way to be able to control the future. For people in these cultures, things move fast. There is more tolerance, even acceptance, of ambiguity and differences; and thoughts and feelings, in the form of information and emotion, are usually more freely expressed.

In relation to other countries in the studies, the United States has a fairly low need for certainty, but not the lowest. Among the countries with even lower needs for certainty (more risk-taking, more entrepreneurial, more comfortable with uncertainty) are Jamaica, certain Nordic nations, Hong Kong, and Singapore (which has the lowest need of all). It is important to remember that low risk-avoidance does not necessarily mean high risk-taking. Many of these cultures have to learn to survive in the face of great uncertainty. For them, therefore, uncertainty is not necessarily something to put great energy into avoiding, since it is daily and inevitable. The dynamic Pacific Rim dragons, like Hong Kong and Singapore, have risk-taking and entrepreneurship as part of their Chinese cultural heritages, in addition to a powerful drive to keep the ever-threatening disasters of the unpredictable future at bay.

For Americans, the experience of working in their companies' overseas offices — particularly in more conservative risk-avoidance cultures — can be extremely stressful. They often find themselves caught in the middle between how they know things really are in their new home and how headquarters wants them to be. The American in the middle knows, for example, that things will simply take more time in the country of assignment, while it may be difficult to explain exactly why to the home office. The home office may understand none of this and therefore will not understand why, ever since Smith was sent abroad, his quarterly results have fallen. Despite Smith's insistence that things simply take more time here, that he needs headquarters' cooperation in sending him more data and information, and perhaps even some assistants with certain expertise in the new country (or an expanded budget that enables him to have some local country nationals as assistants), headquarters thinks he is not doing his job, certainly not as well as he did back in the States, that he has "gone native," and that he needs to return.

4. Masculine Versus Feminine

This choice of terminology is based on the degree to which cultures value certain gender-associated qualities (and ascribe these qualities to men and women in that culture): self-assertion and task orientation (traditionally thought of as "male" traits) or nurturing, quality-of-life, and relationship orientation (traditionally thought of as "female" traits). Those cultures that are more "masculine" tend to value self-assertion and task orientation and usually ascribe such traits quite specifically to men, while the women in such societies are associated with the nurturing, quality-of-life aspects of society and are so ascribed these responsibilities. Such societies tend to favor a sharp, rigid division of sex roles. Those cultures that are more "feminine" tend to value the relationship and quality-of-life values, and, in such cultures, these values are usually shared among both men and women. In these societies the division of sex roles is not as sharp since these societies are less clearly based on the traditional male/female traits described above.

"Masculine" cultures subscribe to "live-to-work" theories. "Feminine" cultures subscribe to "work-to-live" theories. "Masculine" cultures are more advancement-oriented; "feminine" cultures are more accepting of the given situation, especially if it fulfills quality-of-life concerns. The style of work in a "masculine" culture can be more competitive, while in "feminine" cultures the work style can be more collaborative.

Relatively speaking, the United States is not as "masculine" as one might tend to think; while certainly ranking on the task-oriented side, it is not significantly so. The more "masculine" countries surveyed include Mexico (machismo and its effects on sex role division) and certain other Latin American cultures, Spain, Switzerland, the Philippines, Italy, and Jamaica.

The most "masculine" culture surveyed was Japan. In Japan, women on career paths are still uncommon (although this is changing), and the male work ethic in Japan is fierce. There are long hours at the office and then after work at the bars. While there is some dispute about the overall efficiency during such long working days, there is no doubt that the Japanese are extremely task-oriented. So are the Koreans, and yet they score as being significantly more "feminine" than the Japanese in the study, meaning that there is a higher value put on quality-of-life and relationship concerns and that the Korean man must assume some of the responsibility for those issues in family life (certainly more than the Japanese man does). Accordingly, the sex role differentiation in Japan is much more rigid. A Korean friend of mine described the difference this way: "Look," he said. "In Japan, the man can stay out all night at the bars with his office buddies and come home whenever he wants, and the wife doesn't say anything about it. In my country, if the man's not back home by ten o'clock, you can be sure his wife will go out and bring him home herself." The Koreans and the Japanese offer yet another example of the dangers of generalizing—so tempting at great distances—about cultures that share certain overarching similarities. In fact, Japan and Korea are culturally and historically quite different; both the Koreans and the Japanese would be offended if they were lumped together in the Western point of view.

The most "feminine" cultures, on the other hand, include most of the Nordic countries (the term "house husband" is a Swedish word, and quality-of-life issues there, such as day-care, the environment, and old age security, are always hot topics of concern). This, too, is changing somewhat, as middle-of-the-road Scandinavian socialism is currently being reexamined for the 1990s and beyond.

Let's look at an example of a negotiation that is foundering specifically because there is a cultural difference between a "masculine" and "feminine" perception of work:

Gary Harris, representing an American chemical manufacturer, is getting increasingly impatient with Peter Laarsen, his Swedish buyer. "We have requirements here in Sweden that prevent me from buying your company's chemicals unless you can prove that you have not contributed to the degradation of the environment in the manufacture of these chemicals," Peter is saying. "I will need an affidavit from your company stating this." Harris did not expect to have to provide such data before he came over from the States; he just wanted to close what looked like a simple, straightforward deal. Peter continues, "It's OK if you don't have that information ready now. We are in no rush, really; we've done business with your company before, and we will do more together, I'm sure. Besides, I'm taking four months off for paternity leave to be with my new baby so my wife can return to her work. Why don't we talk again in about six months? By then I'll be back at work, and you will have had time to get the necessary papers together.

Quality-of-life issues are extremely important for Peter, as they are for people in most Nordic cultures. And they range from environmental concerns to child care, to a prioritizing of quality day-to-day living over short-term business needs. Additionally, sex role differentiation at work is not as severe. American businesspeople might appreciate some of these values, but often not to the degree that they are appreciated—and enforced—in countries like Sweden, Denmark, Finland, and, interestingly, the Netherlands.

As we can see, there are many areas in which the four Hofstede dimensions have a very clear and definite impact at the negotiating table. We will highlight the effects of these four dimensions as we take a closer look at the aspects of the negotiation process itself. As previously mentioned, recent studies, particularly those done by Stephen Weiss, have identified some features of the negotiation process that are clearly different in different cultures. Let's take a look at some of these important variables, categories, or ways in which all cultures differ in their manners and styles at the negotiating table.

Taking a closer look at the way different cultures view similar aspects of the negotiation process can give us another valuable perspective on how we Americans handle ourselves at the table.

The Basic Concept of the Negotiation

The very definition of *negotiating* can vary culture to culture. What a negotiation is designed to accomplish is seen differently in New York, Paris, and Beijing. Here we are talking about the possibility of mutually exclusive expectations. Before one even comes to the table, such differences in the meaning or purpose of the negotiation affect the negotiation. For example, while Americans generally view negotiation primarily as an opportunity to accomplish or resolve a substantive issue, many cultures view negotiation primarily as an opportunity to build a relationship; resolving a particular issue is simply not the first goal. Such cultures often view the initial meeting as the beginning of a larger negotiation encompassing many meetings. Americans are sorely mistaken if they expect an agreement at the end of their *first* meeting with their Japanese associates, for example. The Japanese view the negotiation as a collaborative process of "mind-meeting," which can mandate several meetings before substantive issues are even discussed. Americans who have traveled halfway around the world to meet their Japanese counterparts for the first time in Tokyo on Monday and expect to be back in their office in Detroit on Friday with a signed deal will surely be disappointed.

Similarly, Americans tend to view negotiating as a competitive process of offers and counteroffers, while the Japanese tend to view the negotiation as an opportunity for information-sharing. Many Americans return from negotiations with the Japanese extremely frustrated: "They just kept pumping me for information," "They wouldn't give me any answers, but they sure could ask questions," "I got nothing I wanted, although they expected me to divulge the most proprietary information," etc. While these issues reflect, as we've discussed, many other values, all of these responses indicate a culture clash between the United States and Japan over basic differences in the *expectations* of the negotiation process. At the beginning of a business relationship between an American and a Japanese, the immediate substantive issue is simply not on the table as far as the Japanese are concerned.

But we Americans are generally not as concerned with building long-term associations as we are with getting our immediate business issues resolved (just as Americans are not as concerned about the long-term business picture as we are about quarterly profits). This means that Americans enter the first meeting expecting an issue-oriented outcome, often through a process of bargaining. For the Japanese, however, bargaining too soon can be a sign of *un*trustworthiness. It is for this reason that Americans in the now classic Japanese-American cross-cultural business scenario lose the deal by bargaining about price just because they are made anxious by Japanese silence.

Bargaining, however, is not a problem for Arab cultures. In fact, if we don't bargain aggressively there, we are considered naive. However, there too, the process of bargaining is meant to establish personal relationships built on a mutual perception of virtue, honesty, and personal merit. Such relationships evolve out of the kind of aggressive and prolonged bargaining that often occurs in Southwest Asia. In fact, these cultures traditionally view the negotiation as a forum for developing a deep personal relationship based not on issues (as in the United States) or even, at first, on mutual business interests (as in Japan), but rather on respect for personal and family honor, dignity, and pride. Americans tend not to realize, when negotiating in these cultures, that they must first prove their "worthiness" and reveal their "mettle" in these terms.

In order for our Saudi counterparts, for example, to do business with us, the Saudis must first feel comfortable about allowing Americans into their psychic "family." The process of extensive bargaining becomes a vehicle for revealing personal merit and honor and for developing the critical personal relationship. It's the same at the souk or the Sheraton. Therefore, when Scandinavians, usually very uncomfortable with aggressive bargaining, negotiate with the Saudis, a serious culture-clash can develop. Saudis will often open with a price much higher than the one they will ultimately settle for. Scandinavians will put forward a price often very close to what they will ultimately settle for. The Scandinavians mistrust the Saudis, and the Saudis think the Scandinavians aren't serious about negotiating.

As well as viewing negotiation in either competitive or collaborative terms, different cultures often display correspondingly different attitudes toward conflict. Americans tend to accept conflict as inherently natural to the negotiation; they expect both sides to "struggle" for what they want, one side getting its way, if necessary, at the expense of the other. We tend to view conflict as functional, sometimes with an accompanying "winner-take-all" attitude, and respond to conflict directly and confrontationally. Not surprisingly, cultures such as Japan and China view conflict at the table as *dys*functional. Correspondingly, these cultures seek to avoid conflict and are indirect, as opposed to confrontational, in their response to it.

The maintenance of *wa*, or harmony, in Japan is such a basic and critical value that it significantly affects much of the behavior during negotiation, as well as determines attitudes toward it. In their effort to maintain harmony, to avoid conflict at the table, the Japanese will employ indirect and avoidant behavior. They will also place priority on face-saving, status acknowledgment, and the establishment of an ongoing system of mutual obligation, expectation, and fulfillment (as symbolized by their often elaborate – and expensive – gift-giving and hosting customs). In contrast, the French view negotiation as a highly competitive process, perhaps even more than do the Americans. Because their expectation and appetite for "conflict" is so keen, the French can give Americans a chance to experience what it's like for less competitive-oriented cultures to negotiate with us.

Mexicans provide us with an interesting paradox. They do not view conflict as dysfunctional but their response to conflict is also indirect and avoidant. While conflict is not necessarily viewed as functional in Mexico, it is seen as inevitable and "the way things are." There tends to be a fatalistic response there to what is perceived as the "nature of things." This results, curiously, in a negotiating style that is essentially competitive, while, because the establishment of personal relationships is a very necessary prerequisite to doing business in Mexico, the general response to conflict is avoidant and indirect. Therefore, while a North American business*man* (and the Mexicans usually do prefer to deal with a man) might find himself doing some very hard bargaining over the price of the deal with his Mexican counterparts, the style in which the entire negotiation takes place would need to be friendly. Each side would be eagerly reinforcing the *simpático* nature of its concern for the other, and each would be appealing to the other's sense of pride and need for reciprocal respect and understanding.

The Selection of the Negotiators

Another aspect of negotiation that can affect the process even before both sides get to the table is the differing criteria various cultures use to select their negotiators. Gender, competence, experience, status, age, even personal attributes can all be used as criteria in choosing individuals to send to the table. If two cultures using different sets of negotiator-selection criteria meet at the table, you can be sure that there will be a clash of expectations about many aspects of the negotiation.

An American recalls, "It seemed natural for me to begin shaking hands with the Japanese as they entered the room. Only later did I realize that I had shaken hands with their most senior member last. I should have waited until he entered and shaken hands with him first." The Japanese choose their negotiators on the basis of seniority and status in addition to gender. It is rare to see a woman on a Japanese negotiating team, let alone in a position of senior responsibility. And while the Japanese may be accustomed to the Western notion of shaking hands, bowing is still very common and is a ritual for showing respect for status and age. Usually the younger, less senior person bows lower and longer as a way of establishing the proper relationship between the two individuals.

The American continues: "At dinner that night, a member of their team discreetly informed me of my *faux pas*, so I made sure for the rest of the negotiation that I addressed all my concerns to the senior man. However, that created its own problems for me, since he never gave me an answer to anything! Was he that hurt over my unintentional snub the first day?" Actually, the American was probably right in addressing his concerns to the senior man. His expectation of getting definitive answers out of him, however, was probably wrong. Because the Japanese choose their chief negotiators on the basis of status and seniority, these people may not be the ones most informed about the details necessary to make a decision. In fact, their assistants may be better equipped with the facts to respond to your question. However, assistants are not usually empowered to approve decisions.

Because Americans typically choose their negotiators on the basis of their substantive knowledge of the issues at the table and on their negotiating experience, the gender or age of the negotiator can be incidental (and using such criteria in the United States might also be illegal). Gender and age, however, often play key roles in the selection of a negotiator in other countries.

I couldn't stand it any longer. It was all I could do to just stay in the room with the Arabs, so how could I care how the deal would turn out? As a manager, I was treated disgracefully, just because I was a woman. I had full decision-making power as the head of my team, but they would barely acknowledge my presence and insisted on speaking, instead, with my male junior assistant. It was an altogether humiliating experience for me and a failure for the company.

One needs to be careful about generalizing attitudes across cultures. We have certainly seen how quickly things do change and how important individual differences are to gross cultural generalizations. It would be unfair to leave the impression, for example, that in Arab cultures women are disallowed in business across the board. Certain fundamental Islamic sects do have this prerequisite, but there are variations within the Arab world. A female associate was recently asked to join a panel of Western men going to speak at a conference in Oman by the conference planner here in the States. The woman had a particular expertise in her field, and it was felt that her information would be useful to the Omanis. I was asked if I thought this would present a problem. In addition to the fact that she was obviously female, and from the United States, she was also Jewish. I suggested that she should go. With adequate preparation given to understanding the culture ahead of time, she should be able to avoid situations that would put her in danger or compromise any Arab and/or Omani values. Besides, she was not having to negotiate or make any deals; she was invited because of her expertise. The Omanis are not radical fundamentalists; in fact, the country is relatively secular in many areas of life and subscribes to a more liberal form of Islam. And while Jews and Arabs certainly have their differences, they also share many similarities. They still regard each other as "people of the Book," who, along with Christians, stand apart from such other groups as Hindus, Buddhists, and many of the African religious identities. Factors that might make her presence an impossibility among the Palestinians would not be a problem among the Omanis. As it turned out, her trip was a success.

A not-so-fortunate example follows: An American woman had done significant business over the phone for her company with her male Japanese associate. She later went to Japan on a business trip as head of her mostly male team. Her Japanese counterpart was so shocked at having to do business with a woman in person that he publicly told her he was surprised that she had come over to discuss things with him. Throughout the negotiations he and his team refused to address her, preferring to speak instead to lower-level males on her team. She was not invited out to the all-important evening socializing events. At the end of the visit, when gifts were exchanged, the Japanese gave all the men on her team brass desk clocks. She was given a sewing kit.

It is conversely difficult for negotiators from cultures where age is a significant criterion for the selection of negotiators to negotiate with young American businesspeople in positions of power. Apparently, it is difficult for them to believe that someone so young has decision-making authority. Generational differences, as well as culture and language, can present communication barriers. One young American entrepreneur had difficulty establishing credibility among his Singaporean and Malay associates because he seemed "too young to be taken seriously." This young American went on to arrange and conduct seminars for political and economic leaders of major Southeast Asian nations. For purely professional reasons only, I myself was recently pleased to notice a few more grey hairs coming in, especially since I was about to speak to an audience of Asian upper managers and executives. In Asian cultures, generally, age carries clout.

Negotiators are sometimes also selected because of their connections, their family, government or business ties. Americans not infrequently can find themselves negotiating with someone in Latin America who may have little grasp of the issues but is at the bargaining table because of his relationship with key industrial or political figures. Expecting immediate answers, carefully considered proposals, or even meaningful discussion of substantive issues under these circumstances would clearly be a mistake.

In France, negotiators are often selected according to their schooling. Managers are highly respected, and often the best come from Les Grandes Écoles. Schooling and social class in France, and in other parts of Europe as well, quite often determine who conducts business. In general, status is highly respected throughout Europe, and an indicator of status (or its absence), be it in the form of an expensive car, a university degree, or a title on your business card, can carry a lot of weight in business. This is especially true in the extremely class-conscious United Kingdom, where indicators of status can be as simple, yet just as significant, as the colors and direction of the stripes on your tie. (The pattern of your tie can indicate which school you went to, and North Americans would be wise to avoid striped ties altogether in Britain unless they are prepared to discuss their alma mater and its standing among the universities in the States.)

The Importance of Protocol

As we've already stated, the United States is probably one of the world's most *in*formal cultures. Even "formal" by our standards is probably deemed informal by most of the rest of the world, with the possible exception of Australia. Americans are "notoriously" casual about their use of first names, physical contact, dress, disregard for titles, use (or lack) of business cards, invitations, conduct at social events, etc. (Remember, this "casualness" is selective. Americans are *not* casual when it comes to some other aspects of the negotiation process, such as time, decision making, format of the final agreement, etc.) Most other cultures conduct the negotiation process within a set of formal constraints, often significantly more complicated than what Americans are used to.

Americans often refer to each other by first name. Last names and titles are disdained. In France, and in much of Europe, however, the use of last names, along with *Mr.* and *Mrs.* is critical, no matter what the length of the business relationship, until the senior indicates that he or she wants to be referred to more informally. (This can be rarely indicated, despite years of working together.) Indeed, the French, Spanish, German, and Italian languages all have a formal and informal form for "you" built right into the language. Americans often take offense when their own informality is not reciprocated, but it is not so much an effort by their European counterparts to remain aloof as it is a cultural difference in the way respect is shown. This is evident also in the use of the handshake. In France, businesspeople in the same office will greet each other each morning, after lunch, and whenever they return to the office after having been away, with a handshake. The style of the handshake is usually distinctive, too. The French handshake is one quick, firm shake, not the endless, sincere "grip and pump" favored by Americans.

Americans don't take business cards all that seriously either, while in many other cultures, the business card is a key form of identification. In Japan, cards are exchanged upon meeting in order for the individuals to learn many things about each other, not the least being each other's status. Just as important as bowing deeply enough and long enough and using the correct style of address, eye contact, and extent of formality (who takes cues from whom, etc.), one must take careful note of the information contained on the business card. In Japan, cards are received with two hands, lovingly examined, and carefully arranged in front of you on the table, in an order that represents the seating of your opposite numbers. They must never be mishandled, written upon, folded, or put in one's back pocket to be sat upon. In Europe, the business card will indicate all titles, educational degrees, and corporate rank of the individual, and titles should be scrupulously used and respected. In the United States many "doctors" do not use their title, unless they are medical doctors. In Europe a Ph.D. is always heralded and announced on the business card and in conversation. Business cards are so key that they should always have the English version on one side and the local language translation on the other. Many hotels in Japan will translate your business card for you, for a small fee, if you send it to them in advance of your trip.

Even social occasions have a protocol overseas that is often more complex than in the United States. For one thing, socializing is often serious business. In Japan, being able to sustain nightly rounds of carousing through restaurants and bars is part of doing business. The evening entertainment is as critical to the negotiation as the sessions during the day. The formalities of the evening activities are important to follow, too, from the drinking and toasting of the first Scotch to the singing of songs, the use of chopsticks, the what and what not to discuss of the day's business, to the forgetting (on a conscious level, at least), of it all by 9 a.m. the next day.

Gift-giving practices differ from culture to culture. *Do* give a small gift in Japan, *never* give one in China. Expect to be invited home in Australia, do *not* expect to be invited home in Japan. If invited home in France for dinner, always bring flowers, but never roses. If invited home in Asia or Africa, do not compliment too much, or your host might feel compelled to give you the item you are admiring, even if it is a family heirloom. Always ask about the spouse and family in Latin America; never ask about the spouse in Southwest Asia. You may have dinner in the United States at 6 p.m., but it won't start until 11 p.m. in Spain. Lunch may be thirty minutes long in Boston, but it's three hours long in Buenos Aires. You might talk business over dinner in Duluth, but you'd better not in Paris. The list goes on and on.

There are often different protocol rules for women in business. Men may shake hands with women, but not in Arab lands. Women may kiss women but not men in Latin America. At the end of business in Latin America men may embrace other men but not embrace women. The area of protocol is filled with many "do's and don't's," and while ignorance of local customs is often a forgivable offense and not a serious deal-killer on its own, combined, as we've said, with other cultural miscommunications, a mistake in protocol may seriously jeopardize a negotiation. The point is, protocol is taken more seriously "over there," and respect for the local customs is an important part of a successful international negotiation. You've got to do your research and homework ahead of time.

The Type of Communication

About 70 percent of all communication occurs nonverbally. This often comes as quite a surprise to Americans, as we believe that clarity resides in language. We trust the word and trust that we can make our facts, feelings, and beliefs known if only we choose the "right" word. The United States is extremely explicit and verbal, and we believe that understanding can occur with the true, direct, and proper use of words. In fact, this is a cultural value, for many other cultures are not nearly as explicit and rely quite comfortably on nonverbal as well as verbal communication. On a continuum of nonverbal to verbal, the United States is strongly on the verbal side, with cultures such as Japan strongly on the nonverbal side and many others straddled in between.

Edward T. Hall has given us the notion of "cultural context."[21] That is, in high-context cultures, information about an individual (and, consequently, about both individual and group behavior in that culture) is provided through words, gestures, body language, and the use of silence and personal space. It is also conveyed through status (the individual's age, sex, education, family background, title, and affiliations) and through the individual's informal friends and associates. Information flows relatively freely within the culture, although outsiders who are not members of the culture may have difficulty "reading" the information because they are not plugged into the required informal networks and do not know the formal and informal "languages" of the culture that carries the information. Such knowledge is often available only to the members of that culture. A low-context culture, on the other hand, transmits information about behavior chiefly through words. Information about the culture is not necessarily embedded in other aspects of the culture. Therefore, in a low-context culture such as America's, things often need to be spelled out quite explicitly, and information is available only through particular lines of communication, although easily "readable" by cultural members and nonmembers alike.

High-context cultures contain and rely on many elements of nonverbal behavior, while low-context cultures rely more or less on verbal communication. The antennae of low-context individuals are often simply not tuned in to receive information being broadcast nonverbally by high-context individuals. This can cause misunderstandings at the negotiating table. High-context individuals are seeking information on many levels in addition to the spoken word, yet when they negotiate with Americans, the spoken word is primarily all they get. Low-context individuals are sometimes quite confused by the ambiguity contained in the spoken or written answers of high-context individ-

[21]Hall, Edward T., *The Silent Language*, Doubleday, New York, 1973.

uals, for high-context individuals are perhaps communicating more information (possibly even contrary information) nonverbally. Each side's inability to accurately "read" the other can send it off with misinformation.

Nonverbal communication takes many forms: the use of silence, eyecontact, body language, body space, greetings, and the nonverbal aspects of verbal communication, such as speed, volume, interspeaker space and pacing, and intonation. Americans are uniquely uncomfortable with silence. We tend to fill up the spaces between us with words. We have a reputation for "spilling" information; that is, others can turn our willingness to talk (and to talk endlessly) against us, by making us so uncomfortable with silence that we often put our foot in our mouth merely by opening it up.

Differences in body language need to be understood culture by culture. In many cultures, beckoning to someone with the forefinger is considered ill-mannered, yet beckoning to them with the palm down is not. Never touch a Malay on the top of the head, for that is where the soul resides. Never show the sole of your shoe to an Arab, for it is dirty and represents the bottom of the body, and never use your left hand in Muslim culture, for it is the hand reserved for physical hygiene. Touch the side of your nose in Italy and it is a sign of distrust. Always look directly and intently into your French associate's eye when making an important point. Direct eye contact in Southeast Asia, however, should be avoided until the relationship is firmly established. If your Japanese associate has just sucked air in deeply through his teeth, that's a sign you've got real problems. Your Mexican associate will want to embrace you at the end of a long and successful negotiation; so will your Central and East European associates, who may give you a bearhug *and* kiss you three times on alternating cheeks. American often stand farther apart than their middle Latin and Arab associates but closer than their Asian associates. In the United States people shake hands forcefully and enduringly; in Europe a handshake is usually quick and to the point; in Asia, it is often rather limp. Laughter and giggling in the West indicates humor; in Asia, it more often indicates embarrassment and humility. Additionally, the public expression of deep emotion is considered illmannered in most countries of the Pacific Rim; there is an extreme separation between one's personal and public selves. The withholding of emotion in Latin America, however, is often cause for mistrust.

Americans tend to speak too loudly for some, too softly for others. In Thailand, the volume is considerably lower; in Hong Kong and Italy, considerably louder. Speed of communication varies too. In Asia, one person speaks, and there may be a considerable pause before the next one speaks. In the United States, we usually wait for our turn to speak but quickly respond to one another. In Brazil, conversations overlap, with much simultaneous talking. Being low-context in the United States, we believe our meaning lies in the word; in Asia, the word is skillfully used to make things more ambiguous, as well as more clear. And in Britain, a subtext of meaning is often simultaneously occurring below the very understated surface of conversation. The degree to which different cultures subscribe to a rich context in which communication occurs differs from culture to culture.

Let's take a look at a clash of high and low context, of verbal and nonverbal reliance, between an American and a Japanese, and try to identify some of the areas of conflict.

Phil Johnson, an American from Chicago, couldn't understand why the Japanese, who seemed so eager to do business with him when he corresponded with them from his Chicago office, seemed so cool toward him now that he was face to face with them in Tokyo. He had thought they really wanted a deal, but when he started talking business, instead of the enthusiastic response he expected, all he got were lots of questions that he thought had already been answered in their previous communications. He tried to be friendly by putting his arm around various members of their team like one of the guys. Johnson tried especially hard to get close to the older fellow who seemed to be their leader, since he felt that two old dogs would have much in common, but he knew he wasn't getting anywhere with him. Johnson insisted on a first-name basis; he was even willing to try sushi one night. But at every turn, it seemed, the Japanese were literally backing away. "Look," he finally said, "if we really agree on everything we've already discussed over these past few months, why are we waiting around now to make a deal?" There was silence. "Ah," he continued, very frustrated now, and a little anxious over what to do next, "I don't have three weeks to kill in Japan. If you needed all this information again, I could have had my secretary send it over before I made this trip." One of the Japanese sucked in a deep breath of air through his teeth. Then there was more silence.

The Value of Time

"My time is very valuable to me," says Becky Weist, "especially when I'm traveling for business. So you can imagine how I felt when, after having arrived on time, I was kept waiting forty-five minutes in a stuffy little anteroom. Forty-five minutes! In New York in my business, ten minutes late, and you're history. Then he finally comes out to greet me all sweetness and light, as if nothing had happened. I guess I was kind of angry, but I also wanted him to know that I wouldn't be able to spend as much time as we had planned because of the delay and another appointment I had later in the afternoon. Everything after that was, shall we say, downhill."

If a negotiation occurs between Americans, we might safely assume that both parties share the same set of beliefs about time; i.e., that it is in limited supply, that one's time should be respected, that it's good for maximum productivity to wrap things up in as short a time as possible. Both parties usually show up for the negotiations on time. Both parties sit down with the expectation of producing an acceptable agreement as swiftly and efficiently as possible. Both parties probably keep formalities and socializing to a minimum, mutually believing that formality and socializing just slow the pace of the negotiation.

But, if the negotiation occurs between an American and, say, a mainland Chinese, differences in values over the concept of time could produce behavior that might jeopardize the negotiation. Producing a satisfactory agreement in as short a time as possible may be one of the *least* concerns of the Chinese. In fact, it might be exactly the opposite for the Chinese, who generally believe that a considerable amount of time should be invested in establishing a general climate of understanding, trust, and willingness to help, in matters quite apart from the specific business issues brought to the table. The Chinese do not mind going over the same point again and again, to the frustration of Americans. They do not view time as a constraint or as a set of limits in which a particular task must be completed. Rather, their values result in a view of time as an endless continuum, a context rather than a constraint, in which we live, and in which, if all other factors cooperate, we can build trustworthy business relationships. Time is simply not the pressing consideration for the Chinese as it is for so many Americans.

Some cultures are "being-oriented"; others are "doing-oriented." Continuing our earlier discussion of differences in the value placed on time, it is not difficult to imagine how differing concepts of time and its importance can affect the process of negotiation. Being-oriented cultures view the here and now as the focus; doing-oriented cultures concentrate on the future. Being- and doing-oriented cultures usually have conceptions that relate to the categories of time we've discussed earlier: monochronic and polychronic. Being-oriented cultures are polychronic; for them, time is multifaceted and a context for life rather than a set of parameters for the completion of tasks. Doing-oriented cultures are monochronic and one-dimensional; they view time chiefly as a framework for task completion. There is usually a connection between a culture's level of economic development and its conception of time. More traditional cultures tend to view time as a polychronic backdrop for life, while more modern, developed, and urban cultures tend to view time as a monochronic series of demarcations for measuring accomplishments ("doingness").

To Americans at the negotiating table, time is money, a commodity in limited supply. We are always and forever planning for the future. In Ireland, time is less important, as "god made so much of it." In Saudi Arabia, it can be foolish to plan, for "only Allah can know the future"; there, one may lose credibility if one is too time-oriented. An American is frustrated when he is kept waiting an extra hour or so beyond the appointed time at the front office in Latin America, especially when he knows that the man he has come to see is in his office. But should the American, anticipating a delay, choose to arrive an hour or so late the next time, so as to not be kept waiting, he would find that his Latin host might be insulted. What the American does not know is that his Latin American host is probably dealing with a great many things at once, among them, busily arranging after-meeting activities for the two of them — activities the American will be expected to partake in, make time for, and enjoy.

An American manager tells of a Thai associate who simply did not show up for work on a very important day. Several days later, the American questioned his associate's disappearance at such a "critical" time. The Thai explained that he had heard that an old friend was in town and so, of course, they went out together to the movies that afternoon. What was a "critical" use of time for the Thai was clearly not so for the American; or, in Hofstede's terms, the American was more task-oriented, while the Thai was more relationship-oriented.

A Latin American manager explained, "You Americans set schedules based on time — 4 o'clock, 9:30, 3 p.m., etc. — as a way of getting things done. We Latins set schedules differently, not based on points on a clock but rather on a series of events: first, we'll do this; then, when it is finished, we'll move on to this; then on to this. That way, we give each task the time it takes to complete, while Americans will move on to the next task, not because the first is completed, but because it's 'time' to, or because the time allotted for the first task has run out. For us, time does not 'run out.'" When time is money, when it is a commodity always in short supply, punctuality becomes critical. Relaxed attitudes toward lateness, or *mañana*, are not appreciated. In Germany, even in social affairs, punctuality is critical. If one is invited to a dinner party at 8 p.m. in Frankfurt, it is not uncommon for all the Mercedes to roll up to the door at five minutes to 8. The guests will step out, and at two minutes before 8, they will begin to walk to the door. All together at the door, at eight o'clock, one will ring the bell.

Perhaps China provides us with the best example of major cultural differences when it comes to time values and negotiating. Certainly a culture several thousand years old has a different perspective on the world from a culture several hundred years old. Patience is the key word when doing business in China. Business is conducted only after one is proven to be a trusted friend, someone with whom a long-term business relationship may be established, someone with whom *guanxi* (a personal connection requiring significant personal obligations) can be established. This can mean years of negotiation before a deal is consummated. However, as in many other cultures, once a relationship is established, once the time and money has been invested in the development of such a relationship, you usually have a reliable partner on whom you can count for many years of business, provided the relationship is nurtured and maintained. The emphasis here is on the long-term relationship and not on the immediate deals at hand.

The effect this has on the negotiation process is important, for, while the Chinese typically seek long-range relationships based on mutual trust and cooperation, they also can be very apprehensive about doing business with Westerners. Therefore, the establishment of the essential trust takes even longer and is always at risk of breaking down. The Westerner must constantly be ready to reinforce the ties of trust and, at the same time, not fall into the traps that the Chinese, due to their apprehensiveness, often lay as a "test" of the Westerner's trustworthiness. Your patience will be tried often while you are being hosted as an honored guest. Information may be provided that should not be in your possession in order to see if you will use such information to your advantage against them in the negotiation. False claims may be made regarding something they have, merely in order to seem magnanimous or "sacrificing" when they offer to give it up—in exchange, of course, for an equally "serious" concession on your side. They may intransigently refuse to budge on a seemingly unimportant point, but be extremely generous on what you view to be significant issues, thereby giving the impression that they have agreed to most of what you want, while not, of course, being able to sign any agreement at all "until everything is sorted out." They might insist on mere letters of understanding, but then quibble over the details for the next ten years, saying that your position regarding the details violates the original spirit of agreement. None of these ploys is meant to destroy the relationship: each is representational of an intense ambiguity on the part of the Chinese about doing business with the West, and as such, each is meant to test your "friendship," your trust, your worthiness, as a Westerner in their land. In China, a different concept of time interacts with such other factors as their bureaucracy, their flip-flopping xenophobia/xenophilia, and their particular versions of the all-important Asian values of face, harmony, and group/individual relationships, to produce a distinctly challenging, yet ultimately rewarding, environment in which to negotiate.

Let's look at a situation in which, after many months of negotiations with the Chinese, an American is finally reaching a point in his negotiations where an agreement is in sight. Then a new, unexpected condition arises:

"Our company has a policy of uniform pricing for all the countries we do business with," explains George Manning, chief financial officer of a global U.S. telecommunications company. Wang Yen Shou, the Chinese government's communications representative, is disappointed. "For some time, we have done business with the Americans—with their companies and their government," Wang says. "There are many opportunities to work together in China, as you know, but special opportunities for friends require special pricing arrangements. This, you would agree, is only fair, in the East or West," he continues. It appears to Manning that he may have trouble maintaining the China market *without* special pricing, yet this request would violate his corporation's requirement for global price symmetry.

In terms of a negotiation analysis, the position being taken by the Chinese is special pricing arrangements. The underlying need is multidimensional; from an economic perspective, the Chinese need to save money, reduce costs, and get more for less. From a cultural perspective, the negotiation has moved successfully to a point where that special *guanxi* relationship is about to be established. In fact, this is a good sign, but the Westerner must be careful: in order to finalize the relationship, the Chinese are asking for some sign of special favors, and they have latched onto special pricing. If Manning can offer some other sign, perhaps, of "doing a special favor for a special friend," the relationship-needs will be fulfilled, while the special pricing request need not be granted.

In fact, this hurdle was successfully overcome. Manning was able to raise a second possibility: to provide the Chinese with some new equipment at a cost he thought they would appreciate. In return, the Chinese agreed to "help him out" with his regulatory mandate and agreed to the pricing of the deal as originally stated. This satisfied Manning's own pricing problems and sealed the relationship of special friendship between his company and the Chinese. In this solution, Manning sought options, recognized the real underlying cultural and economic needs of the Chinese, and looked at his possible chips as needs-satisfiers. In his own way, he had brainstormed creatively for a solution that would satisfy the Chinese need for "special attention." Although he probably hadn't prepared for this possibility ahead of time nor even brought up the alternate equipment as part of the original deal, he realized when the situation arose that this creative solution could get him what he wanted in return. He was flexible, resourceful, and firm, refusing to be put-off and also resisting any temptation to react unconstructively (for which read "emotionally," or with attacking behavior, in this case). He was, above all, tenacious, willing to look beyond his own position in order to satisfy it.

The Propensity to Take Risks

Closely allied with time value differences, are differences in attitudes toward risk. This category is closely allied to Hofstede's uncertainty-avoidance dimension. Cultures can be highly risk-avoidant: slow to make decisions, apparently always in need of more information, dependent on rules and regulations, heavily bureaucratic and hierarchical. On the opposite side, cultures can be very low risk-avoidant: entrepreneurial, making quick decisions based on little information, tending to disregard or find ways to work through or around hierarchy and bureaucracy.

At the negotiating table, more conservative cultures will probably have an intricate decision-making system. Certainly many individuals will probably be required to approve a deal. More risk-taking cultures are more likely to empower individuals to make decisions. We've seen that the United States has a fairly highly risk-taking propensity, although this quality is not necessarily Western: many European cultures are remarkably conservative in their approach to risk. (Greece is one of the most conservative of all cultures in this dimension.) Certain Asian cultures, such as the dynamic dragons, are also very risk-oriented. Risk is a key issue in China and plays a unique role: risky situations may be used to "shame" the other side. Risk-avoidant behavior in the West can take the form of casting "guilt" on the other side. (This is not uncommon in Germany, for example.)

Interestingly, a high level of uncertainty over the future can, in a strange twist, actually promote a high level of comfort with risk taking. In such cultures, the thinking goes this way: "It might be foolish to plan excessively for the future, because we are not ultimately in charge of it. Therefore, since the consequences of today's actions are mitigated by the unknowable, by some other force, let's let the dice roll; we're not responsible." This ambiguous and apparently contradictory relationship with fate and the future explains the often surprising degree of risk taking we sometimes see in basically conservative cultures, the making of serious choices for quite unstudied or unexplained reasons. The Japanese can, for example, require great amounts of information before making a move, yet be dedicated to making such moves for reasons that cannot necessarily be substantiated with data. They may need reams of details in order to plan a step into a particular market, but their decision to enter that market in the first place may have been reached by nothing more than their arbitrary and determined desire to enter that market. In such a situation, they may fail again and again in their specific, risk-avoidant, information-based plans, but they will go back again and again to that market until they succeed there, simply because the larger, perhaps riskier, decision to be there in the first place had already been made. Arabs and certain Africans, such as the Nigerians, as well as the Chinese can often exhibit what, for Westerners, seems a "passive-aggressive" attitude toward risk.

Mexico's low risk-taking propensity is partly based on a fatalistic attitude toward the world. There, "a realist is a pessimist." Since bad things will always happen, one should be extremely careful in one's actions in order to avoid running an even greater risk of bringing on negative situations. In Japan, also low in risk taking, one avoids risk and uncertainty because the unexpected can easily destroy the balanced web of harmony that one is so careful to weave. Our own American "cow-puncher" approach, the "shoot-from-the-hip" attitude of a young and energetic culture unencumbered by the experiences of an older world, is slowly changing. But in one view of many of the cultures we do business with, our continuing enthusiasm and naiveté is sometimes too disturbing to lead to any good.

Group Versus Individual Orientation

Action and work can be conducted for and by individuals or for and by groups, as the Hofstede dimension of individualism versus collectivism demonstrates. In Japan, "the nail that sticks up gets hammered down"; that is, the individual who brings attention to himself or herself will be sharply put back in his or her place. In contrast, as we have seen, the cultural values we are given at an early age in the United States encourage individualism. Children are urged to "do things for themselves." Young people are expected to leave the nest in their late teens and early twenties. Independence is a virtue practiced and applauded at the earliest possible moment. In other cultures, one may not leave the nest just for the sake of leaving; indeed, one may never leave the web of family at all.

Group or individual orientation, therefore, affects the negotiation process in a number of ways. In group-oriented societies, the other side will probably be a team, as opposed to an individual or a few individuals. Decisions will probably not be made at the table, but rather will be discussed among the group members after the meeting is over. Group orientation means that individual initiative, or individual attempts to take extra responsibility, or to do a super job for the sake of getting the credit, will not occur. Merit is bestowed on the entire group, whatever the individual efforts responsible for success. Decisions will probably take longer, and deals will have to be designed so that the group is the beneficiary, as opposed to the individuals that make it up. Individual will, and the expression of individual desires, are generally not appreciated in group-oriented cultures. Highlighting the benefits inherent in the deal for the individuals on the other team in a group-oriented culture will not win you points.

However, this kind of negotiating behavior will be positively received in individual-oriented cultures. In such cultures, one expects decisions to be made more quickly, with positive reactions to the personal benefits to be reaped with the success of the deal. Personal benefits need to be considered as possible negotiation chips. Personal initiative is highly valued in individual-oriented cultures, and you can depend on your opposite numbers to take whatever action they deem necessary to overcome obstacles or press their case. Not only is the business group important in group-oriented cultures, but other groups play a key role as individual stakeholders at the negotiation table. For example, the family, and its impact on the businessperson in a group-oriented culture, plays a significant role in the businessperson's behavior with you. Business in general (or at least the completion of a task, such as a deal with you) may not be as important to him or her as maintaining a strong family relationship. This will affect the amount of time such an individual will give to the negotiation, the stress he or she will place on details, the need he or she may feel that you meet (and maybe become accepted as a "member" of) the "family."

This group orientation is particularly strong in South Asian, South European, and African cultures and is somewhat so in most Latin American cultures. In the United States, we like to say that we want to succeed individually so that we can protect and provide for our families. In truth, we would perform the same way whether we had a family to provide for or not. In this sense, the United States still glorifies the lone, rugged individual, succeeding against all odds (nature, bad guys, and foreigners, to name just a few) as a valid cultural archetypal hero. For Americans, pragmatism and individualism are keys to success. "You can do anything if you try hard enough." The group, for Americans, traditionally is represented as the bureaucracy; it just gets in the way, just messes things up.

Decision-Making Systems

Closely aligned with group or individual orientation in a negotiation is the distinction that cultures make over how decisions are reached. Are they made by the group or by an individual, and, if by a group, are they determined by consensus or by a majority? If made by individuals, are the decisions autocratic and extremely centralized or diffused among many individuals throughout the organization?

In Japan, for example, decisions have almost always been made by consensus. (This is changing, however. The president of SONY announced, a few years back, that Japan could use more nails that "stick up.") The time the Japanese take to make their decisions may seem interminable to the Americans awaiting a decision, but the information exchanged at the table must be taken back to all parties concerned and decided upon in many minimeetings among themselves. This Japanese decision-making system is known as *ringi seido,* or "reverential inquiry about superior's intentions from below." Some have said that the group orientation of the Japanese comes from their eons of work in the rice fields, where teamwork was essential to a good harvest. Whatever the unique combination of factors, the Japanese retain today the need to have the entire group in agreement (harmony, again) on an issue before it is implemented. Therefore, there is always much discussion, but this will inevitably occur out of sight of the other side, and certainly so if the other side is non-Japanese. Traditionally (and this is changing, too, depending on the industry), lower levels "inquire" about the intentions of the next level up. Ideas and decisions move from the bottom up, with each level seeking approval from the next higher level. At each step upward, consensus must be reached by the players before the issue is "recommended" upward again. The final form reaches the decision makers at the top, who then put their stamp of approval (often literally) on it. By this time, of course, all players have discussed the issue at length and have "bought in." Therefore, although the decision-making time in Japan may seem extremely long to the impatient American, once the decision is made, implementation is usually quite rapid, since all concerned with the project are already intimately familiar with it. And it is at this point that the Japanese get their turn to complain about how slowly the Americans move. For Americans may make decisions more quickly, may even decide them directly at the table, but then the project, once decided upon by the top, must move back down through the organization, getting everyone's "buy-in," understanding, and compliance along the way—usually after the decision is made.

We should be careful not to give the impression that the American decision-making process is one-dimensionally centralized and individual. In fact, it is more like a matrix, with a significant degree of consultation at all levels. However, the process is consultative only to the degree that those needing to make the decisions obtain the information they deem necessary. It is not oriented to providing all possible players with all possible information. It does not seek unanimity as much as a majority decision among key personnel. France, on the other hand, is more highly centralized in business decision making, as are many Latin cultures. Individuals there may make quick decisions, but the decisions are usually only those that reflect the limited responsibility of an individual in a particularly circumscribed position within a complex hierarchy, and they usually must fall in line with the goals of the "man at the top."

Chinese decision making, however, can be a unique situation, because of the fact in part that there have developed over the millennia in China several parallel bureaucracies: the current government bureaucracy and the local, historically determined bureaucracies. The whole purpose of the bureaucracy in China is to diffuse decision making so that responsibility is difficult to locate. Nobody wants to be left holding the bag. Ultimately this is done to shield powerful figures from accountability; however, this can result in interminable delays in getting decisions made. Sometimes the delays are intentionally designed to stall, or pass on responsibility. Sometimes, however, the bureaucracies are so complex that your opposite number in China might merely be trying to locate those responsible for or those having the necessary information to help in making a decision to move the project along. Remember, in China you are dealing with a culture with a history of dynastic, bureaucratic rule that reaches back through the centuries.[22]

The Nature of Agreements

Finally, we need to note that what wins the day in one culture may truly blow you away in another. That is, in the United States, for example, we believe that if we present rational, detailed information, the other side will make its decisions based just on that. However, other cultures may use other criteria, such as emotional appeals, ethnic loyalty, or merely just a good feeling about you, as the real reasons for deciding *yea* or *nay*. Clearly, then, along with empirical reason, we must realize that the showing of emotions, intuition, ideological agreement, and even traditional precedents may all present other criteria for agreement.

In Mexico, for example, a clear, rational argument will certainly be appreciated, but ultimately the decision to go with you rather than with

[22]Pye, Lucien, *Chinese Commercial Negotiating Style*, Oegeschlager, Gunn, Hain, Inc., Cambridge, Massachusetts, 1982.

your competitor might not be based on your information, but rather on whether or not you appealed to the Mexican sense of honor and dignity, whether you expressed your emotions freely, whether you were *simpático*. And as we have seen in Arab cultures, the need to become "family" is critical for trust and agreement to occur. In many Asian cultures, information upon which one makes the decision to move forward together or not, is presented, not as an argument or as emotional appeal, but rather as an exposition. It might seem to the Westerner (and certainly to the Latin American) as somewhat cold, sterile, and impersonal.

A final thought on the actual differences in the form of the final agreement. Perhaps not too long ago there was a perfect, unblemished society where a one's handshake was "good enough." Today, most important business deals will require somewhat more formalization. However, the degree of formalization varies considerably. In the United States, we usually wrap up our agreements in 500-page tomes written by our attorneys, detailing every legal possibility that may arise. In many other cultures, however, if you walk into the negotiation with a battery of lawyers, or even bring your attorneys in at the end, you may risk the deal. It is usually taken as a sign of mistrust, as a sign that you are doubting your associate's word. The United States is probably the most litigious country in the world. There are perhaps more attorneys in New York than in all of Pacific Rim of Asia. They are, in most cases, unwelcome at the bargaining table elsewhere in the world. Additionally, the final form of an agreement in many countries may be a brief written synopsis of the outcome of the negotiation. It may be a simple statement of intent.

The Chinese, for example, are fond of issuing "memorandums of understanding." These are statements about the "spirit" of the agreement. Americans may need to negotiate with the Chinese for a long period of time just to get to the point where a memorandum of understanding can be issued. And one of the most frustrating experiences for Americans negotiating with the Chinese is the apparent ease with which their Chinese colleagues "break" the contract almost as soon as it is signed. What is really happening here is a cultural difference in the perceived purpose of the negotiation. Americans tend to view the negotiation process as ending when the agreement is reached. As we've said, the Chinese, however, see the reaching of an agreement as just the *beginning* of the negotiation, for "now that we have determined we can do business with each other—i.e., have come to an understanding and can rely on each other—it should be easy to accommodate each other when special needs arise." And, for many of the various reasons we have stated earlier, special needs can arise surprisingly often.

Models for identifying where and how cultures differ are of greatest help when they aid us in seeing ourselves in relation to the people we are meeting at the table. Our power at the table lies not in overcoming or changing the other side, but in understanding it. And ultimately, we take this power only when we use it to see ourselves. When we take that step, we are truly opening ourselves up to richer possibilities than we would ever have known otherwise. Effective international negotiators may not know exactly what they will ultimately leave the table with, but they work toward getting all that the sometimes vastly different worlds at the table can provide. And they do it by continually trying to see themselves and their needs through the eyes of the people sitting across from them.

9
Coming Home
Out There

I remember a particular social studies class I had in the eighth grade. We must have been beginning a new topic, European history, for by way of introducing what we would be doing for the next few weeks, my teacher asked the class why we thought so many people visit Europe every year. At the time, I didn't know whether or not people actually did this, but since he said so, I assumed it might be true, but I couldn't come up with an answer to his question. If he'd asked why people like to vacation in Florida or the Caribbean, I could have provided an answer, but I hadn't the foggiest idea why people go to Europe. Then he asked each of us to think of the person closest to us in our family—it could be ourselves or our parents or our grandparents—who was born somewhere else. One by one, we mentioned our grandparents, who were born in Poland, Russia, Hungary, Italy, England, Greece, and our parents, who were born in Puerto Rico, Cuba, Panama, the Caribbean Islands, China. A few said they themselves had come from places like the Dominican Republic or Egypt. Some said that they didn't know anyone in their family from another country, but that their family came from the South and before that from Africa. Americans liked to travel, my teacher said, to Europe and to many other places (I think he knew in those days that most of the kids, in our class anyway, had European backgrounds) in order to visit the places that they had come from, that once were their homes. Today, if we asked the same question, the specific countries might be different, but the question and its answer remain the same. Americans abroad are people returning home.

When we, as Americans, conduct business abroad, we are also returning home. Today, though the times might be different, the cultural values of the people we are sitting across the table from, the heart and soul of what makes them who they are, what drives them to do what they do, are not really different from our own...if we acknowledge that our own values and motivations were largely given to us by our parents, our grandparents, their friends, neighbors, and associates and that all these people were the parents, grandparents, friends, neighbors, and associates of the people sitting across from us. As Americans, we have a unique opportunity to know, in the very deepest way, what these people across from us are all about, by looking within ourselves.

If the world today is prying us loose to return to our homes in Europe, to Asia, to Latin America, to Africa, not only to visit, but to do business there as well, then rediscovering the "foreigner within" is an essential first step to understanding the people we are going out to do business with. For a variety of reasons, the entire world is more technologically accessible than it has ever been before. The globalization of American (and world) business is proceeding at an unprecedented rate. New markets and new labor forces, spawned by new technology, are fast making once-domestic companies international and once-international companies global. Once upon a time American businesses saw the limits of their world defined by the Atlantic and Pacific oceans. Differences between peoples were of no concern. Therefore they were not considered. Then these businesses sent their managers abroad to set up offices in Paris and London and Tokyo, and, spiderlike, these businesses became international, with centralized directives and coordination in the United States. Suddenly, differences between people were acknowledged, but as a problem to be overcome. The limits of this centralized arrangement soon became apparent, and today we are seeing the development of organizations which, perhaps a decade or two ago, did not have a single foreign sale but which now organize their operations according to a "think global, act local" philosophy, with autonomous regional units around the world that operate together to provide a definition of what the organization looks like on a global scale. Now it is not enough to acknowledge differences between people as something to be overcome; now differences are to be celebrated as the lifeblood of growth and change itself. Operating according to regionally appropriate standards means that, from now on, successful businesses respond specifically to the different requirements of their region and of their people. And while the global organization helps the regional parts to respond successfully, the response, in order to be successful, must be appropriate to the region.

The new global manager, negotiator, trader, or general businessperson then, is someone who, now more than ever, understands the differences between the peoples of his or her global organization, in order to help them. And Americans, while perhaps relatively new to doing business "out there," are not at a disadvantage. On the contrary, our chronological and cultural proximity to our new associates across the oceans is a unique and precious tool that can help us to do business with them. If we do not see this, it is because we have chosen not to. Just as we have chosen, in so many other areas, not to see that who we are is so very much where we have come from.

As we are learning this about doing business internationally, we are also learning this about doing business domestically. There is no real difference between Americans doing business with associates abroad and Americans doing business with Americans: the cultural differences can be strikingly and increasingly the same. Dealing with domestic diversity issues and dealing with international business issues are two sides of the same coin, and it is not coincidental that both issues are of great concern today. People with a domestic diversity perspective do not merely manage to cope with cultural differences between individuals working in American offices; instead, they celebrate the differences, in order to enrich the possibilities for more fruitful work. The same is true for the efforts at globalization. Those who will succeed are those who do not seek to limit the differences between us but rather to allow for and welcome those differences as new opportunities for working in new and better ways.

We know today, as scientists, and as mere mortal observers, that whether we look out to the stars in the universe or within to the atom in a grain of sand, we are looking at the same structure, the same rules, the same truths. To know one is to know the other. It is the same for us today as Americans and as businesspeople; for whether we look inward to our world at home or outward to the world beyond our borders, we are, more than ever, looking at ourselves. To know one is to know the other.

Appendix

Global Homecoming Exercises©

Analysis and Suggested Interpretations

The goal of these exercises is to help you develop an appropriate, authentic, and constructive approach to intercultural problems—a global mind-set that will help you surmount them—*whether or not you have specific knowledge about the culture in which you're doing business.* For each of the Global Homecoming Exercises©, we will do two things: First, we will illustrate the five-step Global Homecoming Exercise© process with a possible interpretation. This interpretation may or may not be similar to your own, but it will provide you with an example of how the five-step process can help you to discover experiences in your own life that have a bearing on the behavior and values of the people in the exercise that can give you helpful culture-specific information. Then we will discuss some specific cultural facts about the country and the culture in the exercise that you might find useful. Through the interpretation and the facts, we will be building both empathic and technical understanding of the culture in the exercise.

It is strongly suggested that you put some real effort into the five-step process, even if it takes more time than you had expected and even if you have culture-specific information that could help you bypass the steps. Please write down your answers for all five steps before referring to this analysis.

Remember, this is a subjective exercise for developing behavior that works for you. Other people have had different experiences. They therefore cannot provide answers that will necessarily work for you, even if they work for them. Getting the answers from someone else, or even from these analyses, is not the best way to develop a deep, effective understanding. That only comes from finding the answers within your own experiences. Now let's try the first one:

Global Homecoming Exercise© 1: Individualism

Journey to Slovakia

Step 1: Recognize Differences.   The exercise is asking us to stay with the cultural dimension of individualism. Therefore, let's try to identify or recognize the values, attitudes, and behavior of both the Slovaks and the American *in relation to individualism.*

In this case, to start, the American exhibits individualism simply by showing up alone. While there are three representatives from Slovakia, the American is not a member of a team but is acting alone. This should be a clue that, on the individualism scale, the Slovaks are more group-oriented than the American. The degree to which there are differences will be further elaborated as we analyze the scenario.

The style of this, the third negotiation, appears to have started off in a friendly enough fashion, with much ritual sharing on the part of the Slovaks. This indicated that a relationship was being built and that it was appreciated. However, when the Slovaks pressed their demands, the American was put off and began to question whether he should trust these people as he had initially thought he could. In turn, the Slovaks probably began to feel that they too should be tempering their developing trust since the American not only refused to respond to their demands, but rather pressed forward with his own. What we see here is a clash between different views of the way relationships are developed based on different notions of individualism.

For the American, developing the relationship means seeing eye to eye—knowing that the Slovaks are people who agree with him. For the Slovaks, a relationship does not necessarily imply agreement. In fact, they feel that now that a relationship is developing, they can look to and rely on the American's friendship for many things, including favors, special considerations, etc. What they expect can take the form of special generosity on the part of a friend who has the resources with which to be generous and understanding. To the American, this feels as if he is being used or as if his needs are being ignored at the expense of theirs. In addition, the American feels that the unexpected demands damage the developing relationship. To the Slovak, the American's refusal to consider these special needs is a rejection of the new relationship and proof that Americans are only out for themselves after all.

We need to be especially careful not to provide behavioral ammunition by which our non-American counterparts can confirm or justify their preconceived notions about who we are and why we do what we do. We also must be careful not to prejudge or attribute our counterparts' behavior according to our own cultural prejudices. In this scenario, the American is confirmed in his suspicion that "former Communists really can't be trusted after all" and that "their friendship is just a setup." The Slovaks are equally confirmed in their suspicion that the American is just another Western businessman out for himself—not a real friend.

When each of the Slovaks individually puts forward a position or issue, the others support it. Their appeals might appear individualistic, but they are actually part of a group plan for getting the information out on the table for the American. In this case, the Slovaks are significantly more group-oriented, while the American is significantly more of a lone wolf. Along these same lines, we could also say that the Slovaks are probably more comfortable making decisions based on consensus, while the American is more individualist in his approach. (If he were part of a team of several Americans, he might favor majority rule—which is not at all the same thing as group-oriented decision-by-consensus.)

We see the same pattern emerging in the two styles of communication. When the Slovaks make their demands, they are very self-effacing about it, while the American feels justified in making his requests, basing his justifications on what he sees as obvious rational requirements (for information, facts, data, etc.). The Communist official is almost apologetic in his request for a personal payment; the floor manager appeals to what he believes to be capitalist logic (as opposed to personal preference); and the agitator supports his request with appeals to the needs of the people in these unsettled and troubled times. The American wants facts and bases his arguments (or lack of movement) on the need to evaluate. The Slovaks base their positions and demands on what they perceive to be selfless concern for human needs. While the appeals to relationship, human constraints, and so forth may be ploys, referral to such values whether sincere or not, as opposed to other possibilities, reveals the degree of their power and importance in Slovak society. The American appeals to philosophical ideals of standards and logic. The Slovaks appeal to good intentions, human needs, and the obligations of friendship. When it is to their advantage, they express helplessness about being able to do anything else, while being deaf to a similarly expressed condition by the apparently all-powerful American. When it is to their advantage, they become followers of regulations, while the American is viewed as a maker of regulations.

Many of the Slovak attitudes can be attributed to the political facts of life for them over the last forty years. In fact, however, Slovak life has historically displayed a deep collectivist spirit (culturally speaking, if not economically speaking) that goes back for centuries. So communism's encouragement of leader-following (as opposed to self-initiating) behavior is just the most recent political manifestation of a much older cultural artifact. The Slovaks' own awareness of this tradition (if they had, in this example, such awareness) would only serve to increase their perception of how different they are from the American. Therefore, it must seem incredible to them that the American, who they assumed was so capable of making direct, personal decisions and who supposedly has so many resources at his disposal, is asking for more time to reflect on their requests (requests which to them seem appropriate to their budding relationship). Obviously, to the Slovaks, the American's reticence is based, not on inability, but on refusal.

Step 2: Retrace. Try to recall a situation in your life in which you interacted with individuals who perceived you as more individualistic, self-determining, resourceful, and independent than themselves. The individuals should appear to you only as members of a larger group. Their style of communicating with you should be self-effacing, their mode of persuasion based not so much on objective, mutually understood logic as on appeals to human needs and the obligations of association. Under these conditions, they could use their own sense of ineffectiveness (real or not) to justify any demands you might find unjustified.

These people seem to want to have a relationship with you, even to welcome it and work toward it. However, it seems to you that, as the relationship develops, it becomes an excuse for their making unreasonable demands and requests rather than viewing it as an opportunity to build a mutually satisfying friendship based on similarities. You might get the impression, when you do not cooperate, that you are regarded as shallow, insincere, and uncaring. This makes it very hard for you to continue to work toward a relationship. While trust seems to be very important for *them*, you wonder if you'll ever be able to establish a relationship based on *your* needs, as well. Describe these people, and the real-life situation you are in with them.

Step 3: Reclaim. This step is meant to help you identify the facts about your experience, now that you are older and more removed from it. Can you identify the people in your experience? Can you identify their culture? Their country? Their ethnicity? Religion? Sex? Age? Relation to you? Finally, identify your feelings about having to interact with them this way. Describe all your emotions honestly. This is for yourself, and these are your feelings; you are entitled to them.

Step 4: Reframe. OK, so you reacted with many different feelings based on your uninformed reactions to people you did not understand. Now try to use whatever information, maturity, and wisdom you've gained since then and understand those people from a more recent vantage point. That's the purpose of this step: to put our primitive reactions into perspective, tempering them with judgment and information.

Think hard about everything you once felt about the behavior of those people. Ask yourself if there is anything in their culture that might possibly explain why they behaved the way they did with you. Certainly we are individually responsible for our actions, even if our culture determines, to greater or lesser degrees, the values that drive our behavior. Certainly individuals can be very similar or different from the "norm" of their culture. But, more often than not, individuals do exhibit behavior, values, and attitudes that identify them with specific cultures. So *think hard about what aspects of the culture of the person in your past experience might have had a determining effect on their behavior*. List these aspects.

Now comes the reframing part: the challenge of redefining these cultural facts as "gifts." The facts of life in their culture define the ways they, as individuals, behave. These cultural facts, then, are "ways of being," "ways of acting," that could be viable options for you yourself to consider in response to situations you may or may not have encountered before. Is there merit in their behavior after all? Perhaps not in this situation, but could such behavior be used by you successfully in other situations? Put simply, do you understand why they did what they did? Do you see how it "fits" with and emerges from their own culture, their own experience? And could such behavior, under certain circumstances, be a constructive, authentic, and appropriate option for you?

The final step in reframing is to return to your original real-life response and replace it with a modern, informed response from today. That is, *what will you do differently in response to the original situation if you had the chance to do it all over again right now?* This doesn't have to be dramatic. In fact, it may be of no consequence at all. The point is to have your new response appropriate, authentic, and constructive, reflecting your needs and your informed understanding of where your opposite numbers are coming from, culturally speaking.

Step 5: Resurface.   Now let's go back to "Journey to Slovakia." Hopefully, we've gotten a sense of how to deal better with people similar to the Slovaks in our example. Hopefully, this awareness is appropriate, authentic, and constructive, since it should have emerged from our own subjective experience. Now we want to transfer our awareness to the Slovaks in our example.

As you did in your experience, try to identify and reframe the Slovak behavior, attitudes, and values as their cultural "gifts." Can you apply the same positive, effective response used in your own past experience to deal with the current Slovak-American issues? For example, if you were able to identify similar people in your past, recalling how it felt to deal with them, and were able to come up with a better way of dealing with them, could you take this same "better way" and apply it to the Slovak-American case we are discussing? How did you deal with people who were relationship-based, group-oriented, consensus-reaching people who avoided individual initiative, action, and responsibility?

Finally, in order to make your cross-cultural understanding count most, how can you transfer these behaviors from "then" to "now" in a way that preempts, rather than reacts to, the clash of cultures? For example, the American's need for information, data, and specific facts regarding quality control, distribution, etc. could be better obtained, not at this meeting, but rather in a system of longer-term communications begun sooner. By the same token, the American could use his perceived position of being "more resourceful and decisive" than his Slovak associates by setting specific agendas prior to this third meeting. Much can be done in agendas, much can be avoided. Long-distance agenda setting also allows group-oriented cultures to make the decisions they need to make out of your presence without losing face.

The American should not have come to this meeting expecting decisions to be made at the table. Rather, he should have adjusted his expectations of this third meeting in light of what he had already learned about the Slovaks from his two previous meetings with them. With this knowledge in mind, the American could have carefully worked for the information he needed outside of and before this meeting, while anticipating having to meet questions that they as a group would have for him prior to his arrival. In this case, the questions could have been diplomatically raised, once again, in premeeting, agenda-setting communications, so that he could have arrived in possession of certain important facts. At best, this information might have advanced the negotiations. At worst, it would at least have given him some clues as to what was really on their minds, while strengthening and enforcing the relationship-building inherent in his dialogue with them.

The American might have prepared for the negotiation by anticipating the appeals the Slovaks would make to his individual decisiveness and access to resources. That is, he could have come ready with concessions, ideas, or new options that might not have "cost" him much (if anything) but that could have been used as bargaining chips to show good faith and trust, and possibly even fill a Slovak need. The American might also have used the premeeting agenda communications to convey his own constraints (such as financial obligations, stockholders' rights, government regulations, etc.) regarding decision making. This would have helped the Slovaks to better understand his need for additional time to make his decisions, even though he alone has decision-making authority.

There are as many options as there are people reading this case, and the best options should encompass, for Slovak society in particular, not only what is done face to face over the table, but also what is done before and after the actual meeting.

As in many cross-cultural misunderstandings, the greatest problems revolve around the attribution of incorrect meaning to behavior and the incorrect expectations each has of the other based on previous misperceptions, stereotypes, etc. By adjusting their expectations of each other, of the meeting, and of the purpose of the negotiation, based on a real understanding of the cultural requirements of their negotiating partners, Americans can plan for success long before an actual meeting occurs. This can enable them to avoid cultural problems before they occur and to maximize the immutable cultural conditions they will be facing when they get there.

Global Homecoming Exercise© 2: Time

The Time Traveler

Step 1: Recognize Differences. Keeping our focus primarily on the dimension of time, we can identify Jim, the American as rushed, task-oriented, and progress-oriented. He values planning and efficiency very highly, is constantly aware of the time, does things in a one-at-a-time, linear fashion, and in every way exemplifies the monochronic mind-set. In contrast, the Spaniards in this example are extremely polychronic. They have a flexible attitude toward time and feel comfortable handling several tasks simultaneously. They tend to emphasize the human rather than the functional aspects in business relationships and see efficiency as important but not essential to success at work. For them, the business day is more relaxed, the attitude toward risk is more conservative, the business relationship is more long term (if it is to succeed), and maintaining a pleasurable and acceptable status quo is as meaningful a goal as being oriented toward an unknowable future.

The American believes that the Spaniards have the same high regard for efficiency as he does. After all, his secretary had called the previous day to arrange the meeting for 1 p.m. But not only do the Spaniards not share his American perspective on efficiency; they probably resent his ethnocentric ignorance of some of their own basic Spanish traditions regarding time and schedules. For one thing, Jim is unaware of the fact that he had his secretary schedule the meeting for around the time that lunch and siesta usually begin. That is probably the reason the Spaniards rescheduled the meeting for 4 p.m. Earlier they would be out to lunch, and, in their country, so should Jim have been. The heaviest meal of the day is lunch, and dinner isn't usually taken until very late in the evening, especially when hosting special occasions for guests in restaurants. Jim took a small, quick American-style "bite" for lunch at noontime; there was no way he was going to survive until dinner at 11 p.m.

Again, we see here the intertwining of dimensions: the Spanish attitude toward time also determines, along with other values, the nature and importance of relationships in business (and perhaps vice versa). While Jim has a desire to know the Spaniards, his primary concern is getting the job done in the least amount of time. He is practically already back on the plane before he has even landed. The Spaniards may or may not be trying to involve him in their network of socializing and friendships: the example is not clear about their motives for socializing at the beginning of the meeting and for the long delay before getting started. One thing we can safely infer from this situation, however, is the Spaniards' polychronic notion of simultaneous task activity: clearly, while work and the issues that bring them together are important, there is much discussion about other issues at the same time. Jim sees this as distraction and delay; but the Spaniards are just doing things in a polychronic way and perhaps are hoping to see if and how Jim will jump in and join them. He doesn't. Jim has a compartmentalized notion of time which specifies when and how much time should be devoted to work — as distinct from socializing. The Spaniards clearly have a more overlapping notion of tasks. "Work" also involves hosting Jim till all hours, something he has a lot of trouble pulling off successfully since he probably wants to be alone after his long day, what with hunger, fatigue, and a very confused body clock. In fact, in addition to needing to know more about Spanish customs regarding time, he should also have given himself more time to adjust to the jet lag inherent in overseas travel before jumping into an important meeting almost literally the moment he lands.

Some additional thoughts about time-concept differences and their relationship to other cultural dimensions here. Jim is so concerned about efficiency that in typical, traditional U.S. fashion, he has trusted his own instincts to "wing it" (or "shoot from the hip") when it comes to understanding the *Madrileños* customs and traditions rather than taking the time necessary in order to be sure. He pays the price. His Spanish is not adequate (Castillian Spanish is very different from the Spanish spoken in Northern Mexico and Southern California), and he is certainly dressed inappropriately. In a formal culture such as Spain's, such errors do not go unnoticed, and neither wins him any points in this case. While such failings might not be that significant in a multicultural, egalitarian (and hence more informal and lower power-distance) culture like that of the United States, these are critical failings in Spain, where formality and respect for status, hierarchy, role, and protocol are specific and important.

The need for appropriate etiquette, respect, and the kind of relationships that result from such formality and hierarchy (as well as in this case, the unique distinction between independence and individualism we discussed in a previous chapter) also define the pace and form of the meeting. The Spaniards are not particularly interested in a presentation by the American. Rather, they are pleased that he has come so well prepared and are eager to review his information in the privacy of their own offices. Jim, on the other hand, is expecting to make a fairly detailed presentation of his material and, in the best of all possible worlds, to obtain a decision at the table. Neither is a realistic expectation because neither is appropriate to Spanish business tradition.

It should be added before we go any further in our discussions about "traditional" Spanish business that Spain is changing dramatically as this is being written. Therefore, we emphasize the word *traditional* here, and want to use this scenario as a learning tool for an empathic understanding of Spaniards rather than as a lesson on Spanish business methods. There are many harried, time-conscious, task-oriented Spaniards from Madrid and Barcelona in these days of Europe 1992, and Spain is playing a particularly important role (as illustrated by the 1992 Olympics, the Columbus celebration, and the Sevilla World's Fair). Many people in Spain today are struggling to find a way to somehow integrate the traditions of a more refined, slower past with the requirements of a booming, modern, more monochronic, business-oriented future. Remember, however, that research shows that traditional values, more often than not, maintain their hold, even during moments of great social change; it's just that the values may manifest themselves in different ways. I suspect that many of the traditional Spanish values we are highlighting in this example will still have their way for decades to come in Spain; they may just not be as visible as they were in the forms they took in the past.

Step 2: Retrace.   Have you ever had to work, play, build a relationship with (an) individual(s) who appeared too "slow" to you, too concerned about things other than what you thought you were getting together to do, who seemed to be trying to get you to do things their way, which was not at all the way you wanted to do things. And all of this with a warm smile, an intent to serve you, an appearance of having your needs in mind? You may have felt as if these people, while being "so friendly" were also attempting to pull rank somehow. If you are an American, you may have felt that being around them was always a little like being around people who put themselves on a pedestal. Take a moment to describe the situation. It is possible that a coworker may seem to you to be like this, or perhaps a roommate in college. Going back further still, can you recall family members or family friends who seemed to act this way whenever they were around you or other members of the family? Try to create a specific incident in your mind.

Step 3: Retrace.   Recall this scene carefully. Answer the questions for Step 3: define, as best you can, who these people were, their country, their ethnicity, age, sex, religion, relation to you, etc. Most important, ask yourself how you feel about these people (this person).

Step 4: Reframe.   The important question to ask here is if there is anything in the culture of these individuals that might explain their behavior. Once these aspects of their culture are identified, can you reframe them as "gifts," that is, as possible behavioral options that might also be useful to you under certain circumstances? Can you learn from these people and their ways? A possible lesson one could learn, for example, might be that one need not always be so quick to search for the solution or the deal. One can sometimes let the deal emerge out of a more solid association. Another example: maybe you could use your own status and rank in certain business situations where in the past you might have tended to minimize their impact or importance. Returning now to these people and your experience with them, knowing what you know today, think about how you might respond differently to their behavior. Remember, in all relationships—especially those in business—you are looking to maximize and satisfy your own needs. Therefore, knowing what you know about these people today, how could you respond more effectively to their behavior if you put yourself as you are today back in that scene?

Step 5: Resurface.   You are Jim in Madrid. Knowing what you know, and having examined a similar situation in your own past, what will you now do differently? There are many options, and the better ones, once again, are more preemptive than reactive—that is, it would have been better if Jim had reframed his own expectations and perspectives on business life in Spain before he acted the way he did. The damage having been done, however, whatever Jim does now will just get him back to a place where he can begin all over again with the Spaniards, and that's assuming he can pull it off.

Preemptive planning for next time would mean Jim having to modify his expectations of how the meeting would go, what he could expect from it, who the Spanish are and how they might react to him, the degree of relationship building he would be required to participate in and the forms that relationship building would take, etc. To start with, he might want to brush up on his Spanish and try not to be as ethnocentric about it as he was on this occasion. He might want to have his secretary schedule a meeting for a time more convenient to the Spaniards and allow himself a day to recover from the flight over before the meeting. He would have to understand the need for respecting rank and status, in formal ways (not using first names, showing appropriate respect to the senior associate in Madrid) and informal ways (dressing more appropriately).

Once again, however, his own real American needs and constraints would require that he maximize his time while in Madrid. And once again, there might be difficulties there about being as efficient in Spain as he'd like to be. It would be especially important for him to realize this ahead of time and take action beforehand to make sure that his time would be as well spent in Madrid as possible. This would mean agenda planning and communications prior to the meeting about the issues to be discussed. As much information sharing as possible should go on, as much in advance as is reasonable for both parties. This would help Jim achieve his goals while maintaining and building an all-important relationship between himself and his *Madrileños* associates.

Global Homecoming Exercise© 3:
Relationship Building

Bargaining in the Sun

For the remaining two Global Homecoming Exercises©, we'll let you take
yourself through the five-step process, now that you've gotten some practice in how it works. Let's concentrate instead on analyzing what's going on
in these scenarios. You can compare and then apply this information to
your own five-step process afterward (particularly with regard to Step 5).

In this example, we'll be looking at how the Italians and Americans
interact in business over the issue of relationship building. In addition,
this case involves tactics and strategies during a negotiation. Therefore,
we'll be trying to answer the question: How do cultural differences, particularly in the realm of differences regarding relationships, affect the
negotiation process?

Let's begin by comparing some differences between the American
and the Italians in this scene. As with other group-oriented cultures, the
southern Italians in this scene are most comfortable negotiating as a
group (albeit a small group — just two people in this case), while the
American feels confident in being able to negotiate individually.

Some cultural comments about Italy: Southern Italy (the Mezzo-
giorno region) is very different from northern Italy. Neapolitans might
regard the Milanese as "Germans," and the Milanese have some not-
quite-pleasant terms for their more rural southern cousins. It was only
in the last century that Italy was finally united as a republic at all, and
regional alliances and allegiances still are often stronger than national
ones. It is for this reason that we should be careful not to ascribe northern Italian values and behavior to the Neapolitans in this scenario, and
we should use caution about assuming that Srs. Conti and Mondavi exhibit typically Italian behavior. "Typical Italian behavior" is a generalization that exists only outside Italy.

With this in mind, we should begin by recognizing the profound reliance in southern Italy on relationships as the basis for all business.
While we have been stressing this as a value for many cultures, we have
here an example of relationships raised to an exalted level perhaps as
extreme as the American's profound reverence for individualism. This
clash of extremes could be seriously problematic and, in this case in fact,
is the cause of some real misunderstanding. While it may appear to the
American, Paul Stoneworthy (and to the American reader), that the relationships are being manipulated, nevertheless they form the important prerequisite for doing any business at all. As with almost every
other aspect of southern Italian life, the relationship — the group unit,

the clan, the family, the village, the network of associates — is what determines if, what, and how business will occur. Membership in the group means virtual lifetime commitments and trust; exclusion from the group permits the group to treat and perceive the nonmember as a (permanent) outsider. And as an outsider, he or she may be used to serve the best interests of the group. Inclusion in such a rigid, clannish group can be very difficult, yet inclusion is the only way that real trust and, consequently, really successful business can be achieved.

This, then, is the root of the problem between Stoneworthy and his Italian associates. He and they (or more accurately, their companies or organizations) have been doing business together for a long time. But "a long time" in Napoli is different from a similar amount of time in the United States. What may have appeared to be a very tight relationship to Stoneworthy only feels so in contrast to the casual, loose, relaxed kind of American business relationships he might have been more used to at home. In fact, from the perspective of the Neapolitans, the association may not have been close at all. This misperception of the meaning or strength of the relationship makes Stoneworthy feel as if his trust is being betrayed (or at least manipulated), while letting the Neapolitans feel perfectly correct in subjecting him to a range of trickery and tactics reserved for "outsiders." To the Neapolitans, the American is an outsider; as for Stoneworthy, he thought he was well on the inside.

Such negotiating tactics and trickery are not always reserved for outsiders (although there is certainly less compunction felt about using it on them than on one's own). In Italy, other Neapolitans might have just as easily been treated to the kind of blatant manipulation Stoneworthy is experiencing. There are several cultural reasons for this kind of behavior that allow for it by and among Italians, as well as with "outsiders." As we mentioned before in our section on time, certain cultures have an inherent distrust of the future. There is, therefore, support for making the most of today instead. This attitude is particularly strong in Italy. It has developed into the *la dolce vita* syndrome of living for today, of making the most of the moment, of making what is attractive beautiful, of stretching, perhaps to grotesque or at least unrealistic degrees and limits, the meaning of things in order to extract the most meaning and pleasure available from them in the moment. Barzini[23] spends considerable time examining the reasons for this in Italy and believes that it is based on a fundamentally fatalistic view of the world, and on a belief that human attempts at betterment will inevitably fail, that any efforts to achieve a more rational, organized social system are doomed to fall

[23]Barzini, Luigi, *The Italians*, MacMillan Publishing Co., New York, 1964.

apart, and that catastrophe and disorganization are really the natural order of things. Therefore, if we cannot really exercise any control over what happens, we are licensed, in a sense, to get as much as we can right here and now. In a sense, if it weren't for the group orientation of the social system that goes back so very far in Italy, Italians would give Americans a close race for the winner of the individualism contest, in the sense that the Italian (male, at least) can believe he is entitled to whatever he can claim for himself in this life. This leads to a valuing of the cunning, the shrewd, the clever, the one who gets away with something, the one who can put something over on someone else, the trickster. It also leads to a devaluing of the system, the organization, the tax collector, the government official, the plodding bureaucrat. There is the dual notion of playfulness, sweetness, joy in life, coupled with the requirement to get away with whatever one can. Of course, the structure of Italian life, as in all cultures, is the result of and the justifier for these attitudes: the post office does not work, the tax system is unfathomable, and beauty cannot be found in the state. So the wheel keeps on spinning....

In this sense, Srs. Conti and Mondavi are acting in the best Italian tradition of trying to outwit, outmaneuver, and manipulate the American in a playful kind of way. After all, the American is an outsider anyway, all the more ripe for such treatment. From a negotiating point of view, the fickleness and unpredictability of life justify the view of a negotiation as an opportunity for a winner-take-all, or a win/lose mentality. Knowing this, Stoneworthy should either have been better prepared to play a win/lose, competitive bargaining game, planning and playing his moves carefully, or have better prepared to turn the game around to a more win/win, collaborative process. Granted, this could have been the more difficult choice of the two, since, culturally, his associates are more inclined toward the win/lose approach and might have been mystified at or rejecting of any collaborative efforts. The point is, he is prepared for neither. In response to their tactics, he is reactive instead of preemptive. As he offers no alternatives, he simply allows them to play their game.

If he had recognized their game and decided to play it, knowing that eventually they were going to move this way, there would have been several things he could have done. He might have insisted on using precedent as justification for his price. He might have called their bluff, with a bluff of his own about going to their competitors and mentioned what the competitors were willing to offer. He might have called Srs. Conti and Mondavi on their manipulation of his relationship, and expressed relief at now being able to just talk facts without consideration for ongoing long-term relationships. He might have provided information about the plans of the company to move elsewhere. There was much room for hardball. He could have adopted a take-it-or-leave-it stand. He could have determined ahead of time what he would and would not accept and walked away from the table. (There is always the opportunity to return later.)

At the same time, there was much he could have done to try to turn the negotiation into a win/win situation, or at least to test this possibility. Turning a negotiation from a win/lose competitive style to a win/win collaborative style requires the use of certain behavioral techniques that can be difficult to master without considering the cultural differences. If we are dealing with a culture that has a preference for a competitive style, it can be even more difficult. But it can be done, especially since the cultural determinants may be less strong in the individuals actually seated at the table, for a variety of individual and/or situational reasons.

As with any trick or manipulation (and the "good cop/bad cop" game of Conti and Mondavi certainly is a classic manipulation tactic) used in negotiation, style, strategies, and tactics must also be specifically exposed if they are not productive for you. Stoneworthy could have halted the negotiation and focused on the strategies. He might have conducted a mininegotiation around the competitive and abusive tactics of his colleagues. In effect, his occasional remarks of concern and surprise to Conti are efforts in that direction; they just aren't defined enough and employed in a sufficiently constructive manner. Stoneworthy might have said something that recognized their past relationship and pointed out that the current process is, from his perspective, damaging to it. He might have then gone on to state that he was just as capable as they were of playing this kind of manipulative game, and he might have given them a few examples of what that might be like, such as the competitive tactics listed above. He might then have gone on to say that, given their developing long-term relationship, he personally would prefer not to negotiate this way, for it would surely end such a relationship, and to provide his own view that there was much more to be gained by both parties by negotiating collaboratively, seeking common ground and mutually beneficial solutions. He might then have gone on to offer some chips as examples of how the Italians might benefit should they both choose to negotiate collaboratively, chips that would address other issues he knows to be important to them other than the price they are momentarily bargaining over. (Such bargaining chips might consist, for example, for his purposes, of merely opening up the possibilities inherent in a more collaborative negotiating style — easily affordable "concessions" on his part over other, perhaps less important terms such as quantity and frequency of shipments, return policies, and payment terms.) Once Stoneworthy's points were made, he could then have asked for a clear commitment on the part of his Italian associates to move forward in this direction. That way, should the negotiation take a competitive win/win turn, a precedent and agreement over this issue could be called upon to get the negotiation back to the collaborative track.

All this could be difficult to do, however, in a culture where a collaborative win/win approach is suspect and where the successful negotiator is the most clever one who outwits the other. The best hope Stoneworthy has would be to prepare as many chips as possible ahead of time to make *his* way the more attractive one and then to spend his time maximizing the relationship and searching for real needs from the Italians in order to determine which of the chips he's got in his pocket are of most worth to them. They would probably only come around to his style if they see a greater advantage in doing so, and if they have been helped around to it without losing face. It would therefore also be extremely important to keep emphasizing how they would mutually benefit as partners in a more collaborative effort, while providing ways for them to save face as they move away from their original strategic positions.

How to do this involves skill, tact, and a carefully gathered knowledge of what you're up against and where you want to go in the negotiation. It means understanding the Italians opposite you and, most important, understanding how you can be most effective in communicating alternative options. And here's where the five steps of the Global Homecoming Exercises© can help. You've got to act authentically in order to act constructively. Are there individuals in your own experience who are like Srs. Conti and Mondavi, or who have treated you in a similar way? Was it a business deal? Was it a family negotiation? Try to identify the cultural elements that may have played a part in these individuals' behavior. Certainly the capacities of all humans are the same in all cultures, and this includes the capacity to trick and put something over on someone. But this may be emphasized as an acceptable pattern of behavior under certain circumstances and in certain cultures more than in others. Is this a culturally supported behavior? Who are these individuals to you? How can what you know now be applied to that past situation, and what would you do differently if you could relive it again now? Finally, apply this personal experience to the case at hand; put yourself in Stoneworthy's place. What would *you* do (it needs to be authentic to you, "do-able" by *you*) to help find a better solution to the problem?

Global Homecoming Exercise© 4: Egalitarianism

Banking in Buenos Aires

Focusing on the issue of egalitarianism as it is viewed by the Americans and the Argentineans is, as is the case with all cultural facts, a little like trying to hit a moving target. How it is perceived is intrinsically tied up with so many other concepts, such as time, individualism, relationships, etc. For our purposes here, let's try to examine some of the conflicts, in all their subtleties, that arise around the notion of egalitarianism when Americans and Argentineans do business together.

At the heart of it, we find a deep-seated conflict in values. While the Argentineans might profess West European values (and will, especially to differentiate themselves from some of the more indigenous values of their Latin American neighbors), they are more likely referring to traditions that have their roots in European *aristocracy* and its attendant forms, rather than European *democracy*. Americans, as we've seen, however, go to extremes to perpetuate in fact and myth their belief in egalitarianism. And at work, this difference is manifested in differing attitudes toward formality, rank, position, personal responsibility, and initiative.

While the American has been assuming an equal relationship between himself and Juan, Juan may, in fact, have merely been acceding to this perception in order to advance his own agenda. After all, it may not have made that much of a difference to him how the American has been perceiving him, as long as that perception did not interfere with his own desires. And those desires are (to the American's surprise) to leave the bank at some appropriate point in the future and work with the Americans in their company, or to act as the Americans' "agent" in Buenos Aires, either formally or informally, once the operation is set up. From the beginning, levels of relationships and hierarchy have played a key role in the ability of both sides to communicate with each other. For the Argentineans, such communication has been dependent on the clear understanding of and respect for status and hierarchy. For the Argentineans, different authority resides at different levels, and the American appears not to understand these distinctions. They are indicated by the formality of a person's clothes, by the reticence of a person's speech, by a stylishly late arrival, by the importance of the seating plan. All these indicators (and others) reveal a distinct respect for hierarchy and authority. The American and his team have shown a distinct lack of concern for learning these signs and an ignorance of them when displayed by their Argentinean associates. The Argentineans see the

Americans as unknowing and rude; the Americans see the Argentineans (incorrectly) as merely polite versions of North Americans.

Perhaps Juan is familiar with American informality; perhaps that is why he introduces himself the same way. Certainly, he is ingratiating in a studied way that indicates that he is familiar with what would be appreciated by the Americans. It is very easy for him to gain the confidence of the American, particularly in this foreign setting. Perhaps Vienetti is also familiar with American informality and ignorance of Argentinean culture, but he is not as interested in ingratiating himself with the Americans. If he is merely annoyed at their lack of understanding, he is probably downright put out that the American has not arrived with his boss, as Vienetti previously requested. The Argentinean emphasis on rank and status make Vienetti's meeting his counterpart essential to a deal. There is no way that Vienetti, clearly the decision maker, is going to negotiate and make a decision directly with an American at this level. He will only do so after face-to-face conversations with the American's boss. And he is insulted at being asked (in effect by the boss's "pointed" absence) to negotiate with someone of a lower rank and status. In this case, the error alone might cause the deal to fall through. It is just for this and other reasons that Juan is, in fact, correct about the Americans' needing someone like him around to help smooth things for them. Without him, they will keep tripping themselves up. Juan, in fact, might be able to do something in the background to get the deal back on track after this very serious snub, but it will be difficult.

The American however, takes great pride in being able to negotiate directly with Juan and Vienetti. After all, he's been assigned to the case, he has the responsibility, he has the competence; it apparently doesn't matter much to him that Vienetti is his senior. To complicate matters, the American believes that by bringing a Latin along, he will help maintain the relationship between himself and Vienetti. Actually, Susan Lopez has no authority with Vienetti. She is the wrong sex, the wrong age, has the wrong knowledge (is there to assist the American with facts and figures, not Vienetti), and is of the wrong nationality. Perhaps there are no two nations in Latin America more different than Mexico and Argentina. While Mexico prides itself on its indigenous heritage, Argentina all but ignores any reference to its native inhabitants. Argentina looks to Europe for its heritage, while Mexico looks almost as much to its Aztec roots as its Spanish background for its self-definition. Much racial and cultural misunderstanding can exist between Argentineans and Mexicans, and Susan Lopez only exacerbates the already-strained relationship between the American and the Argentineans. Vienetti's paternalistic treatment of Ms. Lopez is evidence of his lack of respect.

Juan tries to position himself through all this in order to maximize the possibilities of his achieving his own goals. He is probably very aware of the many mistakes being made and is hoping that they will serve as an opportunity for him to be able to prove his indispensability to the Americans. The mistake Juan makes, however, is that his perception of personal responsibility and relationships is shared by the American only insofar as it affects the repayment of obligations for personal favors rendered.

Juan is misjudging the American's willingness to reciprocate Juan's warm personal relationship by providing him with a position. Juan is basing his actions on the personal, "one-hand-washing-the-other" type of obligation so necessary in business in Argentina and in much of Latin America (an "arrangement" that also allows for corruption, nepotism, and the like, at least from the North American perspective). But the American's criteria for employment are probably strictly traditional North American (probably a United States-based manager, someone within the company with proven loyalty to it, and an equally well-proven competence as defined by the home human resources staff). Juan's suggestion that the American hire him is too radical, too inconsistent with the human-resource policies of headquarters, and perhaps even perceived as unethical. After all, how can he be soliciting for the job with the American firm while supposedly negotiating for the other side? The American has serious questions about the propriety of this behavior; for Juan, it is just doing business.

Take yourself through the five-step Global Homecoming process. Try to identify individuals like Juan in your own experience. Perhaps you see some of this behavior in yourself. How do you relate to this individual, or this part of yourself, and if there is a conflict here, how do you reconcile it? Recall a specific situation. Identify the players and their cultural backgrounds. Knowing what you know now, if you were interacting with these people today, how would you act differently? Now take this experience and replay it in the above scenario, this time, with you being the American. Is there a better way in which you can achieve your goals with the Argentineans? How would you deal with Juan? With Mr. Vienetti? What would you have done differently beforehand (for example, like *not* inviting Ms. Lopez, or making sure that your boss *did* come, etc.) to make things work out better? And now that there are problems, is there anything you can do to control the damage and repair the relationship to get things back on track?

Index

Index

About the Author

Dean Allen Foster is founder and director of Cross-Cultural Associates in New York, a division of Berlitz International, and a training, design, and marketing consultant for management training organizations. He has conducted training programs for many multinational corporations, academic institutions, and government agencies in the fields of international negotiations and cross-cultural communications. Mr. Foster is also on the faculty of the Department of Sociology, School for Social Resources, College of New Rochelle, New York.